W9-AQV-808

DISCARD

Other books by Jim Mellon and Al Chalabi

Jim and Al have been writing together since 2003. Their first book *"Wake Up! Survive & Prosper in the Coming Economic Turmoil"* (Capstone, Wiley) was published in late 2005. As the title implies, it warned of a coming financial crisis provoked by a housing bubble that was fuelled by debt and advised readers to be prepared by adopting a defensive position, such as accumulating gold.

Their second book, *"The Top Ten Investments for the Next Ten Years"* was published in 2007 and gave investors more specific advice on the asset classes that were likely outperform in the coming decade. These included the Japanese Yen, commodities and the BRIC economies. The book was updated and re-released post financial crisis in early 2009 under the title *"The Top Ten Investments to Beat the Crunch."*

Since 2006 Jim and Al have also been writing their *Wake Up! Newsletter*, which they release every quarter to thousands of subscribers around the world. The newsletter provides a commentary on economic developments and offers suggestions on how readers can protect their assets from potential threats and profit from untapped opportunities. It is free to subscribe to the newsletter at www.wakeupnewsletter.com.

UNDERSTAND AND PROFIT FROM THE BIOTECH REVOLUTION THAT WILL TRANSFORM OUR LIVES AND GENERATE FORTUNES

JIM MELLON & AL CHALABI

WILEY

A John Wiley & Sons, Ltd., Publication

This edition first published 2012
© 2012 John Wiley & Sons, Ltd

Registered office

John Wiley & Sons Ltd, The Atrium, Southern Gate, Chichester, West Sussex, PO19 8SQ, United Kingdom

For details of our global editorial offices, for customer services and for information about how to apply for permission to reuse the copyright material in this book please see our website at www.wiley.com.

Wiley publishes in a variety of print and electronic formats and by print-on-demand. Some material included with standard print versions of this book may not be included in e-books or in print-on-demand. If this book refers to media such as a CD or DVD that is not included in the version you purchased, you may download this material at http://booksupport.wiley.com. For more information about Wiley products, visit www.wiley.com.

Designations used by companies to distinguish their products are often claimed as trademarks. All brand names and product names used in this book are trade names, service marks, trademarks or registered trademarks of their respective owners. The publisher is not associated with any product or vendor mentioned in this book. This publication is designed to provide accurate and authoritative information in regard to the subject matter covered. It is sold on the understanding that the publisher is not engaged in rendering professional services. If professional advice or other expert assistance is required, the services of a competent professional should be sought.

Library of Congress Cataloging-in-Publication Data

Mellon, Jim.
    Cracking the code : understand and profit from the biotech revolution that will transform our lives and generate fortunes / Jim Mellon and Al Chalabi.
        p. cm.
    Includes bibliographical references and index.
    ISBN 978-1-119-96318-9 (hardback)
    1. Biotechnology industries—Finance. 2. Pharmaceutical industry—Finance. 3. Biotechnology industries. 4. Pharmaceutical industry. 5. Investments. I. Chalabi, Al. II. Title.
    HD9999.B442M45 2012
    338.4'76151—dc23

                                                                                    2012002918

A catalogue record for this book is available from the British Library.

ISBN 978-1-119-96318-9 (hardback) ISBN 978-1-119-96936-5 (ebk)
ISBN 978-1-119-96937-2 (ebk)   ISBN 978-1-119-96938-9 (ebk)

Set in 11/13pt CaslonPro Regular by Toppan Best-Set Premedia Limited, Hong Kong
Printed in Great Britain by TJ International Ltd, Padstow, Cornwall, UK

Contents

Acknowledgements ix
Introduction xi

Chapter One   Transformational Technologies   1

Futurists and Scientists Look into the Future 1
The Convergence of Technology and Biology 13

**Chapter Two   The Evolution of Medicine and
the Emergence of Biopharma   23**

From Atoms to Cells to Living Organisms 24
The History of the Pharmaceutical Industry 36

**Chapter Three   The Drug Industry – Reinventing
the Model   55**

Big Pharma, Biopharma 59
Drug Patents 73
The Path to Riches: FDA Approval 79
In Summary 84

**Chapter Four   Curing Disease – Promising Prospects
in the Main Therapeutic Areas   87**

Cancer – Step by Step, Being Beaten 89
Infectious Diseases: New Antibiotics, Hepatitis and HIV
    Drugs Make for a Fast-growing Sector 107
Obesity and its Evil Sisters: Type 2 Diabetes and Kidney
    Disease 118
The Heart of the Matter – Biggest Killer on the Prowl 128
Fading into the Night – Neurodegeneration,
    Rheumatology and Multiple Sclerosis 132
Respiratory Disease – New Drugs: A Breath of Fresh Air 143

Rare Diseases and Rare Profits 146
Drugs for Pain and for the Central Nervous System 150
The Best of the Rest – Ophthalmology, Dermatology,
Gastrointestinal and Bone Disease 153

**Chapter Five   Turning Back the Clock – Stem Cells,
Genomics, Gene Therapy and Regeneration** 157

Stem Cells 166
Gene Therapy and Nano Medicine 170
Organ Growth in and out of the Body 178

Chapter Six   Demographic Changes 181

The Working Age Labour Pool in the World is
Shrinking 191
Can Immigration Solve the Labour Shortage in the
Developed World? 193
The Social Impact of an Ageing Population 195
The United States is the Best Positioned Developed
Country 196
Support Ratios Have Been Plummeting 197
China's Grey Future 198
What Can Governments Do To Avoid Their Country
Becoming a Nursing Home? 200

Chapter Seven   Bioscience's Disruptive Influences 205

Insurance and Healthcare 206
Real Estate 210
Politics 211
Geopolitics 211
Retail Goods and Services 212
The Food Industry 213
The Investment Industry 214
The Law 215
Shortage of Young People in Developed Nations 217

Chapter Eight   Robotics and Nanotechnology   **219**

Robotics   219
Surgical Procedures/Surgical Assistance   220
Medical Monitor/Nurse   223
Housemaid/Domestic Assistance   228
Companion/Pet   229
Nanotechnology   232

Chapter Nine   Lifestyle Maintenance   **235**

It's a Fact: Obesity Shortens Your Life   235
Extending Life Expectancy   237
Common Traits of People who Live the Longest   239
A "Cure" to Ageing   240
Telomeres – Our Biological Clock   244

**Chapter Ten   Investment in Biopharma – Chasing
Those Money Fountains**   **247**

Conservative Portfolio   279
Balanced Portfolio   280
Speculative Portfolio   281
Company Overviews   282

Summary   305
Glossary   315
Appendix – Key Financial Charts of Big Pharma   325
References   327
Bibliography   329
Index   331

Acknowledgements

We owe special thanks in the preparation of this book to the following: Anthony Chow, CFA and Rebecca Allen (Jim's colleagues), Mike Perry of *Bay City Capital*, Declan Doogan of *Palantir Partners*, Chris Anzalone of *Arrowhead*, Bob Palay and Jamie Thomson of *Cellular Dynamics*, Eli Casdin, Brett Robertson, the Bodleian Library of Oxford University, John Arrowsmith of *Reuters Thompson*, Trish Wilson, David Hung and Greg Bailey of *Medivation*, Warren Huff of *Reata*, *Cowen and Company*, *JP Morgan*, *Alliance Bernstein and Jefferies Inc*. Thank you also to Dr Nadia Short for her feedback on the therapeutics chapter.

Introduction

Imagine living in a big, rambling old house, within which there is one remote room, whose door has always remained firmly locked. Speculation abounds as to what lies behind it, and even though generations have peeped through the keyhole, the contents of the room remain almost entirely hidden from view.

After years of persistence, someone finally manages to open the door and discovers that the room contains stacks upon stacks of dusty books – literally thousands of them piled right up to the ceiling.

This hidden room stands for the repository of all knowledge about the human body; the books within it represent the codes that make up all the individual components. The successful locksmith represents the scientists who today have become the first to gain access to the locked room, meaning that for the first time in our history, we have gained access to these "books of life", the *genetic code* that makes us what we are.

Each generation of humankind, at least those for which we have records, has considered itself to be in a golden age of discovery. Even during the Dark Ages, in the worst periods of plague and conflict, humans achieved some scientific or social progress. But compared to where we are today, the pace has been glacial and the progress slight. We are living in the *Diamond Age* of discovery.

Our world stands on the brink of the greatest era of discovery and advance ever seen, and all the tremendous advances of the past two hundred years – the steam-based industrial revolution, the car, the transistor, the personal computer, antibiotics and vaccines – will appear insignificant compared to the advances we are about to witness in the coming decades.

Without a doubt, the two seminal moments that form the pillars of this incredible move forward are the *discovery of the structure of DNA* and the *sequencing of the human genome*, the latter occurring nearly 50 years after the former. These twin achievements are allowing us to see behind the body's own closed door, and to read and understand the books that contain our own particular codes. This ability to "see" the molecular and cellular makeup of our bodies will enable us to take life expectancy to well over 120 years, to repair bodies that are diseased or worn out, and to improve dramatically the quality of life in old age.

From these books of life, comprising our genomes, a vast new industry is about to be born – the industry of human life extension and improvement. This industry, which is loosely called *life sciences*, is about to gain a new prominence, and its biggest successes will dwarf the likes of *Apple*, *Exxon*, *BHP* and so forth that are the current colossi of stock markets.

The book you are reading is about this new(ish) industry and what it will do to transform our world. We identify its key participants and explain how investors can profit mightily from its development.

In addition, we describe the medical advances that will give hope to those who just a few years ago would have had none. We go through all the major *therapeutic areas* and discuss the emerging technologies that are relevant to us as investors.

Our book also concerns how the world as we know it is about to be turned upside down. This will be as a result of these breakthroughs coinciding with a period when the world's human population is undergoing the most ubiquitous and rapid ageing ever. Entire industrial sectors will be disrupted by the achievements of the life sciences, and fortunes will be made by investing in the right companies.

As with our previous books, we describe the amazing developments that are underway without too much of the confusing technical jargon for which this industry is notorious. And of course, these step changes have remained hidden from the public gaze: drugs and medical devices do not have the same wide public appeal as tablet computers, and so our job is to expose them as the modern miracles that they are.

We give a brief overview of the history of medicine up to the present time. We then explain how we are nearing a significant increase in potential *human life expectancy*, and include the specific reasons why this change in our potential life spans is occurring. As well as describing the many aspects of human life and behaviour that will be transformed, we also include a review of most of the companies that we think are going to be the key players in the field.

As the authors of a book about such an exciting field of science, we have a confession to make: we have never donned white coats except in fancy dress, and neither of us can in the slightest way claim to be experts in molecular biology. It was a steep learning curve for us that involved reading a mountain of books, hundreds of published articles and visiting over 100 companies.

In a way, being outsiders is an advantage; we have spent more than a year going "undercover" in the life sciences industry, learning the language of obscurantism that separates the scientific community from the rest of the population, and having done so we hope that we have been able to demystify many of the technicalities that surround the life/bio sciences field.

The principal conclusions from our extensive research are as follows:

- Up to 1975 or thereabouts, medicine was principally focused on keeping people alive to their "natural" life span, that is 75 to 80 years of age, but since then *biotechnological* and other medical advances have been nudging that figure ever higher. What that age will ultimately be is the subject of much debate, but our own view is that the unlocking of the secrets of the human genome will allow life expectancy to climb to at least 120 in the next 20 to 30 years. For the developed world, achieving a 50 per cent increase in life expectancy may appear heroic but it is in fact a smaller increase in life span than the one that took place between 1900 and now.

- The common assumption that the very old are almost universally afflicted by a range of age-related diseases, be it *osteoporosis*, *Alzheimer's*, *Parkinson's*, *blindness* or immobility, is one that will be altered in the next couple of decades. This will be because many of those diseases will be curable or at least their progression halted by new and effective therapies. In much of the literature that we have read, there is a sort of defeatist pessimism about the chances of this happening. But we are optimistic: our research indicates that the major diseases associated with advanced ageing are being addressed at a pace unseen by most. It will not be inevitable that most centenarians will be "illderly" people confined to dribbling in plastic chairs in their dotage. In fact, we think quite the reverse, and we explain why.

The major advances that are needed and that will occur in this area must be in *neuro degenerative diseases*; it is a sad fact that *one in two people over 85 will suffer from* Alzheimer's *or a similar malady*. This would prove to be an unsupportable burden on developed societies as life expectancy increases hugely, and so a change is needed.

Although there is no specific cure *yet* for Alzheimer's, bit by bit the pathways that cause it are being explored and uncovered, and we believe that within ten years there will be a much more effective treatment for this disease, which is possibly the greatest scourge of our age. Blind faith in science is not a great thing, so we will present evidence as to why *neurodegeneration* is not inevitable and why it will be conquered. Already, a blood test to detect the early stages of Alzheimer's is in accelerated development, based on levels of Dehydroepiandrosterone (DHEA) in the brain.

- The mainly age-related diseases that present themselves typically in younger cohorts (the 65 plus) are being slowly strangled by medical advances. Although **metastatic cancers** (i.e. those that have spread from the original location of the tumour) are still difficult to treat, **cancers** that are detected early now have much better prognoses than a few decades ago. One by one, cancers – and there are approximately 200 types of them – are being beaten by the engine of science, and survival rates will rise much further (from about 70 per cent overall after 5 years) in the next 20 years. Cancer – formerly the most dreaded disease – is no longer the biggest killer. That honour belongs to the *metabolic diseases* related largely to lifestyle: **cardiovascular diseases, strokes, type 2 diabetes** and **morbid obesity**. These constitute the biggest causes of mortality in the developed world and are fast becoming a comparable threat in the developing world also. In the developing world, *infectious diseases, infant mortality* and increasingly **lung cancer** from smoking-related causes are the biggest killers.

Although there is not yet a magic bullet to solve the problem of people's sedentary and unhealthy lifestyles, there are many new therapeutics which will in due course become available that will, for example, reduce the incidence and impact of type

2 diabetes, reduce the incidence and impact of **chronic kidney disease**, vaccinate against or treat **hepatitis C** and thereby reduce **liver disease**, and cure many *infectious diseases*, possibly including **malaria** and **HIV**. Additionally, recent Australian research has indicated that there is a way in effect to "vaccinate" mosquitoes against **dengue fever**, an even more prevalent disease than malaria. This process involves infecting mosquitoes with the bacterium Wolbachia.

- *Genetic diseases* will gradually be cured by a combination of *genetic engineering* (i.e., selecting out defective genes in reproduction) and specific new therapies currently being developed. Of course, like all living organisms, human beings keep on evolving, and in a way the addressing of genetic diseases by new therapies is simply an acceleration of our natural evolutionary process. (Harvey Fineberg, President of the Institute of Medicine, calls it "neo-evolution".) Later in the book, we talk about advances in this area and identify the companies at the forefront of their fields. We have also talked with leaders in the field of genetic engineering and as a result are able to identify some investment opportunities.

- *Regenerative medicine* is possibly the hottest and most eagerly anticipated area of medicine today. It is a fact that organs can already be grown outside the human body and whereas at the moment this is limited to simple tissue engineering (such as skin, the windpipe and heart valves), within perhaps 20 years there will be almost no organ that is not reproducible. This is clearly amazing, and will allow, for instance, patients with **renal failure** to avoid dialysis, heart patients to get a brand new heart, lung cancer victims to replace their failing lungs and so on.

  Although there is no prospect just yet of an *age-reversal pill* or therapy, many of the constituent parts of the body will be able to be replaced as they wear out. Advances in hip and knee replacement will alleviate the suffering that **arthritis** and osteoporosis cause for many elderly people, restoring mobility and vitality. And *tissue engineering, stem cell therapy* and *in vivo gene therapy* will all add to the capacity of our bodies to perform longer and better. Age will still be a disease to which everyone inevitably succumbs, but its impact will be lessened, and death, which for many today is an undignified and painful torment, will be much less feared.

Today, about one third of all healthcare expenditures in most wealthy countries take place in the last period of life, typically in the last year. This is because most people in developed countries die in hospitals, and hospitals are the most expensive hotel any of us will ever stay in. One of the reasons that healthcare costs have soared as a percentage of national incomes in most wealthy countries is because of the sheer cost of *hospitalization*; in the US, healthcare now costs the country 6 per cent of its GDP and appears to be on the rise.

If *new drugs*, *therapies* and *medical devices* as well as *preventative medicine* can displace a part of hospitalization costs, then overall medical costs will fall as a percentage of national income. In this way, drugs can be a displacement factor for much more expensive interventions, and advances in drugs are going to keep a lot of people out of hospital.

- Medical advances and *genomic sequencing* will create a much larger group of elderly people in almost every developed and developing society in the next 30 years. The well-advertised collapse in fertility in many European countries as well as in Japan and Korea will be amplified by the rapid rise in the percentage of over-65-year-olds in those societies.

Worldwide, population growth will slow and plateau at almost zero by 2040, with the only areas exhibiting growth being Africa, the Indian sub-continent and parts of the Middle East. Otherwise, most populations, including that of China, will start to decline by mid-century, leaving the world at a peak population of between 8.5 to 9.5 billion people. Barring war, famine or a new form of plague, life expectancy will continue to rise in almost every single part of the world.

This rise will lead to the well-known future that confronts baby boomers today; pensions will be inadequate to keep them in the style to which they might like to be accustomed, so people will have to work longer and harder. But because those very same people will benefit from new medical advances, they will be able to do so without too much hardship; and it will not be surprising to see retirement ages of 80 plus by 2050.

But there will be one gaping hole in this demographic picture: an absence of large numbers of young new entrants into the labour force. In most rich societies, the highest workforce participation rates in history occurred from around 2000 to 2005. This was the result of the baby boomers mostly being at work, the wave of workers born in the 1970s joining the workforce and rising female participation rates.

All those factors will be in reverse in most rich countries, and immigration will not be sufficient to take up the slack, at least not under the current economic and political conditions. This will mean that the so-called *dependency ratio* (the number of people dependent on those in the active work force, notwithstanding rising retirement ages) will grow. *More old people being looked after by fewer young people.* And although old people will be fitter and more active than ever, ultimately they will need some sort of care.

For that reason, we look at *robotic*s in some detail later in the book as a likely solution to the labour shortage. Sounds fanciful, but believe us this is coming to a restaurant, shop or house near you!

The demographic changes we outline will have further major impacts – first on *geopolitics* and second on *industrial patterns*. *Population size* is in itself not a foolproof indicator of global power – the US only has 5 per cent of the world's population, but has the largest economy and huge heft in military might and in world leadership.

Indeed, even though the US currently has 34 per cent of the G20 nations' GDP and that figure will fall to 24 per cent by 2050, it will still remain exceptionally important relative to its population size.

However, the size of a nation's population might well have more relevance in the future. In this respect, the Indian subcontinent, parts of Africa and parts of Asia (perhaps not China) will gain in relative geopolitical importance. Europe, Japan and possibly Latin America will lose relative strength.

Many industries will be disrupted by the wave of advances in life sciences. *Genome sequencing* will, despite ethical considerations, turn the *life insurance industry* on its head. Youth-oriented industries will be squeezed at the expense of those that cater to the elderly, such as nutrition, clothing and entertainment. People looking at the long-term future of their profession should have an eye out for the disruptive trends that are about to change many industrial landscapes.

In this book we also provide:

- A background on medicine and medical advances to the present time, and set the scene for what is likely to happen tomorrow, that is, in the next 10 to 20 years.

- Some basic scientific overview to explain how we are moving into an entirely new quantum of progress, leading to life extension, improved quality of life, and demographic and industrial disruption. Recent books such as *100 Plus* by Sonia Arrison are keen to promote the idea of life spans going to 150 plus, but do not break down the specific science by which this will happen – whereas we attempt to do so. After all, if people are to live to 150 on average, some must live to 200 to achieve that and we think that is a stretch too far for the foreseeable future.

- Interviews and commentaries on the players that matter to investors. This is interwoven into the sections on major therapeutics – cancer, *infectious diseases*, *neurodegenerative diseases*, type 2 diabetes, cardiovascular and other diseases associated with "western" lifestyles.

- Specific recommendations to investors on which areas to be positioned in, what to look for in companies in the bio and life sciences field, and the scope of market opportunities in therapeutic areas and in regions of the world.

- An explanation of the process of drug discovery or device development, including the regulatory hurdles inherent in the process and how that might be changing. We cover the financial risks in drug discovery and how to mitigate them in the construction of a long-term portfolio. We also talk about the interplay between so-called *big pharma* and the newer wave of biopharma companies. In practice, the two disciplines of synthetic chemistry relating to so-called *small molecule drugs* (such as **Viagra** and **Lipitor**), the previous domain of the major pharma names (*GlaxoSmithKline, Pfizer, Merck* and so on), and the engineering of living organisms (biotech firms such as *Genentech* and *Amgen*) are fusing, and we describe why.

By the end of this book we hope that you will agree with us that *life sciences* hold a golden key to unlocking a whole new world for humans; one in which current levels of old age will be considered "normal" and where people's lives will be planned in a totally different dimension.

A world where discovery will advance at a pace too fast for most of us to recognize and where innovation will lead not only to material wealth on an unimaginable scale across the world, but also a world where people will live much longer lives and, importantly enjoy them.

Our first book called *Wake Up! Survive and Prosper in the Coming Economic Turmoil* (published at the end of 2005) forecast a large economic crash; and we have to say that the effects of that crash will probably continue to be felt until at least 2015.

We are pleased to say that this book is an optimistic one and paints a brighter, longer future for all of us. It posits that most people alive today will live far longer than their parents or grandparents, their quality of life will be considerably superior and suggest that almost every affliction from which they might at one time have suffered will be treatable by 2030.

Of course, the people who inhabit this brave new world will also confront other issues such as the depletion of natural resources, environmental damage (with or without climate change) and fiscal issues relating to ageing populations. They will also face an unsettled world order where the postwar hegemony of the United States will be gradually eroded (although not as fast as its detractors would like to suggest).

But because we are living in this *Diamond Age* of discovery, and because the discovery is not just limited to the medical field, but is also occurring in almost every scientific discipline, solutions for many of the problems that sceptics think are intractable will soon emerge.

Robotics, nanotechnology, new energy sources and *commodity substitution* will soon be commonplace – and by soon we mean in the next ten years. When that happens, goods will become abundant, computing power will be far greater than it is today, food will be reengineered to be plentiful and education will be universally more effective. Indeed, we believe that a Malthusian nightmare of food production being unable to keep up with explosive population growth will remain just that – a bad dream unmatched by reality.

This book is principally about how humans will live longer and healthier; how the fusion of *computational power* with *bioengineering* will radically alter the way we think about ourselves, and how in that process we, the early adopters and believers, can make a lot of money.

In our last book, *The Top Ten Investments for the Next Ten Years*, we talked of *Big Ideas* that become *Money Fountains*, and how getting just one *Big Idea* right was all it took to get your *Money Fountain* spouting.

This is our *Big Idea* and we hope you enjoy the book and that you live long and prosper from it.

A Note on the Text

For the reader's convenience, in the first instance in this book company names will appear in italic text, the names of drugs will appear in bold text and types of diseases will appear in bold italic text. After the first instance all terms will then appear in standard text throughout the rest of the chapter.

Chapter *One*

Transformational Technologies

Futurists and Scientists Look into the Future

Futurists tend to be rather unusual folk whose chosen career, to study trends and factors they believe will influence and shape our future, must leave them with a sense of anticipation and, possibly, frustration. From their perch above time, futurists make deductive predictions on what lies ahead for humankind – sometimes right, most often wrong.

We do confess to have studied the work of some of these futurists, particularly those who write about the *convergence of technology and biology* and how it will dramatically enhance and transform our lives. This is largely because we have been seeking validation for our own strong opinion that this convergence is real and that its impact is under-appreciated. The disruptive effects of the fusion of raw computing power and biology are going to be considerable, and are a key feature of this book.

We have also, perhaps less exotically, studied the works of leading scientists in various fields of technology, physics and bioscience to develop a deeper understanding of what is really going on in science generally, and what lies in store for us humans in the next 10 to 30 years.

Some truly breath-taking innovations are just about to be commercialized, and the effect of these will allow us to live longer, healthier and happier lives. Although we will begin to see some of these new technologies within five years, we will have to wait up to 20 years for others, but of course we are all going to live longer, so that's not such a stretch.

As we share our findings, we hope that the technologies we highlight will blow you away, as they have us, and convince you that "the future is already here, it's just not very evenly distributed".[1]

We cannot state often enough how fortunate and privileged we are to be living in the most incredible period of humankind's existence on earth. Already, many things once confined to the realms of science fiction have become fact. Things that did not exist at all not long ago, such as mobile phones and the Internet, are now indispensable (sometimes addictively so) to our way of life.

You might reasonably ask why the biological revolution we are forecasting did not take place earlier, say 5, 10 or 20 years ago. The short answer is that it has taken this long for computer processors to be able to handle the complex work required to study molecular biology and nanotechnology in a productive way.

Allow us to elaborate: one of the futurists whose work we studied is Ray Kurzweil. Mr Kurzweil published a book entitled *The Singularity is Near* (2006). In this book he uses historical data to build a solid case that technological development is growing at an exponential rate. Many people are familiar with "Moore's Law", a trend first proposed by Gordon Moore, the co-founder of chip maker *Intel*, which states that computer processing power doubles every 2 years, and the price halves.

MATHEMATICS FOR BEGINNERS

If you are not too big on mathematics, the vertical scale in Figure 1 is a logarithmic scale, that is, the values are increasing by an order of magnitude, from 100 to 1,000 to 10,000, rather than linearly, such as 100, 200, 300. That is why the line on the graph appears straight. If we were to plot the same points on a linear scale (100, 200, 300 and so on) the line would be exponential and virtually vertical within a few years and we would not be able to fit the plot on a page.

---

[1] A quote by William Ford Gibson, an American-Canadian speculative fiction novelist.

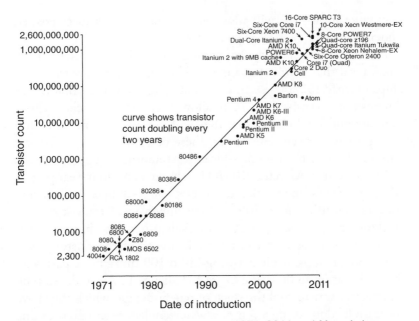

Figure 1: Microprocessor transistor counts 1971–2011 and Moore's Law.
Source: Wgsimon for Wikipedia (http://en.wikipedia.org/wiki/File:Transistor_Count_and_Moore%27s_Law_-_2008.svg)

Moore first came up with his statement in a paper he wrote some 40 years ago, and it still holds true today. The logarithmic chart in Figure 1 displays the number of transistors in a chip since the early 1970s. This has been remarkably consistent with Moore's Law and there is no reason why it will not continue for the foreseeable future, especially as quantum physics and other technologies work their way into computing.

Sceptics argue that we are within a decade of hitting the physical limitations of Moore's Law – that is, it will be impossible to etch transistors smaller than about 30 atoms across and so at that point Moore's Law will cease to hold true. Forecasters estimate that we will reach this limitation by 2020. Technically, they are correct; there will probably be a wall by around 2020 in terms of flat wafer silicon transistors. But Moore's Law is not limited to the current technology of manufacturing silicon chips; it is about the doubling of processing power every 2 years and in that respect we will see new innovations that will allow us to sustain the advances posited under Moore's Law well beyond 2020.

In fact, this is already happening today: in May 2011, Intel announced that it will start mass producing its *Tri-Gate* transistor chips in early 2012. These chips will contain the world's first three-dimensional transistors, which allow them to be packed closer together and Intel claims that they will run 37 per cent faster and use up to 50 per cent less power. These new chips alone will allow Moore's Law to be sustained for at least another couple of years.

In addition, in March 2010 *IBM* embarked on a four-year project with two Swiss universities to develop three-dimensional micro-processors (different to Intel's three-dimensional transistors). By stacking the processors on top of each other, the distances that information needs to travel fall to 1/1000th of the existing two-dimensional chips, while allowing up to 100 times more pathways for information to flow. The biggest challenge has been developing an effective way to cool the stack of red-hot chips, which they have successfully done using a complex water-cooled system. In the same way that big cities tend to start building upwards when they run out of space, chips will also be layered in a multi-storey fashion.

In 2008 Professor Eby Friedman led a team at the University of Rochester that successfully created the world's first three-dimensional chip. When asked if we will get to a point where we can no longer make integrated circuits any smaller, Professor Friedman's response was: "Horizontally, yes. But we're going to start scaling vertically, and that will never end. At least not in my lifetime. Talk to my grandchildren about that." [2]

Then there are other developments underway outside the silicon world: an entirely new generation of computers applying an altogether new technology. These are called *quantum computers* and they potentially have orders of magnitude more processing power than the very best of their silicon versions. Although quantum computers are still in their infancy, a significant milestone took place in May 2011 when it was announced that *Lockheed Martin Corporation* was purchasing the world's first *commercial quantum computing* system to be installed at the University of Southern California. The computer

---

[2] Casey Research: http://www.caseyresearch.com/cdd/3d-computing-way

maker is *D-Wave Systems*, a privately held firm based in British Columbia, Canada. In November, the company's co-founder and Chief Technology Officer, Dr Geordie Rose, was named Innovator of the Year by the Canadian Innovation Exchange. This research is worth keeping an eye on because it may just leapfrog the remaining years of the silicon era and jump-start the quantum one.

By 2020, computer processing power is expected to reach that of the human brain, according to Kurzweil (2006). This is not to be confused with equal intelligence – he predicts this to happen by 2045, an event often referred to as the *singularity*. Futurists define this as being the point in time when *Artificial Intelligence (AI)* surpasses that of human intelligence, making AI computers/machines the smartest and most capable "life forms" on earth.

The term *singularity* is borrowed from physics and means a point of infinite gravity where nothing can escape, not even light. Black holes are singularities. The concept of a technological singularity dates back to 1958 during a conversation between two renowned mathematicians, Stanislaw Ulam and John von Neumann (both worked on the Manhattan Project to develop the atomic bomb).

The thought of a singularity hypothesis coming true is overwhelming on many levels, especially as it is likely to happen within some of our younger readers' lifetimes. The most significant inference of this event is that it marks the point in human existence beyond which we no longer need to invent or make anything else ever again. Think about that: if AI is smarter than the smartest human on the planet, why would we need to use traditional brain power to do "work" anymore?

Another futurist, Dave Evans, is employed by *Cisco Systems*, the American giant technology firm, to gaze into the future and advise the firm on the threats and opportunities ahead. Mr Evans has had this job of Chief Futurist since 1990 – certainly forward-thinking and unusual on Cisco's part!

One of the oft-cited salutary lessons in the tech sector of what happens if you do not anticipate the future correctly is the case of *Microsoft*; it dropped the proverbial ball by underestimating the rapid adoption and impact of the Internet. This opened the door for *Google* to step in and take centre stage. Microsoft remains on the back foot and has yet to re-establish the dominant market position it once had. Its share price has not changed much in 10 years, having increased over 100-fold over the 10 years preceding the dot-com bubble crash in 2000.

In 2010 Cisco's Evans published a list of his top 25 technology predictions. Here are the four that we believe to be the most significant:

- In the next 10 years, we will see a 20-fold increase in home networking speeds.
- By 2050 (assuming a global population of 9 billion), US$1,000 worth of computing power will equal the processing power of all human brains on earth.
- Within two years, information on the Internet will double every 11 hours.
- By 2030, artificial implants for the brain will be possible.

There's no doubt that humankind has achieved some incredible things even in the last 50 years, but to put into perspective the era of rapid change that we have entered, we paraphrase Mr Evans who said in an interview about the future that "In the next 50 years, 95 per cent of everything we know as a species will be discovered".[3]

So the exciting stuff is only just beginning. . . .

In a *post-singularity* world, we would be able to utilize AI to make further technological advancements at a far greater pace than humans would ever be capable of. After all, machines can work non-stop, needing no lunch breaks, coffee breaks or sleep and so on, they can communicate far more efficiently than us and they can build smarter, purpose-built machines to tackle each new challenge they are tasked with.

Most importantly, AI machines would work for free, apart from their energy consumption. Their prevalence would usher in a new post-capitalist era; a golden time in which our standard of living will be dramatically improved and one in which money would slowly cease to have the same meaning or value as we put on it today.

But all that is many years beyond the singularity, and too far into the future to try and understand the consequences of just yet. In fact, as we have said earlier, we think Kurzweil (2006) and his ilk

---

[3] http://blogs.cisco.com/news/cisco_futurist_discusses_internet_of_things_tech_predictions_more_on_talk2c/

are somewhat too optimistic – and that's coming from us, who are bursting with excitement!

Sure, there are those who call the singularity the beginning of the end of humankind (giving rise to apocalyptic scenarios as portrayed in films such as *The Terminator* and *The Matrix*), but we and others hold a more optimistic view.

Most likely, by the time the singularity occurs, humans will already be heavily imbedded with bioscience enhancements, and so we will not be "pure" humans anyway. These enhancements could be in the form of *brain boosting implants* (for instance, for augmenting language or mathematical capabilities), or they could be injections of *nanobots* into the bloodstream to repair damaged tissue, or they could even be biomechanical enhancements and prosthetics to replace damaged or amputated limbs.

So humans are probably going to be *cyborg hybrids* by some distant date in the future, and there will be no clear divide between "them" and "us", that is, pure organic humans versus AI computers.

The previous paragraph may generate scary images of robots patrolling the streets and intimidating "basic" humans, but we need not picture these bionic enhancements to humans as clunky, robot-like limbs; think more of Steve Austin[4] rather than *Robocop*. In all probability, we will still look and feel human, just enhanced versions of ourselves – smarter, healthier, stronger and self-repairing. Who can object to that?

We have already started our journey along this hybrid path, albeit in an experimental capacity – humans have begun to incorporate bionic features and computers have begun to incorporate some human features.

Kevin Warwick is a pioneer in the field of *cybernetics* and a professor at the University of Reading in England. In 1998, Professor Warwick had a small chip transponder implanted in his forearm that allowed his movements to be tracked within his department at the university. Various devices were programmed to detect and react to his presence as he moved around. For example, lights and

---

[4] Steve Austin was a fictional character in the 1970's TV series "The Six Million Dollar Man", played by Lee Majors.

heaters would automatically turn on when he entered a room, and his computer booted-up when he walked into his office. Today, this may seem basic and unimpressive, but in 1998 it was ground-breaking stuff.

Squeamishness aside, a tiny (rice grain size) device implanted just under our skin could come with a multitude of convenient applications. For example, it could serve as our passport/identification, a secure e-wallet that is networked to our bank accounts, and it could contain all our medical records and perhaps be programmed to call for medical assistance if it senses any anomalies in heart rate or blood pressure, giving our exact location at the same time.

Take it one step further and we could have all the current features of a smart phone, including broadband Internet, embedded within us, allowing us to search and retrieve information at will. Fingers are a slow and awkward interface with computer devices and limit the rate at which we can communicate. Keyboards are a legacy from the days of the typewriter; it would be far more efficient to interface with a device through voice or even thought, and we'd still have our hands free to do other things.

But really to have thought-controlled devices, we would need somehow to connect our brain with a computer. Experiments to do just that have already taken place. Following the simple implant procedure in 1998, Professor Warwick underwent another procedure in 2002, as a result of which he technically became the world's first *cyborg*. This time the surgery involved implanting a device into the nerves of his left arm that connected his nervous system to a computer. One of the truly amazing experiments he carried out while wearing the implant involved a robotic hand located some 5,500 kilometres (3,500 miles) away. Professor Warwick went to Columbia University in New York and "connected" his bionic hand to the Internet. Across the Atlantic at the University of Reading, he had a robotic hand also connected to the Internet. Connected to each other in this way, Professor Warwick succeeded in getting the robotic hand to mimic his own hand's movements in real time.

These and other such experiments serve as examples of the inevitable converging paths of biology and technology. Although it is fascinating to learn about what awaits humans in the long-term future, we are more interested in the 5 to 15 year time horizon.

Where are we with AI today?

Based on the current logarithmic path of development (shown in Figure 1), we are within 20 years of being able to get a computer to pass the *Turing test*, which is an assessment of AI that renders it indistinguishable from communication with a human, in a verbal not visual manner. In other words, if a human were speaking to another voice over the phone, that human would not be able to determine whether she is speaking to another human or an AI machine.

AI was once a distant concept portrayed only in Hollywood blockbuster films, but tangible new breakthroughs are arriving with increasing frequency, and as we have mentioned previously, progress is exponential due to Moore's Law. One of the early AI milestones took place in 1997. It involved a custom-built computer by *IBM* called *Deep Blue* that succeeded in winning a chess match against the then world chess champion, Garry Kasparov.

The thinking required for chess, be it human or artificial, is mathematical, logical and empirical. Players need to run through multiple scenarios and sequences of moves before selecting the most favourable one. This does not require any non-chess knowledge or the capability to understand speech and respond appropriately in natural language. So Deep Blue, although impressive at the time, had a very limited sort of intelligence.

It took almost another 15 years before the next major breakthrough in AI was made. Again it was by IBM, but this time it was a computer called *Watson* that in February 2011 successfully won on the popular American TV quiz show *Jeopardy*. Not only did it win, but it beat the show's two most successful and celebrated contestants. For Watson to win, it had to "hear" and understand the voice of the show's host, decide on an answer, buzz before the other contestants and "say" the answer. This was the first time a computer has been able to understand natural language and respond in the same. Furthermore, in Jeopardy the host does not ask a question but rather reads a statement. The contestant's response has to be in the form of a question. This may sound confusing if you have never watched Jeopardy before so here is a simple example:

The host would ask: "He's worth every penny as Alfred Pennyworth in *The Dark Knight*".

The correct answer would be: "Who is Michael Caine?"

The answer is not that straightforward, especially for a computer. First, it has to look up Alfred Pennyworth (that's the easy part as it had many terabytes of information stored on its servers); the search may return that he was the butler in the Batman comic books and subsequent films. Second, Watson has to "deduce" that the "Dark Knight" is the name of a Batman film and this nuance is a potential stumbling block because the host did not say ". . . in the film called *The Dark Knight*". This is reasonably obvious to us humans and extremely obvious to Batman fans, but not so simple for AI.

Watson is by no means flawless – for example, one of the gaffes it made, which would never happen with a human contestant (even an unintelligent one), was to give a response that another contestant had just given for that question and was told it was incorrect. Watson cannot "hear" the other contestants, a feature that its developers will no doubt incorporate into any future upgrades.

Watson is clearly many years from being a household item. For instance, its internal memory is 16 terabytes (that's 16,000 gigabytes) – a reasonably fast home/office computer in 2011 has around 8 gigabytes of memory – so Watson has 2,000 times more internal memory capacity. With today's technology, Watson is still an extremely bulky machine; its servers occupy 10 racks, which is virtually an entire room (see Figure 2). But the main reason why we are unlikely to see Watson in people's homes any time soon is its price tag – the estimated cost of developing Watson is rumoured to be US$1–2 billion.

Nevertheless, it's a wonderful demonstration of what is possible with today's technology, and with Moore's Law at work, today's processing power will increase fourfold in just three years, and so faster, cheaper, smaller is the unrelenting mantra that is driving us towards the singularity.

Even Watson's "brain" power today has incredible capacity to serve society, given the right application, which is what IBM is currently busy trying to figure out.

One such application for Watson could be in the field of medicine; Watson's virtually limitless data storage capability combined with its incredible recall ability makes it a natural diagnostician. Imagine if Watson's memory contained the medical history of every patient, as well as all medical knowledge known to humans

Figure 2: IBM's *Watson* supercomputer.
Source: Clockready for Wikimedia Commons

so far, including experimental treatments. If provided with all the symptoms of a patient with a disease that doctors have been unable to diagnose correctly, Watson could come up with a few likely diagnoses as well as suggest the best course of action given the results from thousands of previous cases.

Better still, if Watson had an additional module installed that allowed it to extract all the information it needs from a patient's blood or tissue sample, it could be an all-in-one medical provider. Taking it one step further, Watson could also be programmed to find certain patterns in disease and treatment. Its vast database would be able to pick up trends and patterns that may be too subtle for humans to detect.

In fact, IBM has already entered into a research agreement with a company called *Nuance Communications*, to explore, develop and commercialize Watson's advanced analytical capabilities in the healthcare industry. Nuance Communications (NASDAQ: NUAN) has a market capitalization of over US$7 billion at the time of writing and is trading at almost 50 times its trailing earnings, so clearly the market strongly believes in the huge commercial opportunity that lies ahead in this sector.

The law would be another wonderfully powerful application for Watson. Totally impartial, Watson the lawyer, or perhaps more controversially, the judge would have access to every case in history as well as all the world's laws and legal systems. Think of how quickly and efficiently cases could be heard and resolved. Most of all, think about the potential billions of dollars saved in legal fees that would otherwise be racked up by using human lawyers!

Incidentally, the fastest computer in the world at the time of writing this book in 2011 is in Kobe, Japan. It is called the K computer and it was developed by Fujitsu. It guzzles almost 13 megawatts of power to run, which is roughly the power used to run 125 car engines.

Consciousness

As the processing power of computers continues to increase and AI slowly progresses from being narrow (i.e., very good at a specific task) to strong (i.e., very good at many things), there will come a time in the next few decades when a computer or machine will experience consciousness. It will then become a *sentient* being – a *synthetic* life form derived from technology. Later in this chapter we discuss *organic synthetic* life forms, so there will be two types of synthetic life forms, and humans will likely be sitting cosily in the middle.

But is consciousness an easy thing to measure? After all, how do we know we are conscious or how do we measure consciousness in others? Through our senses, we acquire and store memories, facts, experiences, knowledge, skills and apply our powers of deductive reasoning and learning. If an artificial life form were to acquire these qualities, would that constitute a form of machine consciousness? It seems somewhat conceptual given that this scenario is still some 30 plus years out, but we believe the answer would be yes.

Once these *synthetic life forms* develop a consciousness, they will eventually need recognition in our society and they will probably expect rights and fair treatment. We will need to find a way to accommodate these new species peacefully and we will have to implement new laws for them. Fortunately that is too far into the future for any of us to have to try and figure out just yet.

The Convergence of Technology and Biology

Author and former *Bell Labs* engineer Andy Kessler published a book with the rather amusing title of *The End of Medicine: How Silicon Valley (and Naked Mice) Will Reboot Your Doctor* (2007). This book was inspired by the rather antiquated medical examination he had when he went for a full body check-up shortly after a close relative suddenly died of a heart attack, and a close business associate was diagnosed with cancer.

In most diseases, especially cancer, the earlier it is diagnosed the higher the chances of survival, which is what prompted Mr Kessler to go for a full medical exam. But he quickly realized that diagnostic medicine was still in its infancy and lagging behind technology. The anecdote he uses to illustrate this point is when his doctor took out a rubber hammer and tapped it on his knee. He could not believe that this practice still went on in the 21st century. As a former microchip designer, he felt that technology was just a few years away from transforming the field of medicine (Kessler, 2007).

Every year microchips become smaller, faster and cheaper and we are at a point now where the chips are small enough (less than 20 nanometres) to be attached to antibodies and injected into the body to detect various diseases at an early stage. At Stanford University, experiments have been successful in detecting **breast cancer** in mice by injecting nano-probes into their bloodstream. The exact location of the cancer cells (in three dimensions) can be found, so that these cells can be irradiated, excised or frozen off when they still number just a few hundred thousand and have not begun to spread elsewhere in the body.

In the next 5 to 10 years, this procedure will be part of a routine check-up and that is where Mr Kessler sees the transformation in medicine – a shift away from treating a disease to one of detecting it early enough before it spreads to other organs and becomes life-threatening (Kessler, 2007). Such a shift in how medicine is practised will save billions of dollars in the long run and free up valuable medical resources. This will mean that our quality of life will improve dramatically and we will have very few medical "surprises" as we get older because all diseases will be picked up in their very early stages and treated effectively.

What is DNA?

DNA is the commonly used abbreviation for deoxyribonucleic acid, which is a polymer or long chain molecule found inside each living cell. DNA contains all the genetic instructions, or blueprints, for the development and functioning of all living organisms.

Did you know that if you were able to lay out a human's DNA flat on the ground, it would measure over 183 centimetres (6 feet long), yet it is coiled so tightly that it fits inside the nucleus of a single cell.

Within just a few years, humans can expect to live dramatically longer lives because we will be able to grow new organs from our own DNA, so there will no longer be the risk of the body's immune system rejecting a donor organ. Also, there will not be a long waiting list for a donor. Within 15 years, we can also expect to have nanobots permanently in our bloodstream working with our own immune system on the lookout for threatening germs, cancers and viruses, while at the same time restoring our living tissue to its optimal state.

Just about all published works that make some sort of prediction about humans' future discuss a convergence of the sciences. *Nanotechnology*, *biotechnology* and *information technology* will become virtually one field. This convergence will provide humankind with unprecedented benefits in terms of healthcare, convenience and quality of life.

The advent of synthetic biology

As a consequence of the human pursuit to decipher DNA, a relatively new scientific field has emerged: *synthetic biology*. The best way to describe synthetic biology is to first consider all living cells as information processors, with DNA as the programming language for those cells.

For several decades now, scientists have been able to engineer genetically or modify the *genome*[5] of organisms such as crops to, for

---

[5] An organism's entire hereditary information.

example, create a strain of wheat that grows faster and is resistant to diseases. Synthetic biology goes one step further than simply altering existing genomes – it creates them from scratch. In other words, synthetic biology is the science of creating entirely new life forms ... and it is no longer a theoretical science.

After more than 10 years of work and a cost of US$40 million, scientists announced in May 2010 that the world's first synthetic life form had been "born". Heading up the team of scientists was Dr Craig Venter (the man behind the first private company to sequence the human genome) who announced that he and his team of some 20 scientists created a bacterial cell controlled by a chemically synthesized genome; that is, its DNA was made from scratch.

This truly incredible milestone occurred almost 60 years after the discovery of the double-helix molecular structure of DNA by James Watson and Francis Crick. But it happened only four years after the completion of the sequencing of the first *human genome* (the last *chromosome* sequence was published in the scientific journal *Nature* in May 2006). This is yet another illustration of the rate of accelerating returns and how we can continue to see progress push forward at an exponential pace. The sequencing of the first human genome in the early 2000s was just the beginning of the race; the use of the technology is in its infancy and will evolve extremely rapidly from here.

Synthetic biology will eventually end up being one of the world's biggest industries and we do not think that we are exaggerating when we say this. Think about the limitless applications – life forms could be customized to serve a specific purpose, such as creating organisms that feed on radioactive or toxic waste and render it harmless. It will be possible to synthesize organisms that feed off certain unwanted pollutants in our atmosphere, perhaps carbon dioxide, methane or sulphur dioxide. The possibilities are endless as we refine our DNA "programming" skills.

Scientists around the world are busy sequencing the *base pairs* of organisms. The human genome comprises some 3 billion *DNA base pairs*. For the past 20 years, *GenBank*, an open access sequence database has been accumulating sequencing information for all types of organisms. Thanks to the efforts of laboratories from all over the world, GenBank's database is doubling in size every 18 months (Moore's Law at work again). Additionally, there is the

European *Molecular Biology Laboratory (EMBL)* and the *DNA Bank of Japan*.

As of February 2012, there were over 137 billion bases in 149.8 million sequence records in the database from over 100,000 distinct organisms. Of course there is still a massive amount of work to do to uncover all the secrets of the genome; only when that happens will it become easier to move from knowledge about what a specific gene does to creating viable therapies for all diseases. This is particularly the case where multiple genes are implicated in a disease, such as in cancer and *heart disease*. The "book of life" is open but still hard to read.

Personalized, or precision, medicine

Another new field of medicine that is developing is *personalized medicine*. Our deeper understanding of our genetic and molecular make-up means that the treatment we receive can be tailored to us specifically. This would result in the treatments prescribed being more targeted and more effective than the existing traditional "one-size-fits-all" approach to medicine.

Personalized medicine is already being used to treat certain types of diseases. A simple example is in the treatment of patients who suffer from blood clots. An effective treatment of this disease is to administer a blood thinner called **warfarin**. Historically, doctors and their patients go through a process of trial and error to determine the correct dose to administer, because each person metabolizes the drug differently. A dose too high or too low can be equally dangerous, and so patients can now undergo a genetic test that determines the rate at which the drug would be metabolized, resulting in the patient receiving the correct dose the first time.

Getting to know yourself . . . genetically

Mass customization is the way medicine is heading. No longer will one drug be used for one disease for all sufferers of that disease; there will be a limitless combination of medicine available to treat each person's unique disease to account for the fact that we all respond differently to various drugs. All we need is our *genetic code* – our blueprint – and getting our hands on this is getting cheaper by the day.

Each human has between 20,000 and 25,000 sets of *genes*, the exact number is not known. The things that make us different from one another are the result of the very small variations in these genes. When we say small, we mean tiny – all humans share 99.5 per cent of their DNA, so just that half a per cent accounts for all the variations in us as a species. Incidentally, we are not that different to chimpanzees, genetically speaking of course; we share 98.5 per cent of our DNA with them.

As recently as 2008, the cost of sequencing a human genome was over US$1,000,000. By 2011, that number had plummeted to a little over US$4,000 – that's even faster than Moore's Law. By the end of 2012, that cost will likely fall to below US$1,000, at which point it will almost certainly start to become a standard part of a full medical exam or check-up.

There is an alternative to sequencing an entire human genome called *genotyping*. Genotyping is an efficient and affordable alternative to *genome sequencing* because the process only involves looking for variations in individual base pairs. These variations are commonly referred to as *SNPs* (pronounced "snips", which stands for *Single Nucleotide Polymorphisms*). There are about 10 million SNPs in the human genome. These SNPs are linked to specific diseases and commercial services attempt to use them to predict the chances of contracting specific diseases.

There are several companies offering human genotype services, one of which is called *23andMe* (www.23andme.com). The 23 obviously refers to the 23 pairs of chromosomes that we each have. It is still privately held and was founded in 2006 by two women, Linda Avey and Anne Wojcicki, the latter being married to Google co-founder Sergey Brin.

At the last visit to the 23andMe website, they were offering a US$99 deal to genotype your DNA. All you have to do is post them a sample of your saliva. After six to eight weeks, they will email you to let you know that your results are ready on the website. You then simply login and view your report.

The report summary is presented in a neat four-quadrant format (you can visit the website to see a sample):

- The first quadrant is your predisposition to certain diseases – a percentage indicating the average risk and one for your risk of, say, **colorectal cancer**, Alzheimer's, **asthma** and so on.

- The second quadrant is your carrier status, that is, whether your genes carry diseases such *cystic fibrosis* (caused by a mutation of the CFTR gene) or *sickle cell anaemia*.
- The third quadrant is a list of your traits, such as hair and eye colour or whether you are lactose intolerant.
- The fourth quadrant is a list of pharmaceutical drugs and your responses to them if you were to take them.

23andMe also have an ancestral lineage offer so you can find your global heritage, distant relatives and so on. It might not offer any health benefits but it is fascinating to learn about nevertheless.

As the technology improves, these reports will become more comprehensive and more accurate. Chances are, by the time you read this book, this will already have happened. And the cost will no doubt have gone down too. This marvellous technology will save millions of lives in the future and billions of dollars in healthcare costs as preventative medicine or early treatment of a disease is both more effective and much cheaper than treating a disease that already presents symptoms.

Tailor-made body parts

There have been a number of films and books released on the subject of cloning including *The Island* (2005), *Never Let Me Go* (book 2005, film 2010) and *The Sixth Day* (2000). All these works share the premise that at some point in the future, humans will resort to cloning themselves so that if accidents or diseases were to injure or damage part(s), they would be able to harvest their clone's organs or even "transplant" their mind to their clone's body.

These would be the ultimate life insurance policies but given how the biotechnology industry is progressing, we think it an unlikely scenario for the future. That is because by the time we will have developed the technology to clone humans, we will certainly possess the technology to clone or grow individual body parts and organs independently. With the availability of this technology, why would we choose to replicate an entire sentient being for harvesting specific body parts if we can grow these body parts in isolation outside a human body on demand? Additionally, cloning an entire human being unnecessarily raises all sorts of ethical and moral dilemmas.

Already there has been serious resistance and objections to using human embryos and *stem cells* in research; can you imagine the public outcry to human cloning? Biologically, cloning is the same as having two identical twins born who possess the same DNA; there would just be an age gap between the clones, whereas identical twins are born within a few minutes of each other. The clone would not be the same person in the same way that two identical twins are different people. But creating a clone purposefully and exclusively to sacrifice his or her life and body parts in the future for the "master" would raise ethical issues concerning human rights and equality among human beings. For all these reasons, we do not believe that it is realistic to expect to see *donor humans* anytime in the future.

Scientists, however, have been working on some ground-breaking technology for creating new organs with the patient's own cells. Doing so overcomes one of the major risks of organ transplants, which is rejection. This is common following transplant surgery where the immune system of the patient starts to attack the new organ and does not recognize it as being one of its own. Rejection is usually addressed by having patients take immunosuppressant medication for the rest of their lives. The side effect of taking such medication is a weakened immune system, which makes a person more susceptible to disease and infection. In some cases, the body rejects the new organ anyway despite the medication.

So would it not be great if we could be certain that the patient's body will not reject the new organ after transplant surgery?

To build a new organ without the risk of rejection, the patient's own cells are used. But these cells have no structure and are unable to develop into new organs, and so scientists have found a way to use a framework or "scaffold" from an existing organ to build a new one.

Dr Harald Ott from *Massachusetts General Hospital* discovered and perfected a method for stripping an organ of its own cells and then infusing the remaining scaffold with new cells from the recipient of the new organ. He does this by taking an existing organ from an animal, such as a pig (a pig has very similar organs to humans, both in size and complexity), or a cadaver and then soaks it in a chemical that strips out all the cells and leaves the proteins that comprise the scaffold.

At the end of this process, the organ looks like a colourless version of its former self. This *cell-less scaffold* is then seeded with cells from another body, such as that of the recipient of the new organ, and placed in an incubator for a few weeks to allow the cells to multiply and to populate the scaffold.

When we started writing this book, the most advanced procedure on a human using this technology was on a patient in Spain who had a severely damaged *trachea* (windpipe), due to **tuberculosis**, making it very difficult for her to breathe. The Italian surgeon, Paolo Macchiarini, performed the procedure by harvesting a trachea from a cadaver and then stripping it of all its cells. He then seeded the *trachea scaffold* with the patient's own cells and incubated it for a few weeks to allow the cells to reproduce.

Once ready, he performed the procedure, which involved first removing the segment of the patient's trachea that was damaged and replacing it with the new part that had been grown in an incubator. The procedure was performed in 2008, making it the world's first such procedure. The patient recovered quickly and today leads a healthy, normal life.

Dr Paolo Macchiarini has since performed over 10 similar procedures, but always until recently with a cadaver trachea that has been seeded with the patient's own cells.

Then in July 2011, a new milestone was reached when Dr Macchiarini and his surgical team replaced a cancer patient's trachea with an entirely synthetic one. Scientists at *University College London* created a perfect copy of the patient's trachea and two main branches (bronchi) from a spongy polymer, providing the scaffold for the patient's own cells to grow. This is further evidence that demonstrates the pace and sophistication of *regenerative* and personalized medicine. No doubt additional breakthroughs will have been made by the time this book reaches your hands.

Performing these kinds of procedures using major organs, such as a heart, is still under development although Dr Ott's progress to date has been truly remarkable, having succeeded in bringing the heart of a rat back to life.

Dr Ott started with the scaffold heart from one rat (stripped of its cells); this was then seeded and incubated with the cells of another rat. The heart was then given an electrical signal, blood pressure and oxygen, that is, all the various things it would have in its normal working environment, and after a week or so, the heart started to beat again. It is probably the closest thing to Frankenstein's monster humankind has achieved to date.

At the *Massachusetts Institute of Technology (MIT)* a synthetic alternative to using actual organs is being tested. *Bio-rubber* as they call it, can act as the scaffold material on which cells are able to grow. For example, bio rubber can be moulded in the shape of a human ear and then seeded with cells from the recipient of the ear. Once incubated, it can be transplanted with no risk of rejection from the patient.

Along these lines, scientists are also working on developing a *three-dimensional bio-printer* that can build the organic scaffold in the shape and size of the organ or body part required. The printer resembles a modern day inkjet plotter, the key differences being that the "ink" is a liquid made from a bio-rubber type material, and the printing needs to be done in three dimensions.

The printer would therefore build the structure from the bottom-up as the liquid solidifies. Once the scaffold structure is completed, it can then be seeded with living cells from the future recipient and incubated until ready for transplantation. Again, there would be no risk of rejection by the patient and no long waits for a donor organ/part.

Chapter *Two*

The Evolution of Medicine and the Emergence of Biopharma

This is not a history book or a science primer, but some context is needed if we are to make our point that the whole field of medicine is entering what we term to be its *Diamond Age*.

In this chapter we provide an overview of the basic jargon and structure of the science we are concerned about as investors and of the history of medicine to date, focusing on the keys to drug development. Also, we explain how *biotechnology* came to be such a prominent part of the medical landscape.

It is no exaggeration to say that in the next 20 years, we are likely to make greater progress in medicine than in all humankind's prior years of cumulative practice. In the forthcoming two decades, many diseases will become curable, if not cured altogether, life expectancy will rise dramatically and the quality of life for older and elderly people will improve.

Already huge improvements are underway in the treatment of the major diseases, such as cancer, *obesity*/type 2 diabetes/cardio disease, neurodegenerative and other age-related diseases, and infectious diseases. Gene therapies as well as organ and tissue regeneration based on stem cells are about to become widespread.

We can thank the two greatest milestones of postwar modern medicine for many of these advances: the discovery of deoxyribonucleic acid (DNA) by Watson and Crick in 1953 and the first draft sequencing of the human genome in 2000. These discoveries together form the "cracking of the code" of this book's title.

Before we delve into the consequences of these and other discoveries, we need to give you a quick introduction to molecular biology. If you know all this already, fast-forward a few paragraphs.

From Atoms to Cells to Living Organisms

Everything on earth is composed of matter, which in its most basic form consists of atoms and sub-atomic particles. Matter that consists of one type of atom is called an element. The periodic table comprises all the known elements. Hydrogen, carbon and oxygen are all different elements.

Atoms bond together to form *molecules* (a widely used word in the drug world). The aggregation of different types of molecules form cells (which is why we are living organisms), which are the basic building blocks of the human body.

The word *cell* dates back to the 17th century when Englishman Robert Hooke saw in wood cork a lattice of what looked like little monastic rooms – or cells – and the term has stuck, although it was many hundreds of years later that we started to understand fully how cells function.

In 1833 a Scottish botanist by the name of Robert Brown discovered that plant cells contained small, seed-like pods, which he termed *nuclei*, hence the word *nucleus*, which is also a widely used term in modern science.

We all start life as a *single (or stem) cell*, a *zygote*, the result of the fusion of one sperm and one egg. *Stem cells* feature heavily in this book as exciting developments are occurring in their use as progenitor cells in *regenerative medicine.*

The first single stem cell from which we are derived goes on to divide and replicate many millions of times eventually forming an entire human. These cells, of which each human has approximately 100 trillion, are formed by large molecules, commonly known as macro-molecules. As cells arise only from other cells, growth can occur either from cell division *(hyperplasia)* or by an increase in individual cell size *(hypertrophy)*. Fat and muscle generally grow through hypertrophy, whereas skin, blood, intestines and the liver usually grow through hyperplasia. As an example, if a heart aortic outlet is blocked, the heart cells normally grow to generate more force, which is why diseased hearts can become very overgrown and eventually stop working – a condition known as **pathological hypertrophy**.

The molecules from which cells are composed fall into four different categories:

- *Proteins*, which are the principal "working" molecules of our cells.
- *Carbohydrates*, which provide energy and structure to cells.
- *Lipids* or fats, which store energy, act as signallers and form membranes.
- *Nucleic acids*, of which the most famous and important is DNA, which contains the entire blueprint for our bodies and is the key to our *genome* – the code defining the way in which we are made up.

So to recap, we have atoms forming molecules which form cells, and in those cells there are four principal types of molecules. Of the four principal types, proteins, carbohydrates and nucleic acids are very long and formed of the same repetitive chain called a *polymer*.

If you already know this information we apologize, but for us non-scientific types, a basic crib sheet is useful to be able to decipher the science that confronts us. So having got to the four key constituents of cellular makeup, let's take a quick look at each one in turn.

Carbohydrates can be *monosaccharides* or *polysaccharides*, simple or complex sugars. Carbohydrates are our main source of energy.

Proteins are made up of one or more long chains of *amino acids* and are essential in all living organisms. They do most of the work at the cell level. As we explain in the next chapter when discussing drug development, a protein's shape is vital to how it behaves. Proteins act as *enzymes*, *DNA binders* and *membrane building blocks*. They control communication, division and transport in and out of cells. Proteins start off as *polymers* of amino acids known as *polypeptides*. Once these polypeptides are folded they are known as proteins.

The *folding of proteins* is of vital importance to humans. A lot of work is being done in so-called *proteomics* and particular attention is being paid to the folding and misfolding of proteins. For instance, it has been posited that Alzheimer's may be partly due to the misfolding of proteins (and indeed that a dye used to identify that misfolding might actually be a biologic agent that may act to prevent it[1]).

One of protein's principal functions is to act as the coordinator of activity at the *plasma membrane* of the cell (the protective barrier between the cell and the rest of the body). The role of proteins as gatekeepers to what can enter a cell is extremely important, particularly for drugs. *Receptor* proteins on the outside of cells receive signals that are then relayed inside. These are chemical signals (sometimes in the form of drugs) that bind to the receptors (called *ligands*). Drug companies sometimes refer to these as *keys* and *locks*, where the *receptors are the locks* and the *ligands the keys*.

Proteins can also be enzymes, which can act as messengers or as catalysts for reactions within *cell membranes*.

There is also a *DNA-binding protein* that is able to control the on-off "switches" of which parts of the DNA are being read and which ones are in the "off" state.

Lipids are the group of proteins that include things such as *cholesterol, fats, oils and steroids* that so many of us try to avoid as much as possible in our lives. Because lipids are hydrophobic and reject water, they can pack a lot of energy. For instance, fats have more than twice as many calories per gram (9) as carbohydrates and proteins (4). Energy storage is one of the principal roles of lipids and too much stored energy results in weight gain.

All the above proteins play vital roles in our bodies, and indeed in every mammalian being, but perhaps the most important of them all is DNA.

DNA and its discovery

DNA is the genetic code of all cells and contains the "blueprint" for the construction of proteins and *RNA (ribonucleic acid)* is the means by which DNA is translated into cellular action. DNA and

---

[1] Buck Institute of Aging, Novato, California.

RNA are incredibly important to modern drug discovery and medicine, which is why so much research attention is being given to this area.

The discovery of DNA's makeup and role has resulted in a huge leap forward in the understanding of the building blocks of all living organisms, including that of human beings.

Contrary to popular belief, DNA was not discovered by the Nobel Laureates James Watson and Francis Crick, but rather by a Swiss, Friedrich Miescher, as early as 1868. While working with white blood cells obtained from wound pus, Miescher managed to isolate a substance he called "nuclein", subsequently renamed *nucleic acid*. This substance contains only four bases, one each in every nucleotide, known as *adenine, thymine, cytosine and guanine* (A, T, C and G for short). Nucleic acid also contains *deoxyribose sugars* and *phosphates*. These bases are what high-throughput machines read in *genomic sequencing*.

The bases combine to create thousands of nucleotides, joining together in a chain of matched pairs and forming long double strands wound into a double helix, although this distinctive shape was not discovered until much later.

Because it is so simple chemically, no one thought that DNA could be the "stuff of life" until 1928, and even then in a tentative fashion. This was when Frederick Griffith recognized that bacteria could acquire something to transform themselves into much deadlier organisms; that something being DNA. These findings were refined by Oswald Avery who recognized that DNA was the "transforming principle".

But it took another scientist, Erwin Chargoff, to recognize that all DNA has a unique factor in common: the amount of *G (guanine)* in organisms varies considerably from one to the next but is always exactly the same amount in each organism as the amount of *C (cytosine)*. And ditto for *A (adenine)* and the amounts of *T (thymine)*. This meant that there was something vital to the structure of DNA, which is what Watson and Crick managed to discover (see Figure 3).

The story of how they discovered the double helix structure is quite well known involving, as with quite a lot of medical innovation, luck and the input of others, in this case from Rosalind Franklin, who pointed out via photographs they were not supposed to have access to, the exact structure for them to model.

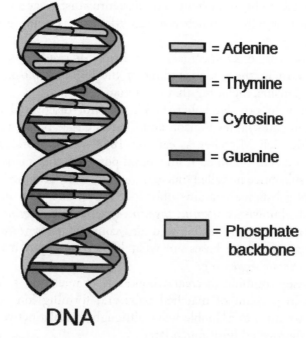

= Adenine

= Thymine

= Cytosine

= Guanine

= Phosphate backbone

DNA

Figure 3: Simple diagram of double stranded DNA.

What they found was that DNA is double stranded, arranged in a helix and its building blocks of nucleotides always match up in a complementary fashion – A with T and C with G. DNA strands always run anti-parallel to each other. DNA is a huge "macro" molecule and is found in three quarters of the cells in our bodies (the exceptions being red blood cells, which have no nucleus), which totals roughly 75 trillion cells. DNA is inserted into our cells in tightly packed coils wrapped around proteins. It has two principal functions: one to contain the code to build proteins and the other to pass on genetic information in cell division.

Strands of DNA are divided into chromosomes, which are present in the nucleus of every single multi-celled organism (which have so-called *eukaryotic* cells). Single-celled organisms, such as bacteria, do not have a nucleus and their DNA sits directly in the cell (known as *prokaryotic* cells).

Chromosomes are threadlike DNA strands and human beings have 46 chromosomes per cell. Of these, two are sex chromosomes (XX for female and XY for male) with the remaining 44 being autosomal chromosomes. Because human beings have two copies of each chromosome (2 pairs of 22), we are known as *diploid*.

All this may seem somewhat removed from the essence of this book, but as we shall see later, the discovery of the shape of DNA and a huge increase in knowledge about its role and action is the key to much of what we are writing about. The revolution in biomedicine taking place literally as we type is, to a large extent based on the unravelling of the "stuff of life". So we have to push on a little bit further.

DNA sits within the nuclei of eukaryotic cells, and within the chromosomes in which our genes exist. These eukaryotic cells divide according to instructions contained within the DNA blueprint. Some cells divide frequently and some almost never. Division is the way in which healthy bodies repair and regenerate. Uncontrolled division of cells forms the basis of cancer.

For example, surface cells such as skin or mucus membranes are constantly being replaced by division to compensate for cells that are shed. Liver cells may divide if they are damaged and needing repair. Cells in the nervous system (tissues) do not normally divide, which is why spinal cord injuries cannot currently be fixed.

Outside the nucleus of a cell is a plasma membrane in which there are a number of parts called *organelles*. These are present in the liquid *cytoplasm* outside of the nucleus. One of the most important of these organelles is the *mitochondria*, which is where most of our energy is created, through the conversion of glucose (from food that we eat) into *ATP* (adenosine triphosphate). ATP is the form in which energy is stored for later use and is found in all animals and plants.

In the human body, there are two types of cells:

- Somatic cells are specialized cells, for instance, muscle, fat or skin cells, which are produced by division in a process known as *mitosis*.
- "Germ" or sex cells are found in the reproductive organs. Here the cells reduce their DNA in preparation for combining with

another cell for reproductive purposes so that they can become base pairs upon conception, a fusion called *meiosis*.

The trillions of cells in the human body are divided into many functional types, most of them containing a nucleus with our entire genetic code (our genome). Many of the cells divide by mitosis and are in a constant cycle of replication. This "cell cycle" is highly regulated (except in the case of cancer cells, which are out-of-control rogue cells); every time a cell divides, all DNA is copied and each of the two resulting cells receives a complete set of chromosomes (23 pairs in humans). In meiosis, only one set of chromosomes is passed to each cell, because another is donated by the other cell it fuses with.

The process by which cells divide is highly complex and involves a number of phases and signals. The main purpose of mitosis (cell division) is to make sure that each new cell is provided with complete DNA containing a copy of all 46 chromosomes (in humans).

At each end of a chromosome is a *telomere* (see Figure 4). Telomeres are regions of repetitive DNA that protect the end of the chromosomes from deteriorating in the replication process or from accidentally fusing with neighbouring chromosomes.

During cell division, key enzymes that duplicate DNA cannot continue their duplication all the way to the end of the chromosome otherwise key information would be lost. Telomeres are therefore disposable buffers blocking the ends of the chromosomes and are consumed during cell division and replenished by an enzyme known as *telomerase*. This enzyme is critical to our health and plays a key role in maintaining chromosome health, which is thought to be related to the ageing process. It is also important in cancers, where cell division is uncontrolled. So if telomerase could be inhibited in cancer cells, the division process would come to a halt.

Within the chromosomes are the genes, which are single blueprints for each type of molecule in our bodies. The *Human Genome Project (HGP)* has identified approximately 22,500 genes in the body, much less than originally thought. The individual genes contain the instructions for our "worker" molecules. Before these molecules can be constructed, the genetic information must be copied into what is known as *messenger-RNA (mRNA)*. That message is then taken to the *ribosome*, a structure on which proteins are

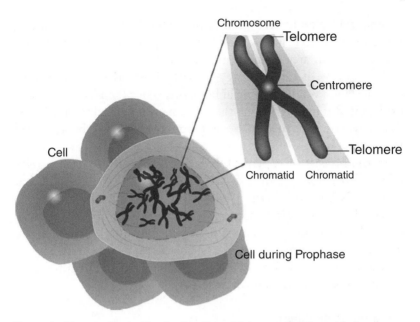

Figure 4: Diagram illustrating the location of telomeres at the end of a chromosome.

Source: (US) National Human Genome Research Institute, National Institutes of Health

made. The mRNA is decoded by a molecule known as *transfer-RNA (tRNA)*. The pathway from DNA to RNA to protein is known as the *Central Dogma of Molecular Biology* and is important in modern drug development. The interference with the operations of RNA is, for instance, a major focus of research.

As a result of the HGP and from prior partial sequencing of DNA, scientists learned that the number of genes in each human chromosome varies widely. Chromosome 1 for instance has 2,968 genes, whereas the Y (or male) chromosome has just 231.

The average gene size is 3,000 base pairs long (AT, GC) and genes are randomly located on chromosomes in clusters and separated by telomeres as we discussed earlier.

Genes seem to constitute only about 2 per cent of DNA with the remainder not being clearly understood. Formerly, this was known as "junk" DNA, but now scientists believe that this non-gene-bearing DNA may have a purpose in regulating the expression (i.e., switching on and off) of genes, and that RNA may have another role in addition to transcribing DNA into proteins. Indeed, there are likely to be many "RNA-only" type genes in the body, and this again is an area of interesting research.

The process of DNA being transcribed into RNA is incredibly complex and even if we were able to, this is not the place to try and explain it. But in that process there are many potential interventions that may have high medical benefit. Some of these will be described later in the book.

In the process of copying DNA from one cell to another, mistakes do occur, and although DNA polymerase (the enzyme that copies DNA in cell division) makes mistakes only about once for every billion base pairs it copies, those mistakes can result in mutations. These mutations can be activated by mutagens, which are generally environmental agents (such as smoking and radiation) that can lead to a serious disease like cancer. These environmental factors are sometimes known as the *exposome*.

Just a few more things

Okay, we are almost done with the technical briefing (phew!) but there are a few other things that are germane to our basic understanding of how new knowledge of the genome is creating the amazing opportunities in drug development that we see today. These things are metabolic and other pathways, the role of hormones and cell signalling. We run through these quickly now.

As we will see later, a lot of modern medicine is focused on understanding "pathways" in disease. Genes within cells all have individual functions but can also act in concert with other genes. Defective mechanisms in these genes (either individually or collectively) can create pathways for disease. These diseases can be of the so-called *Mendelian* type (meaning hereditary, after *Mendel*, the first person to work out the laws of inheritance though his work with pea plants) or complex diseases such as type 2 diabetes or cancer.

A *biological pathway* is any molecular action in a cell that leads to a certain product or change in a cell. Pathways trigger the assembly of new molecules in the cell such as a lipid or a protein. Pathways can also turn genes on and off, or impel the movement of a cell to a different location. There are a multitude of types of biological pathways, and research into exactly what these pathways do, particularly in disease, will be a huge preoccupation for scientists in coming years. Some of the most common pathways are involved in metabolism and in the regulation of genes.

Metabolic pathways are the facilitators of all the millions of chemical reactions that occur in our bodies. A key example is the way in which food is broken down in the body to create ATP.

Gene regulation pathways turn genes on and off. Such action is vital because genes signal the construction of proteins, which is vital to all tasks in our bodies.

Signal transduction pathways move a signal from a cell's exterior to its interior. This is extremely important in drug action. When receptor proteins located in plasma membranes of cells bind to ligands on the outside of the cell, change of behaviour on the inside of the cell can occur. This is "signal transduction" and the signalling molecule (the ligand) is generally a hormone or a paracrine factor.

Hormones are produced in one part of the body and used elsewhere. They are effectively molecular messengers created in certain glands or organs that then travel in the bloodstream to convey messages elsewhere. *Paracrine factors* or *Growth and Differentiation Factors (GDFs)* are also conveyors of biological information, but in the organ in which they are produced.

The principal types of hormones are proteins (such as insulin), steroids (produced from cholesterol) and amines (such as *epinephrine* – found in the famous *EpiPen*[2]).

Protein hormones act as start-stop gene signallers in cells; steroids include the *oestrogens* (the female sex hormones) and *androgens* (the male sex hormones); *amines* are produced by the thyroid and adrenal glands and are important metabolic-rate regulators. For instance, epinephrine is important in controlling heart rate and blood flow.

A *biological network* is when multiple pathways interact with each other, and much research is currently focused on identifying the most critical of these networks. In the lab, bacteria, fruit flies and mice are typically used to discover important biological pathways,

---

[2] EpiPens injections are used to treat signs and symptoms of an allergic emergency, which can be caused by triggers such as food, stinging and biting insects, medicines, latex or even exercise.

because their pathways tend to have many identical characteristics to those of humans. Researchers compare pathways in diseased individuals with those where no such disease is present.

Pathways are the object of a great deal of activity in modern medicine and as we will see, some of the companies we are interested in are heavily involved in their discovery and manipulation.

Metabolism is the aggregate of the processes involved in maintaining our cells. Metabolism is divided into two: *catabolism* and *anabolism*. *Catabolism* is the breaking down of molecules (such as food) and anabolism is the building up of cells. Both processes take place in the mitochondria (the organelle mentioned earlier that sits in the cytoplasm). Metabolism involves energy, either the production of energy *(exergonic)* or the absorption of it *(endergonic)*. The most important energy molecules are ATP, mentioned earlier.

A phenomenal amount of ATP is required daily by our bodies – 140 pounds (64 kilograms). But since the body only contains about one tenth of a pound of ATP at any given time, most of it is recycled about 1,400 times a day. This is the metabolic process.

One of the most important pathways in the body is the *Embden-Meyerhof* pathway, otherwise known as *glycolysis*. For example, all carbohydrates follow this pathway, which converts glucose to two lactic acid molecules in an anaerobic (without oxygen) process.

Common metabolic disorders include **gout**, which is the overproduction of uric acid, and **albinism**, a recessive trait that leads to an absence of skin or hair colour, and is an error of tyrosine metabolism. *Phenylketonuria*, for which most newborns are tested, is a defect of *phenylalanine* metabolism.

So for now that concludes our scientific briefing, and we apologize for its simplicity and non-inclusive nature. By default, more scientific terms will be introduced as we discuss the major areas of disease along with the therapies that have been and are being designed to treat or cure them.

In summary

We are all *atomic beings*, made up of molecules and cells. The processes by which our cells operate and interact make us who we are. Once we understand that we are biochemical beings, albeit incredibly complex ones, it becomes easier to see how the fusion of computing power and chemistry will take humankind way beyond the somewhat crude medical practices that have been in operation to date.

The A, T, G, C composition of DNA provides the platform for this second modern landmark (after the discovery of DNA itself), the development that provides so much of the basis of the optimism we express in this book.

The successful completion of the HGP in 2004–6 culminated with a neat and befitting coincidence with the first sequencing of a human's entire "genomic map" – that of James Watson.

Of course some genes (which we now know to number about 22,500 in every human being) had been individually "sequenced", or decoded (in respect of the "bases" or combinations of A, T, G, C that constitute them), before the HGP did its job. But this 15-year project used progressively improved computer and lab techniques to reveal the entire DNA contained in a single set of chromosomes contained in organisms. The order of the bases (A, T, G, C) is the key to individual DNA and it is the reading of those bases that was the great accomplishment of the HGP. The interpretation and use of that information is the next big step that is currently being taken.

The DNA of most living organisms is quite similar and it is the small differences that make up the great apparent differences between species. Humans do not have the most complex genomes in terms of numbers of base pairs (the salamander does); but we clearly have something special compared to other species.

Since the HGP was completed, the capacity to sequence genomes has increased enormously. So-called *high throughput screening* will make sequencing affordable to most people in the developed world within a few years. Currently, about 40,000 full genomes are being sequenced every year.

The positive results of sequencing the genome cannot be over-exaggerated, from working out which genes do what and how to turn them on and off, to the diagnosis and treatment of genetic disorders, to the production of drugs that have been specifically tailored for individual genomes. It is one of the greatest ever achievements of humankind and will form the basis of much of the advances of which we write later in this book.

The History of the Pharmaceutical Industry

Medicine is the treatment of disease and the provision of relief from pain. It is a field that dates back to the dawn of humans, but the first records date from Ancient Egypt in the form of the *Ebers Papyrus* in which there were 800 prescriptions using plants and herbs written down in hieroglyphics. About a third of these still appear in drug formularies. There are also ancient Chinese and Indian (Ayurveda) medicines, which are still in part practised today in regions well beyond their origins.

The Greeks and subsequently the Romans acquired a lot of their medical knowledge from the Egyptians. As a consequence, much of the nomenclature of medicine today comes from Greek and Latin. The Greek god of healing, Asklepios (in Rome, Aesculapius) had two daughters – Hygeia, the goddess of cleanliness and Panacea, the creator of infallible remedies, names familiar even today.

In temples dedicated to these gods, the treatment consisted of diet (*dieta* in Greek) as well as fasting and sleep. In some temples, teaching and training took place, the most famous under Hippocrates, known as the "Father of Medicine" and famous for his Oath, which laid out the basis for modern medical ethics.

In Homer's *Odyssey* we already find the word *pharmakon* referring to a drug from which pharmacy and pharmacology derive.

The most famous of the Roman medical practitioners, Dioscorides and Galen, lived in the 1st and 2nd centuries AD respectively. Dioscorides produced the first pharmaceutical compendium, the *De Materia Medica* and Galen produced the theory of humoral imbalance, which persisted for centuries. Galen's theory was that disease was an imbalance of the four humours – heat, cold, moisture and dryness – evidenced by four cardinal fluids – blood, black bile, yellow bile and phlegm. He prescribed herbal therapies based on each individual illness.

From Galen's time through the Renaissance and right up to the Industrial Revolution, remarkably little progress was made in medicine. The disastrous principles of Galen continued to form the backbone of what remained pretty dire medical practice, until the golden age of discovery around the turn of the 19th century. Life used to be brutish and short, marked by rampant infections, unsanitary conditions, huge infant mortality and no basic concept of the causes and effects of disease.

The remedies in use before 1800 were generally herbal and taken in the form of tinctures or infusions. None of them would fit the modern definition of a drug and no one at the time understood their chemistry.

At around the same time that the Industrial Revolution was getting underway, advances were being made in sanitation, anaesthesia and infectious disease (vaccines), all of which were to contribute enormously to the rise in life expectancy that was to follow. From the early 1800s to about 1900, life expectancy at birth almost doubled in North America and Europe.

The birth of modern medicine

Although *variolation* (inoculating someone with the *smallpox* virus to produce immunity) had been crudely practised for thousands of years, it was not until Edward Jenner (1749–1823) discovered the *smallpox vaccine* (vaccine comes from the Latin word for cow – *vacca*) that anything effective was done about the decimating effect of infections (see Figure 5). Jenner used *cowpox* pustules (milkmaids appeared immune to smallpox once infected by cowpox) and vaccinated a young boy successfully. This formed the basis of a true revolution in medicine. Thankfully smallpox has now been eradicated, and since 1980 the World Health Organization (WHO) has recommended that countries stop vaccinating their citizens for the disease.

Infectious diseases such as smallpox were the biggest killers of children beyond infancy as well as of adults. Since Jenner's invention many other effective vaccines have come into play, protecting entire generations against what were formerly fatal diseases. These include vaccines against *rabies, cholera, diphtheria*, tuberculosis, *tetanus, mumps, measles, polio, rubella, influenza* and, more recently, *human papilloma virus (HPV), hepatitis B* and now treatments for hepatitis C.

Until 1900 epidemic disease was by far the greatest cause of disease in the world. Indeed in 1900, tuberculosis was the biggest killer in the United States, followed by *pneumonia, diarrhoea* and *gastroenteritis*. The advances made in the previous century in terms of sanitation, including improved water supplies, sewage disposal,

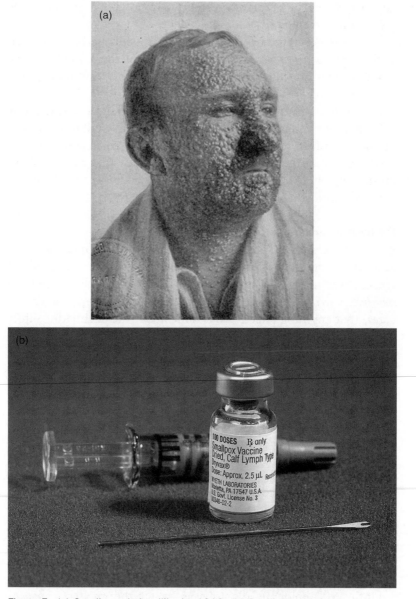

Figure 5: (a) Smallpox victim, Illinois, 1912; (b) Smallpox vaccine.
Sources: (a) Illinois Department of Public Health; (b) Centers for Disease Control and Prevention's Public Health Image Library

anaesthesia and anti-sepsis, were soon to change that. New threats manifested in people who were now living longer, such as heart disease and cancer, and these became the new principal carriers of death.

Surgery became more effective as a result of Scotsman Joseph Lister's understanding of the need for absolute cleanliness in operations, initially using *carbolic acid*. American pioneering work using *ether* as an anaesthetic enabled complex surgical procedures to take place for the first time, improving mortality rates further. All modern surgical procedures and their increasingly positive outcomes stem from these relatively recent inventions.

The first true drugs began to appear in the 19th century as organic chemistry and improved techniques of analysis evolved. Literally up to the late 1800s, **opium** formulated as "laudanum" was the most widely prescribed potion for patients. It was from opium that the first real drug, **morphine** (named after the Greek god of dreams), was discovered in 1806 by a young German pharmacist called Friedrich Serturner.

The first mass-produced drug was **quinine sulphate** in the 1820s. It was derived from *cinchona bark* and used to treat tropical fevers and malaria. This marked the birth of a new industry led by German firms, in particular E. Merck, which began to produce drugs in factories instead of apothecaries. Curiously, the first major products to come out of these factories were drugs that are illegal today, such as **cocaine**, morphine and other opiates.

Nevertheless, their discovery and production represented the start of the first period of innovation in the field of drugs, a period that lasted until the 1930s. During this period the focus was to isolate and purify products that were derived from nature, particularly plants, as well as to develop new compounds by chemical synthesis.

Alkaloids derived from plants, such as *ephedrine* and *emetine*, were in the first wave of products, followed by *serums, vaccines, analgesics and hypnotic drugs*. Much of the progress at the time was derived from a single invention that was made by an 18-year-old English student, William Perkin, who combined nitric acid and benzene in a home-made experiment to create the first artificial dye, *aniline mauve*. This compound acted as a molecular scaffold for other dyes, and soon huge numbers of vivid, easily stored colours that did not bleach or bleed were being produced.

But it was in Germany that the dyestuff industry really took off, based on Perkin's early invention. One of the greatest names in pharmaceutical practice at that time was Dr Paul Ehrlich (see Figure 6), who demonstrated that drugs derived from the advances in dyestuffs could successfully be used to treat infectious diseases. Dr Ehrlich worked with dye compounds being developed in Germany and postulated that in all mammalian cells there are receptors that can combine with chemotherapeutic (meaning any compound, generally synthetic, that acts as a drug) agents to promote an effect, such as a cure.

Figure 6: A portrait of Dr Paul Ehrlich on a bank note from Germany's pre-Euro currency, the Deutsche mark.
Source: http://www.bundesbank.de/bargeld/bargeld_faq_dmbanknotenabbildungen.php

Receptors are proteins embedded in cell membranes which react with active molecules, namely hormones, drugs and neurotransmitters. Drugs typically bind to receptors to promote their action, and the various principal terms for doing so are as follows:

- *Ligands*, which are compounds binding to a specific receptor.
- *Agonists*, which are compounds that activate a receptor.
- *Antagonists*, which are compounds that interact with a receptor and block agonists from activating the receptor.

Dr Ehrlich's work was principally concerned with the effect of dyes on parasitic infections (beginning with *sleeping sickness*) where he stained the *Trypanosome* parasites responsible for the disease as a way of isolating and destroying them. The first product was a lurid red-coloured dye called *Trypan Red*. But although a good part of his work was concerned with *trypanosomiasis*, it was his work with arsenical compounds, more specifically *arsphenamine (Salvarsan)*, that represented his major contribution to medicine.

For the first time, an infectious disease was curable (although rather brutally in the case of Salvarsan). The disease with a cure was **syphilis**, which in the pre-antibiotic age was a major and irreversible scourge, known as the "secret malady". Salvarsan represented the first time a synthetic chemical was used in the treatment of disease.

Dr Ehrlich laid the foundation for a great deal of what happens even today in pharmaceutical research. For the first time ever, he employed the systematic assay of many compounds in laboratory work. Prior to this, luck and judgement had been the main components of research. He used the developing science of organic chemistry to create compounds and his legacy includes the concept of drug targeting, and "magic bullets", which we will see a lot more of later.

Dr Ehrlich also coined a famous mantra for achieving success in innovation in the drug industry: the four Gs: *Geist* (a good idea), *Geld* (money), *Geduld* (patience) and *Gluck* (luck). All these factors still apply today. Later, we give examples where one or more of the four factors have not been in play, leading to enormous losses.

From Dr Ehrlich's work and that of others, particularly in Germany and France, a large number of drugs based on the new field of synthetic chemistry were introduced from 1900 to the 1930s. Prominent among them was **Prontosil**, a product directly derived from *Bayer Corporation*'s work in dye research, more specifically in *sulphonamides*. Prontosil represented a huge advance in antibacterial treatments, particularly in *puerperal fever*, *septicaemia*, *meningitis*, pneumonia and *gonorrhoea*, all of which were huge killers in the early 20th century.

The next wave of discovery in the 1920s and 1930s involved classes of *anti-psychotic drugs*, the precursors of compounds used today to treat mental illnesses of various types. As with so many successful products, the first anti-psychotic drugs came out of innovations focusing on other areas. The first *neuroleptic* (anti-psychotic) drug was **chlorpromazine** marketed as **Largactil** (by *Rhone Poulenc*) in 1950. This drug came as a result of experimentation with *anti-histamines* by French researchers in the 1930s. Anti-histamines are used to dampen allergic effects, and the first anti-histamine to be marketed, **Antergan**, was in 1942, also by Rhone Poulenc.

In many cases, a single drug can end up being used to treat several disease types with either no or little molecule alteration. This was the case with the first anti-histamines. As more powerful anti-histamines were discovered, it was found that they had sedative effects, and so chlorpromazine was initially used to prepare patients for surgery. It then went on to be the foundation for a huge area of drug therapy: mental disorders.

In the wake of the introduction of many variants of Largactil in the US market, the population of people in mental institutions in the US alone went from over 5 million in 1950 to less than 500,000 in 1968. An astonishing achievement that, along with many other drug inventions, demonstrates the potential power of pharmacology in changing the way society operates.

As with many successful drugs, further tinkering with its basic molecular structure was done to make it more effective and have fewer side effects. Thousands of compounds have been introduced from this type of tinkering and some of the most interesting companies we describe later do just that.

Anti-psychotics were joined by *anti-depressants* in the 1940s and 1950s, with most coming out of European labs and companies. Over time, these so-called *tricyclic antidepressants* were progressively improved right up to the mid-1980s, which is when selective *serotonin reuptake inhibitors (SSRIs)* were introduced, the most famous of these being **Prozac**; one of the first class of drugs to be designed "rationally", in other words, a specific biological target *(serotonin)* is identified and a compound is designed to affect it. SSRIs are used to treat anxiety, depression and personality disorders by increasing the levels of serotonin, a neurotransmitter that increases feelings of well-being.

Hand in hand with the development of neuroleptic drugs was an improvement in the performance of anti-histamines; the best known being the compound **Loratidine**, also known as **Claritin** (by *Schering-Plough*). It is still widely in use today as a "generic" drug, meaning its patent protection has expired and it can be manufactured by any company. Claritin is also an example of a drug that has gone from being a prescribed product to one that is available Over the Counter (OTC).

Patents play a major role in drug competition and development. Quite often, as a patent expires, a drug company will tweak a profitable product to try and create a new (but virtually identical) product that will extend its patent life and thus prevent margin erosion from generic competition. Claritin is a perfect example; there is a virtually identical product for sale called **NeoClaritin (desloratidine)** or **Arius** in some markets. It literally lacks only one of Claritin's components, and there is no difference in its efficacy, just a difference in price.

From the 1950s to the 1970s the *benzodiazepine* class of drugs was developed, and the first of these, **chlordiazepoxide**, was put on sale as **Librium** by *Roche* in 1960, followed by **diazepam (Valium)** in 1963, then **triazolam (Halcion)** (by *Takeda*) and then **alprazolam (Xanax)** by *Upjohn* in the 1980s. Until the advent of statins, Valium was the most widely prescribed (and mis-prescribed) of all drugs. It is interesting to note as an aside, that in 2009, a month's supply of branded Valium cost US$177.77, whereas the generic equivalent, Diazepam, cost a mere US$2 per month.

At this point, it is worth explaining that drugs normally have three names in their life span: their laboratory name, which is generally a number; their chemical name; and finally their product name for marketing purposes.

The major drug invention of the mid-20th century period was undoubtedly the antibiotics class, led by **penicillin**. The famous Sir Alexander Fleming stumbled upon an antibacterial substance from the fungus *Penicillium* in 1929. Florey, Chain and Abraham of *Oxford University* recognized its utility as an antibacterial agent in 1940, and a huge effort was made both in the US and the UK to find ways of producing the compound in mass quantity, in part motivated to combat infections in war wounds. At first, production was done by laborious fermentation, but by the end of the 1950s penicillin was being churned out by synthesis, and at extremely low cost.

From the 1940s to the 1970s, many antibiotics were produced to follow on from this remarkable invention. Penicillin itself is effective only against Gram-positive microorganisms and not so effective against Gram-negative organisms, and so new antibacterial agents were needed that are effective against Gram-negative bacteria.[3] Thousands of *analogues* (modifications, improvements) of penicillin have therefore been invented: **Ampicillin, amoxicillin (Augmentin)** and **carbenicillin** followed as broader spectrum antibiotics. Then there followed new antibiotics, with even broader spectrum (i.e., acting on a wider range of microorganisms) in the form of the *cephalosporins*, known as *beta-lactams*.

Other beta-lactams developed in the 1970s including the *carbapenem* and *monobactam* classes of drugs, are still widely in use today.

Different classes of antibiotics invented in the postwar era include the *aminoglycosides*, of which **streptomycin** is best known. **Neomycin** and **gentamycin** also fall into this class. *Tetracyclines* will be familiar to you, including **doxyclicine** and **vibramycin**, as will *macrolide antibiotics*, which are used largely in patients who are allergic to penicillin; **erythromycin** is one example. Many other prescribed classes of antibiotics exist today; almost all of them are generic because patent protection ran out a long time ago. Hence, there is a large financial opportunity for those who can produce a new nonresistant class of antibacterial agents.

As you may know, many bacterial infections, particularly the feared hospital *superbugs*, have become antibiotic resistant, and because of overuse and misuse of antibiotics especially in the developing world, the problem of resistance is getting worse. In Chapter 4 we look at how new work in infectious diseases and other applications of antibiotics is being strengthened to combat this problem. We also examine alternatives in antibacterial agents and some of the companies that look promising in this field.

There is no doubt that as an improving agent for the human condition, antibiotics were among the greatest ever. Given that bacteria reproduce rapidly, however, they are able to evolve to resist antibiotics. Therefore, the search for agents that counter these effective mutations is an interesting one from an investment point of view.

---

[3] Most bacteria can be categorized into one of two groups: Gram-positive and Gram-negative bacteria.

Other exceptionally important drug discoveries that mostly occurred up until the mid-1980s and the dawn of the biopharma era include the *contraceptive pill*, *statins* and other *cardiovascular* drugs, as well as earlier generation cancer therapies including *chemotherapies*, *immunosuppressant drugs* for use in transplants and *gastric* drugs. Additionally, the famous lifestyle drugs such as Viagra and hallucinogenic compounds such as **LSD** were popularized in this period.

Many of the new compounds developed after the war and up to the biopharma age were and still are derived from plants and other natural products. One of the most important areas in which naturally derived substances have been used is in *cardiovascular diseases* of various types.

In fact, so-called *cardiac glycosides* have been employed in the treatment of heart failure, or as it used to be known "dropsy", for centuries. *Foxglove* from which **digitalis** is derived is recorded as being used as early as 1785 to combat poor circulation, a symptom of cardiac failure. Cardiac activity from this class of drugs derives from an *aglycone*, although not until the 20th century was its mode of action in improving circulation discovered, and improved upon, to the extent that it is still in use today. Digitalis and its derivatives were only superseded relatively recently as the drugs of choice by the arrival of a class of drugs known as *ACE (Angiotensin-Converting Enzyme) inhibitors*.

Other cardiac system drugs derived from plants include warfarin (from coumarin clover), originally developed as a rat poison but used as an anti-coagulant. Warfarin and its derivatives are *vitamin K* (the vitamin that promotes blood coagulation, named after *Koagulation* in German) antagonists and used to prevent and treat **thrombosis** (the formation of blood clots) as well as for treatment of **post-myocardial infarction** (a heart attack). Likewise, **Heparin** (from *Hepar*, liver in Greek), another effective anticoagulant, was discovered in nature and became widely used in surgery to prevent pulmonary embolisms.

Organic nitrates – which were first observed in 1877 by W. Murrel of *Westminster Hospital* as having a positive effect on **angina** (chest pain) patients – remain widely in use, in conjunction with more recently developed *beta-blockers* and *calcium channel blockers*. *Nitro-glycerine* (explosive in quantity) has been de-risked and is the most used substance in the relief of angina in the form of **glyceryl trinitrate**.

Other key drug discoveries in the cardiovascular area came from work on microbiological sources. One of the most important of these has been of the fungal secondary *metabolites* known as *statins*, a discovery that took place concurrently in three countries: USA (Merck), Japan (*Sankyo*) and UK (*Beecham*). *Statins* are effective in reducing the risk of cardiovascular disease by reducing the *cholesterol* found in the bloodstream, which can contribute to *atherosclerosis* and coronary heart disease. Atherosclerosis is an arterial condition caused by plaque formation inside arteries where the plaques can undergo calcification, ulceration and bleeding, which can lead to strokes, *heart attacks* and *gangrene.*

Excess lipids in the blood (*hyperlipidaemia*) is a huge problem in the developed world due to sedentary lifestyles and poor diets. The advent of statins has been remarkable in reducing heart disease risk in patients with the condition, and indeed as a *prophylactic* (a preventative measure) for those who might be at risk, especially people over the age of 40. Statins work by reducing the circulating cholesterol plasma levels, inhibiting cholesterol biosynthesis and stimulating the synthesis of hepatic (*Low-Density Lipoprotein – LDL)* receptors so that LDL, also known as the "bad" cholesterol, is returned to the liver and not permitted to accumulate in the arteries.

As an example of just how successful statins have been, prescriptions of all drugs in the UK rose by 70 per cent to 927 million in 2010, from 552 million in 2000. Much of this increase was attributable to statins. On average, both in the US and the UK, the over-60s get over 30 prescriptions each a year.

The first statin to be approved was **Lovastatin** from Merck (known as **Mevacor**), which came onto the market in 1980. Since then statins have become the biggest selling drugs of all time (US$25 billion of sales in 2010 worldwide) with such names as Lipitor (Pfizer) and **Crestor** (GSK), both well known. In fact, so successful have statins become that as their patents expire – and most are expiring around now – the drug companies that make them are facing what is known as a "patent cliff". Generic companies will start producing statins in quantity very soon, significantly eroding the profit margins of the current producers. Once generics start being produced, drug prices typically fall by three quarters, although Pfizer seems to have held on to a large part of its Lipitor sales post patent expiration in November 2011, mostly as a result of effective marketing.

Other key classes of drugs developed for cardiovascular disease in this postwar period were *beta-blockers* and *ACE inhibitors*, still widely prescribed today. Beta-blockers are *beta-adrenergic antagonists* and are used in the treatment of **coronary disease** and **hypertension** (high blood pressure). They act by diminishing the effect of *adrenaline* and other "stress" compounds and they have revolutionized the treatment of angina, for instance. Sir James Black of the UK was the first to produce an effective beta-blocker in the form of **Propranolol**. Since then beta-blockers have become much more powerful, but they all reduce the heart rate and heart work load.

ACE inhibitors are the first class of drugs designed to use an inhibitor of enzymes to cause a *designed* action; the initial drug **captopril** is the first *rationally designed* drug. ACE inhibitors came from work done in Brazil on snake venom, of all things, and they were originally called *bradykinin potentiating peptides (BPPs)*; *bradykinin* being a peptide that causes heart vessels to enlarge and thereby lower blood pressure.

Captopril was approved in 1981 and, over time, its mode of action has been replaced by new antihypertensive agents culminating in 2007 with **Aliskiren**, which acts by inhibiting *renin*, an enzyme that regulates blood pressure. Too much renin leads to vasoconstriction of the *Renin Angiotensin System (RAS)* and retention of sodium and water, leading to hypertension.

Other drugs discovered and commercialized in the postwar period were those used to control *gastric acid secretion* and to treat stomach ulcers. These drugs came out of research into antihistamines, which we mentioned earlier. *Histamines* are present in all tissues of the human body but are present in higher concentrations in the lungs, skin and gastrointestinal tract and live in so-called *mast cells*, which form part of the body's immune system. There are two receptors for histamines, *H1* and *H2*, and classic anti-histamines for allergy have no effect on the *H2 receptor*. When blocked, this inhibits gastric secretions, thereby preventing gastric and duodenal ulcer formation. The first compound doing just that was **Tagamet**, marketed by *Smith Kline* in 1976, and a few years later *Glaxo* produced **Ranitidine** (trade name **Zantac**). Today, these drugs are sold over the counter and their patents have long since expired, but their effect has been hugely beneficial. You will be familiar with the old admonition about worry leading to ulcers, yet we seldom hear of anyone getting ulcers these days.

The *contraceptive pill*, which has also proved revolutionary, is a another postwar innovation. It came out of research into hormones that are produced by organs to regulate themselves or other organs. These are *endogenous* chemicals, meaning that the body makes them itself, but sometimes they are produced in too great a quantity and sometimes in too little, either of which can lead to disease. *Insulin* is the best known of all hormones, and its under-production is responsible for **type 1 diabetes**; resistance to insulin is responsible for type 2 diabetes. Hormones come in two forms: *peptide* and *steroid*. *Cholesterol* is the biogenetic raw material for steroid hormones, and the development of *cortisone* (formerly used in **rheumatoid arthritis**) in 1949 opened the path for the first therapeutic use of steroid hormones.

The isolation of progesterone from the ovaries of 50,000 pigs in the 1930s allowed for the use of a hormone that helps to maintain pregnancy in humans. This led to work in the 1940s and 1950s on the inhibition of ovulation and in 1951, Dr Carl Djerassi (*CIBA* research labs in New Jersey) developed the first oral contraceptive, **norethisterone**. This was further refined into what remains the most common formulation of *oral contraceptives*, a combination of a *synthetic progestional agent (progestin)* and *oestrogen*. By 1963 the first pill was on the market, marketed by *Ortho* under licence from *Syntex* and under the name **Ortho-Novum**. The rest, as they say, is history.

Progestin inhibits the release of luteinizing hormone, preventing ovulation, and oestrogen inhibits release of follicle stimulating hormone, thus making it more difficult for the follicles necessary for conception to develop. Over the years, reduced dosages and improved formulations of the oral contraceptive have been designed to reduce thrombosis in women, especially smokers, and the safety and efficacy of the pill has improved dramatically.

Other steroidal drugs, notably the *corticosteroid* class derived from *cortisone* have improved and are now widely in use as anti-inflammatory agents.

Another class of drugs invented prior to the biopharma age was the *immunosuppressants* such as **cyclosporine** and **tacrilimus**, which are used to prevent rejection in kidney, liver, lung and bone marrow transplantation – all quite common operations now but very dangerous prior to these drugs. Cyclosporines, marketed by *Sandoz* as **Sandimmune** are also used in the treatment of rheumatoid arthritis and in *psoriasis*.

The last major category of drugs invented in the golden period of drug discovery by the big pharmaceutical companies were *anticancer agents*, some of which remain in common usage, but most of which are gradually being supplanted by new drugs emerging from biological sources.

Again, plants are the raw material for a number of these compounds, and indeed, although limited in effect, plant use in cancer therapy goes back many centuries. Dioscorides writes of the use of *Colchicum* in the 1st century AD as a therapy for what appears to have been cancer. As an example of a modern plant derived therapy, the Madagascar periwinkle *(vinca rosea)* still provides the basis for about 10 per cent of all the chemotherapies engaged in fighting cancer: **Vinblastine** is used in *Hodgkin's disease* and in *metastatic testicular cancer*, and **Vinorelbine** is employed to tackle some lung cancers. *Vinca alkaloids* prevent cell division in cancers by blocking *mitotic spindle formation*. These are the formations that allow for chromosome separation during cell division (mitosis).

Paclitaxel and **Docetaxel** are among the bestselling anti-cancer drugs in history, and are derived from the Pacific Yew tree *Taxus brevfolia*. It had been known since antiquity that the European Yew had highly toxic properties, and substances derived from it had been used in murder and mayhem for centuries.

During the 1960s the *National Cancer Institute* in the United States studied more than 100,000 plants and eventually settled on the Pacific Yew as being of interest. It proved very hard to get sufficient quantities of the derived substance, known as *Taxol*, from the Pacific Yew but over time it became possible to derive Taxol from the European Yew, which was much more abundant. By the mid-1990s, after nearly 30 years of development, **Taxol** (*Bristol-Myers Squibb*) began to be used in *ovarian cancer* and then in breast and in certain lung cancers.

Taxol remains a frontline treatment in the fight against solid-tumours, and despite recent new compounds that show some benefit over it, it has been responsible for saving literally millions of lives since its introduction. Life expectancy, particularly in breast cancer, has improved remarkably, largely due to Taxol and **Tamoxifen** and to the more recent biologic **Herceptin**.

Tamoxifen is a so-called *pro-drug*, which means that its own action is not as important as the action it has on catalysing a process elsewhere in the body to create the desired effect. Almost all cancer drugs are *cytotoxic*, that is, their job is to kill cancer cells but they end up killing healthy cells as well as the cancer ones.

Of course, a huge number of other drugs have also been developed since the war, many with highly positive effects. Examples include the first effective *antiviral drugs* (as opposed to antibacterial drugs). Some of these are used to combat the herpes group of viruses. *Wellcome's* **Zovirax** (**acyclovir**) was approved in 1982 and is now a generic OTC product. Undoubtedly, the most famous antiviral drugs of great efficacy come out of the biological age – for example, the *retroviral* drugs for HIV/*AIDS* and for hepatitis C, and we talk about those in Chapter 4.

COX inhibitors were also invented in this period and are in worldwide usage today. Once it became apparent that *corticosteroids* had adverse effects in long-term usage in rheumatoid arthritis, it became necessary to look for new drugs. In the 1970s, it was discovered that new *non-steroidal anti-inflammatory drugs (NSAIDs)* such as **ibuprofen** (**Advil**) and **naproxen**, as well as the old stalwart **aspirin**, inhibited *COX 1*. Incidentally, aspirin is thought to sell at a pace of 100 billion tablets a year, even though its patent in the US expired in 1917.

COX 1 is an enzyme responsible for producing stomach-protecting *prostaglandins*, which is why when these drugs are over-used, stomach difficulties can appear. But in inhibiting *COX 1*, there is a physiological stimulus that relieves the pain associated with arthritis and other conditions.

In examining these drugs and their effects, a *COX-induced isoform* was identified, *COX 2*, which operates mostly in inflammatory cells, and new drugs are being developed to operate in inhibiting this enzyme to avoid the gastric problems typical of *NSAIDs*.

Of course, not all drugs have been as effective and successful as those in the "Hall of Fame" that we have just cited. One good example is **thalidomide**, which although refused approval in the US, was used to stop morning sickness and nausea in pregnant women elsewhere in the world. It was a disaster, and before its withdrawal in 1961, 5,000 to 20,000 deformed babies had been born and thalidomide proved a costly disaster for its maker *Grunenthal* and its licensees (*Distillers* in the UK).

As with many drugs, it proved effective elsewhere, away from the original purpose for which it had been designed. *Celgene* launched it as an effective therapy for **leprosy** and analogues of thalidomide are also being used in **multiple myeloma**, cancer of the plasma cells in bone marrow.

So the story of drug development up to 1980 or so is a remarkable one. Quite simply, the chain of innovation from *Salvarsan*, through to antibiotics, to anti-psychotics, and then ulcer drugs, pain drugs, heart drugs and anti-coagulants is an amazing one. These new drugs built on the efforts of Joseph Lister and others to improve hygiene in medicine and to reduce sepsis, as well as a general improvement in living standards and sanitation, increasing life expectancy to the point where a different set of diseases came into play.

Whereas a trivial wound might have killed a human in 1850, it is extremely unlikely to do so today. Far fewer people die in childbirth or infancy, and far fewer people die of infectious diseases, **ulcers**, or work-related cancers. In short, almost all of us are achieving what was long thought to be aberrant – our allotted life spans.

Biopharma – A new era

Human lifespan is about to change again – and radically so. Innovation will take our average lifespans to over 120 years; it will improve the quality of our lives even further; and it will have the demographic and investment effects that we discuss in Chapters 7 and 10, respectively.

We describe this new era that supersedes the Golden Age, as the Diamond Age, because it marks the fusion of biochemistry with raw computing power.

Around 1975, a new industry was born, an industry that has its roots in the pharmaceutical model of discovery, development and marketing and is the basis of growth of the behemoths of the modern pharmaceutical age. We are referring to the biopharmaceutical industry, or *biopharma*.

What are *biopharmaceuticals* and how do they differ from the drugs we have described in this potted history so far? They are simply drugs derived from or using living organisms. Already, in the 35 or so years of the biopharma industry, over 400 products have come to market and biopharma drugs now account for over 40 per cent of all new drugs being marketed around the world and they are prevalent in the developed world. There are an estimated 1,200 private biopharma companies and about 300 publically traded companies worldwide. As many as 2,000 strategic alliances between big pharma, biopharma, academic institutions and other research organizations are estimated to currently be in existence.

In contrast to drugs discovered in the period up to about 1975, all of which were so-called *small molecule drugs*, largely based on *synthetic chemistry*, biopharma drugs are *macro molecules*, forming proteins. Their range includes *enzymes, monoclonal antibodies (MAbs), hormones* such as *insulin* and *growth hormone (GH)* and *cytokines (signalling protein molecules)*, where *recombinant* technology is used in the production of quite a number of the products.

It is true that the first biopharma drugs were probably antibiotics from the 1940s, because they were derived from living organisms. But the reality is that biopharma drugs, or *biologicals*, are normally proteins where their value in many ways lies in their production. In other words, they are inordinately difficult to make by conventional methods. These are "black box" [4] drugs, in many ways, and neither the *FDA* nor the manufacturer normally publishes the process by which they are made.

Because we will be talking about most of the different ways in which these drugs are made in subsequent chapters as we review the work of specific companies, we do not go into too much detail here. But suffice it to say that from 1972, when the first restriction *enzyme Eco RI* was used to *divide DNA* in the laboratory, *recombinant or rDNA* became possible.

This is basically early *genetic engineering*.

As we mentioned earlier in this chapter, DNA produces RNA, which in turn makes proteins (although this can sometimes reverse in a process known as *reverse transcriptase*).

---

[4] In this context, "black box" is a term used to describe a drug whose inner workings are either not understood or not disclosed by the owner of the intellectual property. Please note that this is totally different from "black box label", a term we use later to describe drugs that can have adverse side effects, which have to be considered against the severity of the disease from which the patient is suffering.

Messenger RNA's CODONS are recognized by transfer *RNA (tRNA)* and a *peptide* chain is formed.

Recombining DNA means synthesizing a gene that is combined with a *plasmid* (fast dividing bacterial DNA) and put into a "factory cell" *(E. coli* or *Chinese Hamster Ovary (CHO) cells)* and allowed to grow. That process uses *biological scissors* called *restriction endonucleases (enzymes)* to site the human gene in exactly the right spot in the *vector (the host E. coli* or *CHO cells)*. This sounds a bit complex, and it is.

The bacterial cells, as they are designed to do, then multiply and the human protein expressed (made by) the gene is produced in quantity. This is "cloning" of the human protein and it has revolutionized medicine.

Cloned human insulin was the first drug to come out of this new technology in 1982, largely replacing the pig (porcine) insulin used up to then. Many other drugs have subsequently been produced by *recombinant DNA*, and many more are in development. Among them are **interferon**, used for cancer treatment, **hemopoietic factor (Epo)** used for *anaemia*, **Factor VIII** for *haemophilia* and the vaccine for HPV (human papilloma virus) to protect against *cervical cancer*.

Monoclonal antibodies (MAbs) came out of a technique developed at *Cambridge University* in the UK in 1975 called *cell fusion*. Here, *mouse spleen B lymphocytes*, which can produce a wide range of *antibodies* that recognize a specific *antigen*, such as a virus or bacterium, are merged with *immortal myeloma cancer cells*. The immortal myeloma cells mean that the cells keep dividing and producing more antibodies – a so-called *hybridoma*.

Using mouse (murine) antibodies that have been altered by breeding special mice to avoid rejection in humans (called "chimeric" antibodies), large scale production of human antibodies by MAbs has been enabled. Monoclonal antibodies are targeted proteins designed to attack foreign antigens, be they bacterial or viral, or tumours.

Examples of MAbs drugs include **Rituximab** for *non-Hodgkin's lymphoma* and rheumatoid arthritis, Herceptin for breast cancer and **Avastin** for colorectal cancer.

Herceptin is famous because it has significantly improved outcomes for patient survivability in the aggressive form of breast cancer that is indicated by the overexpression of the *HER2 receptor*, and is seen in about a quarter of all breast cancers. Here, *HER2* acts as a growth factor for cancer, and Herceptin binds to *HER2* and disrupts its signalling pathway.

Quite often, MAbs are *conjugated* (added) to toxins to be more effective at killing cancer cells.

Finally, *Polyethylene glycol (PEG)* and *Polymerase Chain Reaction (PCR)* are two biopharma era inventions that are of importance in new drug development.

PEG is a process by which proteins are modified. Hence, the term PEG becomes *PEGylation*. Quite often PEGylated proteins are more effective than their native parent molecule, and although the chemistry is complex, a whole variety of new drugs are emerging from this technology.

In Chapter 5, we talk about *stem cells* and their potential, and while at the moment they have limited therapeutic use, they undoubtedly will play a large part in bioscience in the future.

We also talk in Chapter 5 about *genetic engineering* at a higher level than MAbs. In other words, using pre-selection to remove hereditary genetic faults through *in vivo* (i.e., in the body) methods to alter genes and change disease outcomes.

None of this is science fiction; everything we are writing about is within grasp if not already here. The changes that are about to happen are going to be phenomenal. We have come a long way since even the 1970s, and the pace is accelerating.

This has been a long chapter, but without giving some basic overview of the principles of modern drug development, as an investor you can easily get waylaid, lost or bamboozled.

We also needed to go over some of the terms and set the scene in an historical context.

But before we get into the meat of our investment ideas and the therapeutic areas, we need to explain in Chapter 3 how the drug industry used to work, how it works now and how the whole model is shifting, offering the once-in-a-lifetime investment opportunities we will be describing.

Chapter *Three*

The Drug Industry – Reinventing the Model

You may have seen the movie *Love and Other Drugs*, which came out in 2010 and starred Anne Hathaway and Jake Gyllenhaal. In it, Gyllenhaal plays a Pfizer rep selling lots (and lots) of Viagra, the famous blue pill iconic of the 1990s. The year is 1996, and the selling process seems to involve drunken conferences, pretty girls, inducements to doctors and a generally Bacchanalian atmosphere that would not have been out of place in Ancient Rome.

This was *big pharma* and one of its biggest blockbuster drugs,[1] Viagra. It was a period in which profits were high, pipelines of new drugs were full and no really large-scale competitor had emerged for decades. Highly automated research into millions of compounds attempted to find the "lock and key" of Dr Ehrlich fame – the small molecule compound that would bind to a cellular receptor, have the desired effect without too many side effects and make tons of money.

In the 1980s and 1990s, drugs such as Prozac, **Zoloft** (*anti-anxiety*) Viagra, (*erectile dysfunction*), Lipitor, Crestor (statins), **Plavix** (anti-platelet) and **Singulair** (asthma) were cash cows for the major pharmaceutical companies dominating the industry.

Today, the big pharma companies, most of which have reorganized themselves through mergers and acquisitions over the past 15 years into even bigger pharma companies, are different beasts. The

---

[1] A blockbuster drug is generally regarded as one having over US$1 billion in annual sales.

majority moved from a business model that focused on *small molecules* targeting specific diseases to one that de-emphasizes in-house research and adopts partnerships with newly emerging as well as established biopharma companies. In addition, most big pharma companies still generate vast sums of cash that allows them to be generous dividend payers and substantial buyers of their own stock for cancellation. It is expected that the US-based big pharma companies alone will have total free cash flows from 2012–2017 of at least US$35 billion per annum, and will end up with over US$75 billion in net cash by 2017.

The pipelines of many of the major pharmaceutical companies are beginning to thin out as they face a patent cliff, where the intellectual protection afforded to them by patents on their key products begins to expire. As these patents expire and they become "generic", the drugs that once commanded princely prices and funded lavish research and marketing budgets, sell for a fraction of the price, exerting pressure on profits. The patent cliffs are for the most part exaggerated, but nonetheless they have been important factors in the reshaping of an entire industry.

So it is not surprising that most of the big pharmaceutical companies are downsizing, farming out research and entering into partnerships with, or outright acquisitions of, biopharma companies. In these, they see a more innovative and entrepreneurial culture, where big pharma provides the medical marketing clout that the smaller companies lack, as well as the money to bring drugs to market.

In truth, the model is not quite as simple as that, and the profiles of each big pharma company can differ significantly. However, for most companies the reality is that the glory days of high growth, superb margins and easy pickings appear to be over.

The *US Food and Drug Administration (FDA)* defines a drug as

> a substance (other than food) recognized by an official pharmacopoeia or formulary that is intended for use in the diagnosis, cure, mitigation, treatment or prevention of disease, and that is intended to affect the structure or any function of the body.

The drug industry worldwide is estimated to have had sales of US$762 billion dollars in 2010 according to *Alliance Bernstein*, a research provider. Total sales by 2015 are estimated to reach US$880 billion, a growth of 15 per cent. That is equivalent to the Gross Domestic Product (GDP) of Switzerland or Belgium, and is equal to about 1 per cent of total world output.

The combined market capitalization of drug companies around the world in 2011 was about US$1,500 billion, equivalent to the GDP of Russia or Spain. The market capitalization of drug companies represents the bulk of the value in the whole health sector, and is approximately five times that of the medical device business and five times that of healthcare services (hospitals, managed care, pharmacies and so on).

Research and development in the drug industry is second only in terms of total outlays to that of the technology industry, at an estimated US$135 billion worldwide in 2009. Many major drug companies have enjoyed high returns on equity and strong margins for many years. However, productivity from research and development has been declining for years, despite having a worldwide 7 per cent real increase for the past decade. In the 1950s, it cost about US$5 million to get a drug to market, by the late 1990s, it had gone up to US$300 million, and today it is around US$1 billion. Only one fifth of drugs entering Phase 1 trials are approved at the end of a typical eight year period.

The US spends more on drugs per capita than any other country.

In 2009, US per capita drug consumption amounted to about US$780, compared to US$620 in Canada, US$420 for the *Organization of Economic Cooperation for Development (OECD)* countries on average and between US$10 and US$20 in each of Russia, China and India. Overall, the US spends more than twice as much on healthcare per capita than other OECD countries, US$7,538 in 2009 versus the average of US$3,060. Therefore, drugs account for about 10 per cent of total healthcare spending.

Drug prices in the US are typically higher by 60 to 70 per cent than in other developed countries, but US patients have the widest choice in the world and typically get access to new drugs a year before patients in other countries. Indeed, it is expected that drug prices will increase by an average of around 5 per cent a year over the next few years in the US, according to *Cowen and Company*, an investment bank. That stands in contrast to the 10 per cent price erosion likely in the decade to 2020 in Europe.

Notwithstanding that high level of expenditure in the United States, US life expectancy remains relatively low for a highly developed country; 78 at birth, compared to 83 in Japan and 80 in the United Kingdom. This is possibly explained by the fact that a sixth of the US population currently has no medical insurance, by the high incidence of obesity and, speculatively, by too many medical procedures being performed relative to necessity. In addition, over one third of Americans (about 130 million people) suffer from some form of chronic serious condition, persistent illnesses that consume vast resources.

In 2010, the major categories of disease were cancer and haematology (about 18 per cent), antibiotics and antivirals (15 per cent), respiratory (7 per cent), central nervous system (10 per cent), cardiology (18 per cent), *diabetes* (7 per cent) and rheumatology (7 per cent), with the balance made up of other categories including *multiple sclerosis*, gastrointestinal, bone disease, *epilepsy* and ophthalmology.

The fastest growing sectors up to 2015 are expected to be diabetes and rheumatology, with the greatest decline expected to be cardiology, largely because of the patent expiration of several key cardiovascular drugs. The fastest growing part of the drugs business is in the "new generation drug companies" and in particular the *biopharma* sector.

In this chapter, we examine the business models of big pharma going forward, and compare them to those of the biopharma companies, which are emerging as the most potent forces in drug medicine. We also look at how the distinction between each sector (small molecule big pharma and large molecule biologic companies) is blurring, and what the future is likely to look like. Later in the book, we discuss the investment merits of both sectors.

We also write about the drug development and approval process, the critical role of the FDA in the United States and the *European Medical Agency (EMA)* in Europe (although not in detail), and the ways in which drugs and devices are regulated.

We talk about the capital requirements needed to get a new drug to market, the failure rates in that process and how new techniques are likely to accelerate the time to market for fresh drugs.

We look at the changes in the global pharmaceutical market and the potential growth in the major regions; we discuss why drug prices are generally much higher in the United States than elsewhere, and we touch on how drugs are paid for. We look at models showing how a blockbuster drug, both small-molecule and biologic, can transform a company's profit outlook.

We discuss the ways in which new drug and medical device companies are financed, and how the composition of that finance is changing. We look at the management characteristics of successful drug companies and where the greatest clusters of research and company start-ups exist in the world.

Big Pharma, Biopharma

First, we need to explain the difference between *big pharma* and biopharma. It used to be quite clear: big pharma concentrated on mass testing of compounds to generate one-size-fits-all drugs designed for specific targets, and biopharma made drugs from living organisms, so-called *biologics*, employing more complex manufacturing processes.

Companies of note on the big pharma side of the ring are Pfizer, Merck, Bristol-Myers Squibb, GlaxoSmithKline (GSK), *Astra Zeneca*, *Eli Lilly*, *Sanofi-Aventis*, Roche and *Novartis*. Almost everyone will have one or more of their products at home in their medicine cabinet. These companies, mostly American, but also British, French and Swiss, have dominated the pharmaceutical business for decades. The new products coming from these companies are a relatively small part of their sales, reflecting slowing innovation and the stronger position of newer entrants.

Somewhere in there are hybrid companies, such as *Johnson & Johnson (J&J)*, which make drugs in quantities but also have a device side and/or a consumer products business.

Blurring the distinction further are companies that derive a significant portion of their revenues from a combination of small and large molecule drugs. *Roche Genentech* is a good example of that; since Roche acquired Genentech in 2009, it has become the largest biopharma company.

In fact, few of the original biotech companies formed in the late 1970s and early 1980s remain, most having been subsumed by the major drug companies as they grew. These include *Chiron*, which was acquired by *Aventis* in 2006, and *Genzyme*, also acquired by Sanofi-Aventis.

Today, the two major pioneers that remain independent are Amgen and *Biogen Idec*, with Celgene being an anomaly since it was spun out of *Celanese* in 1986. Behind these three are hundreds of publicly listed biopharma companies worldwide, some successful, some pedestrian and many on life-support. And of course there are thousands of start-ups and non-listed companies.

All these companies tend to be categorized as *biopharma companies*, even though they may not be actually producing large-molecule drugs derived from living organisms. The nomenclature has become skewed so that any entrepreneurial drug company, or even gene therapy, drug delivery or stem cell company, is denominated as "biopharma".

The first biopharma company, as well as the most successful in history, was Genentech, based in San Francisco, which as a city remains among the three most important hubs for biotech in the United States, and where a lot of the research for this book was conducted.

Genentech was formed in 1976 by venture capitalist Robert Swanson and biochemist Dr Herbert Boyer. Boyer was a pioneer in the field of *recombinant DNA technology*. In 1973, Boyer and Stanley Norman used "restriction enzymes" as biological "scissors" to cut DNA fragments from one gene and fuse them into a similarly cut plasmid vector (as we describe in Chapter 2). Boyer and his colleagues carried on this research and with others became the first successfully to express (switch on) a human gene in bacteria when they produced *somatostatin* (a hormone) in 1977. In 1978 they did the same with human insulin and this formed the basis for the new company. Genentech was founded on the principles of recombinant DNA and it remains the leader in this field, as well as in monoclonal antibodies (MAbs).

The principles of Genentech's early achievements are still widely used today: biologic drugs are most efficiently produced by cells or within other living organisms, and biotech companies use bioreactors where cells are specially engineered to produce specific types of human proteins in quantity. Most of these products are delivered intravenously to patients.

Like so many biotech companies, Genentech's roots lay in academia, in this case the *University of California in San Francisco (UCSF)*. In fact, Genentech ended up paying a substantial amount to UCSF in resolution of a patent dispute some years ago.

The fusion of academic research and biotech start-ups has suited US academic institutions very well, and several of them derive significant income from patents on work done by in-house research teams, which then goes on to be commercialized by external companies. Good examples include *Stanford*, the *University of Wisconsin*, *Harvard* and of course UCSF.

The huge success of Genentech (it first went public in 1980 to almost rock-star acclaim) encouraged huge investment and hype in the sector. Genentech's model, where early on it partnered with large pharma companies for distribution and funding of its products, was widely adopted, and remains in place today, albeit somewhat modified.

Companies such as *Cetus*, Chiron, Celgene, and Amgen became the poster children of the new *recombinant DNA/MAbs* drugs that were coming in thick and fast onto the production lines during the 1980s and 1990s. These drugs offered new therapies with much greater efficacy and quasi "personalization" to patients whose choices were limited, or they produced "old" products such as insulin in a more efficient and safer fashion.

In the 1980s, Amgen provided the template for today's biotech companies. It raised both private and public money, building cash piles to take its drugs through the development process. It sold rights for some markets to large pharma companies, and by forging alliances and raising cash through these mechanisms, it slowed its burn rate until its first drug, **EPO** for anaemia, could be successfully marketed. This is more or less the same model employed today.

Most biotech companies that end up being successful are one-hit wonders, and quite often the profits resulting from their hit product are reinvested fruitlessly. Of course there are exceptions, such as Amgen, Celgene and *Gilead*, but investors should certainly watch for any "splash the cash" activity in companies that have one successful product and roll the dice with the fruits of that success.

However, the overall picture from an innovation point of view for biotech is very positive. The drugs from biopharma have been so successful that by 2014, the leading seven biotech drugs are expected to be on the list of top 10 blockbuster pharma products globally. By then, the top six drugs worldwide are expected to be **Avastin, Humira, Rituxan, Enbrel, Lantus** and Herceptin, all from biotech.

Evaluate Pharma, which pools consensus data from the world's drug companies, expects Avastin (Roche) for colorectal and other cancers to be the world's bestselling drug, with 2014 revenues of US$9 billion; and this despite it likely losing its role to treat certain cancers.

The next five positions will likely go to *Abbott*'s Humira (for arthritis), Roche's Rituxan (for *leukaemia* and transplant rejection), *Wyeth* (Pfizer) and Amgen's Enbrel (for *autoimmune disease*), Sanofi-Aventis's Lantus (**insulin**) and Roche's Herceptin (for breast cancer).

Additionally, Schering-Plough (Merck) and Johnson & Johnson's **Remicade** (for rheumatoid arthritis) will take ninth position, and so a total of seven of the top 10 drugs in 2014 are forecast to be biotech in origin, compared to five in 2008 and just one in 2000. This means that the entire pharma industry will have been upended in the 20 years or so since the Viagra apogee.

As you will note, some of those drugs will be marketed by big pharma, or indeed owned outright by big pharma. This is the result of the big companies' policy of feeding their depleted pipelines by buying or licensing drugs or companies in the biopharma area.

Taking a wider perspective, biotech drugs will account for about 50 per cent of the top 100 drugs in 2014. Even the drugs coming to market in 2011 are, in many cases, from biopharma sources: **Telaprevir** (recently approved as a drug for hepatitis C) and **Benlysta** (for *lupus*) come out of the industry and are expected to be among the bestselling of the new drugs.

Through the middle of 2011, 30 new small molecule drugs in total were approved by the FDA, compared to 62 for the whole of 2010. Additionally, 234 generics or modifications of existing drugs were approved in the first half of 2011 and five new biologics. This compares to 417 generic/modifications in 2010 and 14 biologics in 2010.

Notable also is that the sales of the blockbuster biotech drugs will still be less than those of the big pharma blockbusters of yore, largely because the marketing of biotech drugs is generally to smaller and more specialized patient populations. As an example, Avastin sales will be only half of Lipitor's (statin) peak sales, which in 2009 approached US$22 billion globally.

Notwithstanding the smaller relative sales, the trends are such that among established and still patent-protected therapies, biotech will be on its way to relative domination. And of course, the pipeline in biotech companies or perhaps more appropriately "new generation drug companies" is apparently fuller than that of the established large pharma companies. This of course means that the balance of power in the drug industry is shifting markedly.

The large pharma companies, still generally highly profitable but facing their imminent patent cliff, will be more inclined to use their substantial cash resources to buy drugs or companies that are currently in the biopharma area. The big pharma companies have not been afraid to acquire the largest of the biotech companies. For example, in January 2012 Bristol-Myers Squibb acquired *Inhibitex* (a Phase 1 hepatitis C compound owner) for US$2.6 billion. This indicates a willingness to spend big money even at earlier stages of drug development. Inhibitex's compound, believe it or not was only going into Phase 2 trials at the time of acquisition.

There were four big biotech and specialty public companies with market capitalizations of US$25–49 billion at the end of 2011 in the US compared to only one in 2002. After Genzyme was acquired, there were still nine players in the next tier below valued in the US$10–25 billion range, compared to only five in 2002. In the valuation range of US$1–10 billion in 2010, there were 62 listed companies in the US, versus 41 in 2002, and this excludes the 35 American companies valued over US$1 billion in the biotech sphere that were acquired in that same period.

Worldwide biotech companies raised a total of US$23.4 billion in 2011, up from US$19.3 billion in 2010. The bulk of the amount came from public company financing, with the venture capital element relatively small at US$4.5 billion.

Although many biotech companies are acquired by big pharma, and indeed some are specifically set up to be acquired, the model is not straightforward. That is because some of the larger biotech companies are themselves becoming aggregators and building scale by acquiring smaller competitors. Notable among these are Celgene,

Vertex Pharmaceuticals and Gilead Sciences, as well as Biogen Idec and *Teva.*

As an example, Gilead (which is a hugely profitable biotech) has built itself on first-in-class science in the antiviral (HIV/AIDS and *flu*) space. But it also has tried to build new franchises through aggregation by acquiring *Arresto Bio Sciences Inc.*, which plays into *Gilead's* efforts to build franchises in liver, *pulmonary* and cardio-vascular diseases (*Pharmasset*).

Celgene's success came from an old molecule, thalidomide, and its reformulations. But more recently it has built a position in *kinase* (signalling enzymes) inhibition, among other areas. Celgene also played aggregator when it acquired *Abraxis Bioscience Inc.* in 2010 in a cash and stock deal valued at US$2.9 billion. The deal added the breast cancer drug **Abraxane (nab-paclitaxel)** to Celgene's oncology portfolio.

But the major trend remains the partnership of big pharma with biotech as a model for funding innovation, especially so following the financial crisis of 2008. Since then capital markets and venture funding for biotech have become more difficult to access and big pharma companies have in effect become the sugar daddies of the biotech industry. Overall, funding for biotech has improved in recent years, but it is highly skewed.

Indeed, *BioWorld Insight* data show that the biotech industry raised US$17.6 billion in 2009, US$19.3 billion in 2010 and US$14.2 billion through mid August 2011. However, *Ernst & Young* has raised concerns that while overall biotech fundraising is increasing, so is the gap between the haves and have-nots, with 82.6 per cent of 2010 funding going to 20 per cent of US biotech companies, and the bottom 20 per cent of companies raising just 0.4 per cent of the funds.

It is a symbiotic relationship; biotech feeds big pharma with products and big pharma is a way in which research and development gets funded. Indeed, big pharma is receptive to buying biopharma companies outright, and many such deals are done, increasingly with so-called *Contingent Value Rights (CVRs)*, which confer some additional upside to the former owners of the biotech companies through what is a form of earn-out.

Medical device or drug entrepreneurial start-ups in the industry, especially in the United States, are quite often unashamed in stating their desire to be acquired and monetized by the big pharma companies.

It is certainly not impossible for a brilliant idea to get funded by venture capitalists (VC), but the important VC firms are much more selective than they once were and are not looking for companies that require 12 years and a billion dollars to get a product to market. Rather they are trying to invest in biotech companies that can bring promising compounds or products to market in much shorter time frames and to do so much more cheaply.

As an example, *Epizyme* is tackling cancer via a family of epigenetic enzymes called histone methyltransferases (HMT) and it recently raised US$54 million from *Kleiner Perkins Caulfield and Byers, MPM Capital, Bay City Capital, NEA, Astellas Venture Management* and Amgen Ventures. These firms are among the most important biotechnology venture capitalists. Nonetheless, it is estimated that the VC industry has contracted by 50 per cent since 2008.

Worldwide, hundreds of companies have been set up in the past 10 years or so, many in a scramble to find large pharma partners. Some of these companies have been based on academic research, some based on hopeful experimentation and some based on rehashed drug compounds. Many have failed, which has understandably dampened enthusiasm for investment in the sector, especially at a time when money is tight. All of them hope to corner a niche, to commercialize a new technology and most hope to be acquired for untold riches. Indeed, although funding has been tougher for biopharma companies since the 2008 financial crisis, the industry has still raised over US$100 billion of fresh money since 2005.

For every success in biopharma there are at least 10 failures. In a way, the biomedicine industry is a bit like the mining industry: it's a capital intensive industry full of thousands of small companies trying to strike gold or other commodities; it's an industry where travelling hopefully is often better than arrival; it has a fair share of charlatans; and when small exploration companies are successful, they often partner with mining giants, or sell outright to them. Mining is an industry where the time lags are long between the enterprise's creation and the first mine (though not as long as in biotech) and, like biotech (although again, not to the same extent) it involves regulatory processes that create barriers both of time and of money.

There are many different business models in biotech, and there are examples of success in all of them. There are fully integrated biopharmaceutical companies such as Gilead Sciences, Biogen Idec, *Dendreon* and Vertex Pharmaceuticals; these seek to capture the entire value chain for themselves by discovering, developing and marketing their own products.

There is the platform technology play (such as *Alnylam*), where a company has a novel technology that it licenses to numerous partners that use the platform to try to develop multiple products. Alnylam's skill lies in *siRNAs*, which we cover in Chapters 4 and 5. There are virtual companies that have no labs, but form small teams of scientists and developers that push one or two drug candidates through some critical early tests. *Trojantec*, which we talk about in Chapter 4, is an example of this model.

The odds are ferociously poor in drug development, whether it is in biotech or in small-molecule development. It is estimated that for every 5,000,000 compounds initially tested, only one makes it to the marketplace. In the developed world, the healthcare industry is the most regulated and the drug industry subset even more so.

By far the most important market for drugs remains the United States. About half of all drug sales are generated there, even though the US only accounts for about 5 per cent of the global population. In contrast, Europe accounts for about 30 per cent of worldwide drug sales and Japan for about 10 per cent, leaving just 10 per cent for the rest of the world. The fastest growing markets are the developing ones, including China and India, but for the near future, the US will remain the key market.

That having been said, China is growing as a market very rapidly. *IMS* reckons that China's drug market has been growing at 20 per cent per annum for the past several years, and is now the second largest individual drug market after the US. *Citibank* believes that China's drug sales will rise to over US$200 billion by 2020, a five-fold increase. However, doing business in China is difficult for drug companies, and generics dominate. One company worth looking at is *Sinopharm Group Company Ltd* (Hong Kong Stock Exchange: 1099). Sinopharm is the largest drug distributor in China. One reason why you should consider it for your portfolio is that it has no exposure to US cuts or potential US dollar depreciation because it generates over 95 per cent sales and profit in China and does not hold many financial assets.

Gastric, oesophageal and *liver cancers* are seven times more prevalent in China than in the US. The number of newly diagnosed patients with lung cancer in China is four times greater than that in the US, and this is rising rapidly. Even breast cancer, which has a lower overall occurrence rate in China, has three times the number of patients than in the US. Cardiovascular disease rates are moving closer to that of the West and diabetes is growing at very fast rates in China as dietary and other lifestyle factors become more analogous to those of the West. Indeed, Chinese consumers trust western brands in drugs more than native brands and for that reason the big pharma companies in particular could ultimately do very well there.

There are several reasons for the continued US domination in branded drugs, but one is that drug prices are high in the US compared to elsewhere. This is due to

- The need to achieve a return on the capital employed (about US$1 billion for every successful drug brought to market, including the cost of failures).
- The time it takes to get a successful compound through all the hoops to commercialization (about 12 years).
- The high rate of failure.
- The highly regulated nature of the industry.

Also, in developed countries, new drugs are not generally sold directly to patients but prescribed by doctors and hospitals, with pharmacy chains and wholesalers providing the products. If you watch US television you will know of the constant barrage of advertisements for drugs, encouraging patients to ask their doctors about what they can do for them. The advertisements never depict disease or people on ventilators, but usually depict hand-in-hand gambolling couples who are the lucky recipients of the miracle potions.

Because US drug prices are so high, there is a general view that the US is subsidizing the healthcare costs of other countries. The innovation and development costs required to bring successful drugs to market weigh heavier on the US patient population than elsewhere. But this is not the whole story – the United States remains the greatest hub of biotech innovation, and many, indeed most, of the greatest companies come from there. Any attempt to reduce drug prices would lead to politically sensitive shortages, as manufacturers become less inclined to make low-margin drugs. Such shortages are now becoming relatively serious in the US.

Without high rewards for taking the risks in bringing a drug to market, there would be little incentive for VCs, angel investors, funds and the others who sponsor the earlier stages of drug development by providing funds. So, in some ways it makes sense to keep drug prices higher in the US, because it has encouraged the growth of a fast-growing industry, with its principal concentrations in the West Coast corridor of San Francisco, La Jolla and San Diego, as well as in Boston and Worcester in Massachusetts, and Raleigh Durham and Chapel Hill in North Carolina. These "clusters" have developed in part because of proximity to universities and medical facilities of note, as well as because of access to funding, high availability of laboratory space and entrepreneurial cultures.

San Francisco is the nearest major city to Silicon Valley, where the longest established and most successful VC industry in the world resides, and because UCSF and Stanford are such world-class institutions, it is natural that the Bay Area has emerged as the top location for biotech in the world, especially as it has spawned the most successful company in the field's history thus far – Genentech.

Other important clusters are to be found in Madison, Wisconsin, in Cambridge and Oxford in the UK, Dublin in Ireland, Munich and Berlin in Germany, Basel in Switzerland, Tel Aviv in Israel, Beijing in China, Tokyo-Kanto in Japan, Bangalore and Hyderabad in India, Brisbane in Australia and the Biopolis in Singapore. Of course there are others, but most world-class companies have originated from these locations. Universities tend to foster innovation and clusters have grown up particularly around these. In the UK, Oxford, Cambridge and *Imperial College* are at the forefront; in the US, Stanford, MIT, UCSF and Wisconsin are in the lead. Others of note are *Singapore University*, *Hong Kong University*, *Tokyo University* and *Trinity College Dublin*.

The worldwide biotech industry has some interesting players outside the US, and of course major pharma companies from Europe or Japan own, have stakes in or deals with biotech companies in the US, but the flavour of the industry remains American. It is likely to remain so for some time.

Overall, it is estimated that sales generated by the biotech industry have been growing at a compound rate of 16 per cent per year since its inception in the late 1970s.

It has been a business of *profitless prosperity* taken as a whole since those founding moments; profits and losses have balanced out to create a zero return on overall capital invested. This reminds us of the airline industry where no net profits have been made since the second world war despite huge capital invested.

But this is misleading for three reasons:

- Airlines generally perform badly or well in synchronized cycles. There are exceptions but generally if one big airline does well, they all do well, and vice versa. This is not the case in biotech. Huge companies have resulted from one or two successful products, generating massive cash profits for their investors – Gilead Life Sciences, Genentech, Amgen, Inhibitex, *Human Genome Sciences* are some examples. These successes have outweighed the many hundreds of companies that have disappointed.
- Unlike airlines, which fly planes and basically all do the same thing, the construction and abilities, as well as the science, of biotech companies is highly differentiated, meaning that some will succeed and others will fail based on divergent business models, to a much greater extent than the airline industry.
- Many biotech companies are a work in progress because it takes so long to get a drug or product to market; they may not show a profit for a very long time, dragging down the profitability of the whole of the measured industry.

Nonetheless, biotech is a very risky business. The purpose of this book, apart from giving you a sense of what the future holds for what is possibly the greatest industry ever to emerge on our planet, is to try and narrow the fields of danger; to change the odds from say one in ten, to perhaps one in three or four, and with those odds to help you construct portfolios that are appropriately diversified.

The choice for investors is now enormous and daunting. Hundreds of publicly listed companies, all competing for the attention of an investment population that for the most part does not have the expertise to evaluate properly the opportunities based on science or prospective sales. One of the key reasons for writing this book was to provide a layperson with a translation of the obscurantism, the hallmark of medical investing.

From its earliest days of Genentech and the fermentation of cells to produce human proteins (*recombinant DNA*), the biotech industry has grown to encompass thousands of companies – an estimated 5,000 or so worldwide, with between 300,000 and 400,000 people working in them.

Products of the industry have multiplied to include *monoclonal antibodies, vaccines, gene-delivery, stem-cells, RNAi (interference with RNA), cloning, proteomics (studies into proteins), phage therapy* (which we discuss in Chapter 4) and *nanotech delivery systems* for drugs.

We do not think it an exaggeration to describe the industry as the most important in the world; there are few people who would not want to have a longer lifespan, especially if the quality in the latter stages of life can be improved. Biotech is on the cusp of delivering just that, and while the path to profitable glory is fraught with dangers – regulatory, financial and scientific – we do believe that the financial rewards, discussed later in the book, will be huge. For companies that develop successful, novel products, intellectually protected (by patents, among other safeguards), and address significant markets of unmet clinical need, the profits can be very large indeed.

To get to that stage, start-ups need to have three key things – money, a product and good people. In fact, they need four things: Paul Ehrlich's Geist, Geduld, Gluck und Geld – idea, patience, luck and money!

Like all other companies, biopharma companies start with an idea. Quite often, that idea comes out of an academic institution, for instance the UCSF work that supported the principles on which Genentech was founded. In the case of "new generation drug companies" (our new definition of biopharma enterprises) often this idea can be quite nebulous, based on casual observations in laboratory settings. Or it can be an idea based on using existing compounds in new areas or be highly rational (the so-called rational drug design – RDD).

The latter is much more common these days and RDD uses complex knowledge of drug "targets" to create compounds that treat specific disease. This approach can be applied both to small-molecule drug development and to biologic drugs. RDD has been around for some time, but because of the sequencing of the human genome and a much greater "library" of targets, as well as increased knowledge concerning receptors and enzymes, it has become much more effective.

RDD involves the application of what is sometimes known as *bioinformatics* or the "lock and key" approach to drug development. In other words, identifying the receptor target in specific diseases and creating compounds from the molecular level up to bind to those receptors in cells and cause action in them. Some companies, such as *Merrimack* use computer modelling and what they call network biology to predict the likely outcome of drug trials in advance.

A technique called *High Throughput Screening (HTS)*, a robotic automated system for synthesizing a large number of huge compounds, is also in widespread use in the modern drug development process. This technique is also known as *combinatorial chemistry*. Drug targets to be tested (such as cancers and infectious diseases) are added by robots to potential compounds that have been arrayed (in so-called *DNA microarrays*) in huge numbers of "wells" in laboratory trays. Those that interact in some way are subject to further automated testing. In this fashion, more than 1 million compounds a week can be tested, up from just 100 a week about 25 years ago.

After the sequencing of the *human genome*, it became apparent that humans have only about 22,500 genes, a considerably lesser number than had been thought previously. Scientists were hoping that the genome would reveal many more genetic targets – up to 100,000 genes – but nonetheless the number of "druggable" targets has at least trebled since the Human Genome Project (HGP). Additionally, the HGP has allowed the examination of biological pathways in much greater details and holds promise for genetic engineering and other techniques that are not drug related.

Because drugs cause complex chemical cascades within human bodies, their engineering is incredibly intricate. It is not just a matter of the key finding the lock; it is also about what happens after that docking of target and receptor has occurred and the body's subsequent reaction. It is also important that drugs do not also target receptors other than the one for which they are intended; that is, are the cause of actions elsewhere in the body that are unwanted.

Equally vital, apart from the obvious one that the drug should work, is that it has no serious unintended side effects (such as with thalidomide, discussed in Chapter 2). Additionally, drugs are metabolized in the body and then excreted, and if metabolized too quickly, the drug might not stay on target for long enough to have the desired therapeutic effect.

At the very beginning of drug research, the focus is generally on finding the appropriate target, and this can be a biological pathway, a gene, a receptor on a cell or a protein. The target is the point where intervention by drugs occurs in diseases.

Once a drug target has been identified, scientists, who can be working for big pharma, biopharma or in academia, will generally look for compounds that have affinity for whatever the targets are. This is where HTS comes in handy. When a compound of promise has been identified, the drug's development really swings into action.

But even at this point, failure is exceptionally likely. Typically, the first line of experimentation is with so-called "animal models", usually mice or rats but sometimes rabbits or primates. Quite often the rodent models are specifically bred to *overexpress* (make more of) or *underexpress* (make less of) a particular target. These "knock out" mice are genetically engineered to achieve this purpose; the large US corporation, *Charles River Laboratories*, is a world leader in breeding these types of mice and rats. These rodents act as useful models for humans because they have DNA in very many respects similar to us and act as useful, though not perfect, surrogates for humans in research.

If researchers find a compound that "binds" to its receptor, the statistics still indicate that the chances of a successful outcome are 1 in 5,000, and although the odds have shortened, the price of narrowing them further begins to rise dramatically.

As mentioned, the US remains the largest drug market in the world, and is likely to remain so for the foreseeable future. As a result, its regulatory agency, the FDA, which dates back to the 1930s, has a budget approaching US$5 billion a year, and is without a doubt the most important such agency in the world.

Drug companies can and often do conduct trials outside the United States on new compounds, although generally some US trialling is required. They can apply for approvals in such countries as Japan or in European jurisdictions without applying in the US, but this is rare, especially for a product of any significance. The US regulatory approval process is extremely complicated and the trials that drugs undergo are rigorous and quite often lengthy. For this reason, we focus on FDA requirements because investors should generally not be interested in companies that are not involved in attempting to sell their products into the US.

Drug Patents

Before any trials are undertaken, the most important priority for a drug company is to patent its invention and thereby secure its intellectual property. Patents comprise a set of laws and legal documents that protect new and useful discoveries and inventions and they exist in most countries of the world. Nations tend to have their own patent laws, but there are conventions that allow for the patents of one country to be enforceable in others. For instance, the European Patent Office has jurisdiction in most European nations.

The most important patent office is the *US Patent Office (USPTO)*, but proper patent protection involves seeking patents in all key countries. Patents typically grant effective limited monopoly protection to a novel product (for instance, new drugs) for a period of time, in exchange for full disclosure of the mode of action and other aspects of the detailed invention.

Biologic drug patents might, for instance, include the manufacturing process for a specific protein, the engineering of the protein-producing organism or the functional aspects of the protein (e.g., its three-dimensional shape). Small molecule patents normally focus on the chemical structure of the compound. Patents in the biopharma area are sometimes highly controversial. It is not possible to patent things occurring in nature (e.g., plants) but it is possible to patent processes that modify those plants (e.g., genetically modified crops).

The laws of nature and abstract ideas cannot be patented; neither can inventions that have no utility (such as perpetual motion machines) or items offensive to public morality. Additionally, a patent has to be for a non-obvious product. Some minor tweaking of an existing product is typically not patentable.

Animals, including humans, are not patentable but transgenic animals, excluding humans ones, are or might be. The so-called *Oncomouse (Harvard Mouse)* genetically engineered for the study of cancer, was patented in 1988. The test as to whether a living thing can be patented is whether or not it is "new" and indeed the patenting of living organisms goes back a long way, with Louis Pasteur receiving one in 1873 for yeast that was "free from organic germs and disease".

The development of genetic engineering has made patent law much more complicated, but the principle that a modified living organism can be patented was upheld when Ananda Chakrabarty received a patent on bacteria modified to degrade crude oil in 1981, and the Supreme Court stated that "anything under the sun that is made by the hand of man is patentable".

The Harvard Mouse patent laid a clear path for the patenting of non-human transgenic mammals, but the really big debate occurs when anything to do with the human body is applied to be patented.

Some patents on genes have been granted on isolated gene sequences with specific functions, but these patents cannot be applied to the whole of a naturally occurring genome in humans or in any other naturally occurring organism. As of 2010, approximately 40,000 United States patents existed that involve an estimated 2,000 human genes, although some of them are now under legal dispute. Approximately one third of these are held by medical or academic institutions and two thirds by private companies or individuals. It is thought that many more genes are "patent pending", almost all of them patented by US entities.

Given that there are between 20,000 and 25,000 human genes, there are patents that relate in part to about 10 per cent of the human genome. These patents cover: (i) some isolated genes; (ii) methods of using the isolated gene sequences (for instance, to manufacture protein drugs); and (iii) methods to diagnose a disease based on an association between a gene and a disease. A good example of this is the patents on the *HER 1* and *HER 2* genes associated with about one third of breast cancers, which are held by Genentech. Any company seeking to produce a molecule targeting the HER 2 receptor is potentially threatened by Genentech's patents.

The patenting of genes has proved to be highly controversial, with many academics and jurists arguing that even isolated genes should not be patentable. For instance, Rebecca S. Eisenberg has made a powerful argument that gene patents produce an "anticommons" at odds with an ideal scientific commons (i.e., open field of play for scientists). Professional societies of medical practitioners have criticized patents on disease genes and exclusive licences to perform DNA diagnostic tests.

Lawsuits have been filed against patents held by companies in respect of genes, to try to have them declared invalid on the grounds that genes are unpatentable products of nature.

The reason the patents were issued in the first place was that such genes are "isolated and purified" to a non-naturally-occurring state. A major case involving *Myriad Pharmaceuticals* and some of the 23 patents it holds on *BRCA1* and *BRCA2* genes (associated in about 10 per cent of breast cancers) is working its way through the US courts and has far reaching implications for the biotech industry. In his decision handed down in this pivotal case on 29 March 2010, Judge Sweet rejected the legal equivalency between "chemical compositions" like purified adrenaline (which was patentable) and DNA and genes. In his opinion Judge Sweet said:

> The information encoded in DNA is not information about its own molecular structure incidental to its biological function, as is the case with adrenaline or other chemicals found in the body . . . this informational quality [of DNA] is unique among the chemical compounds found in our bodies, and it would be erroneous to view DNA as "no different" than other chemicals previously the subject of patents. . . . DNA, in particular the ordering of its nucleotides, therefore serves as the physical embodiment of laws of nature – those that define the construction of the human body . . . the preservation of this defining characteristic of DNA in its native and isolated forms mandates the conclusion that the challenged composition claims are to unpatentable products of nature.

In July 2011, the US Court of Appeals for the Federal Circuit handed down a long-awaited ruling that isolated DNA and complementary DNA (cDNA) can be patented, but that analysing or comparing gene sequences for alterations is not patentable. If the appellate court had ruled otherwise, thousands of patent claims on human genes could have been invalidated. As it is, those patents stand, but no doubt will be continuously contested in coming years, and indeed the Myriad case is still rumbling through the Supreme Court at the time of finishing this book.

It strikes us that the patenting of genes is fundamentally wrong, as Judge Sweet put it, "a lawyer's trick", and that ultimately genes will become public domain.

Increasingly, academic institutions are using the research conducted in their laboratories to generate funds. The models they employ often involve licensing out technologies to private companies or taking stakes in companies in exchange for the use of specific technologies. Quite often, this intellectual property monetization can be of fundamentally important inventions.

This practice, now standard among all major academic institutions, dates back to the 1920s with the foundation of the *Wisconsin Alumni Research Foundation (WARF)*. This is the technology transfer office of the University of Wisconsin in Madison. It is a significant source of research support to the university and currently provides about US$45 million of funds per year, giving the university's research programmes what they term a "margin of excellence". This foundation has an interesting history because it has benefited from three seminal discoveries.

WARF was founded in 1925 by Harry Steenbock, who invented the process for using ultraviolet to add vitamin D to milk and to other foods. He patented it, working with *Quaker Oats* and pharmaceutical companies to commercialize the process, and used the proceeds to fund research at the university, which continues today. WARF currently licenses nearly 100 University of Wisconsin in Madison technologies every year. As of 2008, WARF had an endowment of nearly US$2 billion and a majority of this came from the original vitamin D patent, which was exceptionally important in eliminating rickets in the US (due to *vitamin D deficiency*). By the time the patent expired in 1945, rickets was all but nonexistent.

Warfarin (**Coumadin**), a leading anticoagulant that we discussed in Chapter 2), is named for WARF and the story of its discovery is emblematic of the relationship between academic research and the commercial world.

In 1933, a farmer from Deer Park showed up unannounced at the *Wisconsin School of Agriculture* and walked into a professor's laboratory with a can full of blood that would not coagulate. In his truck, he had also brought a dead heifer and some spoiled clover hay. He wanted to know what had killed his cow. In 1941, Karl Link successfully isolated the anticoagulant factor in the coumarin clover, which initially found commercial application as a rat-killer.

More recently, WARF was assigned the patents for non-human primate and human embryonic stem cells by Jamie Thomson, who we visited in the course of researching this book. Embryonic stem cells were first isolated and purified by Thomson in the 1990s. In October 1999, WARF established the non-profit subsidiary *WiCell* to license its stem cell lines. Thomson was appointed as WiCell's scientific director. In September 2005, WiCell was awarded the contract to develop the first *National Stem Cell Bank (NSCB)*. The NSCB distributes characterized (i.e., categorized) human embryonic stem cells to non-profit researchers worldwide.

The *Bayh–Dole Act* of 1980 *(Patent and Trademark Law Amendments Act)* allowed academic institutions partially or fully funded by the Federal Government in the US to keep for themselves the patents on discoveries made within the institution. This has proved to be a major spur to development of bioscience within universities.

The ownership of patents forms a core feature of successful biotech companies, as well as of academic institutions and the licensing of those patents is a complex and lucrative business.

Patents are issued in the United States, as well as in most other jurisdictions, for 20 years from the date of the application. Typically, anyone can file a patent on just about anything and for the first year while the patent is being evaluated, a provisional patent is issued that allows for temporary enforceability. Patent enforcement is the responsibility of the holder, so drug companies spend a lot of time and money making sure that their patents are not infringed. Because drugs have to go through the FDA process after the patent is filed, and that process can take years, effective patent lives can be short in the biopharma field, sometimes as short as 5 to 10 years. Indeed, a new anti-*prostate cancer* drug **Abaradarone** released into the market in early 2011 at an effective cost of over US$1 billion by Johnson & Johnson will lose patent protection as early as 2014.

Quite often, drug companies therefore try and extend patent life by tweaking the molecular structure of their drugs, changing the dosages or combining their drugs with other therapies to try and create a novel but similar product that allows for patent life to be extended.

US Patent law used to allow inventors to claim (providing they had evidence) that they had discovered or invented something even after other people had filed a patent on the same product. This is about to change and the rule will soon be the "first to file rule" applied elsewhere in the world. This means that whoever files a patent on a product or process first is the holder of that patent, so drug companies clearly have every incentive to keep their compounds secret until they file. This will also mean that US Congress will not be able to siphon off the patent fees that it currently does, leaving more funds with the US Patent Office to speed up the patent application process. The America Invents Act, passed by the Senate in September 2011, represents quite a scope of change and is in our view highly positive for drug innovation.

Patents are expensive to file, typically US$300,000 to $500,000 for full coverage in all the world's major markets, and they have to be maintained and enforced. As a result, a lucrative industry of patent attorneys, translators and other specialists has arisen. Patent infringement cases are common and expensive to prosecute. But because the intellectual property of any biotech company is its principal asset, its legal abilities are almost as important as its inventions.

A famous case, in which Amgen eventually prevailed over the *Genetics Institute*, involved EPO (Erythropoietin – a hormone that prevents anaemia) and centred on the *Freedom to Operate (FTO) Principle*, which is critical to a biotech company's financial outcomes. In other words, if multiple patents are filed for a new product, as was the case with EPO, someone else can claim infringement in one area of the process of making the product, or even on the product itself. This is an area of constant litigation, and if a biotech company cannot demonstrate that it will be able to get or has FTO, its whole product launch can be thrown into jeopardy.

The Path to Riches: FDA Approval

Once the patent is filed, and early animal studies in the laboratory have shown promise for a new compound or process, the inventing company or institution will start following the regulatory path to approval. For the purposes of this book, we will quickly outline the FDA approval process, although equivalent processes are needed for other countries. In Europe, the approval of the EMA as well as individual national agencies is needed. Roughly parallel to the FDA, the EMA was set up in 1995 with funding from the European Union and the pharmaceutical industry, as well as indirect subsidies from member states, in an attempt to harmonize (but not replace) the work of existing national medicine regulatory bodies. These processes are incredibly complex but some knowledge of them is vital to investors in the biopharma area, because any failures along the way in the approval processes worldwide generally mean massive financial losses for the companies concerned.

The first part of the FDA approval process is to agree the "indication" for which the drug is designed, that is, the disease. If a drug seems to have positive outcomes in several diseases, each specific indication has to be approved and go through the rigorous trials. These trials are typically divided into four phases, and the costs of the second and third phases can be extremely high.

The outcomes of the trials are known as *endpoints*, that is, what the drug does as measured against other drugs already established as useful in a particular disease, or against placebos (pills or therapies that have no effect). Drugs must have statistically significant effects with tolerable side effects in order to gain approval.

The results of the testing phases are widely followed by investors in all drug companies, and anyone placing bets in the sector should have a good understanding of how they work:

- *Phase 1* of testing is to check for toxicity and adverse side effects in human patients. These tests are typically done on healthy volunteers, although in cancer trials, terminally ill patients are sometimes enrolled. Typically in Phase 1, 10 to 100 patients are tested, and the whole phase normally lasts for a year before progressing to Phase 2.

- *Phase 2* of testing is to examine further the safety profile of the compound as well as to measure the drug's efficacy at different dosage levels in a wider patient population. Typical Phase 2 studies are with 50 to 500 patients and might involve patient groups who are suffering from whatever disease the compound is targeting, taking three different dosage levels with one group receiving only a placebo. Phase 2 studies normally last for one to two years. Sometimes Phase 2 "b" studies are run to confirm dosage outcomes, which can elongate the approval process further.

- *Phase 3* of testing is the final step in the path to approval. At this stage, which is expensive and more exhaustive, about 50 per cent of drugs fail to pass muster and are rejected by the authorities.

  Phase 3 studies are undertaken in even wider patient populations, numbering from the hundreds to the thousands and are designed to further confirm the efficacy of the drug. These are normally conducted at multiple clinical sites and often in several countries and they normally go on for longer – up to four years. The trials are conducted in a randomized, double-blinded way, so that neither the patient nor the supervising doctors know if they are receiving a placebo or a dosage of the trialled drug. There is a great deal of emphasis placed on the "informed consent" of patients, who are generally compensated by money or free medicine if they participate. Nonetheless, some new drugs stumble because their developers cannot find sufficient patients to recruit into the required trials.

- *Phase 4* trials are sometimes conducted as well, after the launch of a new drug, to assess long-term risks and benefits of a specific drug, but this is not a universal requirement.

The on-going results of trials are held in extreme secrecy, because they can dramatically affect the public market in a company's shares. As an example, US television celebrity Martha Stewart was the recipient of non-public information on the outcome of a trial by *ImClone*, acted on it and ended up in the clink for a year or two.

Generally speaking, trials for biotech companies are conducted by *Contract Research Organizations (CROs)*, which are organizations set up to do research and trialling for external parties; some of these are listed and can be interesting investments.

If the trials appear to be successful, a *New Drug Approval (NDA)* or a *Biologics License Application (BLA)* application is made to the FDA. There is also the *Abbreviated New Drug Application (ANDA)*, which is for the approval of a generic drug product.

In the meantime, the company applying for a new drug approval will have been working on its manufacturing processes, which in the case of biologics can be very complicated and also subject to regulatory approval. It will also have been working out its marketing strategy, whether to develop its own sales force for the product or to partner with another company.

Because many biotech companies partner with other typically big pharma enterprises from a relatively early stage in the development process, quite often the marketing is undertaken, at least in some markets, by the partner.

Partnerships can vary enormously in how they operate, but typically a biotech company will do a deal where it receives some money upfront from its partner, partial funding of the research and development effort, so-called "milestone payments" for specific successes (such as a successful outcome of a Phase 3 trial) and royalty payments on sales if the drug is commercialized. For years, biotech firms seeking to license out their drugs have had to retain an increasing portion of the development risk. However, that has recently started to change, with the average upfront payment in the first half of 2011 rising to US$60 million, considerably higher than the US$29 million for the first half of 2009. Additionally, on-going negotiated royalties are rising, and all this adds up to potentially much better times ahead for the biopharma industry.

Partnerships may involve all the worldwide rights for a drug or only rights in some territories. Also, they may comprise the rights to all the potential uses of a drug or only one or two of them; they may or may not involve the rights to "analogues" of the drugs, slightly different molecular tweaking of the parent compound. Biotech companies need real skill in forging partnerships, and the financial outcomes of any successful product they bring to market can be greatly influenced by this aspect.

Once the FDA has reviewed all the information about the proposed drug – and it will have been in close contact with the company throughout the regulatory process – it will either affirm the application or deny it. This process takes up to 18 months, but for drugs involved in the most "dread" disease for which the alternatives are poor, it can be fast-tracked. The FDA uses outside advisers to opine on drugs, and to help it formulate "labelling" for a drug; more restrictive labelling is clearly less desirable. A "black box" label can severely restrict the potential sales of a drug.

The FDA is risk averse as an agency; it is highly sensitive to deaths or other injurious effects of drugs on a patient population and as such has been accused of being too slow to approve drugs urgently needed in the clinic. It does sometimes, however, react to patient and public pressure; for instance in the case of HIV/AIDS, the first drug for the condition was approved just two years after the disease was identified. In cancers where there is little effective therapy, or in so-called *orphan diseases* where there is a limited number of patients but a high unmet need for an effective therapy, drugs can sometimes be fast-tracked through the process. This is known as the "accelerated development review", but products that go through this process must continue to be tested after approval to ensure safety and efficacy.

Investors in biotech and other pharma companies should watch the results of trials very carefully; they can and often do have a very significant effect on the stock price performance of the underlying companies.

As examples, in 2011 several companies that had promising results in Phase 2 for their proposed products received the dreaded "Complete Response Letter" from the FDA after Phase 3 results emerged.[2] Among them were *Orexigen*, with an obesity drug,

---

[2] A Complete Response Letter is a letter sent by the FDA to a drug company that has submitted a drug for FDA approval when it is not satisfied with the results of the drug trials. It typically asks the drug company to go back and conduct additional trials around certain areas of concern and/or to address certain adverse side effects the drug appears to have. In many cases, a Complete Response Letter can dash all hopes of a drug ever reaching the market.

Mannkind for an insulin inhaler and *Medivation* for its proposed ***Huntington's disease*** therapy, **Dimebon**. For Mannkind and Orexigen, both one-trick ponies, this was a disaster and their shares fell extremely sharply. This was because even if the FDA allows further testing, this can take years and cost many millions, and for a small drug company with limited resources, the one-shot bet that goes wrong can be terminal. Another such example is *Renovo* of the UK, which was knocked back in 2011 on a scar-reduction therapy that seemed highly promising. The company then fired almost all its employees and put its remaining assets up for sale.

Medivation, as we shall see in Chapter 4, did not suffer the same implosion. Its portfolio included at least one other promising candidate, **MDV 3100**, for prostate cancer which has been successful in Phase 3 trials and as a result, this company lives on and indeed prospers mightily. Even so, the percentage of drugs that fail in Phase 3 trials has been rising somewhat, to about a quarter (83 drugs between 2007 and 2010), which makes it even more important to take some precautions before you jump into a product story that may end in tears. The main reasons for failure are lack of efficacy (66 per cent) and safety issues (21 per cent).

It is very difficult to get approval for *neurodegenerative disease drugs*, where the "endpoint" of trials is "soft", in other words where an improvement in patients is observational by judgement rather than by science. An example here is Alzheimer's disease, where existing therapies have limited utility and proposed new drugs can only be measured on whether a patient's cognitive functions have been improved, which is hardly an exact science. This can be frustrating to the drug companies trying to produce drugs for this condition.

It may be that in the case of Alzheimer's the FDA will have to modify its approach because, of all worldwide diseases, this is perhaps the single one that needs most urgent attention. Other examples where the FDA has a reputation for being ultra-cautious is in the area of opioids for pain management or ***insomnia***, where approval and wide marketing can sometimes lead to a prevalence of abuse. Central nervous system drugs designed to deal with obesity or arthritis are also difficult to get approved. **Vioxx**, produced by Merck, was withdrawn from the market in the most expensive drug disaster thus far when heart attack risks were found in a wide patient population. Vioxx was a *non-steroidal anti-inflammatory drug (NSAID)* used to reduce inflammation caused by **osteoarthritis**, rheumatoid arthritis and acute pain conditions. It had gained widespread acceptance worldwide, with over 80 million people having been prescribed the drug when it was withdrawn, generating over US$2.5 billion in sales for Merck each year. Interestingly, having just mentioned the difficulties with getting FDA approval for insomnia drugs, Merck has a very promising orexin receptor **Suvorexant** in the last stages of development for sleep disorders, particularly insomnia. This could be a very big drug indeed, with insomnia affecting 70 million people in the US and standard therapies such as **Lunesta** and **Ambien** (GABA modulators) have side-effects, including some addiction potential. Suvorexant blocks hormones known as orexin pepticles from signalling the body to wake up.

Apart from drugs and biologics, the FDA also regulates the medical device market, which is a huge and growing segment of biomedicine. Such products as replacement hips and knees, cardiac stents or valves, insulin pumps, implants, pacemakers and radiological devices fall into this category. The process for approval in the device area depends on the complexity of the product and whether it needs to be installed in the human body (not all devices are fitted in the body; for example, some hearing aids are implanted inside the ear and some installed outside the ear).

In Summary

In a nutshell, the drug development process can be described as follows:

1. Identification of disease to be addressed.
2. Testing of compounds.
3. Patenting the promising molecule(s).
4. Commencement of preliminary animal and toxicological studies.

If these are successful, the three main phases of seeking regulatory approval are then pursued. Meanwhile, manufacturing processes are developed and approved (resulting in certification for GMP, or Good Manufacturing Practice), and funding is secured through partnership deals with other drug companies, or through raising capital from investors, or both. Not every compound costs US$1 billion to develop or takes 12 years to get to market; that is the average figure that includes the cost of failures as well. Nonetheless, drug development is an enormously expensive and lengthy process. Roche's website suggests that to get one drug to market, it invests US$1 billion, conducts 6,587 experiments and spends 1,874 million hours of work conducted by 423 full-time researchers (see Figure 7).

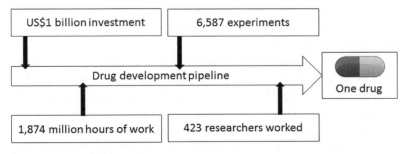

Figure 7: Drug development pipeline.

Genetic testing will also be a way of identifying which patients are likely to have toxicological reactions to specific compounds and as a result accelerating toxicity trials at the outset of the development process.

The huge costs currently associated with bringing drugs to market and the short period of patent exclusivity enjoyed by the companies that produce them, mean that prices for successful drugs have to remain relatively high. Biologic drugs are much harder to make than small molecule drugs and so generic competition in biologics (so-called *biosimilars*) is not normally such a big issue for companies making biologic large-molecule drugs. This tends to add value to the biopharma industry, because it means their own patent cliffs when they eventually arrive are unlikely to be as steep as the ones big pharma currently confronts with small molecule drugs. In fact, the approval process for biosimilars is extremely arduous, although not yet fully clarified, and it may be that a biosimilars industry never develops to the same extent that generics have for small molecule drugs. However, several biopharma companies have joint ventures with generic producers with plans to enter the biosimilar market. It is certain that biosimilars will require extensive trials, and manufacturing will be a big issue given the increased molecular complexity.

There is no simple division to be made between big pharma and new generation drug companies. Big pharma is adopting some of the practices of the more entrepreneurial biotech companies, and indeed some of the large traditional drug companies are among the largest producers of biologic drugs. That is because big pharma has partnered with or acquired many biotech enterprises; and in our opinion they will continue to do so for years to come. Meanwhile, some biotech companies are becoming aggregators themselves, and this trend will persist.

The regulatory approval process, which is among the biggest hurdles to economic success, will continue to be drawn out, but with genetic testing, HTS and computational modelling, the enormous cost of developing successful compounds is likely to fall in coming years, and the time to market will shorten.

There are thousands of products in trials at the moment. The results of those trials are exceptionally important to the economic outcome for drug companies. In the next chapter we examine the most promising candidates for success in the key therapeutic areas. A successful drug can literally change a company's fortunes overnight. Once a drug has been approved, net profit margins can run as high as 50 per cent, so a drug with sales of over US$1 billion, with patent protection and limited price sensitivity (such as in dread disease), can be among the most lucrative products on the planet. The stakes are high and for savvy investors the returns huge.

Chapter Four

Curing Disease – Promising Prospects in the Main Therapeutic Areas

In the previous chapters, we described the history, terminology, principal scientific advances and business of biopharma, as set in the context of the wider drug industry.

There are many diseases that occur in humankind, some trivial, some chronic and some deadly. Clearly, our vision of a world in which people routinely live for 120 to 130 years means that many of the diseases that carry people off today at earlier ages need to be cured, or at least treated effectively.

We believe that the biopharma industry will have a big role to play in this aim, as indeed will big pharma. This book concentrates on the most prevalent of diseases because that is where the greatest potential financial rewards lie and also where the bulk of research and development is concentrated.

Everyone is familiar with cancer, heart disease, arthritis and neurodegenerative diseases as being major categories of drug treatment. In addition, type 2 diabetes, obesity and *chronic obstructive pulmonary disease* are other well-known major categories, but also significant are chronic kidney disease, gastrointestinal/ulcer illnesses, infectious diseases and orphan (rare) diseases, which have more restricted patient populations.

If we believe the maxim that "death is just a series of diseases", then clearly all these illnesses along with others have to be addressed if the grim reaper is to be avoided prematurely. The drug industry is in the midst of some amazing breakthroughs. The biggest drug categories are in cancers, cardiovascular diseases, antibiotics and antivirals, as well as in rheumatology (arthritis), *respiratory illnesses*, diabetes and multiple sclerosis.

The industry's focus on these diseases is primarily driven by patient needs. In other words, if we assume that most of the above diseases are *age-related*, then as populations age, more and more people will contract diseases such as diabetes, arthritis and cancer and will require treatment.

Another reason why these particular disease areas dominate drug sales globally is because other areas do not have as effective treatments (yet), so drug sales are by default smaller. A good example of this is Alzheimer's, where the existing treatments, notably **Aricept**, have limited efficacy.

If researchers do manage to find effective drugs for, say, Alzheimer's or chronic kidney disease, clearly the whole pattern of drug sales would alter. Both of these diseases would probably become major new drug categories by 2020, which would transform the entire landscape of the pharma industry. There are currently 35 to 40 new drugs being trialled for treating Alzheimer's and without a doubt this area will end up being a big revenue generator. After all, if one in two people over the age of 85 develop *dementia* (many cases of which will be due to Alzheimer's), it is pretty clear that this will become among the world's greatest burdens. Other treatments being developed for Alzheimer's include deep brain stimulation, which appears in some trials to promote the growth of new neuron cells.

A disease that affects upwards of 26 million Americans is chronic kidney disease, resulting in dialysis at its end stage. We visited a company called *Reata* that is currently in the late stages of trialling the drug **bardoxolone methyl**, which has the potential to become a "category killer" if approved by the FDA.

In cardiovascular disease, drug sales are declining, not because diseases relating to the heart and circulation are diminishing in importance (they are not), but because some of the key cardio drug products, notably ACE inhibitors, beta-blockers and statins, are coming off patent or are already patent expired. These drugs have had a remarkable effect on reducing fatalities due to heart attacks or strokes; the incidence of fatal heart attacks in the developed world has halved over the past 20 years. Nonetheless, in the US, it is estimated that 500,000 people still die from fatal heart attacks every year. That number is 120,000 for the UK, which is proportionately about the same given the two countries' respective populations.

Future therapeutic areas such as *gene therapies* or *stem cell therapies* are not as yet reflected in sales figures for the pharma industry, but they will surely become major categories in their own right sometime in the next 10 years or so. As we discuss in Chapter 1, *organ regeneration* is now within reach, new organ "manufacture" is at most two decades away (although some organs can already be grown, such as windpipes) and gene therapy is about a decade from becoming a reality. Drugs based on *silencing* or *interference with RNA*, drugs targeted to individual genomes, drugs blocking *pathways* for cancers that were previously unknown are all in development, and in some cases close to realization. We discuss these in more detail later in this chapter.

Although there is not yet a category defined as "anti-ageing" (excluding quackery and cosmetic products such as **Botox**), it will develop into one within 10 years. As "ageing" genes are identified and isolated, we will be able to silence or alter them. Already, a gene in roundworms, *daf-2*, has been identified as its specific ageing gene, and similar longevity genes have been isolated in yeast, mice and rats.

When investors look at the current composition of global drug sales, they should realize that throughout post-World War Two history, there has always been disruption and change, and the rate of that change is likely to accelerate as a new tide of innovation brings cures and treatments in areas that were formerly beyond medical reach.

In this chapter, we review all the major disease areas and talk about the exciting things that are happening now. We highlight those that are potentially profitable, and we give some colour on specific companies that we have met with and like as investments.

Cancer – Step by Step, Being Beaten

Cancer is the second biggest killer in the world after cardiovascular disease. In 2008, approximately 12.8 million *cancers* were diagnosed worldwide, with 7.6 million deaths attributed to the disease. Cancer accounts for approximately 13 per cent of all deaths globally. Approximately one in two people will contract some form of cancer in their lifetime.

Cancer is a genetic disease, but the genetic element is influenced typically by environmental factors. In a normal body state, *proto-oncogenes* and tumour suppressing genes operate in tandem to regulate successful cell division. If cell division (*mitosis*) gets out of control (either because tumour suppressing genes are not doing their job or because oncogenes have emerged from proto-oncogenes), cancers are formed.

The most common cancers are lung (222,000 new cases estimated in the US in 2010 with 157,000 deaths); prostate (217,000 new cases with 32,000 deaths), breast (209,000 new cases with 40,000 deaths) and colorectal (143,000 cases with 51,000 deaths)[1]. Figure 8 is a graphical representation of these numbers.

There are estimated to be approximately 200 different types of cancer, and because there are so many, and because the causes of cancer are so varied, it has proved very hard to treat up until certain key discoveries were made in the past 100 or so years. These were the improved surgical techniques for excising tumours, radiation

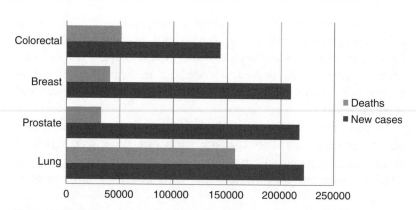

Figure 8: The most common new cases of cancer in the US in 2010 and the number of deaths.
Source: The American Cancer Society

---

[1] Source: American Cancer Society.

therapy, as well as chemotherapy, developed largely after the Second World War.

In general terms, cancers come in different forms; they can be solid tumours (such as a *sarcoma* and *carcinoma*); in the blood (leukaemia); in the bone marrow (*myeloma*); and of the immune glands (*lymphoma*).

Cancer is probably the most dreaded of all diseases based on historical outcomes for survival and also because of the side effects of its treatment, particularly during the earlier era of chemotherapy. The word cancer comes from the Greek for "crab" (*carcinos*), which was what the Ancients thought tumours looked like.

The first understanding of a causal link between cancers and environmental factors that act as *carcinogens* (factors that damage the DNA of healthy cells and cause them to turn into cancer cells) was as early as 1775. This was when Percival Pott observed that scrotal cancers were common only in chimney sweeps and an association was made. The key environmental cancer observations that followed were of the exposure to radiation (Marie Curie died of radium induced cancer, for example) and the discovery that smoking can lead to lung cancer. Lung cancer has a very poor prognosis for survival; currently only 17 per cent of patients survive more than 5 years.

Cancer is very rarely transmissible, and is only hereditary in about 10 per cent of cases. Its major causes are the triggering of genetic changes by outside factors, such as smoking, radiation, asbestos, drinking, diet and obesity, as well as by viruses/retroviruses, such as HIV and Human Papilloma Virus (HPV).

The lifetime probability of developing cancer varies, but 1 in 6 men in the developed world will develop prostate cancer during their lifetime (defined as being up to 85 years), 1 in 8 women will develop breast cancer, 1 in 20 people will get colorectal cancer and about 1 in 39 men and 1 in 58 women will get malignant *skin cancer*.

Cancer is generally age related, with 80 per cent of patients getting the disease over the age of 55.

Cancer is much more survivable today than it was even in 1970. Today, nearly 70 per cent of all cancer patients live to see what is known as remission, which is five years of survival post diagnosis, up from 50 per cent in 1970. Early detection of common cancers, such as skin, prostate, breast and colorectal, through examination,

PSA tests, mammograms and colonoscopies, means an outstandingly higher survivability. If there was ever a reason for people to get tested often – notwithstanding the furore over false-positives in some tests – this is it.

Cancers that are not detected and have *metastasized* (spread) to other sites in the body have had minimal improvement in survivability in recent years, and this is a key area of research and opportunity. In addition, 2 out of 9 patients who have had cancer will relapse after remission, and some of that may be due to the existence of cancer *stem cells*, which are posited to be cancer progenitor cells that lie dormant until relapse occurs. Eradication of cancer stem cells is an interesting area of research, although it is also possible that cancer cells may have the ability to morph into different types of cancer cells, without the presence of cancer stem cells.

Since the end of the Second World War, the major advances in cancer therapy have come in the field of drugs as well as in preemptive testing for early detection and treatment. The *US National Cancer Institute (NCI)* has been at the forefront of providing funding for and engaging in anti-cancer research. The NCI screens thousands of chemical samples a year against about 60 human tumour lines.

The NCI makes its research available to private companies and to academia to enable more effective drugs to be developed along with other not-for-profit medical and governmental agencies such as *MD Anderson, Dana Faber Institute*, the Wellcome Foundation, the *(US) National Institute of Health* (parent of the NCI) and *Cancer Research* in the UK. The NCI is an important contributor to advances in anti-cancer technology.

Cancer drugs represent a huge market for pharma companies, about US$100 billion in total annual sales worldwide; the US alone accounts for half of this figure. The NCI estimates the total annual cancer "cost" to be US$260 billion. Clearly, the argument that we use elsewhere about the effectiveness of drugs as displacing agents for much more expensive therapies (such as surgery or hospitalization) applies to cancer as well. In addition, there is a huge potential market for cancer drugs in developing countries; as life expectancy rises there, so does the prevalence of cancer.

In the 1990s, the FDA softened the approval process for many cancer drugs then in development, seeking to give terminally ill patients access to therapies that qualified for fast-track review. Latterly, there has been some tightening of the process again after the failure of a couple of major drugs, namely Astra Zeneca's **Iressa** and Roche's Avastin for breast cancer. This has made the path for novel cancer drugs a little harder.

Up to the 1990s, most cancer drugs were *cytotoxic*, meaning that they killed both cancer cells and surrounding healthy ones in the process. Many of these cytotoxic agents are still in use, but they are rapidly being superseded by drugs that intervene at much more specific tumour targets. These are still cytotoxic, but they specifically target cancer cells.

At the moment, it is estimated that there are roughly 1,000 new cancer drugs in development in the world. We discuss some of the most promising later in this section.

There are five key sectors in the cancer drug market:

- **Blood cell factors**, where blood cells are stimulated to proliferate and prevent infection and to treat anaemia (iron deficiency) or *neutropenia* (low white blood cell count).
- **Chemotherapeutics**, many of which date back to the pre-genomics age. These include *alkylating agents* that destroy cells by interfering with DNA replication; *hormonal agents* that reduce growth of hormone dependent cancer cells, such as in prostate cancer; *plant alkaloids* that block cell division; *anti-metabolites*; and *anti-tumour antibiotics*.
- **Immunotherapy drugs**, which are designed to boost the immune system to fight cancers.
- **Supportive care/adjuvant agents**, designed to work in combination with other cancer therapeutics.
- **Targeted therapies**, which are the new generation of cancer treatments and the most important for investors. Nassim Nicholas Taleb said that "pharmaceutical companies are better at inventing diseases that match existing drugs than inventing drugs that match existing diseases". This is changing, largely due to advances made in recent times.

Targeted (or "precision" medicine) therapies come out of the genomic progress made in the last 20 years or so, where a whole host of new cancer targets have been identified. Target specific drugs are likely to be the most important therapies in cancer in the next 10 years, and the ways in which they are delivered will also be significant in reducing cancer mortality. Targeted drugs are made both as small and large (biologic) molecules. The targets they address are multiple in cancers because it is such a complex disease. The signalling cascades (pathways) that trigger tumour development in the first place, the tumour's many stages of growth and the metastatic sites to which cancer can ultimately spread all form targets for new drugs.

Of these targeted therapies, there are approximately six subdivisions, mostly to do with cancer, and a lot of blurred edges between them:

- angiogenesis inhibitors;
- epigenetic drugs;
- gene knockout;
- anti-cancer viruses and vaccines;
- cancer pathway blockers;
- kinase and PARP inhibitors.

There are also drugs that fall into these categories, made through recombinant DNA processes or from monoclonal antibodies (i.e., biologics). We discuss each of the targeted therapies subdivisions in more detail in the following sections.

Angiogenesis inhibitors

These inhibitors are designed to block the development of new blood vessels in cancers (so-called *angiogenesis*). Interestingly, more than 70 diseases besides cancer are now recognized as angiogenesis-dependent and may be treatable with the same therapy. These diseases include rheumatoid arthritis, psoriasis, **endometriosis**, Alzheimer's and even obesity.

In 2003, Genentech introduced the first anti-angiogenesis drug, Avastin, for colorectal cancer. Today, 10 anti-angiogenesis drugs for cancer have been approved in the US, and these are being used on more than 1.2 million patients with cancers of the colon, lung, breast, kidney, liver, pancreas, stomach and bone marrow.

We like Roche Genentech as a longer-term investment. Of all the big pharma companies, this is the closest to metamorphosing into a "new generation drug company" and it is relatively cheaply priced and pays a generous dividend. It has a strong pipeline and its patent cliff is less steep than that of most other pharma companies. Roche Genentech is the leader in cancer medicines and is likely to remain so for years to come. Its hostile takeover in early 2012 of *Illumina*, the leader of instrumentation for genomic sequencing, may enable it to better match individual patients to efficacious therapies.

One of Roche's drugs, **Tarceva**, is modelled to attack specific types of lung cancer, the biggest killer of all cancers.

Researchers have discovered two single-gene mutations that collectively trigger lung cancer in about 15 per cent of patients. Patients with the more common one, a mutant form of the gene *EGFR*, have been shown to benefit from Tarceva. New findings indicate that the drug may be useful in people without the *EGFR* gene mutation. Tarceva's sales are expected to peak to about US$1.7 billion worldwide per annum.

Recently, Roche Genentech agreed to pay *Array Biopharma Inc.* US$28 million upfront and as much as US$685 million in milestones, plus double-digit royalties, for rights to the preclinical *kinase ChK-1 inhibitor ARRY-575*.

Genentech has its own *ChK-1* inhibitor in Phase 1 trials, but the economics of the Array deal apply no matter which compound is ultimately advanced. *ChK-1* is important in mitosis or cell division and these *kinase inhibitors* are designed to prevent cancer cell division.

Epigenetic drugs

Epigenetics is the study of changes produced in gene expression (what genes make) caused by mechanisms that do not cause changes in the underlying DNA sequence, hence the prefix *epi* in Greek meaning over, above, outer.

If we may get a bit technical very briefly, such changes can be caused by, for example, *DNA methylation* or by *histone deacetylation (HDAC)*, both of which serve to suppress gene expression without altering the sequence of the silenced genes, and both of which are the focus of considerable drug research.

DNA methylation is catalysed by *DNA methyltransferases*, a process that is sometimes reversible. Cancer is associated with hyper methylation of tumour suppressor genes.

In this area, we like *Pharmacyclics* (NASDAQ: PCYC), a company that has developed a new compound. *PCI-24781* is a best-in-class oral HDAC inhibitor for use in cancer indications. *In vitro* (meaning in test tubes in the lab), PCI-24781 has been shown to have potent anti-tumour activity in many preclinical tumour models, and it also potentiates (increases the effectiveness of) many of the commonly used chemotherapies when used in combination.

Pharmacyclics's drug lends weight to the thought that epigenetics could end up being more important than genetics in producing new drugs. This is because many cancer biologists have come to think that the aforementioned DNA methylation, a process in which enzymes tack methyl groups onto genes and block their activity, as well as other epigenetic changes including HDAC, might be as important as genetic mutations in causing cancer in the first place.

Pharmacyclics announced preliminary results from a Phase 1/Phase 2 trial of its Bruton's Tyrosine Kinase (BTK) Inhibitor Program. BTK is an important cell signaling enzyme that is found in hematopoietic (blood) cells including B-cells, and the trials showed an overall response rate of 69 per cent in patients with relapsed/refractory lymphomas, which is a highly promising result.

New epigenetic drugs are being developed to turn faulty tumour suppressor genes back on, causing cancer cells to fix or kill themselves. Three such epigenetic drugs are already on the market.

Business Insights, a research firm, suggests that the epigenetic market is already over US$560 million in global sales, derived from the sale of three anti-cancer products (**Dacogen** by *Eisai*, **Vidaza** by Celgene and **Zolinza** by Merck). They all target the two key epigenetic pathways, DNA methyltransferases (DNMT) and HDAC.

Other companies involved in this field include *Curagen*, which is testing a compound called *CR011* that acts on HDAC, currently in Phase 2 clinical trials, for the treatment of patients with metastatic melanoma and breast cancer. Curagen is private, but like many biotech companies may go public and so it should be on your radar screens. Roche has a newly approved melanoma product as well, **Zelboraf** (**vemurafenib**) with *Plexxicon* (owned by *Daichi* of

Japan) in the form of a kinase inhibitor for a mutation of the *B-RAF* gene.

Another company *Curis* (NASDAQ: CRIS) has a novel drug in development, *CUDC-101*. This is being designed as a multi-target inhibitor of *HDAC*, *EGFR* and *Her2* and is currently the subject of a Phase 1b expansion clinical trial. Curis is a speculative stock, but worth perhaps a small investment for the more adventurous. We have met the management of Curis and are impressed. Curis Inc. will receive an US$8 million milestone payment from its partner Genentech Inc., assuming the FDA accepts the newly filed New Drug Application (NDA) for **vismodegib** *(RG3616/GDC-0449)* in advanced, ***inoperable basal cell carcinoma (BCC)***, which is the most common form of skin cancer. Although this disease is not normally life-threatening, it can get particularly nasty in about 1 to 2 per cent of cases.

In stark contrast to traditional chemotherapy, epigenetic drugs may also be used in the future as preventative measures against cancer with patients who are at high risk of developing the disease.

Approximately 30 epigenetic drugs are under development by more than a dozen biotechnology companies, according to a Business Insights study on the industry. These drugs focus mainly on the treatment of cancer, and neurodegenerative and infectious diseases, although research is under way to explore the role for epigenetics in cardiovascular, metabolic, ocular and other diseases. Examples of other inhibitors include **panabinostat** by Novartis, which is in Phase 2/3 for ***cutaneous T-cell lymphoma*** *(CTCL)*, breast, prostate and other cancers; and Zolinza, licensed by the FDA for CTCL. Panabinostat is a HDAC inhibitor and is being studied in many hematologic and solid malignancies, including lymphomas (such as ***Hodgkin's lymphoma***), multiple myeloma, ***acute myeloid leukaemias*** and ***myelodysplastic syndrom***es. Novartis (one of the big pharma companies) is a good quality longer-term play, with a strong pipeline and significant vaccine franchise.

The epigenetic silencing of tumour suppressor genes is one of the most important findings in this area, it is found in almost all human cancers.

– Peter Jones, Ph.D., director of the University of Southern California/Norris Comprehensive Cancer Center.

Gene knockout

Tiny molecules called *short interfering RNA strands* (*siRNAs*, which we explain in more detail in Chapter 5) can halt the production of proteins that help tumours grow and survive by interfering with the cell division process. Several companies, including Alnylam Pharmaceuticals (a company we spotlight in Chapter 5) are actively engaged in siRNA strategies. Alnylam's experimental drug **ALN-VSP01** appears to stop the supply of blood to liver-based tumours and halts cell division. The company is seeking a partner to advance it to a Phase 2 Study. Alnylam is an interesting company, which along with **Arrowhead Research** represents the best way of gaining exposure to the siRNA market opportunity.

siRNAs have the potential to become an entirely new class of human therapeutics that could treat many human diseases including cancer. As siRNA molecules are fairly delicate, inserting them into cancer cells before they are destroyed by enzymes is a tricky process. One approach is to package them in a tiny bubble of fat molecules called a *nano liposome*, or to insert them into a silicon-based "carrier". Arrowhead Research is a leader in the field of targeted drug delivery, as well as in siRNA itself (we also cover this company in Chapter 5).

Another company, albeit smaller and private, working on this issue is Trojantec. We like this company too and have visited it on a number of occasions. In 2011, Trojantec presented the first data on its technology using *antennapedia*, a peptide derived from two fruit fly proteins that may provide a way of delivering drugs into cells without causing the body's immune system to reject them.

Trojantec's work has been conducted at the University of Westminster under the supervision of Dr Angray Kang, who believes that "although this is preliminary work, Trojantec's siRNA delivery technology has the potential to target all cells in a non-cytotoxic way and may allow internalization of both the transporter and the cargo, which on this occasion is siRNA". Trojantec has another two products in cancer pathways that are also interesting and it could be that this company goes public in the next couple of years, so keep a look out for it.

Anti-cancer viruses and vaccines

Viruses are a sort of cellular Trojan horse; they can slip into the body and when activated can take over or destroy cells. Some viruses can be introduced into the body as *vectors* by way of vaccination or to kill tumours while leaving normal cells unharmed. Often, these viruses are genetically modified to increase their efficacy.

Tumour cells are different from normal cells in many ways, especially advanced tumours that are highly *immunosuppressive*, meaning the cancer is able to avoid detection by the immune system and therefore continue to thrive. That is where *immunotherapeutics* come in; they provide a way to "teach" the immune system how to fight tumours. Targeted vaccines to prevent and treat cancers are the method by which immunotherapeutics are delivered. So-called *oncolytic poxviruses* or *vaccinia viruses* hold significant commercial and medical potential and may represent a breakthrough technology for cancer, because vaccines are better tolerated than traditional chemotherapies and also possibly more efficacious.

Not only can *oncolytic poxviruses* vaccinate patients against their cancer by inducing an anti-tumour immune response, but also they can disrupt the blood supply to the tumour. Upon entry into tumour cells, *vaccinia* replicate rapidly and efficiently. Infectious *virions* (virus particles) are released as early as 6 hours after tumour cell infiltration and tumour cell destruction occurs in approximately 24 hours, with up to 10,000 particles released upon cell breakdown (known as *lysis*).

In this way, viruses can be used as a bio-weapon against cancer. An important part of the mechanism of action of oncolytic viruses (cancer-killing viruses) through lysis relates to the stimulation of the immune system. This is especially true when viruses are armed with immunostimulatory molecules such as *GMCSF* (to stimulate white blood cell growth), as with the lead clinical agent **CGTG-102** by *Jennerex*, a private US company operating in this field.

These types of viral drugs are not associated with life-threatening side effects because vaccines work by selecting only cancer cells, thus having minimal side effects such as flu-like symptoms. But because these drugs are normally tested in very sick terminal patients, whose immune systems are highly compromised, their effectiveness is greater if combined with other treatments such as oncolytic viruses with standard radiation (now including the much more accurate *Proton Beam Cyclotrons* that are becoming standard care) or chemotherapy treatment.

Immunotherapeutics by way of vaccination or infusion looks like it will be one of the most likely fields for the next major breakthrough in cancer. The first FDA-approved therapeutic cancer vaccine/infusion is called **Provenge**, produced by Dendreon (NASDAQ: DNDN). Provenge is for treating late-stage prostate cancer by using a *dendritic cell* vaccine (*dendritic cells* that interact with *T and B-cells in lymph nodes* to enhance immune response. Interestingly enough, recent research also suggests that dendritic cells might have some effect on cancer's beginnings, so that they are not entirely positive). *Celldex* also has an interesting vaccine for **brain cancer** in late-stage trials. Others have also made their way to late-stage trials, giving a sense of optimism to the field. Researchers expect many new cancer vaccines to emerge in the next decade.

Nonetheless Dendreon's product has been relatively slow to sell so far, partly because it is so complicated to administer and to produce. It requires the patient's blood to be taken to separate out *dendritic cells* and then re-infused. On one day in August 2011, Dendreon's shares fell by over two thirds, which is as good a lesson as any in the need for careful research and diversification when investing! That having been said, sales have once again gained some traction, but competitive drugs, including Medivation's oral MDV3100 are likely to appear and erode the first mover advantage that Dendreon's complex therapy has enjoyed.

Substantial advances are taking place in the anti-cancer virus field. This is a very interesting development, and could add significantly to the traditional therapies of surgery, chemotherapy and radiotherapy (slash, poison and burn in the eyes of some cynics). Pushing the body to create its own immunity is the object of cancer vaccines. One of our favourite larger biotech companies Amgen (NASDAQ: AMGN) recently paid US$1 billion for *Bio Vex*, whose lead product **OncoVex** is an oncolytic virus in Phase 3 clinical trials for advanced *skin melanoma*.

Other companies operating in the oncolytic virus space are *Oncolytics Biotech* (Toronto Stock Exchange: ONC) and *Oncos Therapeutics* (a privately held Finnish company). Oncolytics Biotech is conducting clinical trials in the US, Canada, Belgium and the UK with the objective of developing **Reolysin** as a human cancer therapeutic. The current clinical programme includes a Phase 3 human trial examining Reolysin alone or in combination with chemotherapy. Its first target is refractory (i.e. non-responsive) head and neck cancers, which at the moment have poor patient survivability.

Cancer pathway blockers

The genomic advances of recent years have allowed scientists to identify many *oncogenes* (cancer-forming genes) with names such as *ras*, *src*, *abl*, *myb*, *mos* and *raf*, as well as the proteins that these genes express for (i.e., make), and this has opened up substantial opportunities for compound development. *ras* is implicated in many cancers, because faulty *ras* genes signal for permanent cell division.

Pathways are major targets for cancer drugs. They are the signalling routes that control the development of cell cycles that get out of control in cancers. These signalling routes are responsible for *angiogenesis* (which in cancer turns a tumour from a benign state to a malignant one), *apoptosis* (planned cell death) and other cell activities. New research in synthetic biology is changing the concept of what cells are and what can be done to manipulate them, using them as programmable entities.

Three interesting signalling pathways often implicated in cancers are the sonic hedgehog pathway, the notch pathway and the *P13K/AKT/mTOR* pathway (it is curiously quaint that medical terminology includes such names, especially since the pathways are implicated in such a terrible disease):

- *The sonic hedgehog pathway* is a key regulator of animal development and has been passed down from common human ancestors, fruit flies, to humans. Its malfunction can result in certain cancers and as a result, some companies are attempting to find ways of targeting hedgehog signalling.
- *The notch signalling pathway* is dysregulated in many cancers, and so again research into it is a major focus. As with the hedgehog pathway, humans share the notch pathway with fruit flies. Merck, Eli Lilly and Roche, as well as the aforementioned Trojantec, all have drugs in development to stop cell proliferation (leading to cancer) resulting from rogue notch pathways.

Researchers have recently discovered that many cancers contain a small population of pluripotent "tumour initiating cells" or "cancer stem cells". Trojantec's preclinical product, known as **TR4**, is a therapeutic protein blocking the notch pathway that is a critical pathway for some cancer stem cells, which lurk in the body after normal cancer cells have been destroyed and may be responsible for many cancer relapses. *Verastem*, an American company, recently went public on the back of its efforts to develop small molecule drugs for cancer stem cells.

- *The P13K/mTOR pathway* is an area of even larger research efforts. The P13K pathway represents a family of enzymes that are closely involved with the growth of cells, differences in cellular structure and the movement between cells, all of which are in turn involved in cancer growth. The P13K pathway has been shown to play a significant role in various cancers, including colon, breast and lung cancer. P13K inhibition is considered to be one of the most promising targeted therapies for cancer treatment.

Companies such as Sanofi-Aventis and *Infinity Pharmaceuticals* with its partner *Intellikine*, are developing PK13 pathway inhibitors. They are also developing the necessary biomarkers, the diagnostic "companion" tests that judge whether or not a treatment will be successful. This in itself is likely to be a very large market.

Kinase and PARP inhibitors

Another area of heavy research effort and spending is in the so-called *kinase inhibitor* market. More than 500 *protein kinases* have been identified and they play vital roles as messengers between cells in the body. It is estimated that about a quarter of all drug research is focused on kinases, because they are excellent targets, and not just in cancer.

Protein kinases are enzymes that catalyse the chemicals that regulate the majority of signalling pathways in the body. They play roles in cell division and programmed death (*apoptosis*). If protein kinases are aberrantly expressed, cancers may start forming. *Tyrosine kinase* problems are implicated in many cancers as well as in other diseases, and so inhibiting these is clearly an attractive target. It is estimated that along with monoclonal antibodies, tyrosine kinase inhibitors will account for a market of US$22 billion in sales in the US by 2012, making it one of the largest drug categories.

The first and so far most successful tyrosine protein kinase inhibitor is **Gleevec** (**Imatinib**). It was first commercialized in 2001 for patients with *chronic myelocytic leukaemia (CML)* and *gastrointestinal stromal tumours*. This drug is produced by Novartis and 90 per cent of patients with CML who formerly had a very poor prognosis responded positively to treatment with Gleevec. By 2011, Gleevec was generating sales of over US$4 billion per annum, from a worldwide population profile of only about 40,000 patients. So the race is well and truly on to find other kinase inhibitors in a wide variety of cancers.

Already, Genentech has Tarceva, *Onyx* and Bayer have **Nexavar** and Pfizer has **Sutent**, all of which are small molecule tyrosine kinase inhibitors, and there are many others in the pipeline. Given the astounding success of Gleevec, this is a highly promising area for drug discovery and kinase inhibitors will be a very large factor in cancer medicine in coming years.

Crizotinib (also known as **1066** and **Xalkori**) is an Anaplastic Lymphoma Kinase (ALK) inhibitor being developed by Pfizer used in the treatment of *Non-Small Cell Lung Carcinoma (NSCLC)* which manifest the ALK mutation. The drug was approved in late 2011 and represents another example of how Pfizer is at long last developing a highly attractive pipeline. Pfizer is a favourite investment of ours. A small Canadian company, *MethylGene*, is also interesting in oncology kinase inhibition drug development. It is speculative but well-funded, and has two promising compounds in development.

In addition to kinase inhibition, another new area in cancer research is the PARP-inhibitor market. *PARP* stands for Poly ADP Ribose Polymerase, a protein important for DNA repair and pro-grammed cell death. PARP inhibitors do not appear to affect normal healthy cells, but would obviously be a huge advantage in cancer treatment.

The first PARP inhibitor on the market, Sanofi-Aventis's **BSI-201** has disappointed in metastatic breast cancer, but many more such inhibitors are in development, including drugs by Astra Zeneca, Pfizer, Abbott and Merck. PARP inhibitors can be used to treat ovarian, breast and prostate cancers and they generally target mutations in the *BRCA1*, *BRCA2* genes and other well-known friends of cancer. Agents that act as inhibitors of PARP effectively disarm the ability of cancer cells to repair themselves, leading to the death of those cells.

Additionally, other tumours are targets for PARP inhibition therapy. For instance, BSI-201 (Sanofi-Aventis), mentioned above, is also being studied in *uterine* and *brain tumours*. Astra Zeneca is developing the PARP-inhibiting cancer drug **Olaparib**, where its trials continue in breast cancer, even though they were halted after failure in ovarian cancer. Others include **AGO14699** by Pfizer, **ABT-888** by *Enzo Life Sciences* and **MK4827** by Merck.

Fifty per cent of all cancer cases are related to the *TP53* gene. The *p53 pathway* is the pathway related to this gene and is another area of research. The *TP53* gene is not mutated in these cancers, but it turns out that the *p53* pathway is often partially inactivated. *p53* is a tumour suppressor protein that in humans is encoded by the *TP53* gene. For this reason, *p53* is sometimes referred to as the "Guardian Angel" of the genome due to its crucial role in controlling cell mutations.

The *p53* protein is overexpressed in many cancers, and *p53*-based vaccines are currently undergoing trials. A company called *Aprea* in Sweden (privately held and backed by the world-famous *Karolinska Institute*) is at the forefront of this research, focusing on reactivation of the *p53* pathway, thereby inducing cancer cell death. The compound has been tested in Phase 1 and 2 clinical trials at seven Swedish clinics.

Also involved in research of the *p53* pathway is a US-based company called *Cellceutix* (OTC: CTIX). It has announced that research on **Kevetrin**, its flagship compound against cancers, has demonstrated the potential for a major breakthrough by exhibiting an activation of *p53*. In our opinion, Cellceutix is a company to watch, although it is faced with certain manufacturing difficulties in making the compound.

Other companies to watch

Other companies of interest in the cancer field, which do not fall neatly into one of the six categories detailed above, are *ImmunoGen* and Medivation, both of which are US-based and publicly listed and we shall discuss each of them separately.

ImmunoGen (NASDAQ: IMGN) is a leader in the "antibody-drug conjugate" market, where antibodies that bind to specific targets found on cancer cells are "conjugated"; that is, added to potent cancer-killing agents. ImmunoGen refers to this process as *TAP* technology, which includes engineered "linkers" to keep the antibodies attached to the payload and enables a slow release inside the cancer cells. ImmunoGen is a company we would add to a portfolio of biotech stocks.

COMPANY SPOTLIGHT: MEDIVATION (NASDAQ: MDVN)

Medivation is a San Francisco-based company that we have spent a lot of time with and have made a reasonable investment in. It is run by David Hung, a polymath who not only owns and plays a Stradivarius violin, but also finds time to run a very exciting pharmaceutical project. Medivation and its Japanese funding partner, *Astellas Pharma* (Tokyo Stock Exchange: 4503), have now almost all the data on their prostate cancer candidate MDV3100 from on-going studies, including Phase 3 trials conducted with patients suffering from advanced prostate cancer confirmed anti-tumour effects and a good tolerability profile of the drug. It appears that MDV3100 offers better survivability in patients than Johnson & Johnson's **Zytigal** (Abiraterone) which is on the market already.

Prostate cancer growth requires the male androgen, testosterone. When testosterone, or its metabolite (what it changes to) dihydrotestosterone, binds to its natural receptor, the androgen receptor moves into the nucleus of the prostate cancer cell (known as nuclear translocation) and stimulates prostate cancer growth. The first triple-acting, oral androgen receptor antagonist, MDV3100 has been shown to provide more complete suppression of the androgen receptor pathway than **bicalutamide**, an existing drug used to treat prostate cancer. MDV3100 slows growth and induces cell death in bicalutamide-resistant cancers via three complementary actions: it blocks testosterone binding to the androgen receptor; impedes nuclear translocation; and inhibits binding to DNA.

This is a very exciting new compound and Medivation is a true "new generation drug company" even though it focuses on small-molecule drugs. The company has been astute in getting big pharma companies to fund its research and trials and has retained significant rights for itself in key markets, if and when its drugs are approved. Its key competitors in the end-stage prostate cancer market are a Johnson & Johnson

(Continued)

product, Abiraterone, and Dendreon's Provenge, neither of which seem to work as well as MDV3100.

If MDV3100 is approved, which appears likely the economic impact on Medivation will be considerable, perhaps as much as US$500 million per year in profits, according to our calculations. With an enterprise value of about US$2 billion in February 2012, this makes Medivation seemingly cheap. There is of course, always a risk that something can go awry with the results of the safety trials, but by whittling down the risk factors and recognizing the upside, Medivation is exactly the sort of biotech "gamble" we like to take. This is despite the fact that its Alzheimer's compound, developed in conjunction with Pfizer, named Dimebon, has clearly failed.

Meanwhile, Boston-based Merrimack, a company planning to go public as we finish this book, has extensively modelled key signalling networks regulating the biology of solid tumours, including breast, ovarian and colon cancers. The idea is to use this "network biology" to speed up the drug-development process by predicting outcomes prior to expensive trials.

Merrimack's research, conducted by a large group of PhDs from Massachusetts Institute of Technology (MIT), has developed some novel approaches to shut down the growth signals that drive the growth of tumours. They are testing two therapeutic antibodies, **MM-121** and **MM-111**, both in Phase 2 testing. MM-121, Merrimack's lead candidate, is a monoclonal antibody that targets the *ErbB3* receptor, implicated in many cancers. MM-121 is the first selective *ErbB3* antagonist to enter human clinical development.

An extremely busy field with untold promise

As this section shows, there is no "magic bullet" for cancer and nor is there likely to be one. However, cancer treatment is likely to become more specific, aided by new methods of delivering drugs, as well as by the development of new generations of chemotherapeutics.

The gradualist approach in tackling cancer is likely to continue, with possibly *90 per cent of* cancers being treatable to remission in about 10 years' time. Some of this will result from the development of new biologics, some will be the result of using computing power and genomics to identify and alter a wider range of targets, and some will be by using combinatorial therapies.

Wider scale preventative medicine will play a part in reducing cancer deaths through early screening, and the deadliest forms (notably lung, *pancreatic*, brain and liver *cancers*) are the subject of intense research that is likely to reduce mortality rates considerably.

Cancer is a disease in which biologic and small-molecule drugs can have an equal impact, though for the moment the preponderance of momentum is with the biologics. But the bottom line is that for most cancer victims, the once terrible words "you've got cancer" will no longer come with the previous death sentence.

Infectious Diseases: New Antibiotics, Hepatitis and HIV Drugs Make for a Fast-growing Sector

Infectious diseases, also known as communicable diseases, contagious diseases and transmissible diseases, result from the presence and growth of pathogenic biological agents in an individual host organism. Infectious pathogens include viruses, bacteria, fungi, protozoa, multicellular parasites and proteins known as *prions*.

The infectious disease market can be roughly divided into antibiotics, antivirals, antifungals and vaccinations. Worldwide, the market is very large taking in US$160 billion in sales annually, or about a quarter of all drug sales.

Key infectious diseases are tuberculosis, malaria, pneumonia and other respiratory infections, HIV/AIDS, hepatitis B and C, diarrhoea, measles, cholera, influenza, *the common cold, E. coli, Staphylococcus aureus (MRSA), Pseudomonas, clostridium difficile* and other superbugs. In addition, *fungal infections, sexually transmitted diseases* and *sepsis* are all important disease categories.

This is a fast-growing market, with the most exciting part being new drugs for hepatitis C, new therapies for HIV/AIDS and new drugs to combat resistant strains of bacteria in both hospitals and the wider community.

GlaxoSmithKline (GSK) is the largest player in this category and is likely to remain so for the foreseeable future, with Pfizer and Merck in second and third places. Other companies of note are Vertex, Bristol-Myers Squibb (which has acquired Inhibitex) and Pharmasset (now owned by Gilead) in the hepatitis C market, *Cubist*, *Forest* and *Theravance* in the MRSA superbug market, and Gilead in the HIV/AIDS market.

Infectious diseases usually arise as a result of pathogens entering the body. Pathogens can be transmitted in a variety of ways, including physical contact, contaminated food, body fluids, objects, airborne inhalation, or by vectors, such as mosquitoes, fleas or ticks. These are often responsible for blood-borne disease, such as malaria, *encephalitis*, **Lyme disease** and sleeping sickness.

Table 1: Worldwide mortality due to infectious diseases

Rank	Cause of death	Deaths 2002 (in millions)	Percentage of all deaths (%)	Deaths 1993 (in millions)	1993 rank
	All infectious diseases	14.7	25.9	16.4	32.2%
1	Lower respiratory infections	3.9	6.9	4.1	1
2	HIV/AIDS	2.8	4.9	0.7	7
3	Diarrheal diseases	1.8	3.2	3.0	2
4	Tuberculosis (TB)	1.6	2.7	2.7	3
5	Malaria	1.3	2.2	2.0	4
6	Measles	0.6	1.1	1.1	5
7	Pertussis	0.29	0.5	0.36	7
8	Tetanus	0.21	0.4	0.15	12
9	Meningitis	0.17	0.3	0.25	8
10	Syphilis	0.16	0.3	0.19	11
11	Hepatitis B	0.10	0.2	0.93	6
12–17	Tropical diseases	0.13	0.2	0.53	9, 10, 16–18

Source: The World Health Organization.

Immunity against infectious diseases can be acquired by antibodies and/or T-lymphocytes, and is the goal of many vaccines on the market.

As Table 1 shows, the three biggest infectious disease killers are lower respiratory infections (such as pneumonias, influenzas and *acute bronchitis*), HIV/AIDS and diarrheal diseases (such as cholera, *botulism* and E. coli). The number of deaths due to nearly every infectious disease has decreased in recent years. However, hepatitis B and C, which affect about 670 million people worldwide, can cause extensive liver damage and in many cases, liver failure, and incidences of these have been growing.

Infectious diseases that spread extensively can become epidemics or worse, pandemics, such as the Black Death (plague) of 1347 that killed up to 50 per cent of the populations of Europe, Asia and Africa, or smallpox, which in the 16th century killed 85 per cent of the population of Mexico. An estimated 60 million of European deaths in the 18th century were caused by the same disease.

In the 19th century, tuberculosis was the main killer in Europe, responsible for the deaths of a quarter of all adults; the *Spanish Flu* pandemic just after the First World War killed between 25 and 50 million people worldwide.

In many cases, infectious diseases are now preventable by vaccination, which has led to the eradication of smallpox, a reduction in tuberculosis, cholera, *yellow fever* and measles, as well as a near eradication of polio.

When infectious diseases manifest themselves, they are treated by drugs, which can be antibiotics, antiviral and antifungal. These drugs work by killing the infective organisms, or by preventing them from multiplying. But because of the widespread misuse and over-prescription of antibiotics since their introduction after the Second World War, many microorganisms have developed resistance to antibiotics. If a bacterium carries several resistance genes, it is called multi-resistant or, colloquially, a *superbug* or *super bacterium*.

The largest market opportunity in antibiotic drugs lies in overcoming *resistant bacterial infections*, particularly in hospital settings.

Antibiotic resistance is caused by genetic mutations in bacteria that have evolved defences against antibiotics. Bacteria can do this by evolving their "efflux pumps", mechanisms for expelling antibiotics and toxins, and by modifying the molecules targeted by antibiotics themselves, rendering them useless.

Bacteria have far more "communal intelligence" than previously thought. Not only can resistance develop in a single bacterial genetic line, but also gene transfer means that once a bacterium develops resistance, it can share the genetic information with others. Antibiotic resistance poses a significant problem in the modern world, due to drug companies being reluctant to develop new antibiotics in recent decades because of the relatively poor profitability of the sector, as well as the fact that antibiotics are short-term cures and are therefore not prescribed over long periods.

Among antibiotic resistant infections, MRSA was first detected in Britain in 1961 and is now prevalent in hospitals and beginning to be found in the broader community. In some cases, healthy individuals may carry MRSA asymptomatically for periods ranging from a few weeks to many years, but it is the patients with compromised immune systems who are at a significantly greater risk of symptomatic secondary infection. MRSA is responsible for many fatal cases of *sepsis* and of pneumonia in the US and Europe. The most effective antibiotic against this MRSA, **Vancomycin**, has now started to become ineffective against genetically altered MRSA strains.

Additionally, resistance of pneumonia to penicillin and other beta-lactam antibiotics is increasing worldwide. Other pathogens showing some resistance include *Salmonellas*, *Campylobacter* and *Streptococci*.

Clostridium difficile, also known as *C. difficile*, is a nosocomial (hospital-based) pathogen that causes diarrheal disease in hospitals worldwide. Although in a very small percentage of the adult population, *C. difficile* bacteria reside naturally in the gut, if the normal gut flora has been destroyed (usually after a broad spectrum antibiotic) the gut can become overrun with *C. difficile*, releasing harmful toxins.

Antibiotic resistant *C. difficile* was reported as the cause of large outbreaks of diarrheal disease starting in 1989, and it is now a serious problem. Even today, the better antibiotics, such as **Cipro** or **Levaquin** of the fluoroquinolone class, are becoming less effective against *C. difficile* strains. The *Center for Disease Control &*

Prevention in the US reported a rate of 500,000 cases of *C. difficile* infections annually and that number has been rising in the US since 2000, with the spread of the infection becoming a significant problem in hospitals and long-term care facilities.

Optimer Pharmaceuticals Inc. had its macrolide antibiotic **Dificid (fidaxomicin)** approved by the FDA in 2011 for treating *C. difficile*. This is an interesting company, and one which we cover in Chapter 10. Initial sales of Dificid are highly encouraging, and are helped by collaboration with Cubist Pharmaceuticals. Additionally, *Summit* (AIM: SUMM) of the UK has a promising *C. difficile* drug in development, **SMT 19969**, and is worth watching.

Escherichia coli (E. coli) and *Salmonella* come directly from contaminated food. Of the meat that is contaminated with *E. coli*, 80 per cent of the bacteria are resistant to one or more antibiotics, which can cause bladder infections and possibly death, as evidenced in Germany in 2011, where contaminated vegetables were found to have a drug-resistant strain of *E. coli*.

Another recent and very dangerous pathogen has been found, originating from New Delhi in India. *NDM-1* (New Delhi metallo-beta-lactamase 1) is not a superbug per se, but a supergene – a genetic mutation that can be acquired by a variety of bacteria to make them impervious to any of the powerful antibiotics of last resort. In early sightings of this disease, the mutation had been confined to hospitals. It has been identified in the hospital-associated bug *Klebsiella*, which causes pneumonia; *Citrobacter*, which causes **urinary tract infections** and sepsis; and the intestinal bacteria E. coli.

NDM-1 has been found in the general water supply of Delhi and the implication of this is that it may no longer just be mutating; the supergene can escape and spread quickly to the general population.

The Swiss company, *Basilea Pharmaceutical* (Swiss Stock Exchange: BSLN), has developed a novel antibiotic **BAL30072** in early stage trials that has been shown to be active against multidrug-resistant "Gram-negative" bacteria expressing the *NDM-1* resistance factor, so we suggest that you take a look at this company and follow the progress of these trials.

After years of relative neglect, antibiotics and other ways of treating hospital and community-acquired superbugs are very firmly on the radar screens of public health organizations, as well as of drug companies that are interested in profiting from this series of new worldwide epidemics. Since most older generation antibiotics are generic and therefore not profitable, the newer drugs being developed specifically for the resistant strains of infection are where a lot of the excitement lies in infectious disease.

Drugs for so-called Gram-negative infections, which are less susceptible to treatment by conventional antibiotics, are now either entering the market or awaiting approval. Forest Laboratories (NYSE: FRX), one of the companies we like as an investment, has **CAZ 104** in Phase 2 trials. Cubist Pharmaceuticals (NASDAQ: CBST), another company of interest, has **CAX 201** also in Phase 2 trials. Both of these drugs are positioned to deal with Pseudomonas strains resistant to antibiotics. GSK's **052**, also in Phase 2 testing, appears to be highly effective in treating urinary tract and *abdominal infections* and has the early potential to be a blockbuster drug.

In the MRSA market, Cubist's **Cubicin**, Theravance's **Vibativ**, Forest's **Teflaro** and Pfizer's **Zyvox** are the drugs of choice, but newer and potentially more effective treatments are being developed, a few of which we have discussed above.

In the *C. difficile* market, Merck's monoclonal antibody *CDA-1/ CD B-1* is showing great promise from the data coming out of the Phase 2 trials and is worth watching.

PolyMedix Inc. (OTC: PYMX) has a new compound in development – a small molecule that mimics the action of so-called *defensin* proteins. It attaches to bacterial membranes just as defensins do, and pokes enough holes to cause them to burst. During *in-vitro* tests and in animal models, **PMX-30063** shows a high level of efficacy against MRSA infection, including highly resistant strains. In mice and rats, PMX-30063 has been shown to have comparable or superior performance when compared to Vancomycin. PolyMedix is a very small company and its shares trade in small volumes; however, for investors inclined to take a speculative position in the antibiotic area, it seems attractive.

Another interesting area in the antibacterial field is *phage therapy*, an approach that was extensively used as a therapeutic agent for over 60 years, especially in the former Soviet Union. Phage therapy was employed in the US until the discovery of antibiotics, in the early 1940s. *Bacteriophages* or "phages" are viruses that invade bacterial cells and, in the case of so-called *lytic* phages, disrupt bacterial metabolism and cause the bacterium to *lyse* (break up).

Bacteriophage therapy might turn out to be an important alternative to antibiotics in the current era of multidrug resistant pathogens. An interesting company, in which we have an investment and have met with the management on several occasions, is *AmpliPhi Biosciences* (OTC: APHB), which has a very strong board and about 200 patents in the phage area. AmpliPhi is moving to monetize its expertise in phage by using companion and farm animals as its first customers; bovine mastitis and canine ear infections from pseudomonas are well treated with bacteriophage. For cows branded "organic", antibiotics are definitely off the menu and phage is a viable and effective treatment. In humans, the first and most likely to be approved product is for cystic fibrosis, where phage can be inhaled to clear lung infections. There is likely to be a lot of interest in this area, and we strongly recommend you look at AmpliPhi.

Hepatitis
Hepatitis C is a liver disease caused by infection with the hepatitis C virus. It is transmitted through contaminated blood and the infection can cause *liver failure* and liver cancer and is the leading cause of liver transplants. About 3.2 million Americans are infected with hepatitis C but the worldwide potential patient population is 170 million. Hepatitis C leads to liver disease and *cirrhosis* and is fatal in 2 to 5 per cent of cases.

The FDA recently approved Vertex Pharmaceuticals' (NASDAQ: VRTX) hepatitis C drug, Telaprevir, saying it showed strong effectiveness. In addition, Merck has a similar protease inhibitor **Boceprevir** that has also been approved.

Telaprevir and Boceprevir are effectively cures for hepatitis C and create a so-called sustained virologic response, leading to a reversal of the danger of cirrhosis and cancer of the liver. There are several other protease inhibitors in various stages of development, including by Johnson & Johnson, Roche and Gilead. In addition, Pharmasset (a company acquired by Gilead in 2011 for over US$11 billion) has a nucleotide polymerase inhibitor in late-stage trials, which is likely to be approved for hepatitis C and does not require interferon as an adjunct.

Hepatitis B, another widespread liver-related disease, spreads by blood transfusion or sexual contact and causes up to 5,000 deaths a year in the US alone. About 2 billion people have been infected worldwide with hepatitis B and about 500 million are active carriers, according to the *World Health Organization*. The market for hepatitis B drugs is relatively small compared to hepatitis C owing to the fact that there are already a number of effective vaccines against hepatitis B but none on the market (as yet) for hepatitis C, so the first company to get a hepatitis C vaccine on the market will get 100 per cent of that market. Hepatitis B drugs generate about US$1.5 billion in annual sales and Gilead's **Viread** is the most recently approved drug, which like the other drugs, targets the hepatitis B *polymerase*.

Dynavax (NASDAQ: DVAX) has a late-stage development hepatitis B vaccine, **Hepislav**, which is being positioned as a superior preventative compound. Existing hepatitis B vaccinations are not totally effective and have to be interspersed three times over six months, reducing compliance. Dynavax's product, if approved in around 2012, could be a large selling product and the company is worth looking at.

Cowen and Company, a financial services firm, expects the hepatitis B and C market to explode in size between 2010 and 2015, from US$5 billion to US$13 billion in sales. Inhibitex and Pharmasset have now both been acquired, so the listed alternatives where there is significant direct hepatitis exposure are limited. This is largely due to the stunning advances in hepatitis C treatment options. We favour Vertex and Dynavax in this space.

HIV/AIDS

Another area of likely strong growth for drug companies is the HIV/AIDS market. HIV is an *RNA* retrovirus, unique in that it is a virus that attacks the very cells that are supposed to eliminate it, and thereby suppresses the immune system. Because HIV has a high mutation rate, resistance to a single drug occurs rapidly, which is why treatment normally consists of a drug cocktail, typically involving three compounds: two nucleoside reverse transcriptase inhibitors (NRTIs) and either a protease inhibitor (PI) or a non-nucleoside reverse transcriptase inhibitor (NNRTI).

About 33 million people worldwide carry the *HIV/AIDS* virus, of which over 70 per cent live in sub Saharan Africa. About 1 million live in the US and 500,000 in Europe. Infection rates are rising slightly in the US, to about 60,000 new cases per year, but mortality is falling due to the effectiveness of AIDS treatment. However, it is estimated that about a quarter of all HIV carriers are unaware of their condition in the US and a similar percentage in Europe, and that as many as 40 per cent of US patients do not receive any treatment at all.

In the developing world, greater awareness of the disease and lessening rates of infections are bringing death rates down slowly, to about 2 million worldwide per annum. Infection rates have halved to about 2.7 million worldwide per annum from a peak of about 5 million.

Antiretroviral drugs work to control the viral load in AIDS patients and can lead to a near normal life. However, patient compliance with the drug regimens is vital, and the failures that occur when patients are on drugs are normally due to people not adhering to their regimen. Because so many patients, even in the developed world, are still not treated for the condition, and because AIDS is a life-threatening disease, the opportunity in this market remains very large.

By far the dominant player in the HIV/AIDS market is Gilead Sciences (NASDAQ:GILD), one of our favoured larger biotech companies (Gilead now owns Pharmasset, a highly promising company in the hepatitis C space), which has rapidly taken market share away from GSK, the former market leader. Gilead's lead drug is Viread, which has proved to be much more efficacious than GSK's **Retrovir**, and Viread revenues worldwide are expected to be close to US$1 billion by 2015. When used in combination with drugs such as **Truvuda** and **Atripla** (also Gilead compounds) Viread, is an even bigger seller than when prescribed on its own. Truvuda sales are expected to reach US$3.4 billion by 2015 and those of Atripla US$4.7 billion, making Viread the basis of one of the largest drug franchises in the world.

Gilead is likely to maintain its franchise lead in HIV/AIDS, with a new drug in Phase 3 trials, **Elvitegravir**, an integrase inhibitor. There is also a new **Quad** combination pill expected on the market in the near future. This pill again uses Viread as its backbone and will provide valuable patent life extension to Viread.

NanoViricides (OTC: NNVC), a company based in West Haven, Connecticut, has said that its HIV candidate drug had equivalent efficacy to a highly active antiretroviral therapy triple drug cocktail in an animal study, with no evidence of toxicity. The drug is designed to mimic the cellular structures that HIV uses to bind to cells. The company is small and speculative, but might be worth looking at.

An HIV vaccine that protects vaccinated individuals from the HIV infection is the ultimate goal of many research programmes, although currently there is no effective vaccine against the HIV virus.

There is mounting evidence that a vaccine may be possible in the future. Work with monoclonal antibodies has demonstrated that the body can defend itself against HIV, and certain individuals remain asymptomatic for decades after HIV infection. One of the reasons why an HIV vaccine is more difficult to develop than classic vaccines is that conventional vaccines mimic natural immunity against reinfection generally seen in individuals who have recovered from infection. There is only one recorded case of a person who has recovered from AIDS.

Malaria

Malaria is a leading cause of death and disease worldwide, especially in developing countries. About 300 to 500 million cases of malaria occur annually, and more than 1 million people die of the disease. Malaria can be a fatal disease, but illness and death are largely preventable. In fact, for patients diagnosed early, a cure is possible because one of several medicines that kill the malaria parasite (*Plasmodium*) can be used effectively. Specific medications that are used as a cure include **chloroquine, lariam, malarone quinine** and doxycycline. There are also drugs based on an ancient tree derived remedy, **Artemisinin**.

A great deal of research is going into finding ways of destroying or incapacitating the malarial *vector*, the mosquito, but we can find little evidence of anything that looks like an interesting commercial or investment opportunity currently; most existing drugs are already generic and therefore less profitable. There is a malarial vaccine of some promise, with about 50 per cent effectiveness, being developed by GSK and *Walter Reid Military Hospital* in the US, named **HSTT**. In addition, *Selecta Biosciences Inc.*, a privately held Massachusetts company, has achieved its third significant collaboration with a subcontract from *Science Applications International Corporation*

(SAIC) of Virginia (NYSE: SAI) to develop a *targeted Synthetic Vaccine Particle (tSVP)* product for malaria.

Tuberculosis

Tuberculosis (TB) is a common and in many cases lethal disease caused by various strains of mycobacteria. It mainly attacks the lungs and spreads through the air when people who have an active TB infection cough or sneeze. Most infections in humans are latent and only about 1 in 10 progresses to active disease, which if left untreated kills more than half of its victims.

One third of the worldwide population is thought to be infected with TB and new infections occur at a rate of about one per second. In 2007, there were an estimated 13.7 million chronic active cases, 9.3 million new cases and 1.8 million deaths, mostly in the developing world. About 80 per cent of the population in many Asian and African countries test positive in tuberculin tests, while only 5 to 10 per cent of the US population test positive. Vaccination with the **BCG** vaccine is the most effective way of preventing the spread of TB, but long periods of antibiotic treatment are required to cure patients who already have it, and increasingly the new generations of antibiotics in development in response to resistant infections will be needed in TB. Sanofi Aventis is developing a new TB vaccination, which is showing some promise.

Vaccines

In the field of vaccines, the four most exciting opportunities are for HIV (described earlier in this chapter), Human Papilloma Virus (HPV), influenza and meningitis. Vaccines have been common for a long time and have had highly positive effects in diseases such as tetanus, seasonal flu, diphtheria, polio, measles and rubella. Previously intractable targets such as *meningitis B* and, possibly, *Staphylococcus aureus (S. aureus)* are now capable of being prevented by vaccination. Vaccines are quite difficult to make, because they are normally cultivated in eggs, which creates barriers to entry, and as a result big pharma has a fairly effective lock on the market; Sanofi-Aventis, Merck, GSK, Novartis and Abbott are the dominant players.

In terms of meningitis B, Novartis is in Phase 3 trials with a vaccine for this devastating but relatively low incidence disease. In the HPV market, which is directly linked to cervical cancer (280,000 deaths per annum worldwide), there is an enormous market opportunity in vaccination of adolescent girls. The product doing the best in this relatively new market is **Gardasil** from Merck, although GSK's **Cervarix** (recently on the market) appeared to be more potent in trials, and offers potential cross protection for men from HPV effects, such as *warts*. This is likely to be a US$1 billion market for both companies, and a highly profitable one.

In the influenza field, new forms of seasonal flu vaccines show some promise, particularly in more effective protection of the very young and the elderly, who are most vulnerable to its effect. *Novavax* is an interesting company that is entering Phase 3 trials on a new virus-like particle vaccine, including the *H3N2*, *H1N* and *B influenza* strains. Virus-like particle vaccines are recombinant structures mimicking viruses but lacking genetic material, thereby making them incapable of replication and hence safer.

We can expect a universal flu vaccine within 5 years according to *NIH* Chief Francis Collins, who told *USA Today* that a long-term jab could replace the annual seasonal flu. In fact, the first antibodies that can fight all types of the *influenza A virus* have been discovered, researchers in Switzerland have claimed. In 2011, *Biondvax* (Tel Aviv Stock Exchange: BNDX) announced that it had completed the first Phase 2 trial of the first universal flu vaccine in the world, with promising immunogenic results.

In MRSA infections, a vaccine in Phase 3 trials from Merck looks like the best bet, and since *S. aureus* is the cause of MRSA, the most common form of hospital infections resistant to antibiotics, this could be a very large market, because vulnerable populations and hospital workers would all receive immunizations. Merck's product **V710** is worth watching as it progresses through the regulatory system.

Obesity and its Evil Sisters: Type 2 Diabetes and Kidney Disease

Obesity is the most visible of all the modern medical scourges, but some of its side effects are not so readily apparent. About one third of the US population, and increasing numbers of people elsewhere in the world, are obese. This is defined as having a *Body Mass Index (BMI)* of more than 30 (we explain BMI in more detail in Chapter 9). The percentage of Americans at this level or above has doubled since the 1970s. About 10 per cent of the US population is morbidly obese (BMI of 40 or more), meaning that they are likely to die as a result of the condition or from its side effects. In the United Kingdom, it is forecast that almost half of all males will be obese by 2030, if current trends continue; already, 26 per cent of the population, or 15 million people, are obese. Worldwide, 500 million people are thought to be obese, and a further 1.5 billion overweight.

Researchers at *Kings College*, London have recently discovered that there is a "master gene" for obesity and type 2 diabetes: the *KLF14* gene. They believe that *KLF14* acts as a "master switch" for other genes, which are linked to cholesterol, insulin levels and BMI. As a result, work is proceeding to find ways in which this gene can be affected. However, any success here will take years, and in the meantime, the obesity problem continues to grow.

The film *Supersize Me*, featuring Morgan Spurlock, is a good illustration of the problem. In the movie, *Mr Spurlock* eats nothing but portions of *McDonald's* food for a month, gaining monstrous amounts of weight in the process and ending up with serious health issues. The accessibility of fast food, the use of high fructose corn syrup in soft drinks, ignorance about good nutritional habits and a lack of exercise all contribute to this most modern of medical problems. The fast-food industry in the US spent US$4.2 billion on advertising in 2009, and many schools derive revenue from alliances with the makers of unhealthy foods.

Obesity is the primary contributor to contracting type 2 diabetes and also leads to other conditions such as hypertension, hyperlipidaemia and other cardiovascular problems. Heavier weight can also lead to osteoporosis and respiratory problems, and the overall economic cost of obesity is thought to be US$100 billion a year in the US alone.

Anti-obesity medications or weight loss drugs are agents that try to reduce or control patient weight gain. They suppress appetite and/or metabolism or absorb calories in the form of fat or carbohydrates. Most of them do not work or have serious side effects. The magic pill for weight loss is a holy grail yet to be discovered.

Presently, the main treatment for obesity is will-power, diet and exercise, although surgical options are also possible in extreme cases. The limitation of drugs for obesity is that scientists do not fully understand the neural basis of appetite and how to modulate it. Appetite is clearly a very important instinct that has evolved to promote our survival. Arguably, any drug that could abolish appetite would carry a high starvation risk and be unsuitable for clinical use.

Only one anti-obesity medication, **orlistat** (**Xenical**), is currently on the market and approved by the FDA for long-term use in the US, and it is now an OTC product. Orlistat reduces intestinal fat absorption by inhibiting pancreatic lipase; that is, by stopping the pancreas from converting fat.

Another drug, **Acomplia**, based on blocking the endocannabinoid system (related to cannabis), has been withdrawn from sale in Europe and is not approved in the US. **Sibutamine** (by *Meridia-Abbott*), which deactivates neurotransmitters in the brain to decrease appetite, was withdrawn from the US in 2010 due to cardiovascular risks.

Orexigen and *Vivus* are two companies that were recently knocked back on their obesity drug trials, and their share prices collapsed as a result. Orexigen's **Contrave** and Vivus's **Qnexa** are combinations of approved drugs but the FDA is extra cautious on weight loss drugs in particular, and it has asked for much more extensive safety information in both cases. Orexigen and Vivus are both conducting additional trials with a view to determining the incidence of adverse cardiac events; our own opinion is that both of the drugs will succeed, but with restricted labels; for instance, restricting women of childbearing age. Orexigen is fully funded and appears cheap, as a speculative bet, and Vivus appeared to be on the path to approval after the FDA panel voted favourably in respect of Qnexa in February 2012. Even with restricted labelling, the market potential in the US for each drug is over 80 million people.

The approval process for "obesity" drugs is littered with failure, and it is clear that a new modality is needed if the safety concerns associated with these types of drugs are to be overcome. One of the reasons the FDA is so cautious is because in earlier times "obesity" drugs were based on *amphetamines*. These worked, but had risks such as heart palpitations, addiction and outright cardiac failure.

The most popular of these was **Fen-Phen,** but it was found to cause heart disease and was withdrawn from widespread use.

Some of the earliest post-Second World War obesity drugs, notably generic **phentermine** and **topiramate** are still prescribed today but for limited periods, due to side effect problems. The one that is not still prescribed is **methamphetamine** – yes, the one that makes you age 40 years in a month – which, believe it or not, was approved for weight loss in 1947!

However, the size of the potential market is clearly large (pardon the pun) and as a result, there remains a fairly full pipeline of hopeful candidates. Funnily enough, it seems that a novel successful treatment for obesity may well come as a consequence of the treatment of other conditions, such as diabetes and renal failure. In other words, a drug that treats these conditions effectively may lead to weight loss.

One of the problems for companies developing weight-loss drugs is the extensive testing required by the FDA. Phase 3 testing requires 4,500 patients to be enrolled, one third on a placebo, and for a duration of at least one year. To gain approval, the patients on the drugs need to lose at least 5 per cent of their body weight. They should do considerably better, on average, than those on the placebo.

A similar medication to orlistat that has been designed for patients with type 2 diabetes is **acarbose**, which partially blocks the absorption of carbohydrates in the small intestine and produces similar side effects to orlistat, including stomach pain and flatulence.

Another potential long-term approach to anti-obesity therapy is through the use of *RNA interference (RNAi)*. Animal studies have illustrated that the deletion of the *RIP140* gene in mice by genetic engineering results in a stop to fat accumulation, even when the mice are fed a high-fat diet.

CytRx (NASDAQ: CYTR), a small US-based company involved primarily in cancer, is developing RNAi therapeutics for the treatment of obesity and type 2 diabetes. This is highly speculative and any investment in this company should be insignificant. The same applies to *Silence Therapeutics* (LON: SLN), a company we have visited at its offices in Berlin, Germany. It has a broad siRNA clinical pipeline but the problem is that the time-to-market for this company is still long, and it requires regular infusions of cash. Nonetheless, it warrants a small investment, and we are impressed by the management and their dedication.

Amylin Pharmaceuticals (NASDAQ: AMLN), a company that we are neutral on as an investment, has developed a drug in this area, **Byetta**. This is currently used in type 2 diabetes for patients who do not achieve adequate control of their blood sugar levels with **metformin** (the most widely prescribed and now generic anti-diabetic drug, sometimes known as **glucophage**) and definitely has a weight loss effect. The drug was approved for diabetes in 2005. Byetta does appear to have some side effects, although they may not be directly attributable to the drug. On average, over a three-year period, patients lose 5 kilograms (11 pounds) with Byetta, although that is not its primary goal. This drug remains to be tri-alled for obesity, but given the problems that have emerged, possible *pancreatitis* and *thyroid cancer*, it is unlikely to be accepted as an obesity treatment.

Amylin and its partners Lilly and *Alkermes*, however, now have US and European approval for **Bydureon**, the first once-weekly injectable drug for diabetes, which is a reformulation of Byetta and has reasonably good prospects. Bydureon will go head to head with *Novo Nordisk's* **Victoza** which worldwide is close to blockbuster status. Amylin's stock price is relatively expensive which is why we have a neutral view on it.

The most promising drugs in the pipeline for obesity are those already submitted by Vivus and Orexigen, as well as modifications of those. Amylin has recently abandoned a compound for obesity, **Pramlintide**, which was in Phase 2 trials with Takeda as partner. *Arena's* **Lorcaserin** has also received the dreaded FDA Complete Response Letter and in our opinion this drug is less likely to succeed than Contrave or Qnexa, both of which might eventually get across the line.

Transoral gastroplasty (TOGA) is a new form of restricting food intake by surgical means. It is still in the early stages of obesity studies. This method avoids large scarring by going through the mouth and seems to be effective, although radical. As of 2010, 300 people had undergone the procedure, 200 in the US and 100 in Europe. The Los Angeles *Cedars-Sinai Medical Center* reported in 2009 that European patients lost an average of 45 per cent of their body weight after 18 months.

The overall market for obesity drugs is at present relatively small – less than US$500 million per annum in the US due to the difficult path to approval and the generic nature of the most prescribed products. However, without a doubt this could be a vast market, if someone could only crack it.

We have seen two interesting obesity opportunities, one of which is related to the treatment of another condition, Chronic Kidney Disease (CKD). CKD affects as many as 26 million American adults and constitutes an enormous market. CKD can progress to kidney failure and eventually dialysis, and because there are nowhere near enough organ donors, the outcome is often fatal. In fact, mortality rates in End Stage Renal Disease patients is higher than in almost any other serious disease including cancers.

Reata Pharmaceuticals is a privately held company based in Dallas-Fort Worth that we have visited, which has an exceptionally promising drug in Phase 3 testing for CKD. Bardoxolone methyl can reverse CKD or halt its progression. One of the side effects of this drug is that patients appear to lose 1 kilogram (2.2 pounds) per month until an optimum weight is achieved, and in due course therein may be a new obesity drug.

Reata's scientists work on the premise that obesity, diabetes and hypertension induce inflammation in the kidneys, which in turn reduces the glomerular filtration rate and increases cellular oxidative stress. Bardoxolone works by activating a transcription factor, *Nrf2*, which increases antioxidant levels and suppresses inflammatory pathways. This new class of drug might be an effective anti-inflammatory across a broad range of diseases, including neurodegenerative and pulmonary disease. Reata is well funded and has partnerships with Abbott, as well as *Kirin* of Japan, and may go public in the next couple of years. If it does so, we strongly recommend that you consider taking a position in this company.

Arrowhead Research, a company we mentioned earlier, also has an interesting angle on obesity. This is a product from its subsidiary *Ablaris* and licensed from the famous MD Anderson medical facility. The drug destroys the capillaries that feed the white fat cells making up adipose (fat) tissue. After receiving subcutaneous injections, rats lose 30 per cent of their body weight in a month. Primates lose somewhat less weight. Dosing may be an issue though, as at high doses there may be marginal renal toxicity (which is reversible). It is scheduled to enter human trials in early 2012, with all trials being funded by MD Anderson. One positive thing about this drug is that it has no effect on the central nervous system, the downfall of so many weight-loss drugs. Consequently, Arrowhead is one of our top picks. It is a small company, but the upside with its nano technology and siRNA businesses as well as its anti-obesity product could be huge.

Diabetes

Diabetes is divided into types 1 and 2. *Type 1* is characterized by an inability to produce insulin, and *type 2* by a resistance or poor response to insulin. The hormone insulin regulates the conversion and cellular uptake of sugars and starches into biochemical energy. About 10 per cent of patients with diabetes have type 1, which typically manifests itself in early adolescence. The balance have varying degrees of type 2, and the total number of people with diabetes in the US is thought to be about 24 million, with only three-quarters of them having been diagnosed as having the condition. Left untreated, diabetes can lead to organ failure, blindness, amputations, and sometimes even death.

Type 1 diabetics have an autoimmune condition that destroys the insulin producing beta-cells in the pancreas, and they are dependent on insulin injections to stay alive. There is no alternative treatment for them currently available, and it is thought that type 1 diabetes has a hereditary element.

Type 2 diabetics typically still produce insulin, but if their disease progresses they may require insulin injections, as well as oral anti-diabetes drugs, special diets and exercise. About 35 to 40 per cent of type 2 diabetics require insulin at some point.

Diabetes is a fast growing disease and the reasons for this are largely due to lifestyle. Its prevalence is rising fast around the world as people have become more sedentary, consuming diets high in fat and low in nutritional value. It is estimated that by 2030, the number of diabetics worldwide will grow from 190 million to 330 million, the vast majority of them having type 2 diabetes. It is believed that a tendency to diabetes can result from poor nutrition in the womb, leading to "catch up" and potentially dangerous growth after birth.

The major players in the diabetes market are Novo Nordisk of Denmark, Sanofi-Aventis, Lilly and Merck. The major products in this area are insulin and GLP-1. Type 2 diabetics who require insulin need higher doses than type 1 patients because of their resistance to the hormone. Novo Nordisk is an excellent company and its shares can be considered a solid long-term investment. Apart from a strong position in insulin in many markets, including emerging ones, it also has a highly prospective agent Victoza, a GLP-1 agonist, which is a competitor of Alkermes/Amylin's Bydueron. Novo will also file for approval of two new types of ultra long acting insulin called Degludec and Degludec Plus in 2012. Lilly, having been a partner with Amylin in Byetta/Bydureon is expected to launch its own GLP-1 agonist, **dulaglutide**, sometime in 2014–2015.

Insulin is divided into different types: rapid acting, short acting, intermediate acting and long acting. Sanofi-Aventis's Lantus is a once daily type of insulin that has a high percentage of the long-acting market, although it has been weakly associated with some forms of cancer. The alternative leading product is Novo Nordisk's **Levemir**, which has not been associated with cancer, but does not have the same efficacy of action as Lantus. Both products use insulin analogues or new formulations to differentiate themselves from generic insulin. The modes of delivery and dosages are also extremely important in the insulin market and Lantus, which uses a pen for delivery, appears to be the better product overall, but it comes off patent protection relatively soon. In the fast-acting market, which accounts for about 40 per cent of the insulin market, **Humalog** by Lilly is the leader with sales estimated to be US$2.1 billion in 2011.

Insulin is a large market, but also a competitive one, with little going on to generate excitement except in the emerging markets. Total sales of insulin products will account for about half of the diabetes-related drugs market by 2015, and run to around US$20 billion.

The other half of the diabetes market consists of so-called *DPP-IV* inhibitors, which reduce the breakdown of GLP-1, *GLP1 analogues* and a large category of other anti-diabetic drugs.

As a target, GLP-1 is the largest in this market. GLP-1 is a hormone controlled by the *proglucagon* gene. It lowers blood sugar levels by increasing insulin secretion from the pancreas, lowering the high levels of glucagon in diabetics. In the brain, GLP-1 attaches to an appetite suppressor and often acts to reduce weight in patients. GLP-1-related drugs, which mimic its action, are used to delay the progression of type 2 diabetes.

GLP-1 itself is not useful as a drug. The drugs used to mimic it need to last a lot longer in the body than the hormone itself, which has a low half-life. Longer acting GLP-1 agonists include Novo's Victoza, approved in January 2010, though with a "black box" warning for thyroid cancer. Other GLP-1 drugs close to market include Amylin's Bydureon, Human Genome Science's **Syncria** (now in Phase 3 testing) and Sanofi-Aventis's **Lixisenatide**.

One of the important aspects of GLP-1 agonists is their usefulness in lowering the weight of diabetics, because there is a strong linkage between obesity and diabetes (*comorbidity*). Byetta has many positive features in this regard, but being injectable is less convenient than other GLP-1 drugs. Victoza is expected to be the leader in the important GLP-1 market for the next few years. Already it is significantly outperforming Byetta in terms of new prescriptions in the key US market.

The diabetes research pipeline is a pretty full one, and includes some new compounds with novel modes of action. Among the most exciting are known as *FGF-21 agonists* for type 2 diabetes. *FGF-21* is a hormone associated with starvation and seems to protect mice from diet-induced obesity. As a result it may have a role to play in weight loss also. It is at a very early stage of development by Merck and *Ambrx*, and Lilly has a compound called **LP 10152** in Phase 2 testing.

Other areas of interest in this field are *glucokinase activators*. As their name implies, they promote *glucokinase*, a signalling enzyme involved in the first step in the metabolization of glucose to ATP – a process called *phosphorylation*. Glucokinase activators act to reduce blood glucose levels by enhancing both insulin release and glucose uptake by the liver. Astra Zeneca has a compound, **AZD 1656**, in Phase 2 trials, and Forest has six early stage products in this area.

Another company worth a mention, even though it is highly speculative and was dealt a severe blow early in 2011, is Mannkind (NASDAQ: MNKD). We have met with Al Mann, a veteran of many biotech companies, and the founder of Mannkind. He is extremely wealthy and tenacious. His company's product, **Afreeza**, which is an inhaled insulin powder, is ultra-rapid acting insulin that completed Phase 3 trials but has been sent back by the FDA for further testing.

The idea is a clever one; by inhaling the insulin, the large surface of the lungs provides faster access to the circulatory system of the body, and the insulin achieves peak action in 12 to 14 minutes, mimicking the action of insulin in a healthy body at mealtimes. The FDA has required Mannkind to do further tests to demonstrate that there are no pulmonary side effects, and needless to say Mannkind's share price plummeted in the meantime.

The difference between Mannkind and other one-shot biotech companies whose products are sent back for further testing is that Al Mann has considerable financial staying power and an almost religious belief in his product. Clearly, safe inhaled insulin would be preferable to an injected form of the hormone, and if Afreeza works, the company's shares could soar. We recommend Mannkind in small measures for those who like a bit of a gamble.

Overall, the obesity epidemic is providing both a challenge and a financial opportunity to the pharmaceutical industry. There is no doubt that the obesity crisis will be a major driver of growth for the industry but at the moment it is difficult to get too excited about these areas, with the exception of a few companies. This is because of the FDA's reluctance to approve drugs in the metabolic area, as well as the fact that in diabetes most treatments are fairly well established and pathways to the disease are not so well understood as to make gene therapy or more targeted drugs a near-term possibility.

This will change over time and so we suggest that you watch carefully for news of breakthroughs in this area. We favour Arrowhead Research in the field of obesity and would also include Vivus and Orexigen in the equation. We favour Reata when and if it goes public for CKD and other anti-inflammatory indications, and in diabetes we suggest a small position in Mannkind. Amylin, although a large company, carries risks and faces severe competition for its key products. Novo Nordisk of Denmark is an excellent business and its shares can be considered a long term safe haven in the diabetes field. Another company worth keeping an eye on is *Keryx* (NASDAQ: KERX), which has three Phase 3 compounds, one of which is **Zerenex** for reducing serum phosphorous concentrations in end-stage renal disease, and which appears to be significantly better and safer than competing products. Keryx also has an interesting collaboration with *Aeterna Zentaris* (NASDAQ: AEZS) for colorectal cancer and multiple myeloma with the fully recruited Phase 3 compound **perifosine**.

We discuss another nasty sister of obesity – hypertension – in the next section on cardiovascular disease.

The Heart of the Matter – Biggest Killer on the Prowl

Diseases of the cardiovascular system account for more deaths in both the developed and developing countries than any other. About one fifth of all deaths in the United States, as an example, are cardiovascular related and 14 million people a year worldwide are estimated to die from the disease. Nearly 60 million Americans suffer from cardiovascular disease, with at least another 100 million cases elsewhere in the world.

The cardiovascular system is comprised of the heart and blood vessels supplying vital organs. Diseases affecting the cardiovascular system are well known; for instance high blood pressure (hypertension) affects 85 per cent of Americans. Reduced blood flow (*ischemia*) often results in *myocardial infarction*, better known as a heart attack, often caused by the long-term build-up of *Low-Density Lipoprotein (LDL) cholesterol* (that's why it is known as the *bad cholesterol*). Many people suffer from angina (pain in the chest) and about 5 million Americans suffer from congestive cardiac failure, which is a failure to pump blood adequately around the body, often resulting in death.

The cardiovascular drug market is enormous and comprises at least 13 different types of drugs. Most of them seek to treat excess cholesterol, high blood pressure, congestive heart failure, *arrhythmia* (irregular heartbeat) and angina. In addition, anti-thrombotic and anti-platelet agents are a large market. These seek to stop either arterial or venous clots from forming in the body, which are leading causes of strokes.

Although the cardiovascular market is enormous in terms of prescriptions and sales, because many key patents are expiring its overall percentage of worldwide drug sales is declining. According to IMS Health, a leading healthcare information services provider, 1.1 billion prescriptions will be filled in the US for cardiovascular drugs by 2015, and although that figure is huge, it is on a declining trend. Those prescriptions are mostly for statins (to reduce cholesterol), ACE inhibitors (for hypertension and *congestive heart failure*), beta-blockers (for hypertension), diuretics (for hypertension) and Angiotensin Receptor Blockers (ARBs) (for hypertension yet again). There are also anti-thrombotic drugs that are used to prevent stroke or thrombosis.

The types of drugs that treat hypertension can be grouped into the following categories:

- **Diuretics** help the body to get rid of extra sodium and reduce fluid in blood vessels.
- **Beta-blockers** block the effects of adrenaline.
- **Alpha-blockers** help blood vessels to stay open.
- **ACE inhibitors** prevent blood vessels from constricting by reducing how much *angiotensin II* (a chemical that constricts blood vessels) the body makes.
- **ARBs** work by blocking the effect of *angiotensin II* on cells.
- **Calcium channel blockers** help prevent blood vessels from constricting by blocking calcium from entering cells.
- **Combinations** combine two medicines, such as an ACE inhibitor or a beta-blocker plus a diuretic.

Sales of cardiovascular drugs in the US alone are expected to be over US$60 billion in 2015, but that figure represents a drop of almost US$15 billion from 2010 due to patent expiration and generic competition. Almost every category of cardiovascular drug is subject to declining sales over the next few years because of the preponderance of patent expirations in this sector, the most famous of which is Lipitor, the Pfizer statin that has been an enormous sales generator.

Statins in general face a gradual decline, and since there is nothing really in the pipeline to challenge them, because they are highly effective at reducing LDL cholesterol, it seems obvious that this is an area of little interest to us in this book. There are new drugs in development that seek to raise the level of HDLs, the "good" cholesterol, but they are unlikely to gain much traction after the failure of Abbott's **Niaspan** to prove efficacy in this respect.

Similarly, ARBs are under threat as a highly profitable category because of generic competition, particularly from analogues of **Cozaar** by Merck, as well as the fact that the category leader, Novartis's **Diovan** is coming off patent in 2012.

A new class of drugs, known as *renin inhibitors*, is appearing in the treatment of hypertension and *cardiac failure*. In the lead is Novartis's **Tekturna**, but this is several years away from commercialization, and Novartis has recently scaled back investment in this compound.

In anti-thrombotic and anti-platelet drugs, the impact from generics is also large, with Plavix, a huge seller by Bristol-Myers Squibb and Sanofi-Aventis, coming to the end of its patent life, although Bristol-Myers Squibb had a promising replacement drug that it partnered with Pfizer to develop called **Eliquis**, which has recently been approved.

To show just how dramatic patent expirations are likely to be in cardiovascular drugs, research by Cowen and Company indicates that Lipitor sales will fall from US$11.5 billion in 2011 to US$2.2 billion in 2015. Generic manufacturers such as *Ranbaxy* are already lined up to provide low-cost identical-to-Lipitor drugs, the day patents expire around the world.

A drug does not have to be out of patent itself to be affected by this problem. For example, Crestor is regarded by the people we have spoken to as the best-in-class statin. It has also been shown to reduce the incidence of non-fatal heart attacks by 65 per cent compared to a placebo, as well as reduce stroke risk by 48 per cent and halve the overall risk of fatal strokes or heart attacks. In addition, it appears that a specific gene that is carried by one fifth of men, the Haplogroup 1, leads to a significant increase in heart attack risk. This discovery has prompted a new area of research. But even though Crestor's patents do not expire for a few years, its profitability for Astra Zeneca will start to decline quickly because of the cost competition from Lipitor substitutes in the near future.

In terms of new compounds that appear interesting in the cardiovascular field, *Anthera's* **Varesplatib** is one worth mentioning. Varesplatib is a small-molecule $sPLA2$-IIa (enzymes involved in cardiovascular inflammation) inhibitor. It is in early Phase 3 trials and could end up being a significant drug, because when used with statins and anti-platelet agents, it seems to reduce mortality risk for cardiovascular patients even further.

For hereditary *hypercholesterolemia*, a disease characterized by very high levels of LDL cholesterol, a drug that has completed Phase 3 testing, **Mipomersen** (**Kynamro**) from *Isis*/Genzyme, has considerable promise. This drug targets the *ApoB-100* protein and inhibits it. This protein seems to be a good indicator of cardiac risk. Genzyme has been taken over by Sanofi-Aventis, but Isis is a good investable company. Kynamro is on track for filing in 2012, and Isis has over US$350 million in cash.

For drugs serving the hypertension/congestive heart failure market, most patients are prescribed two agents: one is a generic **thiazide** diuretic drug and the other an ACE inhibitor; the latter include Pfizer's **Accupril**, Bristol-Meyers Squibb's **Capoten** and Merck's **Vasotec**. In congestive heart failure, which becomes an end-stage disease, there is no current cure and a heart transplant remains the only option.

Gilead, a company we like and mention earlier, has taken over the marketing of an anti-angina compound **Ranexa** that shows high promise. Six million American patients have angina, and typical treatment includes *nitrates* and *beta-blockers* that widen blood vessels or lower heartbeat rates. Ranexa addresses the market of about 2 million patients with angina who do not respond to these types of drugs and it is the first new angina treatment for about 20 years. Ranexa patents have been challenged but it is the view of experts that these challenges are unlikely to succeed. Ranexa has the potential to be a US$1 billion per annum drug worldwide, adding to the already considerable allure of Gilead, which is the market leader in HIV/AIDS drugs.

In the thrombosis/platelet market, the already-mentioned Plavix's US patent expires in 2012 and so sales are likely to plummet. Lilly has a newly approved product in this area, **Effient**, but it does not appear to be superior to Plavix and has a higher risk of associated bleeding. Astra Zeneca similarly has a new(ish) product, **Brilinta**, in the anti-platelet market, which generally seems comparable or slightly better than Plavix. Sales in 2015 of Brilinta are expected to be over US$1 billion, but in the context of Astra Zeneca this is not a blockbuster drug because the company is already so large. In addition, Astra's key drug for *schizophrenia*, **seroquel** has recently come off patent which will lead to significant sales pressure.

The leaders in new drug development for cardiac indications are Merck, Takeda of Japan, Astra Zeneca (the outright leader), Bristol, Lilly, Novartis and Pfizer. All these are big pharma companies and nothing in the cardiovascular area appears likely in the immediate future to make a substantial difference to their bottom lines.

Treatment for cardiac-related patients has improved remarkably over the past 30 years, with the advent of statins, beta-blockers and other agents. However, what these have done in a sense is to counterbalance the lifestyle effects on the cardiovascular system of "modern living". In Chapter 5, we look at how stem cells and gene therapy could have a remarkable impact on the cardio area and provide impetus to further improvement in the prognosis for the most common deadly disease – cardiovascular disease.

Fading into the Night – Neurodegeneration, Rheumatology and Multiple Sclerosis

The ageing of the world's population, as we have said before, brings to the fore diseases that tend to manifest later in life. Among the most prevalent of these are Alzheimer's, Parkinson's, rheumatoid arthritis and osteoarthritis. Not all of these manifest themselves exclusively in older age, but the overall prevalence rises as populations age.

All these diseases represent large and growing patient populations, and in the case of Alzheimer's and Parkinson's, treatment that is effective is urgently required if a catastrophe of unbearable proportions is to be averted.

It is undoubtedly true that people who are 65 years of age in the developed world are comparably much healthier than their ancestors who reached that age. But by the time they reach 85, half of them will end up in a nursing home or equivalent, and half of them will also suffer from some form of neurodegenerative disease, most probably Alzheimer's.

People with Alzheimer's typically live for 8 to 10 years postdiagnosis, which is a long time to suffer from this awful condition. A whole new cohort of "illderly" people is emerging in the developed world – alive but with a very poor quality of life. The goal of modern medicine is to create a class of "wellderly" people, and we believe that this is achievable within two decades.

Parkinson's is the second most common neurodegenerative disease in the developed world. The disease is characterized by a depletion of *dopamine*, which causes dysregulation of the body's motor circuits, resulting in the well-known manifestations of Parkinson's, including tremors and *bradykinesia* (slowness of movement). Parkinson's typically affects older people, although younger adults can also be afflicted, such as the actor Michael J. Fox, who was diagnosed with the disease when he was just 30 years old.

A disease that does affect mostly younger people, and is the major cause of non-injury related trauma in people under 40, is multiple sclerosis (MS). About 1 million people are affected by MS worldwide, and half of them are in the US. About 50 per cent of MS patients have a form of the disease that comes and goes, and the other half have a progressive and degenerative form.

Meanwhile, the diseases of the *rheumatology* family are also expanding at an epidemic rate. This area encompasses many autoimmune and musculoskeletal diseases, inducing joint pain, destruction of bone and cartilage and ultimately disability.

By 2030, the US-based Center for Disease Control estimates that 67 million people in America will be afflicted by a rheumatologic disorder, most of them less than 65 years old, and that worldwide, already 450 million people suffer from these types of diseases. The most common of these diseases are osteoarthritis (OA), rheumatoid arthritis (RA), lupus and gout.

There are no cures for any of the above diseases, although in some there are effective therapies that halt progression; all of them represent huge unmet clinical need and are the focus of large scale research efforts.

Any one of these diseases could be the subject of a book on its own, and so we will briefly review what appears to us to be the interesting developments in each of them, and highlight some companies worth watching out for.

Alzheimer's

Alzheimer's is a debilitating disease, characterized by a slow death of neurons in the brain, leading to progressive loss of memory and cognitive function. Communication between neurons in an Alzheimer's victim is impeded by the formation of *amyloid plaques*, which are largely composed of a protein called *beta-amyloid*. In addition, neurofibrillary tangles, formed from a protein called *tau*, are visible in the brain of Alzheimer's sufferers, and these appear to have a "stranglehold" effect on normal brain cells.

A protein is described as being *amyloid* if, due to an alteration in its secondary structure, it takes on a particular aggregated insoluble form. As a result, the cerebral cortex, the outer surface of the brain responsible for intellectual function, shrinks dramatically over time.

There is no cure for Alzheimer's or as yet any effective treatment to slow the progression of the disease. There appears to be no real pattern of inheritance in Alzheimer's, and age appears to be the principal cause of the disease. About seven genes have been implicated in Alzheimer's, the most important one being the e4 version of the *APOE gene*, which when overexpressed seems to indicate a 400 per cent increase in the chances of developing the disease.

Diagnosis is possible by spinal tap and by new forms of brain scans (see Figure 9), but normally Alzheimer's is recognized by

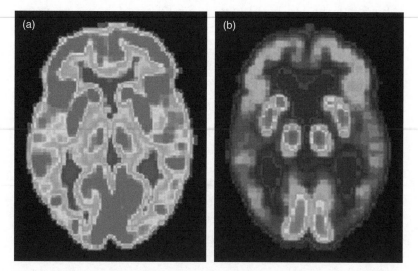

Figure 9: (a) PET scan (visualizing brain activity) of a normal brain compared (b) to one with Alzheimer's.
Source: National Institutes of Health

behavioural symptoms, including memory loss and loss of language skills. Alzheimer's eventually leads to total loss of memory and an inability to function at almost any level.

Drugs approved by the FDA for Alzheimer's are designed to raise the level of *acetylcholine*, a chemical that helps to transmit nerve signals to the brain. Aricept by Pfizer, the most prescribed of these drugs, has limited efficacy. Like others, this drug is an *acetylcholinesterase* inhibitor and is the mainstay treatment at the moment for Alzheimer's and likely to remain so for a while yet.

The new generation of Alzheimer's drugs that are lined up for regulatory approval, attempt to focus on the underlying mechanisms of the disease, although these are not yet fully understood. The areas these drugs target include *beta-amyloid*, via immunotherapy (either with monoclonal antibodies or by vaccination), and the activation or inhibition of *secretases* (alpha, beta and gamma). In addition, drugs designed to prevent *tau* accumulation are in development.

A long list of companies is involved in this field, which in itself gives us grounds for optimism. Furthermore, because of the high unmet need, the FDA is likely to give promising compounds fast-track status. Pfizer, Eli Lilly and Forest are the leaders in the category and likely to remain so for some time to come. We think Pfizer is a relatively cheap stock paying quarterly dividends and can be considered a "big pharma" play that should provide solid, if unspectacular, returns in coming years.

Alzheimer's is a fast growing disease with over 5 million sufferers in the US, and that number is expected to grow to 15 million by 2030. Worldwide, 15 million people have the disease today, and again that number will treble in the next two decades. About 10 per cent of people over 65 will contract Alzheimer's.

Poor clinical results for novel compounds, including Pfizer's **Flurizan** and Medivation's Dimebon have slowed the progress of new drug development in the field. The Alzheimer's drug market was worth about US$5.5 billion worldwide in 2010 and is expected to grow by 50 per cent by 2015, making it one of the fastest growing pharma categories, even though the drugs are not yet effective treatments.

Aricept, which has 50 per cent of the market, has gone off patent and will be eroded by generics, but Pfizer's **bapineuzunab**, expected to be marketed by 2014, will allow it to maintain the highest market share, with Lilly in second position. Pfizer, which will offer bapineuzunab along with *Elan* and Johnson & Johnson, has a drug that seems to prevent beta-amyloid accumulation, and actually may clear beta-amyloid from the brain.

Another area of promise is in the *beta-selective APP Cleaving Enzyme (BACE)* inhibiting drugs, which although fraught with difficulty and still in very early trials, are demonstrating considerable promise. Astellas of Japan and its partner *Comentis* are the furthest along the path in this area, and investors would do well to monitor the progress of their development compound **CTS-21166**.

Genentech scientists are pursuing a line of thought that *APP* is a ligand (signal) for *Death Receptor 6* (DR6), which may be responsible for neuronal death. Lilly will bring out key data on its Alzheimer's compound **Solanezumab** (a beta amyloid antibody) sometime in 2012, and that is a process well worth watching.

New tests for Alzheimer's are expected to represent a significant market opportunity, and in particular Lilly's **Florbetapir F18** and *GE*'s **Compound B**, both imaging agents, are likely to do well.

Our own view on Alzheimer's is that you should take special note of developments in potential new drug therapies. We will keep you updated on our most recent research findings through our newsletter,[2] but as yet the safest "plays" in this area (bearing in mind it is as yet an intractable condition) are Pfizer and Astellas.

Multiple sclerosis (MS)

MS is a disease that can be held at bay, or at least kept under control reasonably effectively. It is also a disease that is not growing faster than the general population. However, it is thought that only 80 per cent of those who have intermittent MS and only 30 to 40 per cent of progressive MS sufferers are being treated. MS originates from the degeneration of the *myelin sheath* that surrounds the *axons* of *neurons*, which are responsible for the conductivity of brain signals. It can be a highly debilitating disease, leading to a life in a wheelchair and a lack of control over bodily functions.

---

[2] You can subscribe to our free newsletter at www.wakeupnewsletter.com.

Until recently, there were four key drugs in the MS arsenal, three based on *beta-interferon* (Biogen-Idec's **Avonex**, *Merck Serono*'s **Rebif** and *Novartis Bayer*'s **Betaseron**) and one *immune-modulatory peptide*, **Copaxone**, by the Israeli company Teva. Interferon-based drugs have significant side effects, and so the only non-interferon approved thus far, Copaxone, has enjoyed significant market share gains. Teva is an interesting company, and we discuss it more later in this chapter.

Beta-interferon was first approved for use in MS in 1993, and since then it has been the mainstay treatment, although its mode of action is not understood. The mode of action of Copaxone is also unclear.

Two new drugs have recently appeared, Novartis's **Gilenya**, approved in 2010, and Biogen's **Tysabri**. Biogen is the leader in the MS market with about a one third share of worldwide sales and looks like it will maintain its leadership with its blockbuster drug Tysabri.

Tysabri (**Natalizumab**) is a humanized monoclonal antibody used to treat both MS and *Crohn's disease*. It is co-marketed by Biogen Idec and Elan and is administered by infusion once a month. The drug is believed to work by reducing the ability of inflammatory immune cells to attach to and pass through the cell layers lining the intestines and the blood brain barrier.

Natalizumab was approved in 2004 by the FDA but subsequently withdrawn after it was linked with three cases of a rare neurological condition called *PML*, but then re-marketed recently with great success, after a test was developed to identify a predisposition to PML. The drug is expected to address the needs of at least 100,000 patients, making it one of the most successful speciality products ever.

Biogen is also rolling out **Fampyra** (**fampridine**) in Europe following conditional approval in 2011. Biogen has licensed the European rights to the drug, which aims specifically to improve walking ability in MS patients, from *Acorda Therapeutics Inc.*, a company that markets the drug as **Ampyra** in the US. Initial sales of Ampyra have been good and Acorda is well funded.

The market for MS drugs is extremely large, currently much bigger than the Alzheimer's market, and is expected to be worth US$15 billion in global sales by 2015.

In terms of new drugs in the pipeline, the ones that show the greatest promise are Biogen Idec's **BG12**, a drug originally marketed for psoriasis in Germany. Teva's Phase 3 compound, **Laquinimod**, has failed in testing, which is a positive for Biogen, reinforcing the dominance of its portfolio in the MS space.

Overall the MS market is growing because more patients are being diagnosed and because more new drugs are coming to the clinic. However, no cure is in sight.

Parkinson's

As previously mentioned, Parkinson's is a disease characterized by the depletion of dopamine. The disease is also characterized by the accumulation of a protein called *alpha-synuclein* in what are called *Lewy* bodies in neurons. Dopamine is a *beta-phenyl ethylamine* involved in the synthesis of *adrenaline* from *L-tyrosine*.

The disease normally affects men and women over the age of 60 equally. Its symptoms include shaking and slowness of movement, as well as difficulty with walking. Patients normally experience cognitive and behavioural problems, about 10 years after the onset of the disease, with dementia commonly occurring in the advanced (post-15 years) stages. About 1 per cent of over 60 year olds will get the disease, and 4 per cent of over 80 year olds.

Parkinson's is not a hereditary disease, but certain genetic mutations have been implicated in its development and are currently being researched. Evidence suggests that there is an increased risk of Parkinson's in people exposed to certain pesticides (Agent Orange, for instance) and a reduced risk in tobacco smokers. This smoking link is leading to research into the effect of nicotine as a therapy for Parkinson's.

Mainstay treatments for Parkinson's are effective at managing the symptoms of the disease, mainly through the use of **levodopa** (generic) and *dopamine agonists* that promote dopamine. As the disease progresses and dopamine neurons continue to be lost, the point comes, usually after 10 years, when these drugs become ineffective and at the same time produce a complication called *dyskinesia*, marked by involuntary writhing movements. Surgery can be performed to promote brain stimulation and reduce the motor symptoms as a last resort in severe cases.

We bring up Parkinson's disease again in Chapter 5 on regeneration, involving stem cell and gene therapies, as quite a lot of research in this area is being undertaken.

No lab tests exist to diagnose Parkinson's firmly; the disease is usually confirmed as its symptoms emerge. Other drugs used to treat Parkinson's apart from levodopa (which has been around for 30 years or more) include *dopa decarboxylase* inhibitors such as **carbidopa** and **benserazide**, usually in conjunction with levodopa. These counteract the fact that only 5 to 10 per cent of *L-dopa* reaches the brain, with the rest causing problems elsewhere in the body. **Entacapone** is also useful in degrading dopamine outside the brain. In addition, **Requip** and **Mirapex** are used as *dopamine agonists* to encourage dopamine in the brain.

Stimulated in particular by a new drug from Teva/Lundbeck, **Azilect** (**rasagiline**) and successful reformulation of leading dopamine receptor agonists, the Parkinson's disease market value is set to grow strongly, reaching over US$3 billion in 2013. Azilect is a potent, second-generation, irreversible *monoamine oxidase type B (MAO-B)* inhibitor with demonstrable neuroprotective activities. It has a once-daily dosing and high tolerability thereby addressing a significant unmet need in the treatment of Parkinson's. *MAO-B* may also have disease-altering results with the possibility that early treatment with Azilect slows the development of disability.

The market for Azilect is shared with *Lundbeck* (a Danish public company), and so the overall impact for Teva, the world's leading generic drug manufacturer, will not be significant, with sales of about US$500 million for the drug. But Teva's Copaxone franchise is exceptionally strong in MS and sales for that could reach US$5 billion by 2015. For this reason we regard Teva as a good investment because it is a fusion of strong generic production with novel compounds, both on the market today and in development in key areas of unmet patient need.

Rheumatology

Rheumatoid arthritis affects about 2 million Americans and a similar number of Europeans. It is a debilitating autoimmune disease manifested by severe joint inflammation. It diminishes life expectancy by causing a variety of side effects, including cancer.

Females are twice as likely as males to contract the disease and it seems that it may be partly heritable.

Recent drug launches have improved the quality of life for rheumatoid arthritis sufferers in the form of *disease altering anti-rheumatic drugs* (known as *DMARDs* for short) that slow the progression of the condition. *Non-steroidal anti-inflammatory drugs (NSAIDs)* are used often in the treatment of rheumatoid arthritis, as is **Prednisone**, a generic corticosteroid that relieves severe symptoms. Biologic drugs used to treat the disease include Enbrel (by Amgen/Pfizer) and Humira (by Abbott), the latter being the most popular in the space. Most rheumatoid arthritis drugs are targeted as *anti-cytokine* agents. Remicade and **Simponi** (by Johnson & Johnson and Merck) are other drugs in widespread use. For the most difficult cases, Rituxan (by Biogen-Idec/Roche) and **Orencia** (by Bristol-Myers Squibb) are among the medications used.

The relatively new *Tumour Necrosis Factor (TNF)* inhibitors target the *TNF alpha*, which is produced by *t-lymphocytes* and *macrophages*. TNF plays a key role in what is known as the "inflammatory cascade", and so inhibiting it causes a significant decrease in inflammation. As a result it is expected to continue to be the dominant therapy in rheumatoid arthritis.

A new line of drugs called *JAK1/3* inhibitors are being trialled. Pfizer has **tofacitinib**, an oral small molecule drug that targets the *JAK 1/3* enzyme, the effect of which is to inhibit the *IL-6* regulator of inflammation. This drug is in Phase 3 testing, and although unlikely to replace the biologic TNFs, it will have a role when patients fail with TNF drugs. Eli Lilly and *Incyte* are in a Phase 2 trial of a *JAK2* inhibitor that has had some preliminary success.

Overall, the rheumatoid arthritis market is expected to be about US$7 billion in 2015 and its leading players will continue to be Pfizer and Biogen, along with Abbott.

Pfizer and Biogen are on our "buy" lists for the more conservative investor.

Lupus – Systemic Lupus Erythematosus

Lupus is an autoimmune disease that primarily affects women in their 20s and 30s. It is particularly prevalent among people of

African descent, and although it reduces mortality for sufferers, long-term survival rates are generally good. Immunosuppressants are the first line of attack for lupus to put patients into remission. Its symptoms include arthritis, renal and blood disorders.

The first drug for decades to treat lupus, Benlysta, has recently been approved by the FDA. Human Genome Sciences and its partner GSK have recently begun marketing this drug, a *monoclonal antibody* which has *anti-BLys* action. Patients with lupus have elevated levels of *BLys*, which is a protein necessary for the maturation of *B-lymphocytes* into plasma cells. Decreasing *BLys* is effective in treating lupus, and possibly in other autoimmune diseases. There are 1 to 1.5 million lupus sufferers in the US, and so this is a large market opportunity. About half of these will see some positive responses from Benlysta over conventional therapies, and by 2015 Benlysta is expected to be a US$1 billion per year drug in the US. European sales are expected to be between US$300 and 500 million per annum. However, Benlysta is not greatly efficacious, and for that reason we do not recommend Human Genome Sciences as an investment.

There are other drugs in development for lupus, including **Lupuzor**, developed by *ImmuPharma* (LON: IMM), which is worth looking at. Overall, the standard of care for years to come is likely to remain conventional immunosuppressants and NSAIDs, supplemented in about half of cases by Benlysta.

Gout – A form of chronic arthritis

Gout is an inflammatory condition in which the symptoms are very swollen joints and painful movement. The old myth about gout being caused by drinking too much port has some veracity, given that lifestyle has a high linkage to gout. People who are obese and have type 2 diabetes are much more likely to contract gout. It is estimated that about 2 per cent of people over the age of 30 are gout sufferers, and as many as 8 per cent over the age of 80. Most people who get gout are men or post-menopausal women.

About 3 to 5 million people in the US have the disease, and the numbers are growing fast. Similar numbers exist in Europe, and it is believed that the figures are even higher in Asia Pacific. As a result, this is a large market for the pharma industry, especially since new and effective medicines are coming into play.

Gout is caused by deposits of *uric acid crystals* in joints; when uric acid levels rise above normal solubility levels (due to diabetes, hypertension, alcohol abuse and so on), urea begins to form as crystals in joints, leading to painful inflammation. In the early stages of gout, palliative treatments such as NSAIDs can be effective, and indeed steroids are useful to a limited degree.

However, the key to treating gout is in lowering uric acid levels and thereby controlling what are known as "flares" of the disease. **Allopurinol**, a generic product, is considered to be the main treatment for gout patients whose flares regularly recur. It is an inhibitor of *xanthine oxidase*, the enzyme that produces uric acid. It does have some side effects, however, and for that reason the market is open to new therapies.

Savient Pharmaceuticals (NASDAQ: SVNT) has developed **Krystexxa** (pegloticase), a disease modifying agent for gout that was approved in 2010, although with a "black box" label for anaphylaxis. Krystexxa is a *PEGylated recombinant urate oxidase* (a biologic) derived from pigs. It breaks down uric acid and is particularly useful in reducing *tophi*, a painful condition of the joints, cartilage, bones and other places throughout the body resulting from gout.

Krystexxa is used for *refractory* gout patients (i.e., those who do not respond to other treatments) and as a result, because of the side effect issues, has a more limited market (about 5 per cent of gout patients). Sales of this drug, which is expensive at about US$60,000 per annum, are estimated to grow slowly to US$500 million per annum – good, but not a blockbuster. We do not recommend Savient as an investment nor do we recommend *BioCryst*, which is in late Phase 2 developments of a gout treatment.

Companies with more interesting prospects in gout include *Regeneron* (NASDAQ: REGN), which appears to have an effective preventative medicine called **Rilonacept**, and Novartis, which has a new agent in development called **canakinumab** that may have a niche role in tackling gout.

Osteoarthritis

Osteoarthritis affects about 30 million people in the US, and an estimated 100 million plus worldwide. It is a degenerative joint disease involving hips, knees and the spine, and in a small number of patients the hands and feet. Lifestyle is a contributing factor to osteoarthritis, including obesity, diabetes and earlier joint injuries. The US market is estimated to be worth US\$8 billion in osteoarthritis drug sales by 2015.

No drugs exist at the moment that can modify osteoarthritis, and principal drugs used are NSAIDs, anti-inflammatory creams (such as **Voltarol**) and patches, corticosteroids and narcotics. *Cox-2 inhibitors* used to be very widely prescribed for this condition, notably Vioxx (by Merck) and **Celebrex** (by Pfizer), but Vioxx has been withdrawn and Celebrex is much more tightly controlled due to an elevated cardio risk in patients. NSAIDs with Cox-2 inhibitory action were also given "black box" warnings, including ibuprofen and naproxen.

Amgen's **denosumab** is going into later trials for osteoarthritis. It is potentially a disease-modifying drug targeting the pathways that cause cartilage and bone erosion. If this drug works, it has the potential to be a blockbuster, because at the moment there is nothing else that can slow the progression of the disease, which though not life-threatening, is highly debilitating. Denosumab is a further reason why we like Amgen as a core holding in the biotech sphere.

Another interesting drug under development in this area (especially since Celebrex is about to go off patent) is **Naproxcinod** from **NicOx** (Paris Stock Exchange: COX). Naproxcinod is a modified naproxen designed to reduce cardio risk, and it has completed Phase 3 clinical trials, but the FDA has asked for further tests and the future of the drug is in doubt.

Respiratory Disease – New Drugs: A Breath of Fresh Air

Diseases of the respiratory system are growing in the developed world and affect many millions of people. The principal conditions are asthma, chronic obstructive pulmonary disease (COPD), seasonal and other allergies, and *pulmonary arterial hypertension (PAH)*. There is currently no cure for COPD and PAH.

Respiratory diseases are mostly caused by environmental factors such as pollution or irritants. The most common is asthma, which is a chronic inflammation of the airways prompted by the release of histamines and leukotriene from mast cells. Worldwide incidence of asthma is increasing, especially among children, although the exact reasons for this are still unknown.

About 20 million people suffer from asthma in the US, although very few die from the condition. Major therapies include long-term *corticosteroids, leukotriene modifiers* such as Singulair (by Merck) and *long-acting beta agonists*, as well as **Xolair** (see below), *short-acting beta agonists* and *anticholinergic drugs*. Combination therapies are often used in asthma, incorporating *anti-inflammation agents* (inhaled *corticosteroids* or *anti-leukotriene drugs*) with *bronchodilators* that are either *beta agonists* or *muscarinic antagonists*. Asthma treatment is often the same as that used for COPD, a much more serious, and often fatal, condition. About half of asthma sufferers do not respond to standard care, particularly those who do not have high levels of eosinophils, a type of white blood cell, leaving a large unmet medical need.

Asthma drugs are a large market, but increasingly subject to generic competition. It is thought that asthma product sales will reach US$20 billion per annum in the US by 2015, with Merck's Singulair, the number 2 product after GSK's **Advair**, which is losing its patent protection in 2012.

Xolair is a monoclonal antibody that inhibits the inflammatory pathways responsible for asthma symptoms. It is a Roche product, but its high price (US$10,000 per person per year) and the fact that it is injectable, constrains its market size to only the worst affected asthma patients.

Cephalon (Teva) has an interesting Phase 2 product for asthma, **Cinquil**, with a bigger market potential than Xolair.

The asthma and COPD markets are dominated by GSK (Advair, with **Relovair** to follow), and its market share is expected to increase in coming years. Principal products include steroids and long-acting beta agonist combination inhalers, including Advair, with estimated sales of US$8 billion worldwide in 2011.

A new combination drug from Forest Labs, **LAS 10097**, in partnership with *Almirall*, has significant promise in the inhaler market. This is another beta agonist combined with *corticosteroid* and with another Forest product for COPD, **Daxas**, showing great promise also, Forest appears to be the best bet in this sector.

Overall the asthma sector is a reasonably attractive one, based on higher incidence of asthma around the world, particularly in children, and the fact that many millions go untreated. What is not so attractive from an investor's point of view is that the disease is intermittent, and that existing inhalers and treatments work well to mask the symptoms. As yet, there is no cure in sight.

Asthma is a condition where patient compliance is a particular problem; one of the features of prescription use is that quite often patients do not take them at the appropriate time or dose, and it is thought that up to two thirds of asthma patients are non-compliant either all the time or inconsistently.

COPD is a progressive and nasty disease, linked to smoking in 80 per cent of cases. Airways become obstructed and lung tissue is inflamed and eventually destroyed. *Bronchitis* and *emphysema* are linked to COPD and can lead to death. In fact, in the US, COPD is the fourth leading cause of death and it is expected to climb higher in the grim reaper rankings over the next 20 years. As many as 600 million people suffer from the disease worldwide, and most are untreated. About 20 per cent of smokers will develop the condition, which is irreversible.

Treatment is with *anticholinergic* drugs, including *Boehringer Ingelheim*/Pfizer's **Spiriva** and GSK's Advair (which is about to morph into Relovair). These, along with Forest's Phase 3 *muscarinic agonist*, **BID**, relieve the symptoms of COPD but are not disease altering. Many new drugs for COPD, which are combinations of *long-acting muscarinic agonists* and *long-acting beta agonists (β₂ agonists stimulate β₂ receptors* on airway smooth muscles, causing them to relax), are in Phase 3 trials.

Perhaps the most exciting of them are GSK/Theravance's **GSK 573719** and **vilanterol** combo and Forest/*Nycomed's* Daxas (**Daliresp**). The latter is close to launch in the US and could well be a US$1 billion per annum drug for COPD, adding to the allure of *Forest* as an investment.

Pulmonary hypertension is relatively rare with perhaps only 100,000 patients worldwide, but has a high unmet need for treatment. The disease ultimately leads to right side heart failure due to excessive pumping of oxygenated blood through the lungs. It is progressive and terminal unless lung transplants can be performed. The standard care has been prostanoid drugs, with GSK's **Flolan** and a newly approved compound from Gilead, **Letairis**, seeming to delay progression of the disease. Letairis, like its competitor

Tracleer (by *Actelion*) is an oral endothelin receptor, which acts to widen the arteries of the pulmonary system. Actelion also has another drug, **Macitenan**, in development.

Seasonal and other allergies suffered by large and increasing numbers of people are treated by anti-histamines. These are now almost universally OTC generics, dominated by GSK's **Veramyst** and Merck's **Nasonex**.

Among the companies involved in respiratory diseases, GSK and Forest are our preferred investments.

Rare Diseases and Rare Profits

An *orphan or rare disease* is one that affects a small percentage of the population. Because there are upwards of 7,000 such diseases, the percentage of the population who suffer from one or more of them is high, estimated to be between 8 and 10 per cent in the US and Europe.

Most rare diseases are genetic and thus chronic, meaning that they are present throughout the patient's life even if symptoms do not immediately appear. However, many such rare diseases do appear early on in life, and about 30 per cent of children with rare diseases die before they turn five years old.

Drug companies have been encouraged by tax breaks and market exclusivity, as well as by very high pricing, to develop therapies for the more prevalent of rare diseases. With these incentives, a successful drug in this area can make large amounts of profit, even with small patient populations.

The *Rare Disease Act of 2002* in the United States defines rare disease according to its prevalence, that is, "any disease or condition that affects less than 200,000 persons in the United States". This definition is essentially the same as that of the *Orphan Drug Act of 1983*, a federal law that was enacted to encourage research into rare diseases and possible cures by pharma companies and other entities. They are offered tax incentives on clinical trials and seven years of marketing exclusivity for drugs developed for conditions that occur only rarely. Since then, more than 360 orphan drugs have been approved by the FDA, and most are on the market today. Similar legislation has been adopted in Japan and Australia. EU law provides for 10 years of marketing exclusivity, but no tax incentives (because there is no centralized EU taxation system).

The *European Commission on Public Health* defines rare diseases as "life-threatening or chronically debilitating diseases which are of such low prevalence that special combined efforts are needed to address them". This is later defined as generally meaning fewer than 1 in 2,000 people. In Japan, the legal definition of a rare disease is one that affects fewer than 50,000 patients in Japan, or about 1 in 2,500 people.

Many rare diseases are known as *lysosomal storage disorders (LSDs)*. All LSDs have a similar origin: a genetic (inherited) problem that causes a deficiency or malfunction of a particular enzyme in the body, so that the enzyme cannot properly rid cells of waste material. Waste products accumulate in the lysosomes of cells, leading to disruption of cell function. However, although all LSDs have a similar underlying cause, there is great variety among signs and symptoms of the individual diseases. As a group, LSDs can affect nearly every part of the body in people of all ages and races.

The first of these diseases to be identified was *Tay-Sachs disease* in 1881, but the lysosome itself was not discovered until 1955 by Christian de Duve; in 1963, *Pompe's disease* was identified as a storage disorder. This paved the way for discoveries about the intracellular biology of the lysosomal enzymes, which culminated in the first successful treatment of an LSD, *Gaucher's disease* in the 1990s, with **b-glucosidase**, an enzyme replacement.

Some names of the more well-known orphan diseases include *Fabry disease*, which is an LSD characterized by failing kidneys and leads to early death if untreated by enzyme replacement. As an example of how orphan diseases are in many cases being treated successfully by enzyme replacement, Fabry in the US is now treated with a Genzyme product **Fabrazyme**, and in Europe typically with a drug by *Shire*, **Replagal**. Both are formulations of *alpha galactosidase*, and the average cost of therapy is over US$200,000 per annum per patient, which is likely to make the two drugs combined US$1.3 billion per annum by 2015. For a total of only 8,000 patients in the US and in Europe, that is lucrative.

Equally, enzyme treatment is the only effective treatment for Gaucher's disease, manifested by skeletal damage and possible mental retardation. Some patients with particular types of the disease do not live beyond 2 years old, while some will live to a maximum of 40. However, with enzyme replacement, the majority of Type 1 Gaucher patients will live full lifespans. About 6,000 people around the world suffer from Gaucher's. **Cerezyme**, Genzyme's recombinant enzyme launched in 1991, was the first effective treatment, but today new enzymes from Shire and *Protalix* are expected to erode Cerezymes's franchise, which at one point made more than 50 per cent of Genzyme's profits (US$700 million).

As you can see, even though these diseases are small in terms of patient numbers, they can be highly profitable to companies that successfully address them. In fact, Shire is expected to make upwards of US$350 million in sales per annum for its Gaucher's product **Vpriv** by 2015.

Duchenne Muscular Dystrophy (DMD) is a disease characterized by progressive muscle degeneration, affecting young children, mostly boys. It leads to paralysis and death in young adulthood and is caused by mutations in the dystrophic gene leading to a failure to produce dystrophin protein, a vital component in muscle tissue. It manifests itself in 1 in 3,500 males, making it one of the most prevalent of rare disorders with about 17,000 patients in the US. It has also been the subject of famous campaigns by parents of victims, particularly by Pat Furlong.

There is a promising new treatment being developed by *AVI Biopharma* that seeks to restore the absent dystrophin protein in DMD patients. Currently, **eteplirsen** (formerly known as **AVI-4658**) is AVI's lead therapeutic candidate for DMD and is intended to skip exon 51 of the dystrophin gene. By skipping exon 51, eteplirsen may restore the gene's ability to make a shorter but still functional form of dystrophin. Data from a Phase 1b/2 clinical trial of eteplirsen presented in October 2010 demonstrated a broadly favourable therapeutic profile with promising safety and biological assessments.

Prosensa Therapeutics BV of the Netherlands and GlaxoSmithKline are trialling three *exon-skipping antisense oligonucleotides* as part of their alliance on DMD. One of them, **PRO051**, addresses about 13 per cent of the DMD population, who have a frame-shifting mutation at or near exon 51 of the gene encoding dystrophin, the large protein required for maintaining muscle integrity, the absence of which causes progressive loss of muscle function. Interestingly, Summit Corporation of the UK has a very interesting compound for DMD that is still preclinical. We have had a closer look at this compound, which is a utrophin upregulator designed to balance out the absence of dystrophin. We like Summit and suggest readers consider making a small investment in it.

Other rare diseases for which new drugs are being commercialized or are in development are *hereditary angioedema (HAE)*, *Hunter Syndrome, Sanfilippo Syndrome, Morquio A syndrome* and *paroxysmal nocturnal hemoglobinuria (PNH)*.

PNH is an autoimmune disease involving the destruction of the red blood cells, resulting from mutations of the *PIG-A* gene. About 8,000 to 10,000 people are affected by PNH worldwide, which manifests itself in the 30s and severely reduces life expectancy if untreated.

A new drug, **Soliris**, by *Alexion* (NASDAQ: ALXN), is an antibody designed to stop the destruction of the red blood cells. The drug has had a dramatic effect on PNH patients' lives. Alexion is already selling nearly US$800m on an annual basis and is expected to have sales of over US$1 billion by 2015, making it a potentially very profitable company. Soliris is likely to be the most successful orphan drug ever and it has potential in other rare disease treatment as well. In October 2011 it was approved for *atypical Hemolytic Uremic Syndrome (aHUS)* in both the US and Europe.

In Hunter Syndrome, a fatal disease with a small patient population, one single drug, **Elaprase** from Shire, dominates the worldwide market, and again it is a specific enzyme replacement therapy. Treatment per patient (and there are about 2,000 worldwide eligible for this treatment) costs about US$400,000 per annum, and Shire is expected to generate about US$600 million per annum in sales for this product alone by 2015.

Shire has about 25 per cent of the total orphan drug market, which is expected to reach US$8 billion by 2015. The other key player is Genzyme-Sanofi Aventis with about 40 per cent of the market, and *BioMarin*, with a compound in late stage trials for Morquio Syndrome and Pompe disease, is an interesting play. Despite the extremely high cost of therapies, the orphan drug market is likely to grow strongly in coming years. Our favoured stocks in this area are Shire, BioMarin, Alexion and, as a more speculative vehicle, AVI Biopharma.

Drugs for Pain and for the Central Nervous System

Drugs for such conditions as *depression, anxiety, bipolar disorders, attention deficit disorder, migraine,* schizophrenia, *addiction* and of course pain constitute an enormous and varied market for drug companies. These conditions are not normally life threatening (except where they lead to suicide), and therefore by implication the drugs used to treat them are not life extending, but palliative.

The broad *central nervous system (CNS)* and pain markets stand in contrast to each other: CNS sales are expected to fall sharply in coming years due to patent expirations whereas the pain market is expected to grow strongly due to demographic factors and novel compounds entering the market. According to Cowen and Company, CNS sales in the US are projected to fall from US$41 billion in 2010 to US$27 billion by 2015, largely due to the expiration of Lilly's patent on **Zyprexa**, the leading antipsychotic drug. This is one of the reasons why we do not favour Lilly as a long-term holding.

The key parts of the CNS market comprise antipsychotic drugs (accounting for over a third of sales), antidepressants, migraine treatments and addiction therapies. Half of the antipsychotic market is accounted for by schizophrenia and the rest is consists of bipolar disorders, dementia and *severe depression.* The key mainstay drugs are Zyprexa and Bristol-Meyers Squibb's **Abilify**, although the patents on both expire in 2014.

New compounds in testing for schizophrenia include Roche's **RG1678**, a glycine transporter inhibitor in Phase 3 testing. This is the first drug to treat the "negative symptoms" of schizophrenia, such as the lack of pleasure and poor social interactions. If this drug succeeds, it could be a blockbuster, which is why we like Roche Genentech as a core long-term investment.

Nearly 20 million Americans suffer from depression, and although many remain untreated, this is a huge market for drug companies. About twice as many women as men are diagnosed as being clinically depressed. There are also a substantial number of people who suffer from *manic-depression*, now described as bipolar disorder. These are known as depressive illnesses, and their exact cause remains unknown.

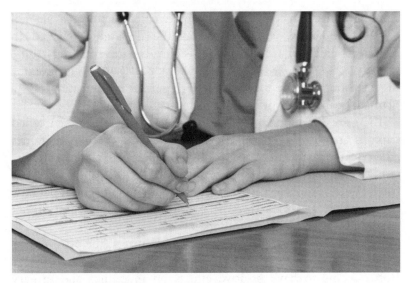

Figure 10: Dr Feelgood, dispensing with depression.
Source: Sheff/Shutterstock.com

Xanax (alprazolam), a generic drug, remains by far the most commonly prescribed psychiatric medication in the US, with a staggering 44 million prescriptions written for it in 2009 alone. **Lexapro (escitalopram)** by Forest had over 27 million prescriptions.

Since all these drugs are more or less the same, only novel compounds with new modes of action are likely to do well in the antidepressant market. Astra Zeneca/*Targacept*'s **TC-5214** which is in Phase 3 testing is one such novel drug, and is a nicotinic channel blocker.

In terms of addiction therapies, a large and growing market exists worldwide. Alcohol dependency affects at least 8 million Americans and smokers number 45 million in the US, plus the obviously huge numbers elsewhere, especially the enormous market of heavy smokers in Asia. Currently, alcohol abusers who seek treatment are given *SSRIs*, **naltrexone** (an opioid receptor antagonist) or *Odyssey Pharma*'s drug **Antabuse**. Smokers seeking help are given nicotine patches or GSK's **Zyban** or Pfizer's **Chantix**, neither of which works very well. An exciting company involved in the anti-smoking field is *Star Scientific* (NASDAQ: CIGX), which has an interesting smoking substitute product that could gain traction. In alcohol therapy **Topamax**, which decreases the dopamine released in response to alcohol, works well but is already a generic drug. Additionally, *22nd Century Group* (NASDAQ: XXII), which is developing very low nicotine tobacco, through genetic modification of the plant, appears interesting, though speculative.

There are 30 million migraine sufferers in the US alone, so-called triptans are the therapy of choice. It is estimated that migraines affect nearly 8 per cent of the world's population. Migraine sufferers tend to get progressively worse headaches over time, and the disease can be quite disabling. In the US, only about 25 per cent of patients seek medical treatment for the condition, leaving a high unmet need and a potentially large market.

Triptans, NSAIDs, acetaminophen and opiates (the usual palliatives) are the standard of care, but peculiarly enough *Allergan*'s Botox seems to have positive effects on migraines and urinary incontinence. These could add as much as US$1 billion to Allergan's sales and give a new lease of life to its Botox product. *MAP Pharmaceuticals*' **Levadex** is expected to be approved in 2012 for migraines and has had some excellent results in trials. MAP is a company we like, and sales of Levadex may end up being much higher than analysts are currently forecasting (US$500 million per annum in the US) making MAP an excellent investment.

Among triptans, there is little differentiation and increasing competition from generics.

In the pain market, there is fairly vibrant growth, and encouraging development of novel products by pharmaceutical companies. As everyone knows, there are many types of pain, but about 10 per cent of adults tend to suffer from persistent or chronic pain. This can take the form of back pain, neuropathic pain or post-surgical pain, as well as of cancer-related pain. Neuropathic pain, caused by nerve damage, affects about 8 per cent of adults, and work is progressing in knocking out or suppressing the HCN1, 2 and 3, which appear to code for proteins implicated in pain pathways. As populations age in the developed world, the pain market is expected to significantly expand. In the US, pain-management drugs are expected to sell at a rate of US$8.5 billion per annum in 2015.

Purdue's **Oxycontin** is the market leader in prescription opioids and *Endo Pharmaceutical's* **Lidoderm** is the number two. Pfizer,

Astra Zeneca and Johnson & Johnson, as well *as Cephalon* (now Teva), are also big players in the pain market.

The latest developments in pain drugs are the introduction of tamper-resistant opioid analgesics to reduce abuse, which is not a particularly riveting change. Oxycontin goes off patent in 2013, and generics will no doubt eat away at its substantial market share.

Nektar Therapeutics (NASDAQ: NKTR) is strong in oncology but also has an intriguing new pain medication, **NKTR 181**, undergoing Phase 2 trials. This is a product as effective as Oxycontin but without the euphoria, respiratory depression or sedation typical of Oxycontin and its equivalents. This strongly reduces the addictive potential of the opioid and in our view will find favour with physicians and the FDA. We recommend a small investment in Nektar, a well-funded company whose management we have met. They also have a strong candidate for breast cancer.

In cancer pain, the largest segment of the pain drug market, Johnson & Johnson and Cephalon are market leaders, but UK privately held *Archimedes Pharma*'s **Lazanda** has just been approved and will be launched shortly in the US. It is nasally administered, which gives it an undoubted edge over the other fentanyl drugs for breakthrough cancer pain.

The Best of the Rest – Ophthalmology, Dermatology, Gastrointestinal and Bone Disease

Failing vision and blindness caused by *glaucoma, age-related macular degeneration (AMD) or* diabetes is a significant yet slow-growing market for drug companies, bringing in about US$8 billion per annum in sales worldwide. Allergan is the market leader and is particularly strong in treating glaucoma. Regeneron, another company we like, has a product in the market called **VEGF-Trap Eye (Eylea)** that has multibillion dollar market potential in treating the so-called wet form (the worst kind) of AMD and *diabetic macular oedema (DME)*. Eylea appears to be more efficacious than the standard of treatment today, Roche's **Lucentis**. Eylea is a recombinant protein that prevents the formation of new blood vessels and could be a company maker. A small investment in Regeneron is recommended as the best option in the crowded ophthalmic market, along with Allergan, which also benefits from the new indications for its Botox franchise.

In the gastrointestinal (GI) market, generic competition is leading to reduced levels of sales. The principal categories of treatment in GI are ulcers (gastric or duodenal), *gastric/acid reflux (heartburn)*, *irritable bowel syndrome (IBS)*, Crohn's disease and *ulcerative colitis*. Astra Zeneca dominates the sector with almost half of all worldwide sales, and is expected to remain the key player in coming years.

Ulcers are lesions that form in the duodenum or stomach, and about 4 million Americans get one every year. Reflux or heartburn is caused by acid in the oesophagus and affects about 2 per cent of all adults. Both are treated by a combination of H2 antagonists (such as Zantac or Tagamet) and proton pump inhibitors that suppress acid. These drug categories are subject to very heavy generic competition and there is little opportunity for investors because at the outset, they were enormously successful. By way of example, Zantac (now generic ranitidine) was introduced by GlaxoSmithKline in 1981, and by 1986 had become the world's biggest selling drug.

IBS and *chronic constipation* are potentially better bets from an investment point of view, and Forest Labs, one of our favoured companies, has a promising new compound in this field, **Linaclotide**, a type-C-receptor agonist that appears safe with few side effects. Over time, Linaclotide could be a US$1 billion plus drug, because over 10 per cent of the population of developed countries suffer from either IBS or chronic constipation. *Ironwood* (NASDAQ: IRWD) developed this product and retains about 40 per cent of the worldwide rights. There is a comparable product, about two or three years behind in development, although apparently with lesser diarrheal side effects from *Synergy* (OTC: SGYP), whose management we met and like. This compound has recently started enrolling in Phase 3. Synergy stock, although very thinly traded, is worth picking up because the difference between its valuation and that of Ironwood is immense despite the fact that they have roughly analogous products, and Synergy, headed up by Gabriel Cerrone and Gary Jacobs, retains all of the worldwide rights to its product.

In dermatology, growth is relatively strong in what are wide-ranging markets covering psoriasis, *eczema*, warts, skin cancers, *acne*, and *dermatitis*. Generics are a big factor in the category due to the extensive use of antibiotics and corticosteroids for several conditions. Enbrel from Pfizer/Amgen is the leader in psoriasis (an overproduction of skin cells) and it is expected that there will be further growth for this drug as new international markets are penetrated. Abbott's Humira is also widely prescribed for the condition which affects about 2 per cent of people in the developed world. Further biologic drugs are under development for psoriasis, which is the largest part of the dermatology market amounting to about US$5 billion in sales in 2015 worldwide, in a category expected to be US$8 billion in total.

In acne, *Medicis* has a strong, relatively new product, **Solodyn**, an oral minocycline antibiotic, and the company seems like a good long-term investment to us. Other treatments for acne include **Accutane** generics and oral contraceptives for acne in women.

In cosmetic dermatology, Allergan dominates with Botox, with Medicis's **Dysport** a distant second. Although Botox is not patented, because it is a natural substance, it retains a strong and growing franchise. Allergan is one of our preferred larger investments, partly because of the new indications continuously being evolved for Botox.

Osteoporosis (meaning "porous bones" in Greek) is a bone disease leading to an increased risk of fractures – typically occurring in the hip, spine and wrist – particularly evident in women over 50 years old. About 10 million people, 8 million of them women, have been diagnosed with osteoporosis in the US, a figure expected to double by 2020. Multiple vertebral fractures lead to a stooped posture, loss of height and chronic pain with resultant reduction in mobility. Bisphosphonates are the main drugs used in the treatment of osteoporosis and they work by limiting bone breakdown.

The most often prescribed bisphosphonates are generic versions of **Fosamax** (**alendronate**) by Merck, though Amgen has a new drug **Prolia** that is expected to gain traction. This is a fully humanized monoclonal antibody, known as a *RANKL* inhibitor. Additionally, there are selective *oestrogen receptor modulators (SERMs)* led by Lilly's **Evista**, which although going off patent in 2014, is expected to be a strong seller for years in the future.

Screening for osteoporosis is inadequate worldwide, and most patients remain undiagnosed. This opens opportunities for some modest market growth, especially as post-fracture patients are very vulnerable to further illness and death. Additionally, about half of all hospital beds occupied by the elderly are for patients with osteoporosis-induced falls and so an effective treatment or cure would have an enormous effect in freeing up valuable healthcare resources. Merck has a new compound **odanacatib**, likely to be filed for approval in 2012, whose mode of action is to inhibit cathepsin K, which in involved in bone resorption.

In cancer-induced bone disease, Amgen's new drug **Xgeva** is capable of sales worldwide of about US$1.5 billion per annum by 2014, adding to the allure of Amgen as a high-quality investment, and approval is likely to be sought in 2012. Trials of Xgeva in bone metastasis in prostate cancer victims appear to have been disappointing however.

Chapter *Five*

Turning Back the Clock - Stem Cells, Genomics, Gene Therapy and Regeneration

The amazing advances in medicine that we have been describing will sweep away conventional wisdom on ageing, life expectancy, health and quality of life for the elderly.

A key element of this change lies in the pharmaceutical industry, which is beginning to be driven by "precision" targeting based on advances in genomics and by the development of *biologic* compounds. Many diseases will fall to science in the coming two decades as drugs for treating or curing conditions once thought impossible become a reality. These new drugs will reverse or halt disease, enable people to live a higher quality of life and enjoy remarkably longer lifespans. Already the average 50 year old in the developed world can expect to live to be over 90 years old, and life expectancy is rising by about 1 per cent per year.

But the advances in pharmaceuticals are only part of the story. Eli Casdin of *Casdin Partners*, an investment firm, believes that we are living in an era of "molecular medicine", and we totally agree with him. Conjoined to the advances being made by pharmaceutical companies are the amazing developments in stem cell research, genomic sequencing and interpretation, as well as in the use of gene therapy and tissue and organ engineering and regeneration, which is progressing towards being able to effectively rebuild entire bodies.

A world of sprightly centenarians is more than just a possibility; it is extremely likely. But before we are able to get to that point, some understanding of why humans age and die is necessary. This is because even if drugs were able to eliminate all cancers and heart disease, the two main killers in the developed world, it is thought that this would add just six years to today's human life span. More advances will therefore be required to extend life spans to the 120 to 130 year range that we expect many people will be able to enjoy in the future.

"Biological death" is not a certainty in nature. After all, some cancer cells are immortal. A good example is *HeLa cells* (taken from Henrietta Lacks): these cancerous cells were removed in 1951 and are still used in hundreds of research sites around the world today (see Figure 11). But with the exception of cancer cells, all other cells die and eventually so do we. Humans are not the longest lived

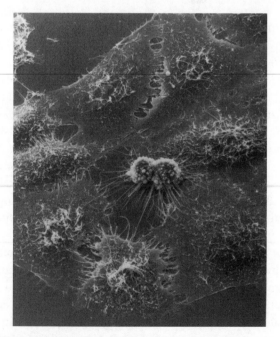

Figure 11: *HeLa* cells dividing under electron microscopy.
Source: National Institutes of Health

of species; certain types of whales, koi fish, tortoises and sea urchins all live far longer. Indeed, hydras and a type of jellyfish (*turritopsis nutricula*) are believed to be immortal.

Ageing or *senescence* is the progressive deterioration of virtually every body part over time, and it seems to start in humans as early as the age of 11 or 12. From that age on, the probability of dying appears to be ruled by the law of eight; that is, every eight years our chance of dying doubles. A mouse's mortality doubling time is three months and a fruit fly's is 10 days. Men's life expectancy, although increasing, is still less than that of women at every age group, but women suffer disabilities in old age at a rate two and a half times greater than men.

There is no evidence that the ageing process has changed much over the past century or so. Of course people are living longer due to reduced infant mortality and better medical treatment, as well as better nutrition, sanitation and less harsh environments, but these expedients have served to prolong life to its natural span rather than to reverse the ageing process itself.

There is certainly a genetic component to ageing. Good evidence of this is that despite major efforts to breed a long-lived mouse, none of them has ever lived over five years. In humans, only one person in recorded history has lived to over 120 years. There appears to be some hereditary link to long life, but it is not a strong one, perhaps about 25 to 30 per cent. People who claim to have "good genes" because their grandparents or parents lived a long life may be indulging in wishful thinking.

There is also a genetic predisposition to some diseases that can influence life span, but again environmental factors (such as smoking, lifestyle, obesity), which act as the triggers to most diseases, generally have a much higher impact on lifespan outcomes than genetics.

One example of genes affecting life expectancy is the *apolipoprotein E (APOE)* gene and its variants. People who have a mutation called *e4* of this gene have much higher LDL (bad) cholesterol than those without. It is no coincidence that since this gene is related to the processing of dairy products, the Finns, who have a high prevalence of the *e4* variant, have high rates of atherosclerosis (calcium deposits that lead to the thickening of the arterial walls). This stands in contrast to the Japanese, who have low rates of *e4* gene mutation, and hence low rates of atherosclerosis. Indeed, the *APOE-e4 gene* is also heavily implicated in Alzheimer's. Conversely, those with the *e2* variant of the gene seem to live longer than those without.

The *Hayflick Limit*, which posits that adult cells are capable of a finite number of divisions before dying (believed to be 50 to 60), was a fashionable explanation for ageing and death until recently. However, it is now believed that cells die in order to protect themselves from a limitless division that would result in cancers.

The key to cell longevity appears to reside in the length of their *telomeres* (discussed further in Chapter 9), which sit at the end of all chromosomes and act as a sort of disposable buffer as cells divide. The enzyme *telomerase*, found in reproductive and cancer cells, adds back *telomere* length after each division and is the subject of intense research, both in anti-ageing and in cancer medicine. Nobel Laureate Elizabeth Blackburn, who has done the most acclaimed work in *telomere* research, has set up a company called *Telome Health* (www.telomehealth.com) to offer *telomere* measurement tests. These indicate whether individuals have longer or shorter *telomeres*, and it is thought, though not definitely proven, that the longer the telomeres the healthier and biologically younger the individual. In the future, it might be possible to use *telomerase* as a tool to partially reverse cell ageing.

Other explanations for why we age and eventually die include the *Rate of Living* hypothesis, which suggests that faster-paced organisms relative to body weight and size have a shorter life expectancy than slower paced organisms. For instance, mice scurry around and live at a constantly fast pace and have much shorter lives than turtles. Raymond Pearl, active in the 1930s, and father of the rate of living theory, suggested that higher metabolic rates and higher energy consumption per gram of body weight meant foreshortened life spans for animals. Lazy people lived longer than active individuals, he postulated, due to lesser levels of energy metabolism. As a side note, Pearl also felt that anyone over the age of 50 should be deprived of the right to vote, as they would by then have become foolish!

Over time Pearl's thesis has been disproved; the rate of living is not linked to longevity in any consistent fashion; if you work hard your whole life, for example, you do not necessarily die earlier than couch potatoes. But from this work came the undoubted fact that a restricted calorie diet – not a starvation diet – does indeed increase life expectancy in most mammals, including humans. We discuss calorie-restricted diets for longevity in more detail in Chapter 9.

There is also a well-established "cost" attributable to reproduction. *Testosterone*, the male hormone, contributes to heart disease and prostate cancer. Castrated men seem to live many years longer than non-castrated males. *Oestrogen* has a similar effect on women. For example, breast cancer is linked to oestrogen levels. In dogs, neutered animals live three years longer on average than non-neutered ones.

In the 1970s, Denham Harman discovered that *free radicals*, highly reactive molecules that are a by-product of normal metabolism, have an effect on ageing. Excessive oxygen in the form of oxidants creates free radicals, and these are now firmly implicated in diseases such as atherosclerosis, arthritis, **cataracts** and cancers.

As we mentioned earlier, we firmly believe that future breakthroughs in *stem cells*, *gene therapy* and *organ replacement* (such as with artificial organs) will eventually enable humans to have much longer lifespans, through rejuvenation to a relatively youthful condition. We do not, however, agree with the likes of Aubrey de Grey and Ray Kurzweil's view of achieving immortality any time soon. Technological advances will be rapid, but nowhere near as fast as they suggest. Our analysis suggests that advances in biomedicine will take life expectancy up by about 20 to 25 years in the next three decades, but the idea that people will be living to 1,000 years is speculative and reflects the somewhat "cultish" nature of many of the longevitist crowd.

Figure 12 is our scenario of how life expectancy will increase from roughly 80 years today in the developed world to around 120 years as new cures and breakthroughs are made.

Certainly, most people want to live longer, and this is reflected in consumption patterns: anti-ageing products such as skin care, hormone replacements, vitamins, supplements and herbs are a lucrative global industry, with the US market alone worth about US$50 billion of sales a year.

The science related to taking antioxidants as supplements (such as *vitamins C* and *E*) and products like *resveratrol* (a natural chemical that appears to increase lifespan in simple organisms) is unproven. Similarly, *hormone therapies* to reverse ageing are probably

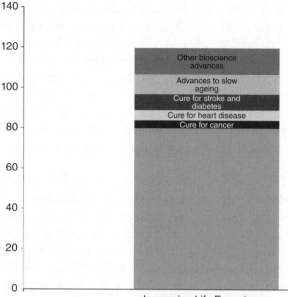

Figure 12: Scenario of how life expectancy is likely to increase between now and 2025 in the developed world.

downright dangerous, as they can induce cancers. However, *hormone replacement therapy* for post-menopausal women, although increasing the chances of ***gynaecological cancers***, significantly reduces heart attack risk (the latter outweighing the former in benefit terms).

Much more promising than anti-ageing notions and potions are *stem cell usage, gene therapies, organ and tissue regeneration*, as well as *nano medicine*. All these take the science of extending human life to a new level and are complementary to the advances being made in drug development. Later in this chapter, we explain the mechanics by which tissue can be grown, organs "manufactured" and how stem cells can be used to alter the course of disease. But before that, we provide a brief review of the technological leaps currently underway in the sequencing of DNA that are essential in producing the new generations of drugs.

A large part of the advances in modern medicine, both those already made and those about to happen, are because of the computer revolution and quantum theory. Quantum theory provides detailed models of how atoms and subatomic particles work to create molecules, and how these molecules go on to create life.

DNA sequencing involves using a variety of technologies for determining the order of the nucleotide bases *A*, *C*, *G* and *T* in a molecule of DNA. The first DNA sequences were partial, and were obtained in the early 1970s by academic researchers using laborious techniques based on chromatography. Following the development of automated analysis and dye-based technology by Frederick Sanger and others, DNA sequencing has become orders of magnitude faster and more accurate.

Today, a whole genome sequence can be delivered to a client in about 30 days with extremely high accuracy by *Complete Genomics* (NASDAQ: GNOM), a US-based company that is our preferred speculative investment in the sector. Complete Genomics operates central sites in which its proprietary machines sequence about half of all the genomes being read on an annual basis around the world.

At the moment, almost all genomes (including those of animals and plants) are sequenced for research projects for new drugs, crops, or for academic or commercial purposes. The price of a full genome sequence at Complete Genomics currently runs at about US$4,000 but is likely to fall over the next few years.

Partial DNA sequencing by companies such as 23andMe (discussed in Chapter 1) also seeks to discover traits likely to lead to disease or to trace ancestry. This approach tends to produce mixed results and they are less comprehensive than those from a total sequencing by companies such as Complete Genomics, but for the time being offer a more affordable option.

As the price falls, genome sequencing will become a matter of routine in doctors' clinics in order to better personalize drug and treatment regimens. In the near future, it is quite likely that many newly born children will have their genomes sequenced at birth to provide parents and doctors with indications of genetic aberrations, such as a disease with no symptoms, or an increased likelihood of contracting a disease(s) later on in life (for example, diabetes or cancer). This information would be useful for guiding parents in helping their child to adopt a lifestyle that minimizes the chances of such a disease from manifesting itself, as well as to provide preventative treatment.

COMPANY SPOTLIGHT: COMPLETE GENOMICS (NASDAQ: GNOM)

Complete Genomics, which we favour over competitor *Life Technologies*, is a company we have met with and like. The company employs its own proprietary means to sequence genomes known as *nanoball arrays* and *combinatorial probe-anchor ligation reads* and we explain what these terms mean.

Complete Genomics reproduces each DNA fragment, and then connects all the copies together in a head-to-tail configuration, forming a long single molecule of connected nucleotides. The system then causes each long single molecule to consolidate (or "ball up") into a small particle of DNA that the company calls a *DNA nanoball (DNB)*. The DNBs are approximately 200 nanometres in diameter.

The small size and biochemical characteristics of the DNBs allow them to be packed together very tightly on a single silicon chip. Using photolithography processes developed in the semiconductor industry, silicon chips with a grid pattern of small spots are created. The small spots are approximately 300 nanometres in diameter and the centre of each spot is separated by approximately 700 nanometres from neighbouring spots.

Each silicon chip has approximately 2.8 billion spots in an area just 25 millimetres wide and 75 millimetres long. Complete Genomics's proprietary process makes the DNA adhere to these spots, known as "sticky" spots, and when a solution of DNBs is spread across the chip the DNBs stick to the spots (one DNB per spot). The silicon chip filled with DNBs is a DNA nanoball array. Each finished DNA nanoball array contains up to 180 billion bases of genomic DNA prepared for sequencing.

To read the sequence of nucleotides in each DNB, the company uses a proprietary ligase-based DNA (an enzyme that catalyses a chemical bond) reading technology called *combinatorial probe-anchor ligation (cPAL). cPAL* technology uses the naturally occurring ligase enzyme, which accurately distinguishes between *A*, *C*, *G* and *T*, to attach fluorescent molecules that light up red, blue, green and yellow to the nucleotides in each DNB.

The sequencing industry is expected to grow to be very large indeed over the coming decade; by 2015, *Strategic Directions International*, a market research firm, expects annual sales to be close to US$5 billion, doubling again by 2020. Because of the capital intensity of the industry and the technical complexity of its product, we believe that Complete Genomics has a good chance to be a leader in providing genome sequencing services. This is all the more the case because, as sequencing becomes more accurate and less expensive, the interpretation of sequences is still at an early stage of development. In other words, though producing the genome "book" is getting to be quite commonplace, the reading of it remains an art with high value-added potential.

This science is called *bioinformatics* and is poised to be at the centre of a large and vibrant industry. Bioinformatics is the curation and interpretation of the vast amounts of genomic data being unleashed by the new technologies at humankind's fingertips. In an article in Nature Biotechnology in 2011, involving a performance comparison of whole-genome sequencing platforms, Complete Genomic came out best.

COMPANY SPOTLIGHT: PACIFIC BIOSCIENCES OF CALIFORNIA (NASDAQ: PACB)

Another company of note in the field of genome sequencing is Pacific Biosciences of California, though it is in our view a more speculative investment than Complete Genomics. Pacific Biosciences uses a proprietary *SMRT* transcription process to read protein transcriptions and its business is manufacturing the machines that do this. It is a different business model to Complete Genomics, which operates a

(Continued)

service rather than selling hardware that could be leapfrogged in the near future by a superior sequencing technique.

Pacific Bioscience's technology involves the replacement of the DNA polymerase used in other technologies (employed by Roche subsidiary Illumina and Life Technologies, for example) with an RNA polymerase (enzyme) that provides the ability to observe directly in real-time the transcription of a gene into an RNA message, the first phase of protein expression. According to the company, which has already gone through nearly US$600 million of funding in its short life, the combined power of direct observation of transcription and the sequence context that SMRT sequencing provides has the potential to replace present transcription assays and enable transcription analysis on a whole genome.

Stem Cells

There are over 200 types of human cells, all generated from a single fertilized egg *(zygote)*. This egg, known as a *stem cell*, is the only cell that is *totipotent*, meaning that it has the capacity to become every type of cell in the body. After five to seven days, the zygote has divided hundreds of times to become a *blastocyst* (see Figure 13).

Stem cells are found in all multicellular organisms that have cells that can divide through mitosis. They then generally change into specialized cell types, such as heart, liver or brain cells. Stem cells can also self-renew and produce more stem cells.

In humans there are two broad types of stem cells:

- Embryonic *(pluripotent)* stem cells that are isolated from the inner cell mass of blastocysts.
- Adult *(multipotent)* stem cells that are found in various tissues.

In adult organisms, stem cells and *progenitor* cells (meaning they can only produce one form of cell) act as repair systems for the body. In a developing embryo, stem cells can differentiate into all the specialized cells, but also maintain the normal turnover of regenerative organs, such as blood, skin or intestinal tissues.

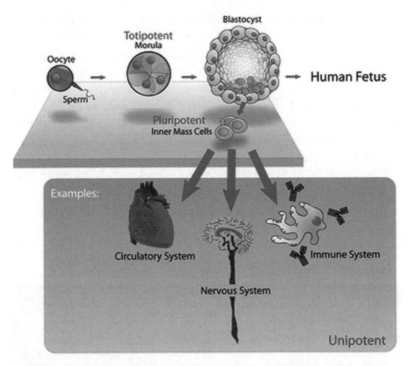

Figure 13: The origin of pluripotent stems cells from developing embryos.
Source: Mike Jones for Wikimedia Commons

Stem cells can now be artificially grown and transformed into specialized cell types such as muscle or nerve cells through *cell culture*. Stem cells can also be derived from a variety of other sources, including umbilical cord blood and bone marrow.

To sum up then, stem cells have two crucial properties:

- *Self-renewal:* The ability to go through numerous cell divisions while maintaining an undifferentiated state.
- *Potency:* The capacity to differentiate into specialized cell types such as heart cells.

There are currently no approved treatments for using embryonic stem cells. The first human medical trial with stem cells started in Atlanta in October 2010 for spinal injury victims, but the results so far have been disappointing. However, stem cells used in macular degeneration of the eyes appear to have very promising efficacy, according to recent research at *Moorefield's* in London. By exploiting their combined abilities of unlimited expansion and pluripotency, embryonic stem cells are a potential source for regenerative medicine and tissue replacement after injury or disease.

Adult stem cell treatments have been successfully used for many years to treat leukaemia and related **bone/blood cancers** through bone marrow transplants. Additionally, research has indicated that liver stem cells can be injected into patients' bodies with regenerative effect on diseased livers.

The use of adult stem cells in research and therapy is not as controversial as that of embryonic stem cells because the production of adult stem cells does not require the destruction of a human embryo. Additionally, because in some instances adult stem cells can be obtained from the intended recipient (known as *auto-grafting*), the risk of rejection is essentially nonexistent in these situations.

COMPANY SPOTLIGHT: CELLULAR DYNAMICS INC. (PRIVATELY HELD)

Induced pluripotent human stem cells (hIPS) are not adult stem cells but rather normal cells that have been reprogrammed to have pluripotent capabilities. Using genetic reprogramming with protein transcription factors, pluripotent stem cells equivalent to embryonic stem cells can now be derived in quantity from human adult skin tissue. Junying Yu and Jamie Thomson and their colleagues at the *University of Madison* were among the first to induce such cells in 2007 (concurrently with Shinya Yamanaka of *Kyoto University*), and the technology has now been commercialized.

The company that Jamie Thomson co-founded, along with Robert Palay, a successful bio investor, is called Cellular Dynamics Inc. (CDI). We visited this still private company and its two founders in Madison as part of our book research. In 1998, Dr Thomson became the first person to isolate human embryonic stem cells and as a result, a new field of study was created.

The development of hIPS cells manages to bypass the legal controversy surrounding the use of human embryos in stem cell research. However, it is still not completely clear whether hIPS cells are equivalent to human embryonic cells. To overcome this uncertainty, CDI employs what it calls the *IPS 2.0* method, where two or three *plasmids* (self-replicating circular DNA molecules found in bacteria) containing multiple reprogramming genes are introduced into the cells to be induced.

Although the plasmids turn genes in the cell on and off, reprogramming them into stem cells does not integrate the cells with genome itself. This method should address the concerns arising from the potential risks associated with the insertion of foreign DNA – *oncogenes* (cancer genes) to induce reprogramming – which was the method used with earlier iPS.

If the use of induced pluripotent cells can move from being purely for research purposes to being used *in vivo* in humans, the outlook for companies such as *CDI* is going to be phenomenal.

Already *CDI*, which is a highly impressive company, produces several types of cells from stem cells including *cardiomyocytes* or heart cells. These human cardiac cells are specifically designed to aid drug discovery by improving the predictability of drug efficacy and toxicity screening, thereby weeding out ineffective and toxic compounds at an early stage. Additionally, *CDI* is commercializing *hepatocytes* (liver cells) that are to be used in preclinical drug research as well as in neural cells.

hIPS allow *CDI* and others to manufacture any type of human cell. Currently, the focus is on making healthy cells for research purposes and removing any potentially harmful elements in the process. In the near future, diseased cells will be made, which is very exciting because it will allow drug companies to test novel compounds more directly and efficiently.

The industry evolving around stem cells is called *cellular biology*, and it is about to take off. The invention of recombinant DNA in 1975 presaged the first biologic drugs to emerge in the 1990s. These are now the basis of US$65 billion a year in sales from biologic drugs. Similar growth curves are posited for the stem cell industry in which CDI is one of the clear leaders. This is a company to watch if and when it goes public.

All around the world, large scale research is taking place in stem cells, including in Singapore (with its research and development "biopolis" dedicated to the biomedical sciences where everything is ready to "plug and play"), Cambridge (UK), Qatar, California and Boston, as well as in other centres of medical and scientific excellence.

One key area for potential stem cell therapy is in heart medicine. In a heart attack, a common cause of death, about a quarter of the cells of the *left ventricle* (one of the heart chambers) die from lack of oxygen – that is about a billion heart cells. If the patient survives the attack, scar tissue forms making it harder for the heart to work effectively. Some animals such as *Zebra fish* are able to regenerate heart tissue, which is creating interesting research into how stem cells could be used for regenerative purposes. The injection of stem cells, typically *endothelial progenitor* cells found in bone marrow and blood, directly into heart tissue appears to have a catalytic effect on the regeneration of heart tissue. A company called *Soligenix* (OTC: SNGX) has an interesting product being tested in Phase 3 to treat acute **gastro intestinal graft-versus-host disease**, an inflammatory disease that occurs in almost all patients who receive a hemopoietic (blood) stem cell transplant.

Diabetes is another disease that may lend itself to reprogramming of some of the body's cells *in vivo*. Diabetes in both of its types is an area where stem cells may have a positive effect. Rejuvenation of the *islets of Langerhans* (the part of the pancreas that produces insulin) is being heavily investigated. Researchers from *North-western University* in the US have used injections of patients' own stem cells seemingly to reverse successfully the course of type 1 diabetes.

In the future, we anticipate that stem cells will also be used to treat a wider variety of diseases including cancer, Parkinson's, Alzheimer's and multiple sclerosis, as well as to repair muscular damage, for instance, in the heart (see Figure 14).

Gene Therapy and Nano Medicine

Gene therapy, in which artificial genes are integrated with an organism to replace mutated or otherwise deficient genes, is the subject

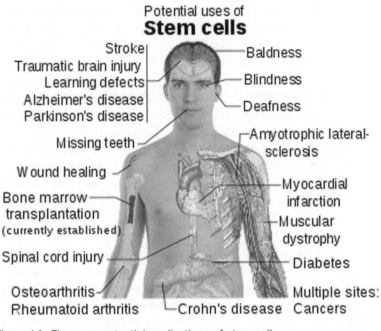

Potential uses of
Stem cells

Stroke
Traumatic brain injury
Learning defects
Alzheimer's disease
Parkinson's disease

Missing teeth

Wound healing

Bone marrow
transplantation
(currently established)

Spinal cord injury

Osteoarthritis
Rheumatoid arthritis

Baldness

Blindness

Deafness

Amyotrophic lateral-
sclerosis

Myocardial
infarction

Muscular
dystrophy

Diabetes

Multiple sites:
Crohn's disease Cancers

Figure 14: The many potential applications of stem cells.
Source: Mikael Häggström for Wikipedia

of major research efforts. Although the technology is still in its infancy in human applications, it has been used with some limited success.

Most gene therapy studies today are aimed at cancer and hereditary diseases, such as cystic fibrosis or sickle cell anaemia, which are linked to a single genetic defect. *Antisense therapy* and *RNA interference (RNAi)* using *short interfering RNA strands (siRNAs)* are other areas of great promise, as are so-called *Zinc Finger Nucleases (ZFNs)* (more on them shortly). Furthermore, the ways in which genes are delivered into cells to create positive alterations are being improved in exciting new ways, opening up huge opportunities in nano medicine.

There are two types of gene therapy: *germ line* and *somatic*:

- *Germ line* therapy occurs as a way of changing genes before conception to stop hereditary disease or to make other adjustments to future human life.
- *Somatic* therapy is applied to existing patients.

In the case of germ line gene therapy, *germ cells* (meaning sperm or eggs) are modified by the introduction of *functional genes* that are integrated into their genomes to alter, for instance, a genetic defect. As a result, the changed DNA becomes heritable and is passed on to later generations. This approach, theoretically, should result in the elimination of genetic disorders and hereditary diseases such as sickle cell anaemia, cystic fibrosis and Tay-Sachs disease.

In fact many diseases have a partly heritable factor; Alzheimer's and **high blood pressure** are about 60 per cent hereditary and prostate cancer is about 40 per cent inherited. That is, of course if individuals are exposed to environmental factors that promote them. If germ line therapy in the future could be used to select out the hereditary components of such diseases, then clearly a major leap forward will be made in addressing them.

Identical twins are a good example of how disease is in part heritable; they have a 9-fold greater risk of a heart attack than the general population if their sibling has had one and a 12-fold greater risk of prostate cancer given the same condition.

Many jurisdictions, however, prohibit germ line therapy in human beings for a variety of technical and ethical reasons, although we firmly believe that within a few years, germ line therapy will become widely used and will be an important component in adding time to human life expectancy.

With somatic gene therapy, the therapeutic genes are transferred into the cells of a patient. The modifications that result are therefore restricted to the individual patient only, and not passed down through the generations. As an example, in a recent trial, Parkinson's disease patients who had viral particles carrying genes inserted into the brain showed a 23 per cent improvement in motor skills, albeit on a temporary basis.

For the time being gene therapy is difficult to effect in so-called multigene disorders, where several mutations of genes conspire, such as in heart disease, Alzheimer's or arthritis. Single gene mutations are the readiest candidates for gene therapy, both of the germ line and somatic types.

Gene therapy trials using retroviral vectors (delivery agents) to treat X-linked severe combined immunodeficiency (X-SCID) (also referred to as "boy in the bubble" syndrome) are the most successful applications of gene therapy to date. This is where a healthy version of the defective gene is inserted into a "vector" or carrier, which in this case is a harmless virus, to introduce the "good gene" copies into the patient. More than 20 patients were treated in France and Britain, with a high rate of patient recovery, although side effects were observed, including the induction of leukaemic cancer in 4 of the 20 patients. This was due to the inherent problems with the viral vectors used until recently in gene therapies, which can generate toxicity and immune system reactions. Furthermore, there is the possibility that the virus might change the DNA of tumour-suppressing genes, thereby leading to the formation of cancers.

To limit tropism (the aberrant mutation of cells) caused by gene therapy, newer versions of these "transfection agents" are being used. The human body maintains a sophisticated series of barrier defence mechanisms to guard against infection and toxicities. Unfortunately, these mechanisms can prevent some therapeutics from reaching their intended sites of action. A variety of white blood cells are present in the blood stream to engulf infectious agents like bacteria and viruses before they can infect sensitive tissue.

Consequently, new forms of delivery are being developed, including silicon-based nanoparticles, liposomes (tiny fat bubbles) and ZFNs, all of which are designed to penetrate cells and deliver their gene-altering payloads. These could be siRNAs and miRNAs or the delivery of drugs.

Improving the bioavailability of whatever drug or molecule that is being put into the patient is a key component of success, in other words, making sure that the amount of the drug/molecule being administered actually gets to the specific site of the disease.

Nanoparticles have unusual properties that can be used to improve drug delivery. Whereas larger particles would be purged from the body before they can make their "delivery", nanoparticles can be ingested by cells relatively easily because of their small size. Several complex new drug delivery mechanisms are being developed with the ability to get molecules through cell membranes and into cell cytoplasm. Indeed, active robotic pill-sized capsules are being developed for screening, diagnostic and therapeutic procedures; the work of Paolo Dario and Arianna Menciassi at the Scuola Superiore Sant'Anna in Pisa, Italy, is of particular note in this regard.

In recent years, the benchmark for so-called transfection agents has been "cationic lipids" or nano liposomes. The most common use of liposomes has been transfection into cancer cells, where the implanted genes have activated tumour suppressor genes in the cell and decreased the activity of oncogenes. Recent studies have shown liposomes to be useful in transfecting respiratory epithelial cells, so they might be effective for treatment of genetic respiratory diseases such as cystic fibrosis.

Every existing method of gene transfer has shortcomings, which is why there have been some hybrid methods developed that combine two or more techniques. Virosomes are one example. These combine liposomes with an inactivated influenza virus and the process has been shown to have more efficient gene transfer properties than either viral or liposomal methods alone.

Equally exciting is a new form of drug delivery being developed by *Leonardo*, a subsidiary of Arrowhead Research (NASDAQ: ARWR), a company we recommend as an investment. Leonardo designs and produces multi-stage silicon-based nanoparticles that circumvent the body's natural barriers to foreign agents (called transport oncophysics) and provide dramatic increases in access to tumour cells.

Leonardo has a library of first-stage nanoporous silicon particles of specific shape, size and surface properties. The first stage, using silicon, can be loaded with different nanoparticles that act as second-stage delivery vehicles to generate custom drug delivery solutions. The second stage can be loaded with pharmaceuticals, ranging from cytotoxic chemotherapies to more fragile biological molecules.

In addition, major progress is being made with derivatives of ZFNs called Zinc Finger Protein Transcription Factors (ZFPTs). ZFNs are artificial restriction enzymes (biological scissors) that normally and naturally regulate genes in humans and can either activate or repress genes. As therapies, they seem to have an excellent safety profile.

By precisely targeting specific sites along a chromosome, ZFPTs deliver a replacement gene into the correct cells in the body. By targeting the ZFPT towards a specific DNA sequence, it is possible to down-regulate or up-regulate the expression of the gene(s), affecting the production of its protein, while leaving the core DNA unaffected.

Therefore, ZFNs edit genes by inducing double-stranded DNA breaks at specific sites in the genome, then repair those same breaks with template DNA provided by the ZFN complex itself. They are therefore clearly more specific than vector-based gene therapy, which delivers its therapeutic payload into patients' DNA at essentially random places.

Sangamo BioSciences (NASDAQ: SGMO) makes use of genetically engineered ZFTPs that they describe as acting as "molecular word processors", editing mutated sequences of DNA. They design ZFTPs that are custom-matched to a specific gene location. For instance, ZFTPs specific for the factor 9 gene (F9), the haemophilia gene, were designed and used in conjunction with a DNA sequence that restored normal gene function lost in the blood disease.

Sangamo's leading drug, **SB-509**, is a ZFTP that up-regulates the gene for the vascular endothelial growth factor-A (VEGF-A) gene. (The *endothelium* is the thin layer of cells that lines the interior of blood vessels.) The VEGF-A gene has been shown to have angiogenic properties, (meaning it promotes the growth of blood vessels) and to have a protective and regenerative effect on nerve tissue.

SB-509 may well prove to be useful in the treatment of strokes, spinal cord injuries and traumatic brain injuries, but for the moment it is being tested in Phase 2 clinical trials for ***diabetic neuropathy*** (nerve damage as a result of high blood sugar levels). *Sangamo* is a fairly speculative investment, but nonetheless one worth watching.

There are also some relatively new technologies that are rapidly evolving around two linked areas: siRNA (short interfering RNA) and *antisense synthetic oligonucleotides*.

RNAi – the concept of *RNA interference* – was discovered in 1990 as naturally occurring in animals and it has been the focus of research ever since, albeit with mixed results. However, it seems to us to be on the point of major breakthroughs, offering significant hope in the treatment of certain conditions. RNAi differs from *antisense therapy* because it uses double-stranded RNA fragments called short interfering RNA rather than the single stranded DNA or RNA fragments that antisense uses, though both are similar in terms of objective, which is to change gene expression.

As we explained earlier, RNA is the factor that transcribes DNA into proteins. Interfering with RNA (RNAi) allows scientists to control which genes are active and for how long. Two types of small molecules, *micro RNA (miRNA)* and small interfering RNA (siRNA), are central to RNAi.

COMPANY SPOTLIGHT: ALNYLAM (NASDAQ: ALNY)

A company that we like, Alnylam, is a leader in the *RNAi field*, and its technology platform accounts for 50 per cent of all the drugs being developed using RNAi. Furthermore, it holds about 700 patents worldwide related to RNAi.

Alnylam and other companies using RNAi employ methods of gene silencing already within our own bodies. The technique uses short lengths of siRNA to interrupt gene transcription and prevent the production of proteins produced by the gene, thereby preventing disease. There are many drugs now in clinical trials using RNAi, including for liver cancer, Huntingdon's disease and for respiratory infections. In addition, Alnylam is testing a *cholesterol lowering agent* in Phase 2 clinical trials at the moment, which appears to have high efficacy.

RNAi could be a very significant industry. One of the factors that has limited the progress of the technology so far has been the difficulty in delivering "naked" siRNAs to the body, except in easy-to-reach tissues such as the lungs or the eyes. This is on the way to being solved, opening up massive opportunities for RNAi technologies. Putting siRNA into the cells where it is required is challenging in several ways, not least of which is that RNA is not a stable molecule.

Calando Pharmaceuticals and Leonardo, both subsidiaries of Arrowhead Research, are heavily involved in delivering RNAi to specific disease sites in the form of siRNA, and it is worth looking at this small company's technologies. Chris Anzalone, the CEO of

Arrowhead Research, has a vision of making the company a leader in siRNA and its delivery mechanism. It seems to us that Arrowhead is a good long-term investment in the field, encompassing both delivery and production of RNA silencing materials.

Gene therapy using *antisense* attempts to inactivate directly the genes involved in disease. So-called antisense molecules consist of small RNA or DNA segments *(oligonucleotides)*, which attach to messenger RNA so that they cannot be read in the ribosome (where the RNA is translated into proteins). The big problem with RNAi has been the delivery of gene silencing compounds. Merck spent US\$1.1 billion on the acquisition of *Sirna* and has probably blown most of it, because it has shuttered its RNAi facility in San Francisco. Roche (which has sold its RNAi assets to Arrowhead), Abbott and Pfizer have also been retreating from their RNAi activities. If Arrowhead can solve the delivery issue for RNAi, it may end up being a huge success. In this respect, research using three-way junction scaffolds at the *University of Cincinnati* is worth watching because it may be a partial solution to the RNA delivery problem.

Antisense nucleic acid gets its name from its base sequence, which is the opposite of the gene's *messenger RNA (mRNA)* (the "sense" sequence). Antisense thereby "blocks" mRNA by preventing its translation (see Figure 15). Since there are between 20,000 and 25,000 genes in the human body, it is estimated that there are about

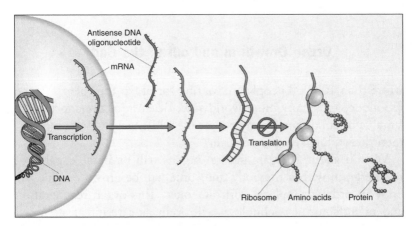

Figure 15: Antisense molecule's role in blocking mRNA.
Source: Robinson R, *Public Library of Science Journal*, Biology **2**(1) e28

85,000 types of mRNA, all leading to the production of different proteins.

Most potential antisense therapies have not yet produced significant clinical results, though one antisense drug **fomivirsen** (marketed as **Vitravene**) has been approved by the FDA as a treatment for *cytomegalovirus retinitis* (a viral inflammation of the retina of the eye).

Isis Pharmaceuticals (NASDAQ: ISIS), another company we like, is the leader in antisense therapies. Isis licenses its drugs, including Vitravene, to partners prior to late-phase development and commercialization, thereby eliminating the high costs associated with sales and marketing. Since 2007, Isis partnerships, particularly for Mipomersen, an anti-cholesterol drug licensed to a company called Genzyme (owned by Sanofi-Aventis), have generated an aggregate of more than US$830 million in licensing fees, equity purchase payments, milestone payments, and research and development funding. In addition, for partnered drugs, Isis has the potential to earn more than US$3.5 billion in future milestone payments.

A German privately held company, *Antisense Pharma* (also worth following), has an interesting antisense drug, **Trabedersen**, which inhibits the formation of *transforming growth factor beta 2 (TGF-B2)*, overproduced by aggressive tumour types, particularly in the most common types of brain cancers.

Organ Growth in and out of the Body

More than 100,000 people are waiting for organ transplants in the US alone, and many more worldwide. Because of the shortage of suitable organ donors, many people die while waiting for a replacement heart, lungs, kidney or liver.

Within about 10 years, several organs will be made capable of regeneration within the body, and some will be grown outside the body in order to replace worn out ones. This organ regeneration and manufacturing technology will occur as a result of stem cell technology advances and improvements in artificial organs, anti-rejection drugs and "scaffolding" methods.

Synthesized organs can now be grown from the patient's own cells, and although as yet the science is limited, it is advancing at a prodigious pace. Already, many patients have received lab-grown bladders, windpipes and ears. Jawbones, lungs and rat hearts have been artificially grown, although these are some way off from implantation into live humans or animals.

The technique for growing artificial bladders was developed by Anthony Atala of the *Wake Forest Institute for Regenerative Medicine* in Winston-Salem, North Carolina. Healthy cells are removed from a patient's diseased bladder, multiplied in petri dishes and then added to a balloon-shaped scaffold using collagen, the protein found in cartilage. Muscle cells go on the outside and urothelial cells (which line the urinary tract) on the inside. The bladder is incubated for around eight weeks at human body temperature until the cells form functioning tissue, after which a functioning bladder is ready for transplantation.

The greater challenge is with organs that are rich in blood vessels and dense in structure, such as the liver or kidneys, but even with these some significant progress is being made.

In addition, artificial hands will become biocompatible with normal hands, using techniques called *osseointegration*, where the hand will be implanted directly into the bone of the arm.

A small San Francisco-based company we like is called *BioTime* (AMEX: BTX). It has received a critical second patent covering its hydrogel technology. *Hydrogels* are the basis of the sculpted scaffolds or matrices of living tissue that are employed in the regrowth of organs and injected directly into patients, for instance in the knee. This matrix substance is described by the company as "living cement". Once injected into the body, it can be shaped precisely to fit individual patients. Setting up or polymerizing quickly, the matrix becomes permanent.

Another company, *Nanotope*, has a peptide-based self-assembling matrix of nanofibres that may be capable of actively directing surviving cells in, for instance, an injured spinal cord, to re-grow damaged tissue. The customizable matrix, or gel, of nanofibres is three-dimensionally bioactive or "smart" scaffolding in which cells and tissues may grow and differentiate.

Nanotope is yet another subsidiary of Arrowhead Research, a company we discuss earlier in this chapter. The firm has used this technology to reverse paralysis associated with spinal cord injuries in rodent models, and although this is a long way from commercialization, it vindicates our view that Arrowhead is one of the more interesting, albeit speculative, of the smaller companies involved in the bio medicine sector.

In addition to the amazing advances in stem cells, gene therapy and nano medicine, new techniques are evolving in surgery. These seek to minimize the time of "invasion" of the surgeon into the body in complex procedures such as heart surgery, and knee and hip replacement.

We discuss robots in surgery in more detail in Chapter 8.

Chapter *Six*

Demographic Changes

Demography is the study of human populations. Understanding the current demographic trends is a key driver of the drug industry's research and development efforts. The biggest market opportunities will in part depend on the demographics of the target markets/countries. Companies can put a value on the lifetime revenues derived from a new drug based on the potential market size.

We are in the midst of a demographic change like no other in human existence and many drug companies are busy trying to capitalize on this. No doubt, you are aware of the trend in population ageing that has been a topic in the mainstream media since the turn of the century, increasingly so over the past few years. But what you may not know is that this change is not cyclical in nature; it is a pervasive trend that will continue for the foreseeable future. The speed and extent of the ageing population is being underestimated, as are its consequences, meaning that many governments, corporations and individuals will be caught by surprise.

Up until recently, elderly people (generally defined in the past as being over 65 years old) accounted for only 3 to 4 per cent of the population. Even as recently as 1900, only 1 person in 25 was lucky enough to reach 60 years of age. Women lived shorter lives due to complications during childbirth.

In fact, life expectancy at birth remained below 65 years in most developed countries until around 1950. Before then, it was the exception not the norm to make it to what has become known as the *retirement age*. In the developed world today, the elderly (generally now defined as being over 60) account for 16 per cent of the population. In fact, around two-thirds of anyone who has ever reached 65 years of age is alive today. Just take a moment to absorb this incredible statement!

It is probably no coincidence that life expectancy and the ageing of the population in the developed world increased not long after a patent was granted to mass produce penicillin (in May 1948).

Medical knowledge (a major factor in life expectancy) has progressed rapidly over the past half-century, and according to the United Nations (UN), by the year 2010 there were over 100 countries with a life expectancy at birth of over 70 years, the highest being Japan with 82.6 years (females are even higher with a life expectancy at birth of 86.1 years). Interestingly, the *CIA World Factbook*'s 2011 life expectancy at birth estimates are even higher than the UN's 2010 figures (UN 2011 figures not published at the time of writing), with the highest at 93.8 years for a girl born in Monaco.

The person who has lived the longest life on record was a French woman by the name of Jeanne Calment. Although she died in 1997, she lived to be 122 years, outliving her daughter and grandson. Her husband died in 1942 in his 70s! She was wealthy enough never to have needed to work for a living and so led a relaxed life of leisurely pursuits, such as tennis, swimming and playing the piano. (Her genome would certainly be worth sequencing and studying as it might reveal some incredible information about human health and longevity.)

Even with the medical know-how available so far in the 21st century, living for 122 years is exceptional, but it does provide an indicative natural limit of the human lifespan under 20th century technology when combined with a healthy lifestyle. We will almost certainly see this record broken in the coming decades by some margin. Within a decade, we can expect to see several countries reaching a life expectancy at birth of at least 100 years, with many more people living to beyond 120 years.

At the other end of the longevity spectrum, the African nation of Swaziland has a life expectancy at birth of only 32 years – just a couple of years longer than life expectancy in Medieval Britain. Sadly the country has been ravaged by HIV/AIDS, leaving more than a quarter of the adult population infected with the disease, the highest rate in the world. Swaziland's very survival as a nation is under threat, because social stability is virtually impossible to attain under such grim circumstances.

The maps in Figures 16 and 17 are a good visual overview of life expectancy around the world for males and females based on the latest map data from the UN (2009). It is worth noting that the differences in life expectancy at birth between the two sexes can

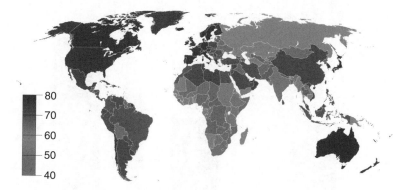

Figure 16: Male life expectancy at birth.
Source: The United Nations Development Programme: Human Development Report
2009

Figure 17: Female life expectancy at birth.
Source: The United Nations Development Programme: Human Development Report
2009

vary significantly between countries, but in just about every country
women outlive men. One extreme example of this is in Russia,
where women can expect to live almost 11 years longer than their
male comrades (72.6 versus 61.8 years).

In developed countries where life expectancy is high for both
sexes, women still live longer than men. In fact, there are twice as
many women octogenarians as there are men. This difference gets
more pronounced as people age further, and by the age of 100, there
are over 80 per cent more women than men.

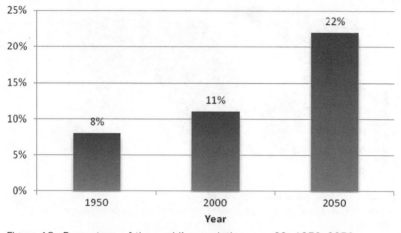

Figure 18: Percentage of the world's population over 60: 1950–2050.
Source: The United Nations Development Programme: Human Development Report 2009

So far we have only discussed the world's demography as it is today; older than the past, yes, but still young relative to what is in store for the global population. With every passing day, the median age of a person living on this planet increases; and in all likelihood this trend will never reverse. By around 2045, there will be more over-60s on the planet than there will be children for the first time in human history.

Figures 18, 19 and 20 give you some broad percentages and numbers of how rapidly the population is ageing, not just as a percentage of the population but also in absolute terms. Imagine two billion over-60s on the planet by 2050, bearing in mind that the entire human population in 1950 was only 2.5 billion. (2050 is not some hypothetical date in the distant future; you may well be alive then and certainly any young children you have will be. We are, after all, closer to 2050 than we are to the year in which *Neil Armstrong* became the first man to set foot on the moon.)

Just as there will be a record number of over-60s, there will also be an unprecedented number of over-80s whose numbers are set to grow fourfold by 2050 from today's 100 million (see Figure 20).

Figure 18 also disguises the severity of the problem in the developed world where the proportion of over-60s is already at 20 per

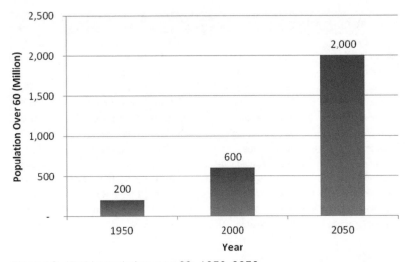

Figure 19: World population over 60: 1950–2050.
Source: The United Nations Development Programme: Human Development Report 2009

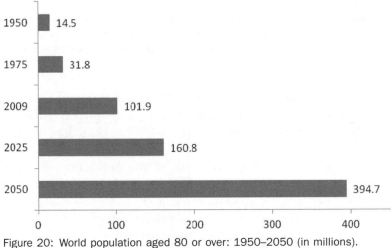

Figure 20: World population aged 80 or over: 1950–2050 (in millions).
Source: United Nations World Population Ageing 1950–2050 (2009)

cent. The oldest population today is in Japan and it is set to remain thus; by 2050 the elderly there will make up 45 per cent of its population and its working age population will fall by 39 per cent. These changes are substantial and will definitely have a negative impact on the country's economy and society in many ways.

Already Declining		Decline Beginning: 2009-2029		Decline Beginning: 2030-2050	
Hungary	(1981)	Italy	(2010)	Azerbaijan	(2030)
Bulgaria	(1986)	Slovakia	(2011)	Denmark	(2031)
Estonia	(1990)	Bosnia &	(2011)	Belgium	(2031)
Georgia	(1990)	Herzegovina		Thailand	(2033)
Latvia	(1990)	Greece	(2014)	North Korea	(2035)
Armenia	(1991)	Serbia	(2014)	Singapore	(2035)
Romania	(1991)	Portugal	(2016)	Netherlands	(2037)
Lithuania	(1992)	Cuba	(2018)	Switzerland	(2040)
Ukraine	(1992)	Macedonia	(2018)	UK	(2044)
Moldova	(1993)	Spain	(2019)	Hong Kong, SAR	(2044)
Belarus	(1994)	Taiwan	(2019)	Puerto Rico	(2044)
Russian Federation	(1994)	South Korea	(2020)	Kazakhstan	(2045)
Czech Republic	(1995)	Austria	(2024)		
Poland	(1997)	Finland	(2027)		
Germany	(2006)	China	(2029)		
Japan	(2008)				
Croatia	(2008)				
Slovenia	(2008)				

Figure 21: Countries facing declining populations; the number in brackets indicates the year in which the population decline began or will begin.

Source: Jackson, Richard and Howe, Neil (2008) *The Graying of the Great Powers: Demography and Geopolitics in the 21st Century*, Center for Strategic & International Studies.

Western Europe is not far behind Japan and its population will only be about 5 per cent younger on average than Japan's in 2050. Its working age population will see a 27 per cent drop by the same date.

Globally, the annual growth rate of the population of older persons is outpacing that of the overall population: 2.6 per cent versus 1.2 per cent. By 2050 we can expect the world's median age to have increased from 28 years today to 38 years.

Many countries have populations that have already been in decline for several years (see Figure 21), among them being the big exporting economies of Germany and Japan.

Within the category of the elderly, the sub-category of over-80s is set to sky-rocket. Already the world has over 100,000,000 people over the age of 80 and that number is set to reach almost 400,000,000 by 2050 (see Figure 20).

Even though it is the over-60s or over-65s who are typically categorized as pensioners and elderly by demographers, most people in their 60s could comfortably continue to work. We are still in the early stages of the chronic ageing of populations, but already around 60 per cent of retirement income is provided to the pensioner by the national governments of OECD member countries, according to a 2011 report on pensions (OECD, 2011).

With so much of pensioners' livelihoods dependent on the state, how will governments ever be able to afford to pay the hundreds of millions of additional pensioners in the coming decades under the current system? Governments will go bankrupt very quickly unless drastic changes are made. Legislation to increase the retirement age to be closer to 70 has been met with substantial resistance by many people in the developed world, and governments are therefore dragging their heels, even though unfortunately they do not have the luxury of time.

Every year that a government fails to increase its nation's retirement age to around 70 years, means a bleaker prognosis for that nation's future finances. Sadly, in politics doing the right thing is often doing the unpopular thing, especially when the over-60s are the ones with the highest voter turnout and the ones to most likely resist any efforts that would reduce their state entitlements (see Table 2).

Increased life expectancy is only part of the reason why the world's population is ageing. Falling fertility rates is the other (see Figure 22). Most developed countries' fertility rates are below the rate required to sustain a stable population size, known as the "replacement rate". This is due to a combination of factors, namely that more women are pursuing careers and opting not to take time out to have children. The high costs of raising children is another factor holding down fertility rates.

The transition of the world's demography is well underway; moving away from high fertility, high mortality rates and towards populations characterized by low fertility and longer life expectancy.

Population ageing is now expected to accelerate in the near future, particularly in developing countries. As a result, governments of developing countries have less time to adapt to a society with an ageing population, and so there is an imperative for them to take steps that try to address the consequences and challenges of older population bases.

At the same time, the world's population as a whole is set to continue to increase, albeit at a more modest rate. It is truly

Table 2: Countries with the highest percentage of over 60s

Rank	Country	Percentage of population over 60
1	Japan	29.7
2	Italy	26.4
3	Germany	25.7
4	Sweden	24.7
5	Bulgaria	24.2
6	Finland	24.0
7	Greece	24.0
8	Portugal	23.3
9	Croatia	23.1
10	Belgium	23.0
. . .		
17	United Kingdom	22.4
42	United States	17.9
65	Mainland China	11.9

Source: United Nations, World Population Ageing (2009).

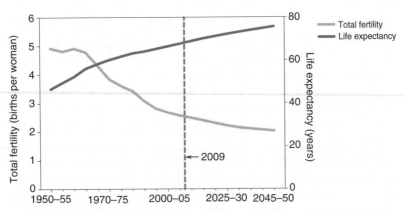

Figure 22: Total fertility rate and life expectancy at birth: world, 1950–2050.
Source: United Nations World Population Ageing (2009)

incredible to think that there are 7 billion humans living on this planet today, especially when compared to the population of only 1 billion back in 1800. That's quite a growth spurt.

According to UN forecasts, the world's human population is expected to reach its peak at 9.22 billion by 2075. However, our view is that fertility rates will be lower than predicted because the major emerging economies of today are developing rapidly, and as they do, their fertility rates will tend to trend downwards.

Consequently, we are of the opinion that the human population will peak by around 2030, much earlier than the UN's forecast year of 2075. We are then likely to experience a small but steady population decline for the next hundred years, barring any global catastrophes.

Before we discuss some of the more specific problems individual countries face, we give a brief explanation about fertility rates. If a country or region does not wish to rely on immigrants to sustain its population, it must have a fertility rate of 2.1; that is, every couple resident in that country needs to have, on average, 2.1 children. This number is the afore-mentioned replacement rate. Unfortunately, pretty much every developed country in the world is already below the replacement rate and forecast to fall further all the way to 2050 and beyond. A good example of this is in Russia, which is forecast to fall from 4th place in world population rankings in 1950 to 16th by 2050.

Table 3 is a table containing the latest fertility rates of the world's 10 largest economies. Apart from India, each country listed has a fertility rate below the replacement rate, although the United States' fertility rate is only a fraction below 2.1, thanks largely to a steady influx of immigrants who tend to have more children.

If we repeat this exercise, but this time use today's 10 most populous countries, we see half of the countries in Table 3 re-appearing in Table 4. This tells us that the world's largest economies tend to have large populations, but there is by no means a consistent correlation between the two.

Comparing Tables 3 and 4 also reveals that only developing countries have fertility rates greater than the replacement rate, the highest being Nigeria with 4.82, followed by Pakistan with 3.52 (the 7th and 6th most populous countries, respectively). When countries have a high fertility rate, it can be a boon for a steadily growing economy because it increases the size of the potential

Table 3: Fertility rates in the world's 10 largest economies

	Country	Fertility Rate 2005–2010
1	United States	2.06
2	China (Mainland)	1.54
3	Japan	1.20
4	Germany*	1.42
5	France*	1.97
6	UK	1.92
7	Brazil	1.90
8	Italy*	1.38
9	Canada	1.58
10	India	2.81

*The EU average is 1.50.
Source: United Nations Department of Economic and Social Affairs, Population Division.

Table 4: Fertility rates in the world's 10 most populous countries

	Country	Fertility rate 2005–2010
1	China	1.54
2	India	2.81
3	United States	2.06
4	Indonesia	2.28
5	Brazil	1.90
6	Pakistan	3.52
7	Nigeria	4.82
8	Bangladesh	2.65
9	Russia	1.54
10	Japan	1.20

Source: United Nations Department of Economic and Social Affairs, Population Division.

Ranking	1950	2005	2050
1	China	China	India
2	India	India	China
3	*United States*	*United States*	*United States*
4	Russian Federation	Indonesia	Indonesia
5	*Japan*	Brazil	Pakistan
6	Indonesia	Pakistan	Nigeria
7	*Germany*	Bangladesh	Bangladesh
8	Brazil	Russian Federation	Brazil
9	*UK*	Nigeria	Ethiopia
10	*Italy*	*Japan*	Dem. Rep. Congo
11	Bangladesh	Mexico	Philippines
12	*France*	Viet Nam	Mexico
		(14) **Germany**	(18) *Japan*
		(20) *France*	(26) *Germany*
		(21) *UK*	(27) *France*
		(23) *Italy*	(32) *UK*
			(39) *Italy*

Figure 23: The world's most populous countries in 1950, 2005 and 2050.
Source: Jackson, Richard and Howe, Neil (2008) *The Graying of the Great Powers: Demography and Geopolitics in the 21st Century*, Center for Strategic & International Studies

labour pool. By 2050, the 4th, 5th, 6th and 7th most populous nations will be Indonesia, Pakistan, Nigeria and Bangladesh (see Figure 23). All are predominantly poor nations with a history of instability, although Indonesia's economy has been growing rapidly in recent years as a result of China's insatiable appetite for commodities, namely oil, gas and coal.

High birth rates in poorer countries that are already burdened with high unemployment can be a destabilizing force that can ultimately affect the world as a whole, in the form of tensions and conflicts. Young people who enter the labour pool and cannot find work become demoralized, frustrated and eventually disaffected as they lose hope of ever earning a decent living.

The Working Age Labour Pool in the World is Shrinking

It may come as a surprise to some that the number of people in the world who are of a traditional working age has been falling. The peak was reached in 2005 at 60 per cent of the world's population.

Several large countries have already begun to experience a contraction in their working age population including Germany, Italy and Japan. By 2015, pretty much everywhere else in the developed world will see a contraction in its working age population, with the notable exception being the United States. We mention earlier that by 2050, the major economies of Japan and Germany will experience severe contractions in their working age population; Japan's falling by 39 per cent and Germany's by 27 per cent.

Naturally, a declining labour pool is potentially very negative for a country's economic prospects. Many countries will experience a slowdown in their economic growth; some will even undergo an economic contraction. Governments need to initiate policy changes today to prepare their nation's economy to one that is economically sustainable against a backdrop of an ageing population. Economic collapse is a very realistic prognosis for countries that do nothing to address their demographic trends. It is worth repeating that the trend of population ageing is expected to continue for the foreseeable future – this is not a generational blip in the statistics, it is the new status quo.

The chart in Figure 24 shows that by 2050, the world's two largest working age populations will be in the Indian sub-continent

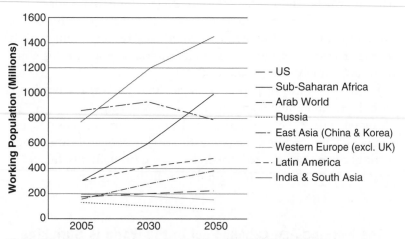

Figure 24: Size of working population by region (2005–2050).
Source: Jackson, Richard and Howe, Neil (2008) *The Graying of the Great Powers: Demography and Geopolitics in the 21st Century,* Center for Strategic & International Studies

(1.5 billion) and sub-Saharan Africa (just under 1 billion). China's working population will fall as the effects of its one-child policy take hold in the coming decades. Although there are signs that Beijing is starting to relax this policy under certain circumstances, it will not be enough to prevent China's population and workforce from falling in the future (we talk more about China towards the end of this chapter).

Can Immigration Solve the Labour Shortage in the Developed World?

With the chronic ageing of the developed world set to continue for decades to come, governments face spiraling healthcare and pension costs. A society with more elderly means more demand for healthcare, more demand for pensions and less tax revenue generated from an ever shrinking work force. So to prevent the inevitable fiscal meltdown that lies ahead, governments need to look to innovations in the biotech sector to save the day. If new drugs and technologies can provide cheaper and better preventative treatments and disease cures, it could reduce their healthcare liabilities by an order of magnitude. At the same time, governments should be looking for ways of luring overseas workers to prevent their own labour pool from shrinking, and with it their tax revenue.

Adopting a pro-immigration policy in countries facing falling populations may be part of the solution. It is a delicate matter that carries a great deal of risk, both societal and economic. It can trigger a social backlash against immigrants, especially those who do not integrate with mainstream society. We see evidence of this throughout the United States and Europe. In the US, there are tensions in states that border Mexico about the extensive number of illegal Latin American immigrants. In Germany, there are over 3.5 million Turkish "guest workers" who are still discriminated against and tend to have low social status, even though they make up the largest ethnic minority. In France, the law on secularity that bans the wearing of conspicuous religious symbols in public schools has been interpreted as targeting Muslim girls who wear headscarves. This has only increased the tensions between France's significant Muslim population and its non-Muslims.

These examples highlight how delicate and difficult such a challenge is for governments, particularly if the immigrants are from very different cultures. The quandary is that countries with declining populations need additional people but cannot and should not simply open their borders to immigrants without a more thorough societal integration plan. Doing so will almost certainly create deeper divisions within a country's society.

The effectiveness of immigration integration policies will ultimately determine whether immigrants become assets or liabilities to society. In Britain and some mainland European countries, there is a growing backlash against immigrants living off state benefits who take up no employment and remain detached from mainstream society. Yet adopting an anti-immigration policy has virtually guaranteed dire long-term economic consequences among countries with low fertility rates, and they do not come much lower than in Japan, which is a country with an anti-immigration stance.

Japan is very picky about its Japanese-ness, its distinct race, ethnicity, language, culture, food, emperor and so on and does not want all that diluted or lost as a result of immigration. Becoming a Japanese citizen is virtually impossible unless you are of Japanese ethnicity, that is, one or both parents are native Japanese. It is also difficult to immigrate to Japan. As a result of its strict immigration policy, Japan has to rely almost exclusively on its fertility rate to maintain its population.

Unfortunately, Japan's fertility rate is currently at 1.2, which means that unless Japan opens its borders to immigrants, it must resign itself to a future with a steeply declining and rapidly ageing population. In economic terms it translates to a shrinking economy that can no longer sustain its standard of living or support its elderly. To make matters worse, Japan's government debt is already the highest in the world as a percentage of GDP, with a total debt well over 200 per cent of economic output. Faced with a shrinking workforce and an ageing population, how can Japan realistically ever expect to repay its national debt, support its elderly and achieve a sustainable economy?

Although Japan faces the greatest demographic challenge of all, by the mid-2020s we can expect growth in the total population of every major developed country other than the United States to stall or reverse.

The Social Impact of an Ageing Population

As people's average ages increase steadily towards 2050 and beyond, we as a society will change with it. Older people think differently, buy differently, invest differently and vote differently.

First, consider the likely economic impact of an ageing society: older people are typically more set in their ways, less innovative, less entrepreneurial, less mobile and more risk-averse. This last point will have a dramatic effect on financial markets, where equity investments will decline because they are considered to be too risky when compared to income-linked investments that are more preferable, such as bonds and time deposits. The over-60s typically work less, save less, pay less taxes and are more likely to draw on government financial support of some sort (that is, pensions and healthcare). And it is the healthcare costs that seriously threaten to bankrupt many governments in the future; as this chapter explains, there is going to be an ever increasing number of elderly people in society, and the older we get, the more likely we are to need medical assistance. The healthcare bill that governments face in the future is insurmountable and the biotech revolution is the only hope to save the day. Innovations in disease prevention, early detection and effective, cheap cures are all likely to provide relief to government coffers in the medium term. Without such breakthroughs, governments face a very difficult set of circumstances and in most developed nations, it will simply not be possible to balance a budget, particularly when we see the current unsustainable deficits and ballooning debts in many of the major developed economies. Some economists estimate the demographic crisis will cost 10 times more than the global financial crisis that began in 2008.

We can also expect the overall social mood to change as countries age. Psychologically, societies under greater influence of the elderly would be more conservative in their outlook and most likely be more risk-averse in how they vote and who they support in politics. On a positive note, there will likely be fewer wars in which the scarce young are sent off to fight. This may not mean fewer wars overall, however, because advances in technology would permit drone and robotic warfare against poor, unstable hotspots with high populations of disaffected youth.

The United States is the Best Positioned Developed Country

With most of the world's population growth coming from what we call developing nations today, the population of the current developed world is forecast to fall to below 10 per cent of the world's population by 2050. Yet, despite this, the population and economy of the United States is expected to expand steadily as a percentage of the developed world. This will also likely mean that America's influence within the developed world will likely increase.

Two hundred years ago, when the US was a young country, its population accounted for only 6 per cent of the developed world. Today, the US accounts for 34 per cent of the developed world's population. That proportion is expected to rise further to 43 per cent by 2050. Of course this number does not include any countries that may become developed nations by 2050 – we are referring to the categories assigned to those countries today.

It is also worth pointing out that although America's influence over the developed world will be increasing, its overall influence of the world as a whole will be decreasing because India and China's economic expansion will lead to greater influence by them over the rest of the world. That said, the United States is expected to remain the world's third most populous country by 2050, as it is today and as it was in 1950 (see Figure 23), although interestingly India's population is expected to surpass that of China by then. Note how "old Europe" countries that were in the top 10 back in 1950 struggle to make even the top 30 by 2050.

In the very long term, the United States' prospects look more promising than other developed or developing countries, thanks largely to its higher fertility rate and steady flow of immigrants. Under such an outlook, the United States looks set to reinforce its position as the global hub of the biotech industry as a whole – the centre of research, innovation, investment and talent. It is also likely to remain the largest market size for the sector well into the second half of the twenty-first century.

Support Ratios Have Been Plummeting

Although today Japan is often cited as the oldest nation when illustrating the future that awaits many developed nations, it has not always been a nation of retirees; quite the opposite in fact. In 1970, Japan had the highest *support ratio* – the ratio of workers to retirees – of all the major countries. Obviously, the higher the support ratio, the smaller the economic burden of the elderly on a nation's economy. Figure 25 illustrates how in just 40 years, Japan's accelerated ageing turned it from the youngest to the oldest major country.

The ratio of 8.6 that it enjoyed in 1970 started to fall rapidly as Japan industrialized, having the steepest rate of decline among major OECD nations. Conversely, the chart shows the US as

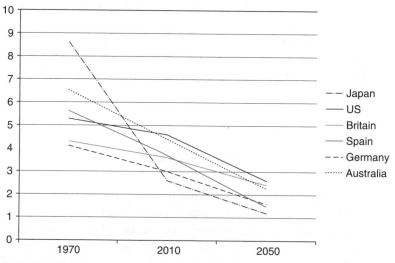

Figure 25: Past and projected support ratios across major OECD countries.
Source: OECD

having the slowest rate of decline in support ratios within the OECD countries, thanks to a higher fertility rate and a steady flow of immigrants.

Japan's support ratio today is 2.6, that is, there are 2.6 workers for every retiree. That ratio is expected to fall to just 1.2 by 2050, which is effectively saying that there will be almost one worker for every retiree. In other words, the contributions from one worker's income must fully support the state's pay-out to one retiree. This notion is inconceivable and yet is certainly in Japan's future, and so its government needs to seriously think through the implications for its society and economy. Although every Japanese citizen is aware of the continued greying trend, no bold steps have been taken to address this chronic condition, hoping instead that robots will be developed in time to save the day (we talk more about this in Chapter 8).

Once a global production power house admired and revered by the world, the land of the setting sun seems to be sitting quietly accepting its fate much in the same way that an elderly person does in a nursing home. It should serve as a reminder to all other nations just how important a young, steady population is to the economic prosperity of a country.

Japan's healthcare system is comprehensive and costs 8.5 per cent of GDP (versus around 16 per cent of GDP in the United States). However, its rapidly ageing society means healthcare costs are set to double in the next 20 years. Reform is badly needed, including the speeding up of time to market for new drugs. That said, Japan remains the world's second largest pharma market after the United States.

China's Grey Future

As the world's most populous nation, China is worth covering separately in more detail. According to the latest figures released by China in April 2011 following its census in 2010, the population of mainland China is 1.34 billion. The population growth rate is the really interesting number. Over the past 10 years, it has averaged a rate of 0.57 per cent, implying a replacement rate of 1.4. The one-child policy measures are obviously working, but at what economic and social cost in the long term?

The census data also reveals a perverse statistic on newborns: for every 100 baby girls born in 2010, there were 118 boys. The natural sex ratio at birth is around 105 boys for every 100 girls, so the noticeably higher number of boys births can only mean infanticide of some sort. Boys, for traditional reasons relating to manual labour and perpetuating the family name, are more desired by couples, so if a family is only allowed to have one child by law and the expectant parents discover that they are going to have a girl, some couples resort to finding a way to give away their baby girl, having a discreet abortion or, the worst option, killing their baby girl after she is born so that the authorities do not record the birth and the couple can have another chance at getting a boy during the next pregnancy.

The longer-term consequence of this perverse behaviour on a national scale is a distorted male-to-female ratio. Having a "surplus" of men in a country with a huge population like China creates significant social tensions. The proportionately smaller female population will potentially leave hundreds of millions of men without a partner. The social impact of this phenomenon can be felt today in some of the more remote parts of China where men resort to kidnapping women from other regions, or even from neighbouring countries, to take or to sell as wives because there simply are not any young women available for them in their local villages.

These disturbing behavioural patterns are set to worsen unless China relaxes its one-child policy so that ignorant couples do not have to resort to such extreme measures to have a boy in the first place.

The census report also reveals that the number of people in China over the age of 60 is around 180 million. There were only 41 million people over 60 years of age in 1950, and by 2050, the over-60s in China are expected to reach 440 million[1], which will be almost a third of the country's total population. This is an inconceivably large number – only slightly less than the entire population of the European Union today and well over the entire population of the United States and Canada combined. How will a country cope with almost

---

[1] United Nations Department of Economic and Social Affairs, Population Division.

half a billion people aged over 60? When faced with such a monumental challenge, what steps can China's policy makers take today to limit the social and economic impact of its new demographic landscape? How does a country even begin to ready itself for a rapidly ageing population? Surely its entire economy and society will be fundamentally different from what it is today; it will probably more closely resemble Japan today, although by then Japan will have an even older population.

Guangdong Province, China's richest, is located in the southeastern part of the country and borders Hong Kong. It is also China's most populous province but has been experiencing a fall in its population. Concerned by its future economic prospects and a rapidly ageing population, Guangdong officials have been lobbying Beijing to relax the one-child policy to allow couples to have two children. Unfortunately, even if Beijing were to grant this request, it would be little more than a token gesture and it would have no demographic impact on the country's ageing population problem.

The prospect of half a billion over 60s in China presents an enormous market opportunity for drug companies that are successful in developing cures for diseases that predominantly affect the elderly.

What Can Governments Do To Avoid Their Country Becoming a Nursing Home?

If a country is experiencing a shrinking working age population, it should ring alarm bells for political leaders. Clearly, in order for an economy to prosper and grow, it needs a sustainable labour force, or better still, a growing labour force (suitably skilled, of course). More workers lead to more economic output, more consumer spending and more tax dollars in the government coffers.

With an increasing proportion of the population becoming elderly, the strain on government finances in terms of pensions, elderly care and medical fees will simply be too much to bear. Decisive, visionary actions need to be taken, and the sooner the better.

If the working age population is declining, what can governments do to maintain or increase the potential labour pool? The following basic equation shows the components that make up a country's working age population:

(Children becoming adults + Existing working-age residents + Immigrants) – (Children not yet adults + Emigrants + Retirees + Disabled + Infirm + Deaths) = Potential labour pool

In order to maximize the working age population, governments can adopt sustainable policies that encourage:

- residents to have more children (longer-term impact);
- citizens working overseas to return to their home country to work;
- citizens of working age from other countries to immigrate and work;
- those reaching retirement age to keep working;
- those already in retirement to come out of retirement and re-enter the labour pool;
- citizens and residents to remain in that country to work.

Although there are other resources that are necessary for a sustainable society, such as economic, environmental and social, we are focusing on the human resource part as this poses the greatest long-term threat to our future welfare.

The number of children becoming adults is determined by the fertility rate of some 18 years prior. So a fall in a country's fertility rate today (all other factors remaining constant) would reduce the potential labour pool in 18 years' time. Equally, a sudden increase in a country's fertility rate would have no impact on the labour pool for about 18 years. This means that even if a country were to experience some sort of new baby boom starting today, it would do little to address the labour shortage in the future unless the higher fertility rate was sustained – an unlikely scenario as fertility rates move very slowly over time and tend to drift down as countries develop. Government should therefore not expect to find the solution to their future labour shortage here.

If developed countries facing declining populations are serious about increasing their fertility rates to a level above the replacement rate, radical steps are needed to make it less burdensome for would-be parents to have children so that they would be encouraged to. Such measures could include offering:

- Accessible and affordable daycare facilities, more flexible working hours and telecommuting. Families that can afford to have one parent stay at home to look after the children are fortunate, but in most cases either both parents need to or want to work or in the case of single-parent families, a parent is the only one who can work.
- Incentives for families to have children in the form of cash or tax breaks.
- Financial support to young families, particularly to subsidize or pay for daycare facilities.

In the long term, the size of a population translates to economic influence and power. Sustaining a nation's population should be an important priority. Even so, the returns on this investment are decades out, beyond the political life of prime ministers and presidents.

Governments could also embark on a campaign to attract some of its overseas citizens back to their homeland. There are two approaches that could be taken: one is a "quality of life" value proposition – the prime case being Australia where cities like Sydney, Melbourne and Perth are seeing a lot of migrants and returning citizens. Despite high taxes and the high cost of living, migrants are flocking down under to make it their home.

The other value proposition is a "financial" one, where there is an environment that encourages business owners and entrepreneurs to set up offices through favourable tax conditions and good infra-structure to support commerce and trade. Unfortunately in recent years, the US has become a good example of how to put off prospective talent – the country has a tax code that is some 75,000 pages long! Not only does it put off talent from moving to the US, it is also a drain on the country's existing talented people who are sucked into the tax industry. Think about all the smart people whose job it is to understand the tax code and to advise their clients on tax optimization and the best tax avoidance strategies. If a simple flat tax of say 22 per cent were introduced for corporations and individuals, with no loop-holes, calculating taxes would be simple and take only minutes to file. At the same time it would "release" so many talented people from a career in taxes to one that could be more productive in an economy, such as bioscience. A flat tax may actually generate more tax revenue for the government as corporations and individuals cut down on their elaborate tax minimization practices and simply pay the low flat tax. Multinational companies would increasingly likely recognize more revenue through their US operations and American citizens would probably repatriate more of their overseas funds and invest it in the US.

The outlook for most developed countries is grim, which should serve as an incentive for governments to do all they can to stimulate and nurture the biotech sector; not only will it create and secure jobs (and tax revenues) for the future, but it will also help reduce its healthcare liabilities through innovations in early detection, prevention and cures of many diseases that currently cost governments billions of dollars a year to treat.

Time is running out. The longer governments do nothing, the narrower their options become.

Chapter*Seven*

Bioscience's Disruptive Influences

The exciting revolution in bioscience and technology currently underway is set against a backdrop of a rapidly ageing global population (as we describe in Chapter 6); this is naturally going to cause some major disruptions to many aspects of our everyday lives.

Some of these seismic shifts will be unexpected; others will be easier to anticipate. These disruptions will affect governments, corporations and individuals alike, and it is incumbent on each to take steps today to minimize and soften any negative impacts of these effects. Some of the radical changes about to occur will be very positive to our health, wealth and quality of life, others less so.

One way to visualize the types of disruptions resulting from living in a super high-tech, ageing world is to use the following simple quadrant diagram that classifies a disruption into one of four types: expected, low impact; unexpected, low impact; expected, high impact; unexpected, high impact.

High impact, Expected	High impact, Unexpected
Low impact, Expected	Low impact, Unexpected

The main area we explore in this chapter is the high impact and expected disruptions. To the extent that it is possible, we also speculate on some of the unexpected disruptions, although by their very definition they are not easy to predict.

Given that we have no historical references to draw upon that come even close to either of these major trends, it is extremely difficult to predict accurately the way they will change our lives. Nevertheless, your brave authors will endeavour to do just that.

There will be vast changes across the public and private sectors and for individuals as a result of these disruptions. Some disruptions will be one-off shocks that will result in permanent change; others will have a large impact but will occur over many years. The impact of these shocks or disruptions will be felt differently depending on a country's demographics (see Chapter 6), technological sophistication, laws, government policies as well as public and private sector finances. It is probably safe to assume that governments will always do too little too late. For example, the global financial crisis was easy to predict several years before it happened and yet governments did nothing to try and avert it because they did not want to be seen as the ones taking away the punch bowl from the party. They only acted after contagion had set in.

Similarly, new media such as *Facebook* and *WikiLeaks* are global entities that in many ways are beyond the existing laws in any country, and governments do not know how to legislate something that is nebulous and pervasive. Governments will continue to find themselves on the back foot, not being able to keep up with the many breakthroughs we can expect to see in bioscience, especially ones related to synthetic biology, genetic engineering and genome sequencing.

We use a quote in Chapter 1 that is worth repeating here to set the tone for the scale of the change that is on its way: "In the next 50 years, 95 per cent of everything we know as a species will be discovered" (Dave Evans, Chief Futurist at *Cisco Corporation*).

Insurance and Healthcare

Without a doubt one of the industries that will be transformed in a world with personalized genome sequencing is insurance.

Once the cost of sequencing one human genome falls to a thousand dollars or less, medical and life insurance companies will want their policyholders to have their genome sequenced for analysis.

Naturally they will want to know more about the person they are insuring before setting the annual premium.

Insurers will no longer be satisfied with referring to actuarial tables for calculating their policyholders' annual premiums; they will want to adopt a "mass customization" approach to setting policy premiums that will allow them to better manage their risk and liabilities.

When submitting an application form for health or life insurance, we can expect insurance companies to request the applicant's DNA sample (such as cheek swab) along with a basic physical examination by a doctor. They will cross reference the findings from this exam with the results from the sequenced genome. They will be able to see which diseases the applicant is predisposed to and which ones the person has inherited. The insurer will then set the policy premium based on the likelihood of contracting the diseases that showed up in the sequenced genome analysis.

This may sound like an invasion of privacy but from the perspective of the insurance companies, they are simply acting responsibly as a business to manage their risk. If a for-profit, private company was considering underwriting the cost of a person's medical expenses and technology was available that allowed them to "see" the person's likelihood of contracting, say cancer, it is in that company's interest to assess the risk thoroughly before issuing medical cover. In fact, a shareholder or group of shareholders could sue the company if it transpired that it took big losses because it did not analyse the genomes of its policyholders. This will lead to insurance companies cherry picking which policies to underwrite, declining to provide insurance cover to people who look like they will be expensive in the future, leaving these people without access to medical or life insurance.

If that were to happen, it would be especially tough on people with inherited (congenital) diseases, because insurance companies would certainly not provide cover for them. There is also the controversial question of who should pay the medical bills for people who contract diseases as a result of living an unhealthy lifestyle, such as smokers or alcoholics.

In a capitalist, free-market situation, insurance premiums for the lucky ones born without congenital diseases, or born with less likelihood of contracting a disease in later life, will get much cheaper;

conversely, premiums charged to those born with congenital diseases, or who have a higher probability of contracting a disease in the future, will skyrocket.

Even today, there are many cases in the United States where families go bankrupt, having sold their homes and exhausted their life savings to pay the medical bills for a family member. In fact, prohibitively high medical expenses are already the number one cause of personal bankruptcy in the US.

From a broader societal perspective, this issue raises big-picture policy questions about if, when and how governments should intervene with the free market and whether it is a policy decision to ensure that all citizens have access to medical insurance at an affordable price.

Governments of countries such as the United Kingdom and the United States would like to offer their citizens affordable, quality healthcare but somebody has to pay the bill in the end. The question is how much of it should be "socialized", that is, people's insurance contributions are pooled together and used to pay the medical expenses for anyone in that pool who falls ill.

Opening this can of worms sooner rather than later will give policymakers time to establish a system that can address this point before we start seeing insurance companies insisting on genome screening prior to issuing cover. The fundamental question is whether it is a basic human entitlement to have a right to affordable, quality healthcare. We believe the answer is, of course, yes but it should not be unconditional. We all know providing healthcare costs money, lots of money, and someone has to foot the bill, be it in the form of higher taxes, through pooled risk insurance or even if it is directly paid for by the patient. Remember that all healthcare systems will already be feeling the extra load from the ageing population and longer life expectancy.

If citizens are to have a right to affordable, quality healthcare, it should come with a "but" clause on it. This clause should state that citizens should equally have an obligation to take reasonable care of themselves. Clearly if a person is born with a disease, affordable, quality healthcare should be granted to that person. But if that person is a smoker or a heavy drinker or obese, these are lifestyle choices that are directly linked to a multitude of diseases that will require expensive medical care in the future. Would it be fair that such people pay the same taxes or insurance premiums as those who do not smoke, are not obese, drink in moderation and exercise regularly? There is no question that every person has a right to smoke, drink and eat copious amounts of fatty food should they choose to, but who will pay the big medical bills that person no doubt accrues as a result of leading an unhealthy lifestyle? How much of a subsidy, if at all, should healthier citizens contribute?

The entire healthcare industry will be turned on its head because the current system cannot cope with the ageing population and the emerging genome sequencing technology. The trouble is that governments of just about all developed countries are heavily indebted as part of their efforts to support the banking system in the 2008 financial crisis, so any new policies that require additional financial outlays are very unlikely. Through inaction by governments, many people will fall through the cracks and end up having to self-insure; that is, use their savings to pay the full cost of treating their medical conditions if and when they arise.

There is another aspect of medical insurance we have not mentioned yet that relates to employers (companies). Many companies provide medical insurance to their employees; the extent of coverage varies enormously but it is a cost to the company and a benefit to the employee. What if there was a situation where a company employs two people with similar jobs and similar performance levels and pays them roughly the same salary. But, one person costs the company 30 per cent more in medical insurance premiums due to a genetically customized policy. Should the company give the more expensive person a pay cut or should it grant a pay rise to the employee with the lower insurance premium?

Perhaps we will enter an era where we have to submit our DNA with our job applications, similar to the 1997 science-fiction film *Gattaca*, where employers constantly sample their employees' DNA to ensure they have no genetic defects.

The behaviour of employers and insurers in the future will be unpredictable and the longer governments fail to implement new policies on genome sequencing and its uses, the more harm it is likely to do.

In the long-term future, perhaps in 25 years' time, this entire issue will vanish because we will have discovered cures to virtually all diseases that are currently expensive and often terminal. Beyond

25 years, technology will enable parents to screen for and "turn off" all diseases in the genome of their child before birth.

Real Estate

Another area in which we can expect to experience disruptive change is the real estate sector. Although for many families the ideal home is a house with a garden in a quiet suburb, this no longer has the same appeal to people as they grow older. There will be a shift towards convenience and accessibility, and so properties requiring too much upkeep will become less popular, as will those that are too far from a major town or city. Retirees will increasingly move away from colder climates to those that have warmer, more pleasant weather. These migrations already happen today on a smaller scale, such as retirees from Canada or the American Mid-West moving to warmer states such as Florida and the Carolinas. In Europe there are many Scandinavians, Germans and Britons who retire in Mediterranean countries such as Spain and Portugal. This will result in many colder climate cities seeing a decline in their populations, negatively impacting real-estate prices there.

Accommodation design will start to change to meet the tastes of an older society. Stairs are a danger to the elderly, so we are likely to see more single-storey houses, called bungalows in the UK and ranch-style houses in the US. Apartments will become more popular; they have lifts and no garden to look after. They are typically in more urban locations offering the convenience of town living without having to drive around. Suburban living will probably decline as the age of an average household increases and urban living will probably increase as older people move to enjoy the many amenities offered by city living, such as parks, museums, theatres, restaurants, courses in languages, cooking and so on.

Assisted living communities will pop up everywhere (there are already over 36,000 of them in the US alone). Although they have been around for many years, especially in older-aged states such as Florida, such communities will become more sophisticated and will offer complete lifestyle living. These places will be nothing like the nursing homes we know and hate today; they will be designed to be fun places to live for those in their senior years.

Politics

As people get older, their needs and expectations change. In a society with a growing and rapidly ageing population, the influence of the elderly will steadily increase because they are the ones who tend to be more vocal and have higher voter turnout. A political rift will develop between the wishes of the young versus those of the old because the elderly have a shorter time horizon than the young and hence their priorities will be different. A classic example is the retirement age; clearly this should be raised to at least 70 years for both men and women within the next few years, and yet today's influential elderly will not hear of it. They all accept that retirement ages need to go up, they just do not want it done until their early retirement has been secured. Increasing the retirement age to 70 years will save governments billions in future liabilities and yet they choose not to fight that battle.

Another example is healthcare. The elderly are bigger users of doctors and hospitals and so they vote against anything that they see as reducing the quality or increasing the cost of care they receive today.

The elderly are also more risk averse and, as a result of their increasing influence in politics across all democracies, elected officials are less likely to be visionaries or leaders who are prepared to undergo major structural reforms for the long-term good of a nation. We will probably end up in a stale political environment with ineffective politicians, just like we see in Japan today (a nation with the oldest population) – a country whose politicians have mastered the art of doing nothing in perpetuity.

Geopolitics

On a geopolitical level, the changing demographics will dilute the influence of the developed world and increase the influence of the emerging countries. By 2050, India is expected to surpass China as the world's most populous nation. In fact, the United States will be the only currently developed nation in the top 10 most populous countries by then, so clearly the West's influence over the world will decline significantly over the coming decades.

With India's young and vast population, compared to China's falling and old one, we will probably see India emerge from China's shadow on the geopolitical stage as we approach the middle of the century. We hope by then that India has upgraded its dilapidated infrastructure and enhanced the bureaucratic system of government, or the country will miss out on the opportunity to take centre stage, both economically and politically.

Despite these changes, the United States will probably remain the most influential of the developed nations even 30 years out, but its overall influence of the world as a whole will diminish to accommodate the large emerging economies.

The political hotspots 10 to 15 years from now will be in the developing countries that have a high proportion of young people combined with high rate of unemployment – countries such as Pakistan, Nigeria and those in the Middle East region all meet these criteria. There will literally be hundreds of millions of young people without employment – a sure recipe for trouble. What can these countries do to avert an unstable future and what can developed countries do to help? An incredible challenge lies ahead.

Retail Goods and Services

The changing demographic landscape will greatly impact buying behaviour in two ways: first, older people buy different kinds of "stuff" to the younger crowd. Tastes differ in everything, from clothes to music, food, soap, perfume – even preferences for cars will be different. Second, we anticipate that the world's population growth will slow down, topping out in the next 15 years or so. As a result, companies relying on growing their business by selling more things to more people will have to re-think their business models. Granted there are regions of the world, particularly in Asia and Africa, that still have untapped markets, but by the time the population tops out, these regions are likely to be saturated too.

Retailers will need to anticipate these changes in buying patterns and adjust their product lines accordingly; and we do not mean introducing different colours and styles of adult nappies (diapers), although perhaps this is something that we will see on the supermarket shelves anyway in the not-too-distant future.

Also, the older generation is more money conscious and spends less because the elderly tend to be net spenders rather than savers (with no or a limited income they tap into their savings so that more money goes out of their bank account every month than comes in). That said, they do spend their money, and retailers and service providers need to adjust their offerings to capitalize on this. New sectors will emerge that simply do not exist today to specialize in selling to the elderly.

Older people tend to look after themselves a little better than the younger generations; if not, they probably would not make it to old age in the first place. As a result, food retailers will have to gain a deeper understanding of what drives the elderly's purchasing behaviour. In some cases, it may not even be about the food but the packaging or the proximity of items to the checkout counters. For example, some elderly people may avoid buying food in jars because they find it too difficult to open them, even though they may actually like the food inside the jar. There will be a growth industry in this type of *ergonomics* for the ageing population, which will drive everything from the design of shopping centres to the development of new innovations in easy-grip everyday things, such as toothbrushes.

Another area that will see major change is the tourist industry. The elderly love convenience and a sense of excitement; cruises are already very popular and demand for them will steadily increase as the world's population ages. Other types of holidays for the elderly will emerge too, also in lower price brackets because not all the new elderly cohorts will be lucky enough to be able to afford cruises.

The Food Industry

In recent years we have experienced sharp rises in food prices as a result of increasing demand from emerging countries, such as China, and limited supply. Despite the world's population expected to climb steadily to 9 billion in the coming decades, we expect food prices to fall dramatically. This sounds contrarian but our conclusion is based on what is happening in the field of genetic engineering. Although for millennia humans have altered the genes of plants and animals through selective breeding, it is only since the 1990s that we started doing it through engineering the DNA of organisms.

Genetically Modified (GM) foods have provided one of the answers to the world's food shortages. Already, many plants have been genetically modified to acquire superior properties, such as resistance to herbicides (weedkiller) or increased crop yields. Everything from soybeans to corn to rice is widely grown in its GM form. Animals such as Belgian Blue cattle exist today as a result of an engineered genetic mutation that allows them to grow 40 per cent more muscle than a normal cow would have. We can expect to see an increase in the availability of GM crops, fruit, vegetables and animals for human consumption in the coming years. Scientists have already been successful in producing GM versions of many plant and animal life. For example, GM salmon grows faster and bigger than their regular equivalents.

There has been much negative press regarding GM foods and FDA approval (in the US) and their equivalents in other countries, and this is usually the biggest hurdle for getting GM foods on sale to the general public. Humans are by their very nature wary of any new technology initially, but eventually the benefits become evident and outweigh the concerns.

In practical terms, if a country such as China finds itself in a position where there is a nationwide food shortage and signs of social unrest, will the Beijing government really turn down the GM option if it can provide a solution? Equally, if a person is desperately hungry and is offered the opportunity to eat GM meat, rice and vegetables, would that hungry person really object?

The Investment Industry

Although we expect most people to be working well beyond today's retirement age in the coming years, the world's human population will still be getting steadily older, both in terms of absolute numbers and as a proportion of the population. This will have a disruptive effect on the financial sector as retirees are much more conservative in their investment style, preferring to invest in very low-risk, yield-generating products, such as bonds and interest-bearing accounts, instead of the stock market.

As more money goes out of their bank account than comes in every month, retirees tend to be more consumers than savers, which could mean that retirement capital invested in the financial sector will steadily decline as retirees withdraw their money to spend it.

Even pension money that remains invested is likely to be re-allocated into less risky assets, because people approaching retirement no longer have the luxury of time to ride out any stock market crashes or big economic downswings. This change will reduce demand in equities, which means they will probably trade at lower multiples of earnings than their historical averages. The baby boomers have historically been big fans of equities (when they were in their 40s and 50s), but as they start to retire, they will be reducing their exposure to this asset class in favour of lower volatility, income-yielding asset classes such as simple interest-bearing savings accounts or bonds issued by governments or multinational blue chip corporations. The younger generations entering these age brackets will not be able to replace this investment void because there will be far fewer of them.

As an aside, we do not expect government bonds issued by countries such as the US and the UK to give a yield below inflation for much longer; this situation is unsustainable and interest rates will realign with inflation in the medium term, being three to five years.

Other investment classes that will suffer are venture capital and private equity, which are both higher risk and volatile investment classes that retirees will shy away from or allocate a very small percentage of their portfolio to. Venture capitalists invest in early-stage, fast-growing companies looking for growth capital and a reduction in venture capital funding would most likely mean many great companies not getting off the ground or not reaching their full potential. Companies ready to list on a stock exchange to raise additional capital may also find it hard to generate sufficient investor interest in their stock.

The Law

In this era of accelerating technological advances, the legal system throughout the world will struggle to cope with an increasing number of cases that have no precedents. Earlier in this chapter we mention *Facebook* and *WikiLeaks* as being new technology-based enterprises that are outpacing today's laws and law enforcement. To give some simple and specific examples of what we mean, consider the so-called "Jasmine Revolution" in the Middle East where citizens in countries from Morocco to Bahrain rose up against their long-standing oppressive regimes thanks largely to social network sites like *Facebook* that allowed its members to feel inspired, empowered, united and coordinated in their peaceful uprisings. The rulers of these nations felt powerless to stop their people from protesting, especially when every person in possession of a mobile phone is a potential photographer, able to forward video and still images to news agencies around the world in an instant.

There are also occasions when new technology can result in harmful acts, such as when highly confidential and sensitive documents belonging to the American government were made public through *WikiLeaks*. In this case the government was not able to do anything to prevent their release.

In the world of bioscience, we shall face far more complex matters than these as the subject matter is literally the very fabric of our existence. Take the controversial topic of embryonic stem cell research; an extremely sensitive topic with polarizing views. Some people adopt a fundamentally moral stance that it is wrong to experiment on a potential human being, whereas others are strongly in favour of it because of the amazing advances in medicine that humankind will be able to achieve by undertaking this research. What people think about these issues matters because it drives legislation, which in turn drives the behaviour of the bioscience industry. So when a government decided to ban federal funding for embryonic stem cell research, which is what the United States did under George W. Bush, it opened doors for other nations to catch up and potentially overtake. Thankfully, the ban was lifted in 2009 shortly after President Obama took office.

That is why the law will be one of the main influencers in determining which areas of bioscience are likely to prosper in a particular country.

Now think of the multitude of legal implications that we will have in a few years' time once a human genome can be sequenced for a few hundred dollars and in less than an hour. It will be a "retail" product accessible to all. Yet a human's genome is an incredibly sensitive piece of information. At the same time, there will be many "tools" readily available that will be able to interpret the genetic material from a sequenced genome. When that happens, who will have the right to access a person's genome? How can you stop a person from taking a DNA sample from another person and having it sequenced? A single strand of hair or some saliva would not be difficult to acquire for sequencing purposes. How could you stop someone using something like *WikiLeaks* to post people's sequenced genomes online without their knowledge or consent? Who would want to do such a thing? Usually the same people who bear grudges against one another, such as business adversaries or political rivals, and it could be used as part of a smear campaign to discredit an individual.

Companies may emerge like today's credit checking agencies but for sequenced human genomes, so that a prospective employer or an insurance company can get a detailed health check on an individual as part of the background check. Would that be right or fair? We are not passing judgement, only giving a scenario of what could happen in a world where everyone had their genome sequenced.

Bioscience law will become a major area of practice in its own right. New laws will be introduced and existing laws will be amended to accommodate this new field. What these laws end up being will have an enormous impact on our future, both in terms of the prosperity of a country and in the way all genetic information, especially human, is acquired, stored and distributed and under which circumstances it can be modified.

Shortage of Young People in Developed Nations

Fertility rates that are below the replacement rate (as discussed in Chapter 6) will be the norm for the foreseeable future in developed nations, with the exception of the US where the population will remain more or less flat. How can a country expect to maintain economic growth when its working population is steadily falling? There may be some productivity gains made through the use of new technologies but it will not be enough to compensate for the future shortage of young people entering the labour pool. Never mind the tax revenue implications for governments and pension support ratios, there will be companies out there desperately looking for young workers and there will not be enough of them.

Companies will resort to setting up operations in other countries where there is availability of young workers. Such firms may even consider establishing schools in developing countries with high fertility rates and educating children from an early age all the way to adulthood whereupon they will be made employees. This already happens on a smaller scale in countries such as India, where big multinationals build campuses next to their operations to provide education and training for their staff.

With so many elderly people in the world, they will need a great deal of looking after. But with fertility rates falling in just about all nations, there will not be enough care workers. To address this shortage, we are likely to see the introduction of semi-automated homes for the elderly, drawing on the latest in robotics to take care of much of the everyday jobs associated with looking after older people. Even the elderly who still live at home will be able to acquire a home assistant robot (see Chapter 8 for more details).

Governments of developed nations will find it difficult to recruit a sufficient number of service personnel, which will put the developing countries at a significant advantage. On a headcount basis, the armed forces of China and India will become the most significant in the world. In the old world of the US, Europe and Japan, politicians will not so willingly deploy large numbers of soldiers into combat situations because they would be considered a precious, limited resource. Instead, there will be an increase in the use of drones, droids and other non-human combat machines, only letting the human troops in harm's way after the situation risk has been contained. Even then soldiers are likely to be equipped with technology (such as some kind of robotic suit) that better protects them, effectively rendering them bullet-proof and providing bionic strength.

Chapter*Eight*

Robotics and Nanotechnology

Robotics

Many people's perception of robots is influenced by what they see on television and in films, and so a number of different mental images arise when seeing or hearing the words "robot" or "robotics". Some people associate the word with *Lost in Space* or *Star Wars*, whereas others have a more functional interpretation, such as a robotic arm working at a car assembly plant.

For our purposes, we are more interested in the types of robots that will directly enhance human lives in the short to medium term. They could be robots that assist or perform surgery, robots that can serve as nurses, robots that can help with the housework or simply robots that make great companions or pets. Believe it or not, these robots all exist today at various levels of sophistication.

Love them or hate them, robots are here to stay. As we explain in Chapter 6, there will be too many old people in the world and not enough younger ones to look after them. Robotics is the only practical solution to address this massive labour shortage that countries such as Japan are already experiencing. This trend will only get progressively more pronounced as the world's population continues to age into the foreseeable future.

There have been some interesting applications of robotics over the past couple of decades, particularly in automobile manufacturing, yet it is fair to say that the field is very much in its infancy. We believe that as a result of an increase in computer processing power, the next decade will yield unprecedented advances in robotics across a multitude of applications. This will be thanks to Moore's Law on the exponential relationship of processing power over time: a doubling of processing power at least every 2 years.

To give you an idea of just how significant that is, the processing power we have today is more than a million times greater than it was just 40 years ago, and because it continues to increase exponentially, we are less than 10 years away from having computers with the processing power greater than that of a human brain. To give you a more tangible reference – the mobile phone you use today has more processing power than the whole of NASA during the Apollo missions to the moon.

In this chapter, we focus on the following applications of robotics:

- surgical procedures/surgical assistance;
- medical monitor/nurse;
- housemaid/domestic assistance;
- companion/pet.

We discuss each of these areas in more detail, explaining the near- and medium-term impact on our lives as well as revealing some opportunities from investing in some of the current companies that lead their fields. We also look briefly at nanotechnology, in which matter can be altered at the atomic level.

Surgical Procedures/Surgical Assistance

The introduction of robotics in the field of surgery dates back to the mid-1980s, although the application then was very limited, such as using a robotic arm to hold a needle that was inserted into a specific part of the brain for a biopsy. Not until the late 1990s were robotics being used in major procedures, such as heart bypass surgery. A system known as the *da Vinci Surgical System* was developed. This system comprises four robotic arms and a console from which the surgeon can make precise micro-movements of the surgical tools attached to the robotic arms. The console allows the surgeon to see with a magnification 10 times greater than the human eye. This increased precision means that a procedure can be less invasive than would be possible using a surgeon's hands. As well as the obvious benefit of allowing surgeons to perform procedures that would otherwise be very tricky with their own hands, the post-op recovery time is greatly reduced due to the reduced trauma to the body and patients experience less post-operative pain.

The da Vinci Surgical System is manufactured by a California-based company called *Intuitive Surgical Inc.* (NASDAQ: ISRG). The company's market capitalization is around US$20 billion. Although the company's growth prospects remain solid and there are no current market rivals, it is less likely that the company's share price will undergo another 50-fold increase that it has undergone since 2002. Today, the da Vinci system is installed in hundreds of places worldwide and is gaining popularity with surgeons and patients alike. In the future, Intuitive Surgical may develop an upgraded, smarter system that can perform procedures automatically; this would make the company an even more attractive investment.

We believe that at some point within the next decade we will have surgeries performed by "smart" da Vinci Surgical Systems or their equivalents. In the same way that the corrective eye surgery system *Lasik* can accurately remodel the cornea with a computerized laser to give the patient perfect, or near perfect vision, we can expect the da Vinci and other surgical systems that currently provide a support role to surgeons to take on the surgeon's role completely, leaving the human surgeon with a supervisory role.

If we make a comparison with the commercial aviation industry today, the autopilot that is installed in many commercial aircraft has the ability to take off, climb, cruise to its destination at the optimal speed/course/altitude for minimum fuel burn, avoiding bad weather systems along the way, descend and land safely without a human pilot needing to do anything. Yet we still have pilots in the cockpit because if things go wrong, computers are not yet sophisticated enough to assess situations and react with the best course of action. That will change. Similarly in operating theatres, we will see surgeons become less hands-on as they allow robots to step in to perform procedures. These procedures will be faster, more consistent, more accurate and cheaper. Patients will still benefit from short recovery time due to the minimally invasive incisions made by the robots. The main barrier to making that a reality today is processing power – we need to give robots sufficient artificial intelligence to perform procedures without input from human intelligence, and that will happen by 2020 when the processing power of computers will reach that of the human brain.

Mako Surgical Corporation (NASDAQ: MAKO) is a US orthopaedic medical device company with which we have met and like. Mako markets its *RIO System* and proprietary *RESTORIS* family of knee implants as a minimally invasive procedure called *MAKOplasty*. The procedure is performed through a 10- to 15-centimetre (4- to 6-inch) incision over the knee. Intelligent robotic arm technology and three-dimensional visualization of the knee guides the surgeon in controlled resurfacing of the pre-defined knee disease, saving as much of the patient's healthy bone and surrounding tissue as possible. Patients can walk very soon after surgery, and drive a car within two weeks. As of the middle of 2011, over 8,500 procedures had been performed with Mako systems.

Another company called *Stryker Corporation* (NYSE: SYK), also with a market value of around US$20 billion, has a competing solution to Mako's. Stryker is a well-established, more diversified medical technology company, manufacturing everything from the joint implants themselves to three-dimensional imaging systems that provide surgeons with precise visualization of the area to be operated on. The company is already profitable and pays a regular, albeit small, dividend.

Minimizing the invasiveness of surgery reduces the time for patients to heal, minimizes scarring and can reduce infections, including the dreaded hospital acquired *superbugs*. Robots are not yet at the point where they can take over from surgeons, but in these particular surgeries they considerably reduce the risk of failure, improve precision and reduce strain for the surgeon. They use CT scans to pre-position the surgical instruments and to guide the procedures.

Hansen Medical (NASDAQ: HNSN), another company that we like and have met, is currently the global leader in flexible robotics, and is creating a new generation of advanced medical robotics for heart surgery. The *Sensei Robotic Catheter System* and *Artisan Control Catheter* are currently its principal products; the robotic system overcomes limitations of manual techniques in surgery by facilitating accurate positioning and stable control of catheter and catheter-based technologies during *electrophysiology (EP)* procedures.

The future of surgery will be partially robotic and this should, over time, have the effect of slowly reducing hospitalization times, reducing infections and, possibly, reducing costs.

Although we do not cover biomedical devices to any great extent in this book, it is clearly an area of major interest. Advances in heart-related devices, surgical techniques and monitoring equipment, including the fast expanding wireless, remote monitoring industry *(telemedicine)*, are possible areas of interest to investors that we may cover in the future in our newsletters. It should be noted, however, that biomedical devices are now to a certain extent blending in with the pharma industry, for instance, a new generation of stents from Johnson & Johnson and *Medtronic* are so-called *drug eluting* because they release drugs directly from the implanted stents.

Also in this space is the less developed field of *nano-robots (nanobots)* that are set to revolutionize therapeutics. These are tiny, microscopic robots that are being developed for injection* into the bloodstream. Once deployed these nanobots will be pre-programmed with a specific mission, which may be to seek and destroy cancer cells or certain viruses, or to locate and remove plaque build-up in artery walls. Their potential application is truly wondrous. We are probably 5 to 10 years away from making these smart nanobots a reality, but we can expect to see some basic functioning nanobots within just a few years.

To give you an idea of just how small these nanobots are, consider the following: a micrometre (also known as a micron) is a unit of length that is one millionth of a metre; a human hair is approximately 100 microns in diameter and a red blood cell is 8 microns in diameter; basic nanobots could have a diameter as small as 0.1 microns. Scientists are currently experimenting with attaching the nanobots to harmless bacteria so that they can be propelled throughout the human body, using glucose in the bloodstream as an energy source to keep them active.

Medical Monitor/Nurse

We explain at length the challenges of an ageing population in Chapter 6 and how the elderly will make up an ever increasing percentage of that population. Consequently, there will be a smaller percentage of the population who are of working age. This non-cyclical trend presents an unprecedented challenge and we must find an alternative to human elderly care workers (who will be in short supply). The answer lies in robotics – human care workers will be a luxury available only to a lucky few. The first time one reads such a futuristic sounding statement, it is natural to be sceptical. But the amount of work done, progress made and money invested in this field is far greater than you may imagine.

In this section, we share with you some of the amazing technologies that we have seen during our research, which we hope will convince you that this is the most likely scenario for us in the near future. Believe it or not, there are already several types of robots in people's homes today. Granted they are not yet capable of providing total care for an elderly person, but from what we have seen so far, it is only a matter of a few years.

Japan is already a world leader in robotics, particularly when it comes to car assembly. It is also has the oldest and most rapidly ageing population, so scientists and policymakers alike are acutely aware of the chronic shortage of care workers. They have therefore invested billions of yen into robotic research and prototypes to prepare them for the future.

Honda, the well-known Japanese car maker, has developed *Asimo*, the world's most advanced humanoid robot (see Figure 26). In 1986, Honda embarked on arguably its most ambitious project: to create a bipedal robot that can be helpful in the home in domestic matters and in providing elderly care. Honda has made endless improvements and upgrades to Asimo since the early prototypes and it has also managed to shrink it down to a height of only 130 centimetres (4 feet 3 inches) so that it does not have an overbearing presence and can comfortably fit into people's homes without getting in the way (Japanese people typically live in much smaller homes than people in other developed nations).

The 2011 version of Asimo can walk, talk, run, go up and down stairs, serve drinks/medication and respond to simple voice instructions. Asimo's camera technology can move around solid objects and even recognize people's faces, yet Asimo itself remains faceless. This is deliberate and there are psychological reasons behind it; when a robot becomes too human-like, people find it creepy, and

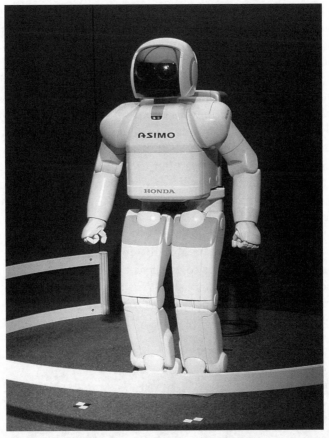

Figure 26: The world's most advanced robot Asimo, developed by Honda.
Source: Gnsin at Expo 2005 for Wikimedia Commons

so its designers have kept Asimo as a humanoid, bipedal robot but not one that could ever be mistaken for a human.

Each year, Asimo becomes more sophisticated and cheaper and we could well see it appearing in people's homes within five years. Once it can retail for about the same price as a simple family car, it will start to become as useful and as essential to households as a car, television or microwave is today.

Pseudo-robotic assistance is available today for those with limited mobility. A "spin-off" product from Honda's Asimo project is the *Stride Management Assist Device*. This light contraption is worn around the hips and thighs and is equipped with a battery pack and small motor. Once strapped in, it provides the wearer with mechanical support to reduce stress on muscles and joints when walking, something that is useful to those who have weak leg muscles, such as the elderly. These devices are being used today to study the impact of their regular use. They offer a wonderful alternative to canes, crutches and Zimmer frames and will probably be used by those who have had leg injuries or leg surgery. They also allow the elderly to get up and move about, something that is essential to staying healthy in later life. Within a few years, we could see a number of elderly people swap out their canes for this device.

In time this technology will evolve to provide mobility to paraplegics and quadriplegics through thought-activated movements. Experiments around the world today have already developed some basic thought controlled movements of limbs. Further out, perhaps within a decade, we will be able to repair damaged spinal cords, which would be a superior solution to Honda's device.

Another popular robot is called *Nao* and has been created by a French privately held company called *Aldebaran Robotics* (see Figure 27). Nao is being increasingly used by those studying and teaching

Figure 27: Nao, the popular robot produced by Aldebaran Robotics.
Source: Jiuguang Wang for Wikimedia Commons

robotics because it is affordable (basic version starts at 1,000 euros), programmable and portable, having a height of 58 centimetres (around 23 inches) and a weight of around 4 kilograms (just under 10 pounds).

Aldebaran Robotics have cleverly embarked on an "open source" approach to programming Nao, encouraging institutions and individuals in the field of robotics to join their developer programme, with a joint set of goals such as AI, social and human/robot interaction, and vision and audio recognition.

In some ways Aldebaran Robotics has taken the same approach as the people behind the *Linux* computer operating system, encouraging programmers and developers around the world to contribute towards the software's continual improvement and enhancement. If Aldebaran's strategy pays off, it could end up being the robot of choice or the robot standard for many applications, because it will have the most sophisticated capabilities and at the same time its price tag has scope for further reduction as sales volumes pick up.

Already researchers have been successful in programming Nao to listen to verbal instructions, read basic words, walk over to its patient and offer the right medication at the right time of day. It can also be programmed to remind you where you put your keys, or what your upcoming meetings/social engagements are for the day. In the same way that the mass computer market developed, it was all about the software and the processing power, and even though robots are not yet in most people's homes, their level of capability compared to just a few years ago is orders of magnitude greater.

Although applications for elderly care are still in the experimental stages, we are only a few years away from being able to buy one for the home. There will be a number of customizable features, such as voice, accent and nature; they will even be available in different shapes and colours. More sophisticated features will emerge, particularly ones related to health monitoring and diagnosis of symptoms and diseases. Robots will be able constantly to monitor their patients' vital signs and flag any abnormalities, either to the patient directly or to a designated 24-hour care centre or doctor. In extreme cases they would be able to call for an ambulance directly.

Elderly care robots will start to appear in homes within five years, probably starting in Japan, which needs it the most. Japan will be pioneering this robotics field and the government is fully backing the acceleration of research and development and the commercial application of household robots, because it may become a new global industry that Japan can dominate in the years to come. Already, Japanese companies make around 7 per cent of the world's industrial robots. Japanese government figures estimate the market to be worth around 6.2 trillion yen (approximately US$75 billion) a year by 2025, two-thirds of which will come from sales relating to elderly care/nursing robots.

Housemaid/Domestic Assistance

Domestic help and nursing care are not so much a luxury as a necessity for many elderly people. It is likely that the nursing/ elderly care robots and the domestic helper robots will converge into one, but that may not happen for 10 or so years. There was a similar situation in the mobile phone industry at the turn of the 21st century when phone manufacturers wanted to incorporate the functionality of a *Personal Digital Assistant (PDA)* into their hand-sets, and PDA manufacturers wanted to add the functionality of a phone to their products (remember the days of the Palm Pilots?).

Although they will start off being for the elderly, robots will become a must-have item by all households, eventually being as indispensable as an automatic dishwasher or a microwave oven in the home.

One of today's leading robot manufacturers is a company called *iRobot Corporation* (NASDAQ: IRBT). The company was founded by Massachusetts Institute of Technology (MIT) students in 1990 and is valued at around US$700 million dollars.

iRobot produces a range of military and domestic robots. Their military robots perform a number of dangerous missions, such as search, reconnaissance and bomb disposal. They even have under-water robots. The public sector, including the military, has acquired over 3,500 of its military robots.

iRobot has also sold over 5 million of its domestic robots. These include a robot to vacuum your home (the *Roomba*), a robot to clean your pool (the *Verro*), a robot to clean your shop floor or workshop (the *Dirt Dog*) and a robot to clean your gutters (the *Looj*). Some of these models sell for under US$100, so they are well within reach for many households, and in the long term it is cheaper than employing someone to perform these cleaning chores manually.

Companion/Pet

There is another area of robotics that is fast emerging – robot pets. As strange as this may sound at first, it is an area of robotics that can help the elderly in a number of ways. First, companionship is a basic human need and as we get older, we are more likely to find ourselves alone and lonely. Living pets are a great companion for many people at all stages of life, but as we get older, we may not be able to look after them as much as we used to, hence the market for robotic pets. Second, robotic pets can also have built-in monitoring features to make sure that their owner is taking his or her medication and is in good physical condition. At the first sign of trouble, they can be programmed to phone for help, something that a real pet cannot do (unless you have a clever collie dog called Lassie).

Although robotic pets are not the real thing, they do look, sound and feel real, and they have the added advantage of not peeing or pooping on your carpet, and so no need to clean up their mess. They also do not eat and so you do not need to feed them. Neither will they knock over your favourite vase or scratch your furniture. It may sound like a pointless concept, but studies have shown that they do make excellent companions for elderly people living alone and reduce stress and anxiety levels in dementia and Alzheimer's patients.

Robotic pets could not only serve as companions, but also help look after their owner. Researchers at *MIT*'s *AgeLab* are hoping that people can form emotional bonds with robotic pets, which would make their owners more likely to obey their instructions and reminders than if they simply prompted their owners to do certain things, such as take their medicine, or call their daughter.

A couple of examples of robotic pets currently on the market today are pictured in Figure 28. The dinosaur in (a) is called the

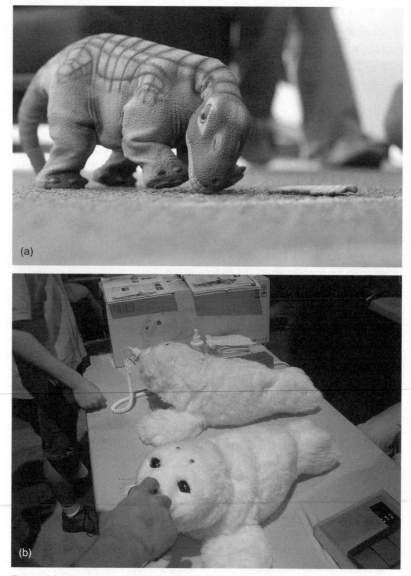

Figure 28: Examples of robotic pets; (a) the Pleo and (b) and the Paro.
Sources: Travis Isaacs (a) and Aaron Biggs (b) for Wikimedia Commons

Pleo, a pet based on a *camarasaurus*, and the one in (b) is called a *Paro*, based on a harp seal pup. Both are designed to be very cute and curious, just like kittens and puppies. They are loaded with sensors that detect and respond to touch, light, sound and pressure.

Makers of these robotic pets carefully chose to make them in the form of animals of which people have no first-hand knowledge and so are not able to make direct comparisons with the real thing, be it consciously or subconsciously.

The Pleo has been designed to have emotions, such as happiness, sadness and surprise. It is playful and lively and big on the cute factor. It retails for around US$400 at the time of our research, making it an affordable pet and comparable in price to buying a live one.

The Paro is apparently the world's most therapeutic robot and it is being used to treat patients with Alzheimer's and mental illness. It is a handmade Japanese robot that is designed to respond to its own name. Paro is programmed to remember behaviour that is rewarded and punished, so that if you hit it, it will not repeat what it was doing before you hit and conversely it will do more of the things that result in you stroking it. In clinical and domestic trials, it has been shown to improve the quality of people's lives. The Paro is still too expensive for most people (around US$5,000 at the time of writing), but the price will no doubt come down as more are sold.

In time, these robotic pets will take on the additional roles of nurse, caregiver and domestic helper. They will help their owners do a variety of things such as:

- dispense medication and ensure it is taken in the right quantity at the right times;
- monitor the owner's vital signs;
- provide assistance in walking or getting in and out of the bath;
- remind owners of their plans and activities for the day;
- make sure that the home is locked and secured prior to going to bed or going out.

Most excitingly of all, owners will be able to chat with their robotic pet/assistant and establish an emotional bond and relationship.

Once again, the likely convergence of the functionality of robots in the home will mean that one type of robot will perform all the domestic help and care needs. It is too early to try and make a guess as to which type of robot will prevail in the home.

Robot ethics

As robots become more sophisticated and autonomous in our society, there will come a time when we will need to hard wire some ground rules or laws that govern them in how they are allowed to behave – their moral code. Isaac Asimov, the American science-fiction author and biochemistry professor set out three laws of robotics:

- Law 1: A robot may not injure a human being or, through inaction, allow a human being to come to harm.
- Law 2: A robot must obey any orders given to it by human beings, except where such orders would conflict with Law 1.
- Law 3: A robot must protect its own existence as long as such protection does not conflict with Laws 1 or 2.

He later added another one that precedes the other three: a robot may not harm humanity or, by inaction, allow humanity to come to harm.

It may sound like it is too soon to start thinking about putting such rules in place for robots, but technology continues to progress at an exponential rate and within the next decade or two, these kinds of debates will come to the fore among society and lawmakers alike.

Nanotechnology

The role of the infinitely small is infinitely large.

– Louis Pasteur

The "nano" part of the word nanotechnology comes from the International System of Units (SI) for one billionth; so, for example, a nanometre is one billionth of a metre (1×10^{-9} m). *Nanotechnology* (or nanotech) is the science of manipulating matter at an atomic level.

Although this field of science is relatively new, there are existing commercial applications of nanotech, such as chemical coatings to improve the properties of a surface or material. These could be coatings that render a material resistant to rust, stains, water or even scratches. Nanotech is also used in airbags, where tiny accelerometers are able to detect a car's sudden braking. This sudden motion triggers a small electrical charge that is enough to set off the explosion to inflate the airbag in a fraction of a second.

Yet even though the word nanotechnology has been in use for some time now, we have yet to tap into anywhere near the full potential of this new industry. For one thing, it is not easy to assemble something atom by atom and we may be a couple of decades away from being able to do so.

Once we succeed, however, the implications are mind-blowing. Imagine being able to re-arrange atoms to make anything we need. Just the slightest modification in how atoms are arranged makes a huge difference to a material and its properties. For example, if you take coal, which mainly comprises carbon atoms, and re-arrange them, you can turn it into graphite, soot and even diamonds (different structures of the same element are called *allotropes*). If you take sand, you would be able to make silicone from it. Being able to make materials and even objects precisely from the atomic level up would mean total efficiency in the use of materials and so there would no longer be any pollution as a by-product of the manufacturing process.

Another allotrope of carbon is in the form of *nanotubes*. *Carbon nanotubes*, as the name suggests, have a cylindrical structure that results in the carbon being incredibly light and strong (see Figure 29). In fact, it becomes the strongest and stiffest material known to humans so far in terms of tensile strength. In tests it has proven to be over 100 times stronger than steel and 30 times stronger than *Kevlar*. Also, carbon nanotubes conduct heat and electricity very well, which means there are potentially vast electronic applications for them.

In the field of *nano medicine*, researchers are competing to develop an effective drug delivery system using *nanotube technology*. Fighting a disease such as cancer with pin-point accuracy offers huge

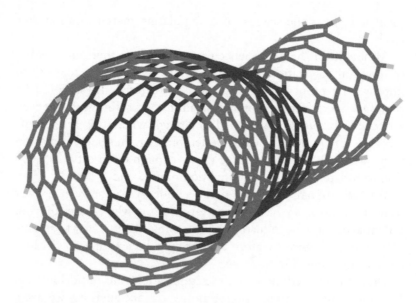

Figure 29: Simulation of a carbon nanotube structure.
Source: Gmdm for Wikipedia Commons

benefits over today's approach. Cancer-killing drugs can be delivered directly to the cancer cells in the body, making the treatment very effective with minimal side effects to the patient.

Carbon nanotubes offer a lot of promise but as yet there are no practical applications for the material; we expect this field really to take off in the next five years or so.

Chapter*Nine*

Lifestyle Maintenance

All humans aspire to live long, healthy lives and as we continue to develop a deeper understanding of the human body, we are increasingly able to do so. In this chapter, we explore some of the current thinking and practices in what scientists are associating with being healthier and living a longer life.

We start with a serious life-shortening disease that is literally eating its way into developed nations across the world; we are of course referring to obesity. The obesity problem has grown to such a point that today, two thirds of the adult population in America and more than half of the adult population in many developed nations is either overweight or obese.

Although there are some potential drugs in the pipeline that are expected to help with this pandemic in the near to medium term, obesity will still pose serious health risks to millions of people for years to come. The average woman in the Western world, for example, now consumes 2,000 calories per day, up from 1,800 in the 1950s, and at the same time has a considerably less active lifestyle.

It's a Fact: Obesity Shortens your Life

It may come as no surprise that it is now a scientific fact that obesity lowers your life expectancy; the more a person is obese, the shorter the life expectancy. A study (Berrington de Gonzalez and Hartge, 2010) involving almost one and a half million adults who were non-smokers with no pre-existing medical conditions, revealed that overweight and obese people have a considerably shorter life expectancy compared to those of a healthy weight. The results showed that obesity had the same negative effect on life expectancy for both men and women. Table 5 displays how with increasing levels of obesity, there is an increasing probability of death for both sexes.

Table 5: The percentage likelihood of death compared with increasing levels of obesity

Body Mass Index (BMI) Range	Women (%)	Men (%)
Slightly overweight (BMI 25.0–27.4)	9	6
Overweight (BMI 27.5–29.9)	19	21
Moderately obese (BMI 30.0–34.9)	44	44
Severely obese (BMI 35.0–39.9)	88	106
Morbidly obese (BMI 40.0–49.9)	151	193

Body Mass Index (BMI) is a simple measurement that is used to measure a person's weight to height ratio; the higher the BMI, the greater the degree of obesity. A BMI between 20.0 and 24.9 is considered to be healthy.

BMI is very easy to calculate:

- In metric, your BMI is your weight in kilograms divided by the square of your height in metres. For example, if you weigh 80 kilograms and are 1.8 metres tall, your BMI is $80/1.8^2 = 24.7$, which falls within the healthy range.
- In imperial, your BMI is your weight in pounds multiplied by 703, divided by the square of your height in inches. For example, if you weigh 200 pounds and are 74 inches tall, your BMI is $200 \times 703/74^2 = 25.7$, which falls into the slightly overweight range.

Although health practitioners acknowledge that the BMI scale is not perfect, it has proved to be a good yardstick in determining whether a person is of a healthy weight.

The *New England Journal of Medicine* study found that the lowest mortality rate was found among men and women with a BMI ranging from 20.0 to 24.9. People who were too thin – that is, those having a BMI below 20 – also had an increased risk of death when compared to people with a BMI ranging from 20.0 to 24.9.

If we plot the study's findings (see Figure 30), it becomes very clear that the risk of dying increases exponentially as the level of obesity increases, even more so in men. So our first tip to avoid a premature death is to get your BMI into the 20 to 25 range. Figure 31 illustrates the obesity problem in different countries.

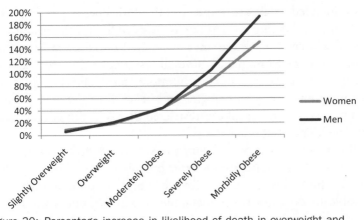

Figure 30: Percentage increase in likelihood of death in overweight and obese men and women.

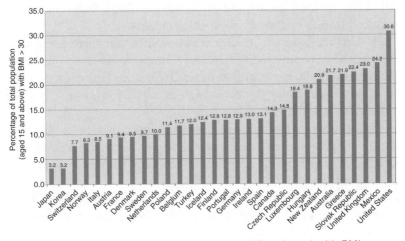

Figure 31: Percentage of total population (aged 15 and over) with BMI greater than 30.

Source: Wikimedia Commons

Extending Life Expectancy

Although there are hundreds of researchers and scientists today looking for a "cure" to ageing (many scientists view it as a disease like any other), for the time being there is only one known method that is guaranteed to work: reducing your daily calorie intake by around 30 per cent. In other words, if 2,000 calories is your daily recommended intake, consume 1,400 calories per day instead (not just during a "dieting" period but as a way of life for the rest of your life). Research along these lines conducted on all organisms, from insects to mice to monkeys, have all resulted in their test subjects having a longer lifespan. Furthermore, test subjects had fewer tumours, fewer cases of diabetes and heart disease. So as counter-intuitive as it seems, a calorie-restricted diet is healthier and makes you live longer, but why?

The generally accepted theory to explain this fact is *energy conservation*. When energy is scarce, organisms go into "starvation mode"; the famine gene is activated, energy is conserved wherever possible to slow down the metabolism, which reduces the rate of cell division and hence slows down the ageing process. Many people have chosen to adopt a calorie-restricted diet as part of their lifestyle, but we have not seen one yet who actually looks healthy; they all seem to look gaunt and malnourished and they experience reduced muscle mass and lower bone density.

So is it really worth it? Our conclusion is that there appears to be a quantity versus quality trade off – sure you can live a bit longer by consuming 30 per cent fewer calories but the quality of your life as a food hermit may not be as high as if you consumed a healthy amount of calories every day.

We suspect that people on these diets are motivated to live just long enough to when we discover a way to arrest or even reverse ageing, at which point they would probably resume a more balanced, healthier diet.

If you are interested in learning more about calorie-restricted diets, there is a *Calorie Restriction Society* (www.crsociety.org) where you can find plenty more information. But note that eating less is much less likely to work as well in humans as in say, mice, because of our slower metabolisms.

Some recent research suggests that calorie restriction leads to an extension of life somewhat by accident; this research suggests the general capacity for growth in a person, useful in early life, can lead to faster deterioration in later life. This particularly relates to the TOR growth pathway, which Mikhail V. Blagosklonny of the *Roswell Institute* in Buffalo, New York, believes becomes an agent of ageing after it has done its earlier work of being an agent of vitality and reproductive capacity. Restricting calories seems to have a "slow down" effect on TOR, lessening its capacity to create dysfunctional mitochondria which leads to free radicals impacting on DNA. In addition, TOR seems to encourage the development of Alzheimers' in certain animal models.

TOR stands for target of rapomycin, and is now the subject of major research as it may be that its inhibition can slow the ageing process. Rapamycin was discovered in a soil sample in Easter Island (also known as Rapa Nui) in the 1960s, but only recently has it become a hot topic in gerontology. Rapamycin itself is thought to be toxic in mammals, so other ways of inhibiting TOR are being explored, including the use of metformin, an oral antidiabetic drug. All this TOR related research is at an early stage, but readers should look out for signs of activity in this area that appear promising.

Common Traits of People who Live the Longest

Author Dan Buettner collaborated with *National Geographic* and travelled extensively around the world to try and identify the parts of the world where people tend to live long lifespans, along with some explanations as to why this was the case. He published a bestselling book revealing his findings called *Blue Zones: Lessons for Living Longer from the People Who Lived the Longest.*

Mr Buettner believes that only 10 per cent of what determines how long people live is dictated by their genes. He believes that the other 90 per cent is due to the lifestyles they lead. By studying and emulating the lifestyles of people who live the longest, we too would be able to maximize the length and quality of our lives.

He finds two locations where people consistently live long contented lives; one is the Mediterranean island of Sardinia and the other is Okinawa in Japan. He describes nine traits and behaviours that residents of these places have, which he refers to as the nine secrets. We provide a summary of these nine secrets below:

- *Secret 1:* Keep moving – these people remained active well into their senior years, doing something every day.
- *Secret 2:* Have a sense of purpose – they all had on-going "projects" or hobbies as part of their life that gets them out of bed in the morning.

- *Secret 3:* Reduce stress – they took life's ups and downs in their stride, never letting anything get to them too much.
- *Secret 4:* Eat wisely – they grazed, eating smaller meals with more frequency.
- *Secret 5:* Eat more plants – their diets included a regular amount of fruit, vegetables and nuts.
- *Secret 6:* Drink alcohol moderately (we like this one) – especially red wine. The health benefits of moderate drinking have been known for some time. Non-drinkers do not live as long, simple as that.
- *Secret 7:* Belong to something – they all tended to belong to a society, a club or religion that gave them a sense of belonging.
- *Secret 8:* Family first – they had a culture of close, multi-generational families, where the elders were admired and respected for their wisdom.
- *Secret 9:* Make lifelong friends who also support a healthy lifestyle – their circle of friends tended to be people who they had known most of their life, sharing common values and healthy lifestyles.

It all makes sense when you read it, but in our current busy lives, it is all too easy to forget these simple guidelines until it is often too late.

A "Cure" to Ageing

In 2000, a group of scientists founded the *Manhattan Beach Project* at an international scientific conference. The project's rather ambitious goal is to reverse the ageing process in humans by 2029. The organization's chairman, Dave Kekich, believes that within 15 years, human life expectancy will be increasing by more than one year, every year. If that proves to be true, it will mean that we will have more years of life ahead of us with every passing birthday.

Kekich has used various data from scientific research around the world and produced a publication called *Life Extension Express* containing what he believes to be the optimal recipe to living a longer, healthier life based on today's knowledge and technology.

There are seven parts to this longevity recipe, the highlights of which are as follows:

- **Diet** – In broad terms, eat more raw food and minimize intake of processed foods. The top 10 *superfoods* based on findings from studies are below:
  - *Tomatoes:*
    - Contain: An antioxidant called *lycopene*. Tomato sauce has five times as much lycopene as fresh tomatoes.
    - Benefits: Lycopene cuts prostate cancer rates by 40 per cent and heart disease by 50 per cent.
  - *Olive oil (extra virgin):*
    - Contains: Monounsaturated fats, most notably *oleic* acid.
    - Benefits: Reduces death from heart disease and cancer.
  - *Red or purple grapes (including red wine):*
    - Contain: An antioxidant called *resveratrol*.
    - Benefits: Increased longevity and inhibits any cancer, heart disease, ***degenerative nerve disease***, viral infections and mechanisms of Alzheimer's.
    - No more than two alcoholic drinks per day.
  - *Garlic:*
    - Contains: Antioxidants.
    - Benefits: Fights cancer and heart disease, and overall is anti-ageing.
  - *Spinach:*
    - Contains: Antioxidants and is rich in folic acid.
    - Benefits: Helps fight cancer, heart disease and mental disorders and may help prevent Alzheimer's.
  - *Salmon and other fatty fish:*
    - Contain: Omega-3 fatty acids.
    - Benefits: Fights virtually every disease and keeps the brain and heart functioning optimally. Also lowers inflammation.
  - *Nuts* (eat over 140 grams (5 ounces) per week):
    - Contain: Mono- and polyunsaturated fats, omega-3 fats, arginine, fibre and vitamin E.
    - Benefits: Can cut heart attack deaths. People who eat about 50 grams (2 ounces) of nuts four times a week tend to live longer. Almonds and walnuts lower cholesterol (unsalted are best); eat them raw if you can.

- *Blueberries and other richly coloured berries:*
  - Contain: Antioxidants.
  - Benefits: Retard ageing and block brain changes leading to fading memory.
- *Matcha green tea and black tea:*
  - Contains: Antioxidant epigallocatechin gallate.
  - Benefits: One cup per day can cut heart disease risk in half (instant or bottled have little effect). Other beneficial effects include improved mental alertness; lower blood cholesterol and triglyceride levels; reduced blood pressure; lower risk of breast, *colon*, lung, ovarian and prostate cancers; protection against type II diabetes; improved exercise performance and lowered risk of obesity.
  - The concentration of the antioxidant in matcha green tea was found to be 137 greater than other green teas.
- *Pomegranate:*
  - Contains: Powerful antioxidants.
  - Benefits: Lowers LDL cholesterol and reduces heart disease.
- **Exercise** – Moderate exercise reduces death rates by 60 per cent. Regular exercise cuts the risk of a heart attack by 75 to 80 per cent over 5 years. They break down exercise into several categories:
  - *Strength training (weights and resistance training):* Benefits include building bone density, muscle, and tendon and ligament strength.
  - *Cardio training:* Benefits include improved breathing, more energy, improved heart health and cardiac output, lower blood pressure, decreased serum cholesterol, reduced stress, better sleep, improved mood and mental functioning, improved digestion and bowel function and more.
- **Supplements** – According to Dr Bruce Ames of the University of California at Berkeley, over 50 genetic diseases have already been identified that can be corrected by aggressive nutritional supplementation. Types of supplements include:
  - multivitamins;
  - low-dose aspirin (80 milligrams per day);
  - omega 3;

- others including coenzyme Q10, carnosine, alpha lipoic acid, vitamin D3, a high-quality absorbable *resveratrol* (not made from *Japanese knotweed*) and folic acid.
- **Anti-Ageing (Preventative) Medicine** – Prevention is better than cure, so get an extensive blood panel to evaluate your present condition and to establish a baseline for yourself. You are recommended to have colonoscopies every 5 to 10 years after the age of 50 or sooner. The 10 most important blood tests are
  - *Chemistry Panel and Complete Blood Count (CBC):* The Chemistry Panel and CBC is the best place to begin your disease-prevention programme.
  - *Fibrinogen:* An important contributor to blood clotting, fibrinogen levels increase in response to tissue inflammation. Increased fibrinogen levels can help predict the risk of heart disease, stroke and other inflammatory disorders such as rheumatoid arthritis.
  - *Haemoglobin A1C:* This test measures a person's blood sugar control over the last two to three months and is an independent predictor of heart disease risk in persons with or without diabetes.
  - *DHEA:* Dehydroepiandrosterone (DHEA) is frequently referred to as an "anti-ageing" hormone.
  - *Prostate-Specific Antigen (PSA) (men only):* Elevated levels may suggest an enlarged prostate, prostate inflammation or prostate cancer.
  - *Homocysteine:* High homocysteine levels have been associated with increased risk of heart attack, bone fracture and poor cognitive function.
  - *C-Reactive Protein:* This is a sensitive marker of systemic inflammation that has emerged as a powerful predictor of coronary heart disease and other diseases of the cardiovascular system. Perhaps an even better predictor of heart disease outcomes, according to a recent study published in *The Lancet*, is the presence of a high level of calcium in arteries, which can be detected in cardiac CT scans.
  - *Thyroid Stimulating Hormone (TSH):* When blood levels fall below normal, this indicates **hyperthyroidism** (increased thyroid activity). When values are above normal, this suggests hypothyroidism (low thyroid activity). Undiagnosed

mild disease can progress to clinical disease states. This is a dangerous scenario, because people with hypothyroidism and elevated serum cholesterol and LDL have an increased risk of atherosclerosis.

- *Testosterone:* Testosterone is produced in the testes in men, in the ovaries in women, and in the adrenal glands of both men and women. Men and women alike can be dramatically affected by the decline in testosterone levels that occur with ageing.
- *Estradiol:* In women, blood estradiol levels help to evaluate menopausal status and sexual maturity. Increased levels in women may indicate an increased risk for breast or ***endometrial cancer***. Estradiol plays a role in supporting healthy bone density in men and women. Low levels are associated with an increased risk of osteoporosis and bone fractures in women and men.

- **Lifestyle** – The type of life you lead greatly impacts your health. A study published in 2004 in *The Lancet*, followed 30,000 men and women on six continents and found changing lifestyle could prevent at least 90 per cent of all heart disease.
- **Stress Management** – Chronic stress kills by weakening your immune system; disrupting your digestive system; causing heart disease, stroke, cancer, Alzheimer's and more. In fact, 80 per cent of all doctor visits in the US are related to stress-induced conditions, and 90 per cent of all diseases are caused or complicated by stress.
- **Attitude** – Be optimistic. In a Mayo Clinic study, optimists:
  - had fewer limitations due to physical health;
  - had less pain;
  - felt more energetic most of the time;
  - felt more peaceful and happy most of the time;
  - had fewer problems with work or other daily activities as a result of their emotional state.

Telomeres – Our Biological Clock

Telomeres are structures found at the tips of all chromosomes. They are often described as being similar to the plastic caps found at the end of shoe laces to stop them fraying. The role of telomeres is to protect the ends of chromosomes by capping them, thus maintaining the integrity of the DNA information they hold.

The research pioneered by Nobel Prize-winning molecular biologist, Elizabeth Blackburn, launched the field of telomere research. It is still a young field of biology that may eventually allow us to control ageing, reduce cell mutations and manage our overall health.

A typical DNA molecule is made up of about 100 million bases, of which the telomere comprises about 15,000 at birth. Over the course of a human life, the telomere's length gets shorter with every cell division until it eventually shortens to about 5,000 bases long, which is when a human dies of old age. There is nothing in science today that can stop telomeres from slowly getting shorter over the course of a human lifetime. Having short telomeres has been linked with premature ageing and many diseases. There are also certain lifestyle-related factors that can accelerate the shortening of telomeres, including smoking and chronic stress.

Telomeres can effectively be viewed as internal human lifespan clocks. Measuring the length of someone's telomeres at the ends of their DNA can give that person's biological age. It can also reveal the age at which the person is likely to die of old age; that is, when the telomeres will have shrunk to 5,000 bases. This technology is available today.

The enzyme responsible for replenishing telomeres is called *telomerase* and the focus for scientists now is to figure out how to control the production of this enzyme because it may be able to slow down the ageing process by slowing down the rate that telomeres shorten throughout a person's lifetime. In a study published in November 2010 in Nature, mice that were engineered to lack telomerase became prematurely decrepit. However, the mice recovered quickly back to health when the enzyme was administered.

There are, however, concerns that increasing the amount of telomerase in a human would increase the risk of cancer, and so further research is being conducted to determine the health risks.

Of course, there is a lot to learn about telomerase and telomeres and their role in human health and longevity, but that is where much of the current hopes lie in discovering the "elixir of life".

Chapter*Ten*

Investment in Biopharma – Chasing Those Money Fountains

We have covered quite a few companies in the book so far, many of which are appropriate for investment, albeit in varying quantities and for varying risk appetites. We ourselves have made a fair number of investments in this sector.

We regard biomedicine as the place where we will find our next "money fountain", the Holy Grail of investing that we describe in our book *Top 10 Investments for the Next 10 Years*.

Let us first say that we are absolutely convinced that a selection of the best investments in bioscience will trounce all other types of investment over the next 10 years, but that choosing the most likely winners is hard, and requires rigorous analysis, constant vigilance and an element of luck.

We also think that anyone looking at this sector needs to have two balancing features in a prospective portfolio: (i) diversification in terms of the numbers of investments and; (ii) a broad spread in terms of the sizes and business areas of the companies chosen.

Not only is it vital to have at least 10 "bets" in the sector, given the high rate of outright or relative failure, but also it is equally important to have a spread of exposures; possibly some to the slower growing steadier large companies, certainly some to medium-sized entrepreneurial companies, and absolutely some to the more speculative companies.

For those investors who only need a modest exposure to the sector and have neither the time nor possibly the inclination to do the necessary research, exchange-traded funds (ETFs) and managed funds are undoubtedly the best ways of proceeding.

In bioscience, we are at the stage that Apple or Microsoft were 20 or more years ago; we are at the inception of the new *Amazon*s and Googles of the world, and that alone makes it important for serious investors to sit up and take note. In the same way that the Internet boomed and crashed in the late 1990s and early 2000s, biotech has had a couple of flirtations with stardom over the past two decades. In recent years, however, the industry has fallen from favour and it has been harder to raise money for biopharma companies, through the venture capital route or through the stock market.

Our preference is to invest our money in *drug companies, gene therapy companies, stem cell companies, sequencing businesses* and in *regenerative medicine.* Money is surely also to be made in the pharmacy sector, in *generic drugs,* in *biomedical devices,* and in *hospital* and other *managed care businesses.* But this book does not cover those in any detail, largely because there is more than enough excitement and opportunity in our preferred areas.

In this chapter, we recapitulate our recommendations, emphasizing that we are looking at these companies for the long term, and talk about some portfolio templates for different types of investors.

We have emphasized that the drug discovery process is arduous and expensive, and littered with failure. But we have also explained that computer technology, sequencing and advances in molecular biology will fit a lot more *new drug locks* into *receptor keys* in the coming years. Although the patent cliff for some big pharma companies is real and imminent, it does not mean that they are all bereft of new products, be they licensed, acquired or home-grown.

In fact, about 1,200 compounds out of big pharma are in Phase 2 and Phase 3 trials at the moment and because the price to earnings ratios (one useful measure of valuation) of the big pharma companies worldwide have been eroding for years, and because the sector is generally out of favour, there will be some clear opportunities for investors to make good money over a long period of time from investing in a handful of the largest companies.

In this respect, our favourite stocks are Novartis (NYSE: NVS), Allergan (NYSE: AGN), Astellas (Tokyo Stock Exchange: 4503), Merck (NYSE: MRK), Pfizer (NYSE: PFE), GlaxoSmithKline (NYSE: GSK), Sanofi-Aventis (NYSE: SNY) and Roche Holdings (OTC: RHHBY).

As an example, Tim Anderson of Alliance Bernstein has reported that he believes Novartis, a Swiss company with US-listed shares, may post a 2020 profit of US$7.67 a share, up from US$5.50 in 2011; this will be led by *Glivec*, *Gilenia*, and *Lucentis*. Similarly, GSK, also traded in the US, could generate earnings of US$6 a share in 2020, up from the US$3.70 estimated for 2011. This places both these companies on what we consider to be relatively low price-earnings ratios.

Novartis and GSK both have substantial non-branded drug operations, which can have the effect of smoothing out earnings over time. Novartis owns *Alcon*, an eye-care giant, and also controls Sandoz, the world's number two generic-drug maker, behind Teva Pharmaceutical (NASDAQ: TEVA).

GSK has a large consumer-products franchise, including Tums, Polident, Aquafresh and Nicorette gum, which provides about 20 per cent of its revenue. GSK is also one of three leading vaccine makers, along with Merck and Sanofi-Aventis. Vaccines offer a near annuity-like business model because generic competition is virtually non-existent due to the difficulty of gaining regulatory approvals given the complexity of the manufacturing process.

Pfizer's US$68 billion takeover of Wyeth has given it access to the latter's vaccines, consumer health and animal products. The move was widely seen as an attempt to boost Pfizer's pipeline in advance of Lipitor, the cholesterol drug that generated nearly US$12 billion in 2010, losing patent protection in the US in 2011. In all, 38 per cent of Pfizer's current sales will face competition from generics by 2013. However, we think that Pfizer is taking all the right steps to rectify this situation; from actively cutting costs, to doing partnership deals with innovative smaller companies, and looking to take Lipitor into pharmacies as an OTC product, which would certainly shake up the statin market. Additionally, Pfizer has an excellent pipeline compared to most major pharma companies; Tofacitinib for rheumatoid arthritis is very promising and is likely to be marketed by 2013, and other drugs for Alzheimer's and *Deep*

Vein Thrombosis (DVT) and stroke all look likely to hit the market in the next couple of years.

Among big pharma companies, none appear to have done as much as Sanofi-Aventis in changing their research and development (R&D) focus. Sanofi's portfolio includes over 60 projects in clinical development, with 17 in Phase 3 or already submitted for approval. Sanofi has reported that it has 65 new molecular entities in its pipeline.

Eli Lilly and AstraZeneca face major patent cliffs in the next few years. Alliance Bernstein suggests, for example, that Lilly's earnings could drop to US$3 a share in 2015 and to US$2 in 2020 from an estimated US$4.28 in 2011, putting at risk its generous dividend. Therefore, Lilly and Astra Zeneca shares should be avoided.

We also like Johnson & Johnson (NYSE: JNJ), which is a curious but effective combination of consumer products, drug brands and medical devices and disposable businesses.

Among the larger Japanese pharma companies, we favour Astellas which, apart from a leading position worldwide in the urology market, is making great inroads in oncology and partnering with some excellent new generation drug companies, such as Medivation (NASDAQ: MDVN) of San Francisco. Astellas, unusually for a Japanese company, also pays a generous dividend.

The above are the companies we recommend as long-term stable investments for the next 10 to 20 years. We believe that they will retain an edge among the big pharma companies, whereas Lilly, and Bristol-Myers Squibb strike as us being less attractive to investors.

Our view is based on evaluating their product pipelines, patent profiles and exposure to consumer products, as well as an assessment of management culture. We also took into account relative valuations, which of course can and do change, so investors should not rely solely on the data we are publishing, because such things as *price-earnings* ratios and *dividend yields* will change over time.

Almost all the big pharma companies have highly robust balance sheets, are well diversified and are cash generative. Margins are typically higher than in other industries and return on equity ranges from 20 to 35 per cent for most, which again represents superior returns. Big pharma companies are engaged in massive share buy back programmes and pay generous dividends. As an example, Pfizer is expected to buy back US$6 billion of its shares in 2012, effectively returning cash to shareholders, along with substantial dividends.

There is a general expectation that, for the biggest pharma companies, growth in *earnings per share (EPS)* will slow and erosion will occur in *margins* and *return on equity*. We believe that this is somewhat exaggerated. Indeed, already, *price-earnings* ratios on major pharma companies are relatively low, averaging about 10 times forward earnings in early 2012, suggesting a limited downside. Biotech companies of significant size have recently tended to sell at about 12 times earnings; again, cheaply priced in our opinion.

One of the reasons for relative optimism for these industry behemoths lies in the potential they have in the parts of the world barely breached by branded medicinal drugs. Because the larger companies are typically the ones with the most extensive sales forces and greatest marketing savvy, they stand to do best in the developing world.

The major opportunities lie in China, India and Brazil. Each of these, however, has their own particular problems. For instance, China insists that every drug has to be re-trialled in China before approval, and Brazil's healthcare infrastructure is woeful. India remains a tale of two countries when it comes to healthcare – highly sophisticated hospitals in some of the big cities and near-feudal healthcare in the countryside. Russia is an extremely difficult market for the big pharma companies and likely to remain so. South Korea is a large and growing market, as indeed are Mexico and South Africa. Generic producers and outright intellectual theft remain rife in parts of the developing world. Nonetheless, it is expected that sales of branded drug products will more than treble by 2020 in the developing world.

In addition, as cash-rich giants, the big pharma companies are capable of – and indeed do – buy the entrepreneurial expertise and culture of smaller biotech companies in order to fill pipelines and create growth. For example, Pfizer bought Wyeth and *Warner Lambert* recently, and Merck bought Schering Plough, and they have been using their cash to consolidate and generate cost savings.

It is estimated that US drug companies have about US$100 billion of free cash overseas, which has not yet been repatriated for tax reasons. If, as seems likely, the US declares a tax amnesty on repatriated profits, this wave of funds could create a cascade of mergers and acquisitions in the US biopharma sector, and investors should follow this potential development closely.

The large European and Japanese pharma companies are also on the hunt for overseas earnings, and a good example is the 2011 acquisition of Genzyme by Sanofi-Aventis, for about US$20billion.

Generally speaking, investors have to recognize that, notwithstanding the attractions of some of the largest drug companies as investments, the overall impact of each individual drug on their financial results is diminished by their sheer scale.

Also, it is undoubtedly the case that big drug company productivity in terms of R&D dollars spent versus drugs coming onto the market has diminished considerably over the past decade. For example, spending on R&D by GSK runs to 15 per cent of sales, Novartis is at 18 per cent, Roche at 19 per cent and Pfizer at 14 per cent. For just those companies alone, total annual R&D spending is US$35 billion per annum, which is equivalent to the size of the economy of a small country! It is thought that at least half of all R&D money is targeted on anti-cancer drugs.

But the "bang for the buck" from R&D spending has been diminishing, despite a massive consolidation by the big pharma companies in recent years. For instance, *Data Search* estimates that in the period between 1999 and 2009, 1,300 mergers and acquisitions occurred worldwide in the pharmaceutical industry, with the largest undertaken by the big pharma companies, and that the total deal value was close to US$1 trillion.

Notwithstanding the consolidation and the massive R&D expenditures, only about 20 genuinely new (as opposed to reworked) formulations coming out of big pharma are being approved by the FDA on an annual basis, reducing the organic growth potential of the major companies.

The larger the company, the harder it is for it to grow. So, if you are a purely growth-oriented investor, we recommend none of the major pharma companies, with the exception of Roche Genentech, which is a hybrid of "old" pharma and biotech, and has a strong and growing pipeline.

COMPANY SPOTLIGHT: ROCHE HOLDINGS (OTC: RHHBY)

Roche is the best placed of all the big pharma/biotech companies for the coming decade, in our opinion. Patent expirations for Roche are the lowest in the sector, at 26 per cent up to 2015, compared to an average of 35 per cent for big pharma generally. The company enjoys an interesting pipeline of potentially blockbuster products. These include extensions of its Rituxan franchise, which is dominant in non-Hodgkin's lymphoma and *chronic lymphocytic leukaemia*. These extensions include the use of the drug for rheumatoid arthritis, where it is gaining traction. Additionally, sales of Roche's massive HER2 franchise should more than double to over US$12 billion per annum by 2020.

Other drugs in late-stage trials that should be monitored by investors include **GA101**, which could end up supplementing Rituxan in non-Hodgkin's lymphoma and is designed using a process called *glycol-engineering* to increase its efficacy. Additionally, a drug designed to raise HDL (or "good") cholesterol levels, **Dalcetrapib**, is in late-stage trials for post-heart attack patients with atherosclerosis.

Avastin, which is dominant in colorectal cancer, has some further opportunities in niche diseases. Herceptin, Roche's drug for *HER2*-related breast cancer, has significant opportunities in emerging markets. Roche is also extremely strong in *diagnostics*, which will be very important in the coming era of personalized or precision medicine.

Overall, the major companies are likely to grow at 5 per cent or so per annum, on average, with perhaps 10 per cent for the better performers. This is a creditable performance given the limiting dynamics of size and the patent expirations that loom ahead, but it is a far cry from the heady days of growth of the past, and indeed of some of the explosive growth that lies ahead for the new generation drug companies that we like.

We do not think that there will be any serious damage done to the drug sector in general by the belt-tightening posture of the governments of major developed governments. However, the larger the drug company, the more prominent it will be in any political wrangling about the price of drugs or about reimbursement in national health services or the equivalent.

In the US, big pharma has had to make some concessions to the Administration in the form of what are effectively special taxes, amounting to about US$90 billion in the next 10 years. This is because of the hotly contentious Obama healthcare reform measures introduced in 2010, where the pharmaceutical industry agreed effectively to subsidize some parts of *Medicare* (medical aid for those over 65 or those with chronic disabilities) and *Medicaid* programmes for the poor. Overall, Medicare and Medicaid cost about US$1 trillion per annum, and they cover about 95 million Americans.

About half of the new special tax on drug makers will be offset by the prospective increase in the size of the market by bringing the previously uninsured part of the population into healthcare schemes. Further pressure is likely on drug pricing, both from the US government, where the reimbursement schemes are fiendishly complicated, and from insurers. In other parts of the world, reimbursement – and indeed approval to prescribe drugs – can be equally complex and price pressures equally severe.

Overall, however, we do not see too much impairment to the drug industry from these reforms. As we have said, drugs are a *displacement* factor – if they work, they can keep people away from the much more expensive surgeries and hospitalization. Drugs are normally only about 10 per cent of the cost of medical treatment, and all governments recognize the need for profits in the industry to foster innovation. In our assessment, the overall impact on the pharma industry worldwide from pressure to reduce prices will result in an approximately 5 per cent reduction in revenues, but will be offset in large part by market growth and by improved efficiencies.

Indeed, US patients who "co-pay" on medical insurance (normally 20 per cent of the total cost of drugs) quite often have their portion funded in whole or in part by the drug companies themselves. As a result, US consumers, who are by far the most important in the world at the moment, are quite often oblivious to the cost of medication.

For that reason, while the patents on them persist, drug prices tend to be relatively stable or even rise. Drugs that work are regarded as among life's most essential consumables, and as a result the drug business is demonstrably less vulnerable to economic downturns than most other industries. As such it is often regarded as a contra-cyclical investment sector.

It should also be taken as a positive for the whole sector that, though there is a perception that the drug approval process has become tougher, molecular biology is likely to make it a lot easier in the future. Technological advances applied to drug trials, including modelling and the use of genomics, will cut costs and shorten development times.

By testing patients with *companion diagnostics* in advance of drug tests, drug makers can eliminate those who are likely to exhibit toxic reactions or are not suitable candidates for a new drug. Herceptin, Roche's blockbuster drug for breast cancer patients who overexpress the *HER2* gene, was tested on a much more limited range of patients than would have been usual because Roche was able to identify the appropriate candidates prior to the trial. *Genomic Health* (NASDAQ: GHDX), a company covered in Table 9 at the end of this chapter, is an interesting leader in cancer genomics testing.

It is estimated that the whole of the pharmaceutical industry will spend US$800 billion on R&D in the years 2010 to 2015, and if just some of that could be saved by more tightly structured drug trials, then large amounts of money could be returned to the bottom line. Similarly, if time to market for a successful drug could be cut from 10 years to 8 years over the next 5 years or so, that will also have a massively positive effect.

None of this will create the conditions for spectacular growth for big pharma as a whole, but with developing markets becoming more accessible to those larger companies, and adding in acquisitions and pipelines being replenished in a more targeted manner, some of the big beasts will prosper.

But the real excitement for investors will lie in the "new generation drug companies", known popularly as *biopharma*. This is where we are concentrating our efforts, and where we are now making significant investments.

We are diversifying our own new generation drug company portfolios, both in terms of the numbers of the "bets" we are placing and also in terms of the sizes and business areas of the companies we are investing in.

The areas that we find appealing as investment opportunities are drugs for cancer, hepatitis, HIV/AIDS, *antibiotic resistant infectious disease*, cardiovascular disease, pain, neurodegenerative disease and diabetes. We also like certain *orphan disease areas* with investment potential. We favour the *gene therapy area*, including siRNA products and *delivery systems, antisense* drugs, and we consider the *stem cell* and *genomics industries* to have exceptionally high potential.

In the context of the larger biotech companies, the superior choices appear to us to be: Roche Genentech, Amgen, Alnylam, Isis, Celgene, Biogen Idec, Medicis, Forest Labs, Gilead Sciences, Medivation, Shire PLC, Cubist, Pacific Biosciences, *Rigel*, Nektar, Onyx, MAP and Vertex Pharmaceuticals. With the exception of Roche and Shire, all these are US companies, reflecting the US preeminence in biotech. Onyx is a company we have increasing respect for, and it appears to us to be an excellent investment with multiple shots on target. **Carilzomib** for multiple myeloma is an extremely exciting compound for a disease with considerable unmet needs, but also **Nexavar** and **regorafenib** are likely to be blockbusters.

Also of note in the "larger" sector (companies with market capitalizations over US$300 million) are: Acorda Therapeutics, Amylin, Savient and Anthera.

In terms of the smaller and certainly more speculative public companies, our favourites are AmpliPhi, Arrowhead Research, Cellceutix, CytRX, Optimer, Dynavax, NanoViricides, Star Scientific and BioTime.

COMPANY SPOTLIGHT: AMGEN (NASDAQ: AMGN)

Amgen is the largest independent biotech of all, and its shares are highly liquid and traded in the US. It recently initiated its first quarterly dividend, and investors should expect a rising level of cash returns in the coming decade. Cowen and Company believe that Amgen will generate as much as US$30 billion in cash over the next few years and that it is virtually immune to the perils of generic competition as a result of strong patent positions.

Amgen's new drug for osteoporosis, Prolia (denosumab), a monoclonal antibody which targets a protein that acts as the primary signal to promote bone removal, has a significant opportunity in metastatic cancer of the bones, where it is branded Xgeva. Existing franchises for **Epogen** (used in dialysis), **Sensipar** (for *hyperparathyroidism*) and Enbrel (rheumatoid arthritis) remain robust. A drug in Phase 3 trials for *head and neck cancers* and for *melanoma*, **GM-CSF**, acquired with Oncovex in 2011, has high promise. Amgen looks to us to be an excellent long-term investment.

COMPANY SPOTLIGHT: BIOGEN IDEC (NASDAQ: BIIB)

Biogen Idec is another very large biopharma company, with robust cash flows and a very strong position in multiple sclerosis (MS), with Tysabri as an extremely fast-growing product. Biogen's core products are Rituxan (co-marketed with Roche in the US, where Biogen has 30 per cent of the rights and is the second highest selling cancer drug worldwide) and Avonex (used in MS, and where Biogen owns 100 per cent).

Tysabri, which has an association with progressive multi-focal leukoencephalopathy (PML) in a small number of users, has been considerably boosted by a companion diagnostic kit that screens out the people likely to suffer the side effect. Tysabri has the potential to be a major blockbuster (US$2 billion per annum), and Biogen's other pipeline drugs in MS should keep it as the dominant player for many years to come. These future drugs include BG-12, which is in Phase 3 trials for late-stage MS patients. Additionally, a *PEGylated* version of Avonex is in Phase 3 trials, which could considerably extend the franchise. The drug Ampyra, co-marketed with Acorda, is also highly interesting, because it increases walking speed in MS patients.

(Continued)

The MS market is, sadly, a growing one, and Biogen's strong position in it makes the company an attractive long-term investment, in our view. Although the average cost of treatment of an MS patient is about US$40,000 per annum, pricing pressures are unlikely to emerge. Biogen also has some highly promising compounds for haemophilia which are expected to get approval in 2012/13.

COMPANY SPOTLIGHT: CELGENE (NASDAQ: CELG) AND SOLIGENIX (OTC: SNGX)

Celgene is a leader in the *haematological cancer* and *inflammatory disease* markets, and is one of the oldest and largest biomedicine companies. Celgene's success has been built on Abraxane for breast cancer, **Thalomid** for myeloma and **Vidaza** for high-risk myelodysplastic syndromes (MDS). Its relatively new compound **Revlimid**, for MDS and myeloma, has very high potential, and with a long patent life (2026) and very strong sales potential, Revlimid could generate upwards of US$6 billion per annum in revenue for Celgene for years to come. Multiple myeloma affects at least 200,000 patients worldwide, and although it is almost universally fatal, Revlimid and *stem cell transplantation* can considerably extend life spans for sufferers, and Revlimid is likely to become a front line treatment option for multiple myeloma in the near future. Celgene will also produce Phase 3 trial data for apremilast (a psoriasis agent) in 2012. Celgene strikes us as a good long-term play on blood cancer science, as well as on arthritis, and we recommend the shares on that basis as part of the "conservative" portion of a biomedicine portfolio.

A company called *Soligenix* (OTC: SNGX), mentioned in Chapter 5, has an interesting compound being tested in Phase 3 to treat acute gastro intestinal graft-versus-host disease, an inflammatory condition that occurs in almost all patients who receive a hemopoietic stem cell transplant for blood cancers and disorders.

COMPANY SPOTLIGHT: GILEAD (NASDAQ: GILD)

Another company to enjoy a dominant position in a single disease is Gilead Sciences, based on the West Coast of the US. Gilead is the leader in the HIV/AIDS market, and also has a strong position in hepatitis B and *fungal infection* drugs. We have already written in Chapter 4 about Gilead's phenomenal success with Viread, either as a standalone or combination drug, and additionally talked about Gilead's upcoming Quad pill for HIV/AIDS. Gilead's patent on Viread (**tenofovir**) expires in 2017, but by judicious tweaking of dosages and combinations with other drugs, the drug should remain highly profitable far beyond that. The HIV market continues to grow worldwide, despite an overall reduction in infections. This is because of better methods of diagnosing the disease and an expansion into hitherto untreated populations. In the US, pricing pressures have led to some diminution of margins for Gilead, but this is not expected to significantly dampen its robust growth. New drugs in the pipeline from Gilead, including an integrase inhibitor Elvitegravir for HIV/AIDS as well as the use of Viread in hepatitis B and HIV, and new compounds for cystic fibrosis (**Cayston**) and for angina (Ranexa) add to Gilead's attractions as a solid, moderately growing investment. Gilead is a cash-generating machine, and by 2015, should be producing upwards of US$5 billion per annum, paving the way for dividends and share buybacks. Gilead has also recently bought Pharmasset, which will likely prove to be highly successful in the massive hepatitis C vaccine space, with late sate compound PSI-7977, which does not require interferon as an adjunct. Even though they paid full price for the acquisition, Gilead's management are skilled at extracting profits. We write of NanoViricides as an interesting and speculative play in HIV, but its drug is years away from even being a threat to Gilead.

COMPANY SPOTLIGHT: ISIS PHARMACEUTICALS (NASDAQ: ISIS)

Isis Pharmaceuticals is the leader in *antisense* technology, and though the company is still not at the money-making stage, it is close to commercial success, in our view.

Isis and Genzyme, its partner, have announced that their cholesterol-lowering antisense therapy, mipomersen, had met its endpoints in a Phase 3 trial on patients with *heterozygous familial hypercholesterolemia (FH)* and *coronary artery disease*. There are lingering concerns in relation to high liver enzyme levels in some trial participants, but because people with a familial history of very high cholesterol do not have many options, we think that mipomersen will get approval. The drug is highly efficacious, and if safety concerns can be overcome, even with a possible reformulation, it is likely that it could rival statins as a cholesterol-lowering treatment in a wider population. Isis also has a late stage oncology compound in alliance with Teva and *OncoGenex* named **OGX-011**. The compound targets clusterin, which is key in clearing cellular debris and apoptosis (cell death). It also has **ISIS-CRPRx**, a compound that targets C-Reactive Protein (CRP), which is highly associated with multiple types of inflammation.

Should mipomersen get approval, Isis will turn out to be an excellent investment. In addition, Isis has a partnership with GSK for developing up to six antisense drugs for rare diseases, and another partnership, this time with Alnylam for the creation of antisense drugs targeting *micro RNAs*. These are single stranded RNAs shown to have an important regulatory effect in gene expression. In our view, Isis has sufficient cash to take it to commercial success, and with an interesting pipeline and a clear lead in antisense technology, it is worth making a longer-term investment in its shares.

COMPANY SPOTLIGHT: ALNYLAM PHARMACEUTICALS (NASDAQ: ALNY)

Alnylam Pharmaceuticals of Cambridge, Massachusetts, is another interesting company. It has completed a Phase 1 trial of ALN-VSP, an *RNAi therapeutic* for solid tumours with liver involvement. Alnylam has said the results demonstrate anti-tumour activity in addition to safety and tolerability. Multiple patients in the study achieved stable disease, and indeed one achieved partial response with 70 per cent tumour regression. Alnylam is a world leader in *RNAi technology* with a significant patent "estate" and multiple licensing deals. It is a medium-sized biotech, and though not as attractive as Arrowhead Research in the *RNAi space*, is nonetheless worth consideration by investors. Indeed, Arrowhead and Alnylam have recently announced collaborations in key aspects of the RNAi science.

COMPANY SPOTLIGHT: RIGEL PHARMACEUTICALS (NASDAQ: RIGL)

Rigel Pharmaceuticals is an interesting play in two areas: rheumatoid arthritis (RA), which is an ageing disease that is fast growing; and *organ transplantation.*

The shares of Rigel have long-term upside potential for new oral RA drugs such as fostamatinib (R788). Fostamatinib reversibly blocks signalling in multiple cell types involved in inflammation and tissue degradation in RA. Rigel is on track for a potential regulatory filing in the US by 2013, to enable a launch of the drug in 2014.

Rigel has partnered with AstraZeneca for this highly promising compound, and also has Phase 2 studies underway in **R343** for mild asthma. Additionally, its *oral Janus Kinase 3 (JAK3) inhibitor* programme on *organ transplant rejection* has
(Continued)

great potential. *JAK3* is critical to immune system activation and has become an attractive target because its expression is limited to key cells in the immune system.

Ninety thousand organ transplants occur worldwide per year and 25 per cent of those are in the US. First year survival rates are 90 per cent plus for the major organs, but chronic rejection rates are high (50 per cent at 5 to 10 years). Current global pharmaceutical sales in the transplant market are approximately US$4 billion, representing a huge opportunity for Rigel, which we recommend as an investment.

Rigel is also considering additional indications for its *JAK3 inhibitor*. The company has plenty of cash, enough to take it to commercial launch of fostamatinib and the *JAK3 inhibitor*, which could be multi-billion dollar products.

COMPANY SPOTLIGHT: VERTEX PHARMACEUTICALS (NASDAQ: VRTX)

Vertex is one of the most amazing successes ever in the biopharma space, and demonstrates the enormous upside in identifying a winner. Vertex has now received approval in the US for **Incivek** (Telaprevir), a hepatitis C *protease inhibitor*. Telaprevir represents a quantum shift in the way that hepatitis C is treated, and seems to have a clear lead over its nearest competitor, Merck's boceprevir (**Victrelis**). Telaprevir is already showing very strong sales growth, and could well end up being a US$4 to 5 billion per year seller, making it one of the most successful drugs of all time. In addition, Vertex has a pipeline of cystic fibrosis drugs, one of which, **Kalydeco**, looks likely to be a strong seller.

Hepatitis C is a worldwide scourge, with about 170 million people infected and a huge unmet need for efficacious treatment. Infection rates, once boosted by tainted transfused blood, but now largely caused by intravenous drug use, are falling, but nonetheless the market is enormous.

Telaprevir is typically used with the former standard of care, interferon, and as a result hepatitis C, which often leads to liver failure, can now be cured. Only about 12 per cent of hepatitis C patients worldwide receive any form of treatment, so this drug, though expensive, has the opportunity to address perhaps the largest market available to a new product. Although there are other competitors to Telaprevir in the market or in the works, including from Merck and from Pharmasset (now owned by Gilead) and its partner Roche, Vertex has a clear lead, with an approved product and good patent life. In Europe, Telaprevir is sold by Johnson & Johnson, in Japan by *Tanabe*. We recommend Vertex stock as a long-term investment, and also note that it is the sort of company that could well be acquired by a larger rival.

COMPANY SPOTLIGHT: SHIRE PHARMACEUTICALS (LON: SHP) & (NASDAQ: SHPGY)

Shire is a British company whose shares trade in London and the US. It is the largest pure biopharma company outside of the US, and the company has a very strong actual and prospective portfolio of drugs, particularly in Attention Deficit Disorder (ADD) and *orphan diseases*. Shire is likely to experience strong growth in the next few years and can be considered a quality core holding for investors. Since Shire has most of its sales in the US, and yet is British, it would make an ideal takeover candidate for one of the largest pharma companies, which adds spice to the story.

Shire is organized into two divisions. Through its *Specialty Pharmaceuticals* division, Shire focuses on small-molecule

(Continued)

medications within the therapeutic areas of *Attention Deficit Hyperactivity Disorder (ADHD)*, including **Vyvanse** and **Intuniv** (where it maintains a leadership position), and *gastrointestinal disease*, with **Resolor**, **Lialda** and **Pentasa**, among others.

Shire's *Human Genetic Therapies* division focuses on *single mutation genetic diseases* such as rare conditions like Hunter syndrome, Fabry disease, Gaucher's disease, Sanfilippo Syndrome and *metachromatic leukodystrophy*. These are treated with infusion products such as Elaprase and Replagel, and as we have seen, the orphan disease market can be highly profitable with a significant barrier to entry. In addition, Shire has a promising new product for hereditary angioedema, a self-administered drug known as **Firazyr**. Last, but not least, Shire has announced top line Phase 3 results for **Dermagraft**, a bioengineered skin substitute, for the treatment of *venous leg ulcers (VLUs)*, a condition that affects 500–600,000 patients annually in the US. This could be a US$600 million a year drug by 2015.

Shire is a highly profitable company, and extremely cash generative; it should make over £1 billion in net income per annum by 2015 and with a strong pipeline, we recommend the stock as a long-term play.

COMPANY SPOTLIGHT: MEDICIS PHARMACEUTICAL CORPORATION (NYSE: MRX)

Medicis is a leading independent specialty pharmaceutical company based in the US focused primarily on the treatment of dermatological and aesthetic conditions. Medicis's mission statement is that it is "dedicated to helping patients attain a healthy and youthful appearance and self-image", which we certainly applaud!

Medicis's products include the acne antibiotic Solodyn, which faces limited generic competition, but also **Restalyne** and Dysport, both cosmetic surgery preparations with very strong franchises. Medicis is a cash-rich, cash-generative business with strong longer-term prospects, and represents a very good way of playing the "anti-ageing" game (along with Allergan, whose Botox is the leading product in the cosmetic dermatology market). We recommend the shares of Medicis for conservative, long-term horizon investors.

More speculative is *International Stem Cell Corporation* (OTC: ISCO), which uses parthenogenetic stem cells, derived from unfertilized human eggs *(oocytes)*, to create a line of cosmetic products called **Lifeline**. The company is working on other therapeutic areas with its stem cell lines as well.

COMPANY SPOTLIGHT: ALLERGAN (NYSE: AGN)

Allergan is a strong and large company in ophthalmology and cosmetic medical products. Its most notable product, Botox, has a very promising new indication for migraine headaches. The Botox cosmetic franchise looks well protected and the headache sales could end up being a near US$1 billion market opportunity for Allergan in coming years. The company should continue to enjoy strong growth in ophthalmology where it is a leader. Returns may not be spectacular, but they should be superior, and there is a chance that Allergan could be acquired by big pharma.

COMPANY SPOTLIGHT: FOREST LABORATORIES (NYSE: FRX)

Forest is a speciality pharmaceutical company of considerable size, which is facing a particularly steep patent cliff with the expiration of some patents on a key product Lexapro (for anxiety) in 2012. This will lead to a reduction in the short term of at least 50 per cent in earnings, and a fall in sales of about 30 per cent.

It may seem strange therefore that we favour this company as a long-term investment; allow us to elaborate. Forest has an extremely strong and interesting pipeline and has at least five new drugs on the imminent launch pad, the combination of which will easily replace the sales lost to generic competition for Lexapro. The company has had some regulatory issues, but these have now been settled.

Forest has a very substantial cash balance, and the launch of Daxas (Daliresp) with **Nycomed**, for *chronic obstructive pulmonary hypertension*, in particular, will generate considerable profits. Additionally, by acquiring *Clinical Data* in 2011, Forest took over the drug **Vilibryd**, a *selective serotonin reuptake inhibitor (SSRI)* for major depression. It is also about to launch Teflaro, for MRSA infections, which seems to have reasonable promise against resistant strains of gram-positive bacteria and may end up being a US$1 billion per annum drug. *Forest* also has other interesting late-stage compounds in irritable bowel syndrome (IBS) and diabetes, and for *chronic pain*.

Overall, Forest is a cash-rich company, which has been buying back its shares, with outstanding management and a rich pipeline. Notwithstanding a fall in earnings for the next few years, the bright outlook for new products makes this a must-have investment in a balanced biomedicine portfolio.

COMPANY SPOTLIGHT: MEDIVATION (NASDAQ: MDVN)

We have already written about Medivation in Chapter 4 and so will not rehash our view here, except to say that its prostate drug MDV 3100 has completed Phase 3 trials and passed the final safety test. This means that it should go forward with commercialisation in 2013 in partnership with Astellas. This is a blockbuster drug in the making, and possible future indications in breast cancer and in front-line prostate cancer (i.e. newly diagnosed men) could add very large volumes to its potential. The company's shares have risen sharply following the announcement of MDV3100's Phase 3 results, but as a long term investment we like this one a lot.

COMPANY SPOTLIGHT: ASTELLAS PHARMA (TOKYO STOCK EXCHANGE: 4503)

Astellas is Japan's second biggest drug company. It has zero debt on its balance sheet and about US$2.1 billion of cash. It has a market capitalization of around US$17.7 billion and offers a dividend yield of over 4 per cent.

Astellas has a solid revenue stream (see Figures 32 and 33) and this has been bolstered by its US$4 billion acquisition of *OSI Pharmaceuticals* in 2010 to boost its oncology business. The company has a nicely diverse source of revenues, and although some of their major drugs, notably **Prograf** and Lipitor, came off patent protection in 2011, it has a healthy pipeline of new drugs at various stages of clinical trials (see Figure 34). Astellas, formerly *Yamanouchi Pharmaceuticals*, is a very smart developer of partnerships and has huge potential in kidney cancer, prostate cancer, and chronic constipation and IBS.

(Continued)

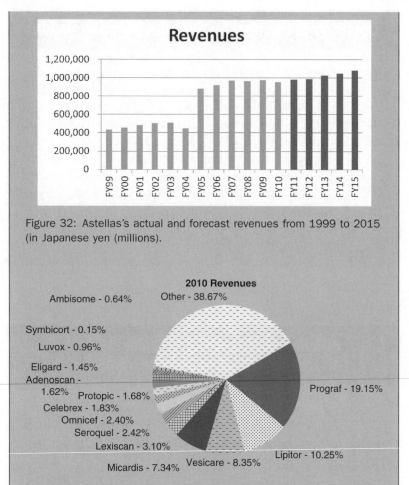

Figure 32: Astellas's actual and forecast revenues from 1999 to 2015 (in Japanese yen (millions).

Figure 33: Pie chart illustrating top-selling drugs by Astellas in 2010.

The three therapeutic areas of focus for Astellas are as follows:

- *Urology:*
  - Growth in sales to be driven by ***Overactive Bladder Treatments (OBT):***
    - **Vesicare** and **Mirabegron** (see Figure 35) – 78 per cent forecast revenue growth (NDA filed in Japan, US and EU).

Drug	2010 Sales (USD)	% of Total Sales	Patent Expiry
Prograf	2,013	19.15%	28/02/2011
Lipitor	1,077	10.25%	28/06/2011
Vesicare	877	8.35%	27/12/2015
Micardis	772	7.34%	07/01/2014
Lexiscan	326	3.10%	22/06/2019
Seroquel	254	2.42%	04/12/2011
Omnicef	252	2.40%	04/12/2011
Celebrex	192	1.83%	30/05/2011
Protopic	177	1.68%	31/01/2012
Adenoscan	170	1.62%	18/05/2009
Eligard	152	1.45%	03/10/2008
Luvox	101	0.96%	NA
Ambisome	67	0.64%	23/02/2016
Symbicort	16	0.15%	17/12/2012

Figure 34: Top-selling drugs by Astellas in 2010 along with their respective patent expiration dates.

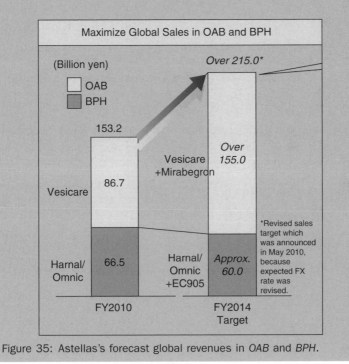

Figure 35: Astellas's forecast global revenues in *OAB* and *BPH*.

- *Benign Prostatic Hyperplasia (BPH):*
  - **Harnal** and **Omnic** (see Figure 35) – 10 per cent forecast revenue decline.
- *Transplantation, Immunology and Infectious Disease:*
  - **ASKP1240** – prevention of organ transplant rejection (Phase 2 in US, Phase 1 in Japan).
  - **ASP015K** – immunosuppressant (Phase 2 in US, Phase 1 in Japan).
  - **Diannexin** – prevention of Delayed Graft Function in kidney transplant (Phase 2 in EU and US).
  - **ASP2408** – Maxy-4 Project – rheumatoid arthritis (Phase 1).
  - **Isavuconazole** – antifungal agent (Phase 3 in EU and US).
  - Fidaxomicin – Costridium difficile (NDA filed in EU and US).
  - **ASP7373/ASP7374** – influenza vaccines (Phase 2 in Japan).
- *Oncology:*
  - MDV3100 – prostate cancer (Phase 3 in EU, US and Japan).
  - **Tivozanib** (in association with *AVEO Pharmaceuticals* of the US) – *renal cell carcinoma*, breast cancer, colorectal cancer has demonstrated superiority in Phase 3 studies over **Sorafenib** (*Bayer-Onyx*) in the US for renal cell carcinoma, indicating a large potential market, currently over US$2 billion per annum.
  - **AC220** (in association with *Ambit Biosciences*) – acute myeloid leukaemia (Phase 2 in US and EU).
  - OSI Projects – *adrenocortical carcinoma*, ovarian and *renal cancer* (Phase 3 in US).
  - Agensys Projects – renal, pancreatic and prostate cancers (Phase 1).

COMPANY SPOTLIGHT: NEKTAR THERAPEUTICS (NASDAQ: NKTR)

Nektar is a leader in *PEGylation*, particularly for the *pain/opioid* market. By tweaking existing molecules, such as Pfizer's **irinotecan** for colorectal cancer, through *PEGylation*, Nektar is overcoming the problems associated with central nervous systems and pain drugs, reducing the potential for habit-formed abuse. This is because the drug is more slowly absorbed than conventional pain drugs such as Oxycontin, thereby reducing euphoria and dependency. Dependency is a huge problem, particularly in the US, and all efforts to reduce abuse by, for instance, using tamper-resistant packaging and gummy formulations can and have been thwarted. A partnership with AstraZeneca for **NKTR-119** (moderate-to-severe pain), for instance *fibromyalgia* and *back pain*, and **NKTR-118** (opioid-induced constipation) looks particularly interesting and could yield upwards of US$500 million in upfront payments, milestone payments and royalties. Nektar also has an interesting drug in ovarian and breast cancer (**NKT-102**) which is entering Phase 3 in 2012, and is a topoisomerase 1 inhibitor with novel action. Nektar has substantial cash that easily outweighs its convertible debt, and looks to us to be an excellent investment in the pain and related sector, as well as in oncology. This company could be a real winner, and there is also the potential for it to be taken over.

Among the smaller, small or tiny, but certainly speculative, we like the following companies that offer enormous potential upside.

COMPANY SPOTLIGHT: CELLCEUTIX (OTC: CTIX)

Cellceutix, which is about as speculative as you can get, has successfully completed a series of animal model tests on two multi-drug resistant non-small-cell lung carcinoma human cell lines. These lines **A549** and **NCI-H1975** have been tested by using Cellceutix's compound Kevetrin. In each mouse cell line, tumour volume was reduced by more than 90 per cent and tumour growth was delayed by more than 100 per cent. In addition, both the tumour volume reduction and the tumour growth delay were greater in each cell line with Kevetrin than with paclitaxel, the standard of care.

Dr Krishna Menon, President and Chief Scientific Officer of Cellceutix, formerly headed up Lilly's research efforts on the very successful **Alimta** and **Gemzar** programmes. Additionally, Cellceutix is trialling **KM-133**, which it is developing for the treatment of psoriasis, a widespread disfiguring condition for which the standard of care is relatively poor. This is a very small company and any investment should be consistent with its size. Kevetrin does seem to have a novel mode of action on both mutant and wild type p53 pathways, so investors should follow the company closely.

COMPANY SPOTLIGHT: DYNAVAX (NASDAQ: DVAX)

Dynavax is a small- to medium-sized US-based company involved in the development of infectious disease treatments. Its most promising product is Hepislav, a hepatitis B vaccine in late Phase 3 trials. Hepislav has higher seroprotection and efficacy, with fewer injections required, than the current standard, **Engerix B**. One single case of a side effect was observed in trials involving over 2,500 patients, and we do not expect this particular incident to prevent the vaccine from going into relatively widespread use among adults, some time in the next few years. The market for hepatitis B vaccines is particularly large among diabetics, who are prone to the disease, and this could make Hepislav ultimately a US$500 million plus product with very high margins. As it is a biologic product, it is hard to manufacture, which means that Hepislav is unlikely to face significant competition from generics. Dynavax also has a collaboration with Astra Zeneca in asthma which holds some promise. The company is fully funded to profitability.

COMPANY SPOTLIGHT: INFINITY PHARMACEUTICALS (NASDAQ: INFI)

Infinity, a US-based biotech firm, is interesting because of its oncology pipeline, particularly in the field of pathway blocking. Infinity is developing **retaspimycin hydrochloride (HCl)**, also known as **IPI-504**, a proprietary protein 90 (Hsp90) inhibitor. Retaspimycin HCl is currently being evaluated in combination with docetaxel (Taxotere) in a Phase 2 trial in patients with non-small cell lung cancer.

Infinity has plenty of cash and alliances with Purdue Pharmaceutical and *Mundipharma International* which should take it through to trial completion, and we believe that an investment in this smaller, but interesting company merits attention.

COMPANY SPOTLIGHT: CUBIST PHARMACEUTICALS (NASDAQ: CBST) AND OPTIMER PHARMACEUTICALS (NASDAQ: OPTR)

Cubist and Optimer are both interesting US companies operating in the same anti-infective space. Cubist is a much larger company than Optimer, which is a pure play on its drug for *C. difficile associated diarrhoea* (*CDAD*) Dificid (fidaxomicin). Dificid is the only FDA-approved treatment for CDAD that has demonstrated superiority to vancomycin in sustained clinical response, and the first new drug approved for the treatment of CDAD in more than 25 years. Optimer is in partnership with Astellas, one of our favoured larger companies, for sales of Dificid in Europe and some other territories, as well as with Cubist to investigate the use of the drug in urinary tract infections.

Patients typically develop CDAD from the use of broad-spectrum antibiotics that disrupt normal gastrointestinal (gut) flora. Older people in particular are at risk for CDAD, most likely because of weakened immune systems. Approximately two-thirds of CDAD patients are 65 years of age or older. CDAD appears to affect more than 700,000 people a year in the US and has a high rate of recurrence. Optimer is worth a smaller investment over the longer term.

Cubist has a much broader portfolio in anti-infectives, including Cubicin (**daptomycin**), for skin and other MRSA-related infections, with sales of US$733 million worldwide in 2011. There remain patent lawsuits surrounding this drug, originally from Lilly, but we believe it to be well protected. In addition it has CXA-201, a *cephalosporin/beta lactamase inhibitor antibiotic* targeting resistant *pseudomonas*, with Phase 3 trials planned for 2012. Cubist is cash rich, and has an interesting early stage pipeline, as well as a useful alliance with Alnylam. We believe that it is an excellent larger scale investment in the infectious disease space.

COMPANY SPOTLIGHT: NANOVIRICIDES (OTC: NNVC)

NanoViricides is a very small and speculative company with an interesting anti-infectives angle. Recently, NanoViricides released animal test results regarding the company's HIV/AIDS drug candidate **HIVCide**, which is positioned as an alternative to *HAART (highly active retroviral treatment)* therapy, the expensive cocktail approach to dealing with HIV, a space dominated by Gilead.

NanoViricides' target is the developing world market for HIV/AIDS where drug resistance to triple cocktail drugs is rapidly emerging and where economic constraints make the current standard of care unaffordable for most patients. *Nanoviricides* are not drugs in the classical sense at all. They are a fusion of nanotech and biological components that create what are, essentially, tiny machines that kill viruses. This means that nanoviricides do not modify the biochemistry of the infected person; they simply devour and disassemble viruses. In animals, the nanotech virus killers, with their cargo of annihilated viruses, are safely excreted from the infected test animals.

One component of these *nanotech* virus killers is the *polymer micelle*. NanoViricides' *micelles*, however, are not simply *nanovesicles*. Nanovesicles are normally just enclosing structures that protect or deliver another substance to a desired destination. NanoViricides' micelles, though, are actually active parts of the nanoviricide technology. The effectiveness of the micelle is reinforced by the second component of the drug, the *ligands*. Ligands are sophisticated "signalling" molecules that bind with the molecules that the viruses use to locate their target cells, and thereby destroy them, be it the HIV product or NanoViricides' other key development compound, **FluCide**, which is set up as a vastly more potent competitor to **Tamiflu (oseltamivir)**.

NanoViricides shares are only suitable for those with strong stomachs and well-lined pockets.

COMPANY SPOTLIGHT: STAR SCIENTIFIC
(NASDAQ: CIGX)

Star Scientific is a controversial and speculative company involved in using a derivative of *nicotine, anatabine*, as a development compound in anti-Alzheimer's trials, as well as in indications for *inflammation*, including rheumatoid arthritis. The company's key product, **Antabloc**, has been trialled in animal models for rheumatoid arthritis, and appears to outperform Celebrex, Voltarol and aspirin, the standards of care. The *Roskamp Institute* has presented a comparison of well-known anti-inflammatories with **RCP006**, the designation of *anatabine citrate*, Antabloc (see Figure 36). (LPS is an endotoxin used to stimulate an inflammatory response and the inflammatory molecule is the IL-1β. Its level was measured after 16 hours of administering the anti-inflammatory being tested and Figure 36 shows that RCP006 is more than four times more effective than the leading drugs Celebrex and Voltarol in reducing inflammation.) Star Scientific is the subject of both hype and incredulity; it has somewhat unproven management and is always short of cash. However, for our money, a small amount in the shares could just – maybe just – work out big time, and we suggest that for more speculative investors, a modest position is established.

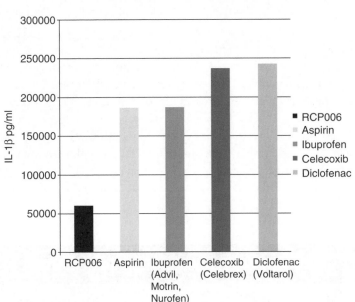

Comparison of anti-inflammatory effects (IL-1β inhibition) of RCP006 compared to NSAIDs after treatment of whole human blood with LPS

Figure 36: Comparison of anti-inflammatory effects (IL-1β inhibition) of RCP006 compared to NSAIDs after treatment of whole human blood with lipopolysaccharide (LPS).
Source: Star Scientific

COMPANY SPOTLIGHT: CYTRX CORPORATION (NASDAQ: CYTR)

CytRx is a small but interesting biopharmaceutical company specializing in oncology. CytRx recently announced initiation of Phase 2 clinical trials to evaluate its highly promising drug candidate **bafetinib** in patients with *high-risk B-cell chronic lymphocytic leukaemia* and advanced prostate cancer. CytRx also has another promising drug currently in Phase 2 clinical trials, **tamibarotene**, which is being evaluated for the treatment of *Acute Promyelocytic Leukaemia (APL)*, a disease with

(Continued)

which approximately 1,500 new patients are diagnosed in the United States annually. The market opportunity for CytRx's tamibarotene in APL for an expanded label, including *refractory*, *maintenance* and *front-line therapy*, is about US$150 million in potential recurring revenue in the US and Europe. There are currently no approved third-line treatment options for **refractory APL**. This same drug, tamibarotene, is also in Phase 2 trials for treatment of **small cell lung cancer**. Additionally, CytRx is involved in very early stage work in RNAi therapeutics for obesity and diabetes. CytRx has some cash, and we like this company as a speculative play in diseases with high unmet need.

COMPANY SPOTLIGHT: BIOTIME (AMEX: BTX)

BioTime is a company specializing in regenerative medicine, and is involved in stem cell and scaffolds for the growth of new tissues. It is the only listed company in this area that we favour, and though speculative, does really appear to have serious science behind it. BioTime has developed the *ACTCellerate* platform, which uses adult stem cells to introduce rejuvenated *endothelial precursor cells (EPCs)* into the bloodstream. Transfused into patients, these stem cells appear to have ability to engraft with the patient's own cells, and to replace the ageing cells of the cardiovascular and immune systems. BioTime uses *endothelial precursor cells* from its *ReCyte* technology, which it claims avoids the problems encountered with some types of *induced pluripotent human stem cells*.

For more complex uses of stem cells, such as in the repair of knee joints, BioTime has developed precisely shaped three-dimensional scaffolds in which stem cells can develop and integrate with the patient's own tissues. This technology is called *HyStem*, and is a matrix using modified *hyaluronic acid*, described by the company as "living cement", injectable into the body and quickly *polymerizing*. After injection, stem cells are added to the matrix scaffold.

In addition, BioTime has a collaboration agreement with Teva for the development of **OpRegen** for the treatment of age-related macular degeneration (AMD). The technology at the heart of this agreement, OpRegen, is a proprietary formulation of embryonic stem cell-derived retinal pigment epithelial cells. The US Center for Disease Control and Prevention estimates that about 1.8 million people in the United States have advanced-stage AMD and another 7.3 million have an earlier stage and are at risk of vision impairment from the disease.

We have already written at length about Arrowhead Research (Chapters 4 and 5) and AmpliPhi (Chapter 4). We are owners of these shares and recommend them as good, though speculative, investments for those who can take the long view. Another company worth looking at is UK-listed *Plethora Solutions Holdings* (LSE AIM: PLE), which has a very interesting late-stage compound for *premature ejaculation*, a large unmet clinical need. In none of these firms should investors have a concentration of risk.

In the next three sections, we have created three "portfolios" for investors to consider based on their risk appetite: a conservative portfolio, a balanced portfolio and an outright speculative portfolio.

Conservative Portfolio

Table 6 shows our suggested portfolio of companies for conservative investors.

Table 6: Suggested conservative portfolio

	Company name	Approximate allocation within portfolio (%)
1	*Allergan*	8
2	*Alnylam*	8
3	*Amgen*	8
4	*Astellas*	8
5	*Biogen-Idec*	8
6	*GlaxoSmithKline*	8
7	*Johnson & Johnson*	8
8	*Medicis*	8
9	*Pfizer*	8
10	*Roche*	8
11	*Shire*	8
12	*Arrowhead Research*	3
13	*Complete Genomics*	3
14	*Infinity*	3
15	*Medivation*	3

Balanced Portfolio

Table 7 shows our suggested balanced portfolio.

Table 7: Suggested balanced portfolio

	Company name	Approximate allocation within portfolio (%)
1	*Alnylam*	6.5
2	*Amgen*	6.5
3	*Astellas*	6.5
4	*Celgene*	6.5
5	*Forest Labs*	6.5
6	*Gilead*	6.5
7	*GlaxoSmithKline*	6.5

	Company name	Approximate allocation within portfolio (%)
8	*ISIS*	6.5
9	*Pfizer*	6.5
10	*Rigel*	6.5
11	*Roche*	6.5
12	*Shire*	6.5
13	*Vertex*	6.5
14	*AmpliPhi*	3.25
15	*Arrowhead Research*	3.25
16	*Complete Genomics*	3.25
17	*Medivation*	3.25
18	*NanoViricides*	3.25

Speculative Portfolio

Table 8 is our suggested portfolio for aggressive and speculative investors.

Table 8: Suggested speculative portfolio

	Company name	Approximate allocation within portfolio (%)
1	*Alnylam*	5
2	*AmpliPhi*	5
3	*Arrowhead Research*	5
4	*BioTime*	5
5	*Cellceutix*	5
6	*Complete Genomics*	5
7	*Cubist*	5
8	*CytRx*	5
9	*Dynavax*	5

(Continued)

Table 8: (*Continued*)

	Company name	Approximate allocation within portfolio (%)
10	*Infinity*	5
11	*Isis*	5
12	*Medivation*	5
13	*NanoViricides*	5
14	*Nektar*	5
15	*Optimer*	5
16	*Pacific Biosciences*	5
17	*Pharmacyclics*	5
18	*Rigel*	5
19	*Star Scientific*	5
20	*Vertex*	5

Company Overviews

Table 9 contains an overview of most of the companies that we mention in this book. Where relevant, we include each company's ticker symbol and stock exchange, as well as some financial data. The market capitalization and revenue figures were correct at the end of February 2012, so they may well have changed by the time you read them. Nevertheless, the figures provide a good general picture of the size of each company and whether it has an existing revenue stream. What we believe will also be valuable to you is the summary of the types of drugs each company currently has on the market along with their respective patent expiry dates and revenue generated by each product. Also included are the drugs currently undergoing clinical trials, which gives a good indication of potential future revenue for each company should they reach the market successfully.

Table 9: Overview of companies mentioned in this book

Company	Ticker	Exchange	Revenue	Market Cap.	PE Ratio	Div. Yield	Top Drugs / Products	Status	Description	Patent Expiration	Annual Sales	% of Revenue
Allergan Inc./ United States	AGN	New York	$5.4b	$26.7b	26.3 x	0.23%	Botox/ Neuromodulator	On Market	Cosmetic and Muscle Spasm	N/A	$1.42b	28.9%
Allergan Inc. is a global speciality pharmaceutical company that develops products for the eye care, neuromodulator, skin care and other speciality markets.							Restasis	On Market	Immunosuppressive – Transplants	2009	$0.62b	12.6%
							Lumigan	On Market	Glaucoma and Ocular Hypertension	2014	$0.53b	10.7%
							Alphagen P, Alphagen and Combigan	On Market	Glaucoma and Ocular Hypertension	2012	$0.40b	8.2%
Astellas Pharma Inc.	4503	Tokyo	$11.2b	$18.8b	19.9 x	3.86%	Prograf	On Market	Immunosuppressive – Transplants	2011	$1.90b	17.0%
Astellas Pharma Inc. manufactures and markets a wide variety of pharmaceuticals including prescription drugs. The company also produces food supplements, health foods and personal care products.							Lipitor	On Market	Cholesterol	2011	$1.14b	10.2%
							Vesicare	On Market	Incontinence	2015	$1.01b	9.1%
							Micardis	On Market	Hypertension	2014	$0.89b	7.9%
							Harnal	On Market	Benign Prostatic Hypertrophy	2007	$0.78b	7.0%

(*Continued*)

Table 9: (*Continued*)

Company	Ticker	Exchange	Revenue	Market Cap.	PE Ratio	Div. Yield	Top Drugs / Products	Status	Description	Patent Expiration	Annual Sales	% of Revenue
GlaxoSmithKline PLC	GSK	London	$43.9b	$112.5b	13.4 x	5.54%	Seretide/Advair	On Market	Asthma	2015	$7.94b	18.1%
GSK is a research-based pharmaceutical company. The company develops, manufactures and markets vaccines, prescription and over the counter medicines as well as health-related consumer products. Products address areas which include infections, depression, skin conditions, asthma, heart and circulatory disease, and cancer.							Flu-prepandemic	On Market	Avian Flu	Unknown	$1.84b	4.2%
							Avodart	On Market	Benign Prostatic Hyperplasia	2013	$0.97b	2.2%
							Epzicom/Kivexa	On Market	HIV	2012	$0.86b	2.0%
Johnson & Johnson	JNJ	New York	$65.0b	$176.9b	12.9 x	3.54%	Remicade	On Market	Autoimmune Disease	2011	$4.61b	7.5%
Johnson & Johnson manufactures healthcare products and provides related services for the consumer, pharmaceutical and medical devices and diagnostics markets. The company sells products such as skin and hair care products, acetaminophen products, pharmaceuticals, diagnostic equipment and surgical equipment in countries located around the world.							Procrit	On Market	Anaemia and Chronic Kidney Disease	2013	$1.90b	3.1%
							Risperdal	On Market	Anti-psychotic	2007	$1.50b	2.4%
							Levaquin	On Market	Antibiotic	2011	$1.40b	2.3%
							Concerta	On Market	Attention Deficit Hyperactivity Disorder	2018	$1.30b	2.1%

Merck & Co. Inc.	MRK	New York	$48.0b	$116.7b	10.2 x	4.39%	Singulair	On Market	Asthma	2012	$4.99b	10.8%

Merck & Co. Inc. is a global pharmaceutical company that discovers, develops, manufactures and markets a broad range of human and animal health products. Merck's products include a treatment for elevated cholesterol, a treatment for male pattern hair loss, a preventive treatment for osteoporosis, a treatment for hypertension and a treatment for allergic rhinitis.

Product	Status	Indication	Year	Revenue	%
Remicade	On Market	Autoimmune Disease	2018	$2.71b	5.9%
Januvia	On Market	Diabetes – Type 2	2022	$2.39b	5.2%
Zetia	On Market	Cholesterol	2014	$2.30b	5.0%
Cozaar/Hyzaar	On Market	Hypertension	2009	$2.10b	4.6%

Novartis AG	NOVN	SIX Swiss Ex	$58.6b	$158.1b	15.0 x	4.37%	Diovan/Co-Diovan	On Market	Hypertension	2012	$6.05b	12.0%

Novartis manufactures pharmaceutical and consumer healthcare products. The company produces pharmaceuticals for cardiovascular, respiratory and infectious diseases, oncology, neuroscience, transplantation, dermatology, gastrointestinal and urinary conditions, arthritis, vaccines and diagnostics, vision and animal health products.

Product	Status	Indication	Year	Revenue	%
Gleevec/Glivec	On Market	Cancer – Gastro and Leukaemia	2015	$4.27b	8.4%
Lucentis	On Market	Macular Edema	2014	$1.53b	3.0%
Zometa	On Market	Osteoporosis	2007	$1.51b	3.0%
Femara	On Market	Cancer – Breast	2011	$1.38b	2.7%

Novo Nordisk A/S	NOVO	Copenhagen	$12.4b	$83.4b	26.2 x	1.76%	Novolog	On Market	Diabetes	2014	$1.39b	11.2%

Novo Nordisk develops, produces and markets pharmaceutical products. It focuses on diabetes care and offers insulin delivery systems and other diabetes products. Novo Nordisk also works in areas such as haemostatis management, growth disorders and hormone replacement therapy.

Product	Status	Indication	Year	Revenue	%
Levemir	On Market	Diabetes	2015	$1.23b	9.9%
Victoza	On Market	Diabetes	2015	$0.41b	3.3%

(Continued)

Table 9: (*Continued*)

Company	Ticker	Exchange	Revenue	Market Cap.	PE Ratio	Div. Yield	Top Drugs / Products	Status	Description	Patent Expiration	Annual Sales	% of Revenue
Pfizer Inc.	PFE	New York	$67.4b	$163.8b	9.2 x	4.13%	Lipitor	On Market	Cholesterol	2011	$10.73b	15.8%
Pfizer Inc. is a research based, global pharmaceutical company that discovers, develops, manufactures and markets medicines for humans and animals. The company's products include prescription pharmaceuticals, non-prescription self-medications and animal health products such as anti-infective medicines and vaccines.							Enbrel	On Market	Arthritis	Biologic Drug*	$3.27b	4.8%
							Lyrica	On Market	Neuropath Pain and Anxiety Disorders	2018	$3.06b	4.5%
							Celebrex	On Market	Anti-inflammatory – Arthritis	2014	$2.37b	3.5%
							Viagra	On Market	Erectile Dysfunction	2012	$1.93b	2.8%
Roche Holding AG	ROG	SIX Swiss Ex	$48.2b	$154.7b	14.5 x	4.27%	Avastin	On Market	Cancer – Colorectal, Lung, Kidney	2017	$6.22b	13.6%
Roche is the world leader in in-vitro diagnostics and drugs for cancer, transplantation, autoimmune disease, inflammatory disease, virology, metabolic disorders and diseases of the central nervous system (CNS).							MabThera	On Market	Immunosuppressive	2015	$6.11b	13.4%
							Herceptin	On Market	Cancer – Breast	2019	$5.22b	11.4%
							Pegasys	On Market	Anti-viral	2017	$1.58b	3.5%
							Lucentis	On Market	Macular Edema	2014	$1.40b	3.1%

Sanofi	SAN	EN Paris	$46.5b	$101.7b	13.1 x	4.71%	Lantus	On Market	Diabetes – Types 1 and 2	2009	$4.66b	11.6%
Sanofi is a global pharmaceutical company that researches, develops and manufactures prescription pharmaceuticals and vaccines. The company develops cardiovascular, thrombosis, metabolic disorder, CNS, internal medicine and oncology drugs and vaccines.							Lovenox	On Market	Deep Vein Thrombosis	2012	$3.72b	9.2%
							Taxotere	On Market	Cancer – Breast, Ovarian, Prostate, Lung	2010	$2.82b	7.0%
							Plavix	On Market	Coronary Artery Disease	2012	$2.76b	6.9%
							Aprovel	On Market	Hypertension	2012	$1.76b	4.4%
Teva Pharmaceutical Industries	TEVA	NASDAQ GS	$18.3b	$42.2b	N/A	2.38%	Copaxone	On Market	Multiple Sclerosis	2014	$3.32b	20.6%
Teva Pharmaceutical is a global pharmaceutical company that develops, manufactures and markets generic and branded pharmaceuticals as well as active pharmaceutical ingredients.							Azilect	On Market	Parkinson's Disease	2012	$0.32b	2.0%
Large Biotech Companies												
Acorda Therapeutics Inc.	ACOR	NASDAQ GS	$292.2m	$1.0b	43.1 x	0.00%	Ampyra	On Market	Multiple Sclerosis	2011	$0.13b	69.7%
Acorda Therapeutics Inc. is a biotechnology company that is developing therapies for spinal cord injury and related neurological conditions including multiple sclerosis. It is also developing multiple approaches to regeneration and repair of the spinal cord and brain.							Zanaflex	On Market	Multiple Sclerosis	2021	$0.05b	25.4%

(Continued)

Table 9: (*Continued*)

Company	Ticker	Exchange	Revenue	Market Cap.	PE Ratio	Div. Yield	Top Drugs / Products	Status	Description	Patent Expiration	Annual Sales	% of Revenue
Alnylam Pharmaceuticals Inc.	ALNY	NASDAQ GS	$82.8m	$685.8m	N/A	0.00%	PF 4523655	Ph II	Diabetes	N/A	N/A	N/A
Alnylam Pharmaceuticals Inc. is an early stage therapeutics company developing technology that can specifically and potently silence disease-causing genes.							ALN RSV01	Ph II	Respiratory Syncytial Virus Infections	N/A	N/A	N/A
							QPI 1002	Ph II	Kidney Disease	N/A	N/A	N/A
Amgen Inc.	AMGN	NASDAQ GS	$15.6b	$54.1b	13.8 x	2.12%	Neulasta	On Market	White Blood Cell Production	2015	$3.56b	23.6%
Amgen Inc. pioneered the development of innovative products based on advances in recombinant DNA and molecular biology. The company introduced two of the first biologically derived human therapeutics (Epoetin alfa and Filgrastim) for the treatment of chronic kidney disease and cancer. Today Amgen has expanded its product base to address anaemia, rheumatoid arthritis and other autoimmune diseases such as psoriatic arthritis and ankylosing spondylitis.							Enbrel	On Market	Arthritis	Biologic Drug*	$3.53b	23.5%
							Epogen	On Market	Anaemia	2011	$2.52b	16.8%
Amgen has 44 products in its clinical pipeline, which includes antibodies, small molecule drugs and proteins/peptides.							Aranesp	On Market	Anaemia	2024	$2.49b	16.5%
							Neupogen	On Market	White Blood Cell Production	2013	$1.29b	8.5%
Amylin Pharmaceuticals Inc.	AMLN	NASDAQ GS	$650.7m	$2.6b	N/A	0.00%	Byetta	On Market	Diabetes: Type 2	2013	$0.56b	83.6%
Amylin is a biopharmaceutical company focused on the therapeutic potential of new peptide hormone drug candidates and the creation of novel therapies for the treatment of diabetes, obesity and other metabolic diseases.							Symlin	On Market	Diabetes: Types 1 and 2	2014	$0.09b	13.7%
							Exenatide	Ph III	Diabetes: Type 2	N/A	N/A	N/A

Company	Ticker	Exchange					Product	Status	Indication	Year	Revenue	%
Biogen Idec Inc.	BIIB	NASDAQ GS	$5.0b	$27.8b	22.5 x	0.00%	Avonex	On Market	Multiple Sclerosis	2013	$2.50b	49.5%
							Tysabri	On Market	Multiple Sclerosis and Crohn's Disease	2017	$1.20b	23.8%
							Rituxan (sold through Roche)	On Market	Non-Hodgkin's Lymphoma and Arthritis	2015	N/A	N/A
							Fampridine	Ph III	Multiple Sclerosis	N/A	N/A	N/A
Celgene Corp.	CELG	NASDAQ GS	$4.8b	$33.0b	24.5 x	0.00%	Revlimid	On Market	Multiple Myeloma	2016	$2.47b	68.1%
							Vidaza	On Market	Myelodysplastic Syndrome	2011	$0.53b	14.7%
							Thalomid	On Market	Multiple Myeloma	2013	$0.39b	10.7%
							Abraxane	On Market	Cancer – Breast	2013	$0.07b	2.0%
							Istodax	On Market	Cancer	2010	$0.02b	0.4%
Cubist Pharmaceuticals Inc.	CBST	NASDAQ GS	$754.0m	$2.7b	26.3 x	0.00%	Cubicin	On Market	Antibiotic	2016	$0.63b	0.1%
							CXA-201	Ph III	Urinary Tract Infection and Abdominal Infection	N/A	N/A	N/A
							CB-183	Ph II	Clostridium difficile-associated diarrhea	N/A	N/A	N/A

Biogen Idec Inc. develops, manufactures and commercializes therapies focusing on neurology, oncology and immunology. The company's products address diseases such as multiple sclerosis, non-Hodgkin's lymphoma, rheumatoid arthritis, Crohn's disease and psoriasis.

Celgene Corporation is a global biopharmaceutical company focused on the discovery, development and commercialization of therapies designed to treat cancer and immune-inflammatory related diseases.

Cubist Pharmaceuticals is a drug company that discovers, develops and commercializes novel drugs to treat infections. The company's lead product is a unique agent with bacterial activity that addresses the critical need for new antibiotics with potent activity against life-threatening infections.

(Continued)

Table 9: (*Continued*)

Company	Ticker	Exchange	Revenue	Market Cap.	PE Ratio	Div. Yield	Top Drugs / Products	Status	Description	Patent Expiration	Annual Sales	% of Revenue
Forest Laboratories Inc.	FRX	New York	$4.4b	$8.6b	7.8 x	0.00%	Lexapro	On Market	Major Depressive Disorder	2011	$2.32b	52.9%
							Namenda	On Market	Alzheimer's Disease	2014	$1.27b	28.9%
							Bystolic	On Market	Hypertension	2015	$0.26b	6.0%
Forest Laboratories develops, manufactures and sells both branded and generic prescription and non-prescription drugs.												
Gilead Sciences Inc.	GILD	NASDAQ GS	$8.4b	$34.1b	12.5 x	0.00%	Atripla	On Market	HIV	2010	$2.93b	36.8%
							Truvada	On Market	HIV	2010	$2.65b	33.3%
							Viread	On Market	HIV	2017	$0.73b	9.2%
							AmBisome	On Market	Fungal Infection	2016	$0.31b	3.8%
							Letairis	On Market	Hypertension	2014	$0.24b	3.0%
Gilead Sciences Inc. is a research-based biopharmaceutical company that discovers, develops and commercializes therapeutics to advance the care of patients suffering from life-threatening diseases. The company's primary areas of focus include HIV/AIDS, liver disease and serious cardiovascular and respiratory conditions.												
Honda Motor Co. Ltd	7267	Tokyo	$104.6b	$69.2b	25.6 x	1.94%	N/A	N/A	N/A	N/A	N/A	N/A
							N/A	N/A	N/A	N/A	N/A	N/A
							N/A	N/A	N/A	N/A	N/A	N/A
Honda Motor Co. Ltd develops manufactures and distributes motorcycles, automobiles and power products such as farm machinery. More recently Honda has moved into the development of humanoid robots and associated technology.												

Isis Pharmaceuticals Inc.	ISIS	NASDAQ GS	$108.5m	$882.6m	N/A	0.00%	Custirsen	Ph III	Cancer – Lung	N/A	N/A	N/A
Isis Pharmaceuticals Inc. discovers and develops novel human therapeutic compounds for diseases that include Crohn's disease, psoriasis, asthma and cancer.							Mipomersen	Ph III	Cholesterol	N/A	N/A	N/A
							Alicaforsen	Ph III	Rheumatoid Arthritis	N/A	N/A	N/A
Medicis Pharmaceutical Corp.	MRX	New York	$700.0m	$2.1b	16.0 x	0.94%	Dysport	On Market	Cosmetics and Muscle Spasm	No Patent	No Details	N/A
Medicis Pharmaceutical Corporation provides pharmaceuticals focusing on the treatment of dermatological, paediatric and podiatric conditions, as well as aesthetic medicine. The company has branded prescription products in therapeutic categories such as acne, asthma, eczema, fungal infections, hyperpigmentation, photoaging, psoriasis and rosacea.							Perlane	On Market	Cosmetics – Wrinkles	2017	No Details	N/A
							Restylane	On Market	Cosmetics – Wrinkles	2015	No Details	N/A
							Solodyn	On Market	Antibiotic	2018	No Details	N/A
							Vanos	On Market	Atopic Dermatitis and Psoriasis	2021	No Details	N/A
Medivation Inc.	MDVN	NASDAQ GM	$62.5m	$2.3b	N/A	0.00%	MDV 3100	Ph III	Cancer – Prostate	N/A	N/A	N/A
Medivation Inc. acquires, develops and sells or partners biomedical technologies in the early development stage of the research and development process.							Dimebon (latrepirdine)	Ph III	Alzheimer's Disease	N/A	N/A	N/A
Merrimack Pharmaceuticals Inc.	MACK	NASDAQ GM	$20.3m	Est. $800m–1b	N/A	N/A	MM-121	Ph II	Cancer – Multiple Indications	N/A	N/A	N/A
Merrimack Pharmaceuticals Inc. is a biotechnology company focused on the discovery and development of drugs using computer models for the treatment of cancer and immunological and autoimmune diseases.							MM-111	Ph I	Cancer – Breast, Lung and Stomach	N/A	N/A	N/A
							MM-398	Ph II	Cancer – Multiple Indications	N/A	N/A	N/A

(Continued)

Table 9: *(Continued)*

Company	Ticker	Exchange	Revenue	Market Cap.	PE Ratio	Div. Yield	Top Drugs / Products	Status	Description	Patent Expiration	Annual Sales	% of Revenue
Nektar Therapeutics	NKTR	NASDAQ GS	$159.0m	$798.7m	N/A	0.00%	Cimzia	On Market	Rheumatoid Arthritis	N/A	N/A	N/A
							NKTR-118	Ph III	Opioid Induced Constipation	N/A	N/A	N/A
							NKTR-102	Ph II	Cancer – Breast, Colorectal and Ovarian	N/A	N/A	N/A
Nektar Therapeutics is a clinical stage biopharmaceutical company that is developing drugs for therapeutic areas including oncology, pain, anti-infectives, anti-viral and immunology.												
Optimer Pharmaceuticals Inc.	OPTR	NASDAQ GS	$1.5m	$590.5m	N/A	0.00%	Dificid	On Market	Antibiotic	N/A	N/A	N/A
							Prulifloxacin	Ph III	Infectious Diarrhoea	N/A	N/A	N/A
							OPT-822 / 821	Ph II	Breast Cancer	N/A	N/A	N/A
Optimer Pharmaceuticals Inc. discovers, develops and commercializes anti-infective products. Optimer's initial development efforts address products that treat gastrointestinal infections and related diseases including diminished efficacy, serious adverse side effects, drug-to-drug interactions, difficult patient compliance and bacterial resistance.												
Savient Pharmaceuticals Inc.	SVNT	NASDAQ GM	$4.0m	$155,093.0m	N/A	0.00%	Oxandrin	On Market	Anabolic Steroid	2012	N/A	N/A
							Krystexxa	On Market	Gout	Biologic drug*	N/A	N/A
							AST 120	Ph III	Hepatic Encephalopathy	N/A	N/A	N/A
Savient Pharmaceuticals Inc. develops, manufactures and markets human healthcare products. The company offers pharmaceutical products for a wide range of medical needs such as weight gain, drugs targeting the control of elevated uric acid levels in the blood and rheumatology.												

Company	Ticker	Location	Col1	Col2	Col3	Col4	Product	Status	Indication	Year	Value	Percentage
Shire PLC	SHP	London	$3.5b	$17.9b	25.8 x	0.41%	Vyvanse	On Market	Attention Deficit Hyperactivity Disorder	2023	$0.63b	18.35%
							Lialda/Pentasa	On Market	Ulcerative Colitis and Crohn's Disease	2020	$0.53b	15.31%
							Elaprase	On Market	Enzyme Replacement Therapy	2019	$0.40b	11.68%
							Adderall XR	On Market	Attention Deficit Hyperactivity Disorder	2018	$0.36b	10.44%
Shire PLC markets, licenses and develops prescription medicines. The group focuses its operations on attention deficit and hyperactivity disorder, human genetic therapies, gastrointestinal and renal disease.												
Sinopharm Group Co. Ltd	1099	Hong Kong	$10.2b	$6.5b	32.2 x	0.91%	N/A	N/A	N/A	N/A	N/A	N/A
							N/A	N/A	N/A	N/A	N/A	N/A
							N/A	N/A	N/A	N/A	N/A	N/A
							N/A	N/A	N/A	N/A	N/A	N/A
Sinopharm Group Co. Ltd is a pharmacy distribution company. It also owns several pharmacy enterprise groups in different industries such as logistics, retail stores, pharmaceutical manufacturing and chemical testing.												
Stryker Corp.	SYK	New York	$8.3b	$20.8b	14.7 x	1.55%	Reconstructive Orthopaedic Implants	On Market	N/A	N/A	$3.55b	42.72%
							MedSurg Equipment	On Market	N/A	N/A	$2.80b	33.74%
							Neurotech and Spine	On Market	N/A	N/A	$0.97b	11.66%
Stryker Corporation develops, manufactures and markets speciality surgical and medical products. The company's products include implants; biologics; surgical, neurologic, ear, nose and throat, and interventional pain equipment; endoscopic, surgical navigation, communications and digital imaging systems; as well as patient handling and emergency medical equipment.												

(Continued)

Table 9: (*Continued*)

Company	Ticker	Exchange	Revenue	Market Cap.	PE Ratio	Div. Yield	Top Drugs / Products	Status	Description	Patent Expiration	Annual Sales	% of Revenue
Vertex Pharmaceuticals Inc.	VRTX	NASDAQ GS	$143.4m	$8.5b	N/A	0.00%	INCIVEK	On Market	Hepatitis C	2025	N/A	N/A
Vertex Pharmaceuticals Inc. discovers, develops and commercializes novel small molecule pharmaceuticals for the treatment of viral diseases, multidrug resistance in cancer, inflammatory and autoimmune diseases and neurodegenerative diseases.							VX-770	Ph III	Cystic Fibrosis	N/A	N/A	N/A
							VX-509	Ph II	Immune-mediated Inflammatory Disease	N/A	N/A	N/A
							VX-765	Ph II	Epilepsy	N/A	N/A	N/A
Biotech Companies												
AmpliPhi Biosciences Corp.	APHB	OTC US	$12.2m	$3.7m	2.0 x	0.00%	BioPhage-PA	Ph II	Otitis	N/A	N/A	N/A
AmpliPhi Biosciences Corporation is a biotechnology company developing and commercializing therapies for the prevention and treatment of diseases using bacteriophage based products.							BioPhage-PR	Pre	Cystic Fibrosis	N/A	N/A	N/A
Anthera Pharmaceuticals Inc.	ANTH	NASDAQ GM	$0.0m	$299.4m	N/A	0.00%	A-002	Ph III	Acute Coronary Syndrome	N/A	N/A	N/A
Anthera Pharmaceuticals Inc. is a biopharmaceutical company focused on developing and commercializing anti-inflammatory therapeutics for cardiovascular diseases, lupus and other serious diseases.							A-623	Ph II	Systemic Lupus Erythematosus	N/A	N/A	N/A
							A-001	Ph II	Acute Chest Syndrome	N/A	N/A	N/A
							A-003	Ph I	Multiple Indications	N/A	N/A	N/A

Company	Ticker	Exchange					Product	Phase	Indication			
Arrowhead Research Corp.	ARWR	NASDAQ CM	$0.3m	$54.4m	N/A	0.00%	Rondel	Ph I	siRNA Delivery Technology	N/A	N/A	N/A
Arrowhead Research Corporation is conducting research projects in the area of the development of nanotechnologies and applications with the California Institute of Technology.							Ablaris	Ph I	Obesity	N/A	N/A	N/A
							Nanotope	Pre	Spinal Cord, Bone and Cartilage Regeneration	N/A	N/A	N/A
							Leonardo	Pre	Drug Delivery Technology	N/A	N/A	N/A
AVI BioPharma Inc.	AVII	NASDAQ GM	$29.4m	$139.8m	N/A	0.00%	Eteplirsen	Ph II	Duchenne Muscular Dystrophy	N/A	N/A	N/A
AVI BioPharma Inc. is a biopharmaceutical company that develops and commercializes products principally based on third generation NEUGENE antisense technology for the treatment of cardiovascular and infectious diseases.							AVI 4126	Ph II	Coronary Disease	N/A	N/A	N/A
Basilea Pharmaceutica	BSLN	SIX Swiss Ex	$75.5m	$526.3m	N/A	0.00%	Toctino	On Market	Eczema	N/A	$28.1m	37.18%
Basilea Pharmaceutica AG is a biotechnology company conducting research into the development of drugs for the treatment of infectious diseases and dermatological problems. The company develops anti-bacterial and anti-fungal compounds that destroy infectious organisms.							Ceftobiprole	Ph III	Antibiotic	N/A	N/A	N/A
							Isavuconazole	Ph III	Antifungal	N/A	N/A	N/A
Biondvax Pharmaceuticals Ltd	BNDX	Tel Aviv	$0.0m	$18.5m	N/A	0.00%	Influenza Vaccine	Ph II	Human Influenza	N/A	N/A	N/A
Trojantec is a biopharmaceutical company focused on identifying, licensing and developing innovative oncology therapeutics.												

(Continued)

Table 9: (Continued)

Company	Ticker	Exchange	Revenue	Market Cap.	PE Ratio	Div. Yield	Top Drugs / Products	Status	Description	Patent Expiration	Annual Sales	% of Revenue
BioTime Inc.	BTX	NYSE Amex	$3.7m	$263.8m	N/A	0.00%	Hextend and PentaLyte	On Market	Blood Plasma Expander	N/A	N/A	N/A
BioTime Inc. researches and develops synthetic solutions that can be used as blood plasma volume expanders, blood replacement solutions during hypothermic surgery and organ preservation solutions. The company also operates in the regenerative medicine sector where it develops stem cell related products and technology for diagnostic, therapeutic and research use.							bES	Pre	Human Embryonic Stem Cells	N/A	N/A	N/A
							iPS	Pre	Induced Pluripotent Stem Cells	N/A	N/A	N/A
							Extracel	Pre	Orthopaedic Disease	N/A	N/A	N/A
Cellceutix Corp.	CTIX	OTC BB	$0.0m	$47.7m	N/A	0.00%	Kevertrin	Pre	Cancer	N/A	N/A	N/A
Cellceutix Corporation is a development stage biopharmaceutical company that develops treatment for cancer.							KM-391	Pre	Autism	N/A	N/A	N/A
							KM-133	Pre	Psoriasis	N/A	N/A	N/A
Curis Inc.	CRIS	NASDAQ GM	$14.8m	$345.4m	N/A	0.00%	Vismodegib	Ph II	Basal Cell Nevus Syndrome	N/A	N/A	N/A
Curis Inc. develops therapeutics for the regeneration and restoration of human tissues.							CUDC 101	Ph I	Cancer – Lung	N/A	N/A	N/A
							Debio 0932	Ph I	Lymphoma	N/A	N/A	N/A

Dynavax Technologies Corp.	DVAX	NASDAQ CM	$24.0m	$632.8m	N/A	0.00%	Hepatitis B Vaccine	Ph III	Hepatitis B	N/A	N/A	N/A
Dynavax Technologies discovers, develops and is seeking to commercialize products based on immunostimulatory sequences. The company is developing products to treat and prevent allergies, infectious diseases and chronic inflammatory diseases using approaches that alter immune system responses in specific ways.							1018 ISS	Ph II	Non-Hodgkin's Lymphoma	N/A	N/A	N/A
Genomic Health Inc.	GHDX	NASDAQ GS	$206.1m	$855.0m	115.8 x	0.00%	Oncotype DX	On Market	Cancer Diagnostics – Breast, Colon and Prostate	N/A	$206.11b	100.00%
Genomic Health Inc. is a life science company focused on the development and commercialization of genomic-based clinical diagnostic tests for cancer. The company's diagnostic services provide information on the likelihood of disease recurrence and response to certain types of therapy.												
Hansen Medical Inc.	HNSN	NASDAQ GM	$22.1m	$191.4m	N/A	0.00%	Magellan Robotic System	On Market	Endovascular Surgery	N/A	N/A	N/A
Hansen Medical Inc. develops and manufactures medical robotics designed for positioning, manipulation and control of catheters and catheter-based technologies.							Sensei X Robotic Catheter System	On Market	Catheter Based Procedures	N/A	N/A	N/A
Infinity Pharmaceuticals Inc.	INFI	NASDAQ GS	$71.3m	$186.8m	N/A	0.00%	IPI-926	Ph II	Cancer – Pancreatic	N/A	N/A	N/A
Infinity Pharmaceuticals Inc. researches and develops cancer drugs. The company uses small molecule drug technologies in the development of its products.							Hsp90	Ph II	Cancer – Lung	N/A	N/A	N/A
							IPI-940	Ph I	Inflammation	N/A	N/A	N/A

(Continued)

Table 9: *(Continued)*

Company	Ticker	Exchange	Revenue	Market Cap.	PE Ratio	Div. Yield	Top Drugs / Products	Status	Description	Patent Expiration	Annual Sales	% of Revenue
Intuitive Surgical Inc.	ISRG	NASDAQ GS	$1.8b	$20.1b	41.6 x	0.00%	da Vinci System	On Market	Robotic Surgery	N/A	$0.66b	46.73%
Intuitive Surgical Inc. designs, manufactures and markets surgical systems. The company's surgical system controls Intuitive Surgical endoscopic instruments, including rigid endoscopes, blunt and sharp endoscopic dissectors, scissors, scalpels, forceps/pickups, needle holders, endoscopic retractors, electrocautery, ultrasonic cutters and accessories during surgical procedures.												
iRobot Corp.	IRBT	NASDAQ GS	$465.5m	$716.6m	19.8 x	0.00%	Home Robots	On Market	Vacuums and Floor Washers	N/A	$0.23b	49.27%
iRobot Corporation manufactures robots that vacuum and wash floors, and perform battlefield reconnaissance and bomb disposal. The company markets its products to consumers through retailers and to the US Military and other government agencies worldwide.							Government and Industrial	On Market	Bomb Disposal & Surveilance	N/A	$0.17b	36.86%
Keryx Biopharmaceuticals Inc.	KERX	NASDAQ CM	$0.0m	$229.4m	N/A	0.00%	KRX-0401	Ph III	Multiple Myeloma	N/A	N/A	N/A
Keryx Biopharmaceuticals Inc. is a biopharmaceutical company focused on the acquisition, development and commercialization of novel pharmaceutical products for the treatment of life-threatening diseases, including diabetes and cancer. Keryx is developing KRX-101 (sulodexide), a novel first-in-class oral heparinoid compound for the treatment of diabetic nephropathy.							Zerenex	Ph III	Erectile Dysfunction	N/A	N/A	N/A

Company	Ticker	Exchange				Product	Phase	Indication			
MAKO Surgical Corp.	MAKO	NASDAQ GS	$44.3m	$1.5b	N/A	0.00%	MAKOplasty	On Market	Osteoarthritis	N/A	N/A	N/A
MAKO Surgical Corporation is a medical device company that offers robotic arm solutions and implants for minimally invasive orthopedic knee procedures.											
MannKind Corp.	MNKD	NASDAQ GM	$0.1m	$371.4m	N/A	0.00%	Insulin Inhalation	Ph III	Diabetes: K327 Type 1	N/A	N/A	N/A
						MKC 1106-MT	Ph II	Melanoma	N/A	N/A	N/A
MannKind Corporation is a biopharmaceutical company focused on the development and commercialization of therapeutic products for diseases such as diabetes, cancer, inflammatory and autoimmune disease.											
Methylgene Inc.	MYG	Toronto	$2.3m	$93.9m	N/A	0.00%	MGCD265	Ph I	Cancer	N/A	N/A	N/A
						MGCD290	Ph I	Fungal Infections	N/A	N/A	N/A
						MGCD0103	Ph II	Cancer	N/A	N/A	N/A
MethylGene Inc. is a biopharmaceutical company that discovers, develops, and commercializes novel therapeutics with an initial focus on cancer and infectious diseases.											
NanoViricides Inc.	NNVC	OTC BB	$0.0m	$110.6m	N/A	0.00%	FluCide-I	Pre	Bird Flu	N/A	N/A	N/A
						HIVCide-I	Pre	HIV/AIDS	N/A	N/A	N/A
						EKC-Cide-I	Pre	External Eye Viral Disease	N/A	N/A	N/A
NanoViricides Inc. is a biopharmaceutical company that researches treatments for viruses such as AIDS/HIV, hepatitis C, influenza and Asian bird flu.											
Navidea Biopharmaceuticals Inc.	NAVB	NYSE Amex	$0.6m	$297.0m	N/A	0.00%	Gamma Detection Device	On Market	Intraoperative Lymphatic Mapping	N/A	N/A	N/A
						Lymphoseek	Pre	Lymphatic Tissue Tracing Agent	N/A	N/A	N/A
						RIGScan CR	Pre	Tumor Specific Targeting Agent	N/A	N/A	N/A
Navidea Biopharmaceuticals Inc. researches and develops a system for the diagnosis and treatment of cancer. The company develops gamma radiation detection instrumentation used in the application of intraoperative lymphatic mapping and development activities related to an activated cellular therapy methodology for the treatment of certain cancers and viral diseases.											

(Continued)

Table 9: (Continued)

Company	Ticker	Exchange	Revenue	Market Cap.	PE Ratio	Div. Yield	Top Drugs / Products	Status	Description	Patent Expiration	Annual Sales	% of Revenue
Neuralstem Inc.	CUR	NYSE Amex	$0.7m	$56.5m	N/A	0.00%	Neuralstem Cell Therapy	Ph I	Amyotrophic Lateral Sclerosis and Chronic Spinal Cord Injury	N/A	N/A	N/A
Neuralstem Inc. is a biotherapeutics company utilizing its Human Neural Stem Cell technology to develop cures for diseases of the central nervous system (CNS).							NSI-189	Ph I	Depression	N/A	N/A	N/A
NicOx SA	COX	EN Paris	$9.8m	$183.0m	N/A	0.00%	BOL 303259X	Ph II	Glaucoma	N/A	N/A	N/A
NicOx develops pharmaceuticals using recently discovered properties of nitric oxide. The company develops drug candidates for the potential treatment of inflammatory, cardiometabolic and ophthalmological diseases.							NLA Nasal Spray	Ph II	Rhinitis	N/A	N/A	N/A
							NCX 6560	Ph I	Myocardial Ischemia	N/A	N/A	N/A
Novelos Therapeutics Inc.	NVLT	OTC BB	$0.0m	$18.5m	N/A	0.00%	I-CLR1404 Light	Ph I	Cancer Imaging	N/A	N/A	N/A
Novelos Therapeutics Inc. is a pharmaceutical company developing novel drugs for treatment and diagnosis of cancer. Novelos's three cancer-targeted compounds, which are selectively taken up and retained in cancer cells and cancer stem cells, versus normal cells, are being developed to find, treat and follow cancer anywhere in the body.							I-CLR1404 Hot	Ph I	Molecular Radiotherapy	N/A	N/A	N/A
							I-CLR1404 Cold	Pre	Cancer	N/A	N/A	N/A

Company	Ticker	Exchange				Drug	Phase	Indication			
Orexigen Therapeutics Inc.	OREX	NASDAQ GM	$1.2m	$200.9m	N/A	0.00%	Naltrexone	Ph II	Depressive Disorder	N/A	N/A	N/A
Orexigen Therapeutics Inc. is a biopharmaceutical company focused on the development and commercialization of pharmaceutical products for the treatment of the CNS disorders and obesity.						Zonisamide	Ph II	Obesity	N/A	N/A	N/A
Pharmacyclics Inc.	PCYC	NASDAQ CM	$8.2m	$1.7b	107.5 x	0.00%	PCI 32765	Ph II	Chronic Lymphocytic Leukaemia	N/A	N/A	N/A
Pharmacyclics Inc. is a pharmaceutical company developing products to improve upon current therapeutic approaches to cancer, atherosclerosis and retinal disease. The company's products are patented agents derived from its technology platform for designing and synthesizing energy-potentiating drugs.						PCI 27483	Ph II	Pancreatic Neoplasms	N/A	N/A	N/A
						Motexafin gadolinium	Ph II	Chronic Lymphocytic Leukaemia	N/A	N/A	N/A
Plethora Solutions Holdings PLC	PLE	London	$1.7m	$13.1m	N/A	0.00%	PSD 502	Ph III	Premature Ejaculation	N/A	N/A	N/A
Plethora Solutions Holdings PLC is a speciality pharmaceuticals company focused on urological disorders.						Striant	On Market	Testosterone Replacement	N/A	N/A	N/A
						hi-Cran	On Market	Urinary Tract Infections	N/A	N/A	N/A
Sangamo Biosciences Inc.	SGMO	NASDAQ GM	$10.3m	$296.4m	N/A	0.00%	SB 509	Ph II	Amyotrophic Lateral Sclerosis	N/A	N/A	N/A
Sangamo BioSciences Inc. researches and develops transcription factors in the regulation of genes. These transcription factors are the proteins that turn genes on and off and regulate gene expression by recognizing specific DNA sequences.						SB 728-T	Ph I	HIV Infections	N/A	N/A	N/A
						SB 313-xTZ	Ph I	Glioblastoma	N/A	N/A	N/A
						NAI	Ph I	Acne Vulgaris	N/A	N/A	N/A

(Continued)

Table 9: (Continued)

Company	Ticker	Exchange	Revenue	Market Cap.	PE Ratio	Div. Yield	Top Drugs / Products	Status	Description	Patent Expiration	Annual Sales	% of Revenue
Soligenix Inc.	SNGX	OTC BB	$1.9m	$6.0m	N/A	0.00%	orBec	Ph III	Graft-versus-Host disease	N/A	N/A	N/A
Soligenix Inc. develops therapeutics and vaccines. The company researches treatments for gastrointestinal graft-versus-host disease and cancer, and develops vaccines for military and civilian applications.							SGX201	Ph II	Radiation Enteritis	N/A	N/A	N/A
							RiVax	Ph I	Ricin Toxin Exposure	N/A	N/A	N/A
Star Scientific Inc.	CIGX	NASDAQ GM	$0.8m	$520m	N/A	0.00%	Ariva	On Market	Tobacco Addiction	N/A	N/A	N/A
Star Scientific Inc. manufactures dissolvable smokeless tobacco products with reduced toxin levels that are made with tobacco cured using the company's patented technology. The company's subsidiary develops nutraceuticals and products that address neurological disorders like Alzheimer's disease and other neurological conditions.							Stonewall	On Market	Tobacco Addiction	N/A	N/A	N/A
							CigRx	On Market	Tobacco Addiction	N/A	N/A	N/A
Summit Corp. PLC	SUMM	London	$1.2m	$21.7m	N/A	0.00%	SMT C1100	Pre	Duchenne Muscular Dystrophy	N/A	N/A	N/A
Summit Corporation PLC is a biopharmaceutical company that discovers and develops therapeutics for the treatment of type II diabetes and infectious diseases. Summit has a broad range of drug discovery programmes in the clinical, pre-clinical, and discovery stages of development.							SMT 19969	Pre	Clostridium difficile	N/A	N/A	N/A
							Seglin Technology	Pre	Alzheimer's Disease	N/A	N/A	N/A

Company	Ticker	Exchange					Candidate	Phase	Indication			
Synergy Pharmaceuticals Inc.	SGYP	OTC US	$0.0m	$237.4m	N/A	0.00%	Plecanatide	Ph II	Chronic Constipation and IBC	N/A	N/A	N/A
							SP-333	Ph I	Ulcerative Colitis	N/A	N/A	N/A

Synergy Pharmaceuticals Inc. is a biopharmaceutical company focused primarily on the development of drugs to treat gastrointestinal disorders and diseases. The company's lead drug candidate is a guanylyl cyclase C (GC-C) receptor agonist, to treat gastrointestinal disorders, primarily chronic constipation and constipation-predominant irritable bowel syndrome (IBS-C).

Vivus Inc.	VVUS	NASDAQ GS	$0.0m	$1,778.5m	N/A	0.00%	QNEXA	NDA	Obesity	N/A	N/A	N/A
							Avanafil	Ph III	Erectile Dysfunction	N/A	N/A	N/A

Vivus Inc. is a biopharmaceutical company developing therapies for obesity, sleep apnea, diabetes and sexual health. The company markets a treatment for erectile dysfunction and has drugs for obesity in clinical trials.

Private Companies

CardioFocus	N/A	Private Company	N/A	N/A	N/A	0.00%	Endoscopic Ablation System	On Market	Atrial Fibrillation	N/A	N/A	N/A

CardioFocus is dedicated to the advancement of ablation treatments for cardiac disorders.

Cellular Dynamix	N/A	Private Company	N/A	N/A	N/A	0.00%	Hepatocytes	Pre	Human Liver Cells	N/A	N/A	N/A
							Neurons	Pre	Human Neurons	N/A	N/A	N/A
							Endothelial Cells	Pre	Human Vascular Cells	N/A	N/A	N/A
							Hematopoietic Cells	Pre	Cancer and Immune Disease	N/A	N/A	N/A

Cellular Dynamics is the world's largest producer of fully functional human cells derived from induced pluripotent stem cells.

(Continued)

Table 9: (*Continued*)

Company	Ticker	Exchange	Revenue	Market Cap.	PE Ratio	Div. Yield	Top Drugs / Products	Status	Description	Patent Expiration	Annual Sales	% of Revenue
Reata Pharmaceuticals	N/A	Private Company	N/A	Private Company	N/A	0.00%	Bardoxolone Methyl Renal	Ph III	Chronic Kidney Disease	N/A	N/A	N/A
Reata Pharmaceuticals is the leader in developing a novel class of oral anti-inflammatory drugs, Antioxidant Inflammation Modulators (AIMs), which are potent activators of the bioloical transcription Nrf2.							AIM	Pre	CNS, Respiratory and Autoimmune Disease	N/A	N/A	N/A
Trojantec	N/A	Private Company	N/A	Private Company	N/A	0.00%	Tr 1	Pre	Cancer	N/A	N/A	N/A
Trojantec is a biopharmaceutical company focused on identifying, in-licensing and developing innovative oncology therapeutics.							Tr 2	Pre	Cancer	N/A	N/A	N/A
							Tr 3	Pre	Cancer	N/A	N/A	N/A
							Tr 4	Pre	Cancer	N/A	N/A	N/A

*Biologics (large molecule drugs) are more complicated to manufacture than the more traditional small molecule ones. Consequently, even when a biologic's patent expires, the FDA currently requires any prospective "biosimilar" to be subjected to full clinical trials before being approved. This means that biologics potentially have exclusivity periods that run far beyond their patent expiry dates, as competing biosimilars could take years in clinical trials before the FDA (or equivalent for other regions) is convinced that they are as safe and effective for patients as the original biologic.

Summary

This book project has been our most challenging and rewarding one to date and the learning curve was steep. We have learned an enormous amount about the fascinating developments in bioscience and technology and enjoyed writing about them. As non-scientists, our layperson's perspective allowed us to break down some of the complex concepts and topics covered into more bite-sized, digestible segments. Some of the material can still come across as complex and overwhelming even in its most basic interpretation, but that is because it is complex. We have delved into some incredibly sophisticated themes in human biology, biochemistry and technology. Some of the cutting-edge research mentioned is still at a developmental stage. All the material covered has been important in providing a context for the subject matter that includes the past, present and likely future.

From the outset, we wanted to focus on two core themes that are very important to us and to everyone else in the world: health and wealth. We have woven these themes together in a unique way by explaining how the emerging technologies that will enhance the quality and length of human lives are also investment opportunities that can make people wealthier.

To set the scene, we started the book with a chapter on transformational technologies. We referred to some of the world's leading futurists to gain from their many years of analysing technological trends and developments. They were all consistent in emphasizing how humans have tended to underestimate the pace of technological advancement. Since the 1960s, *Moore's Law* has been uncannily accurate in predicting the future processing power of computers, which has been at least doubling every 2 years. It is largely for this reason that futurists are able to extrapolate that by 2020, we will have the raw computer processing power of a human brain and by 2045, we will have created a computer with superior intelligence to a human brain, an event often referred to as the *singularity*. Even though the current technology for manufacturing silicon-based microprocessors reaches its physical limitations by around 2020, we revealed some new developments in manufacturing using three-dimensional transistors and where microprocessors are stacked in layers on top of each other. There is also the entirely new field of quantum computing, which opens the door to processing power that is leagues beyond even the world's fastest computers today.

We described the birth of a remarkable new field known as synthetic biology, under which an incredible first was achieved in May 2010, when the world's first synthetic organism was born, a bacterial cell made with DNA that was created entirely from scratch. Synthetic biology has also been used successfully to create body parts, such as a windpipe, from a synthetic polymer that is seeded with the patient's cells, incubated and then transplanted. We are just a few years from performing such procedures on patients using more complex synthesized organs, such as kidneys, livers and even hearts.

Equally exciting are the implications for synthesizing new, tailor-made organisms to perform a specific purpose. Every living thing is essentially an application (an "app"), like a software program on a computer or smart phone. Once we understanding the programming language, we will be able to write programs to do almost anything. For instance, we could synthesize an organism that feeds off carbon dioxide and releases solid carbon and oxygen. Or it could be an organism that feeds off radioactive waste, rendering it harmless. There already exists a type of bacteria that feeds off oil and it has been a natural assistant in the clean-up operations of oil spills.

Chapter 1 on transformational technologies was in part written to convert the sceptics out there into believers because many of the technologies we wrote about are already here today. We are not writing about hypothetical breakthroughs that will take place in the distant future; it has already started and we can expect a lot more within our lifetimes.

With much of the new cures and treatments of disease coming from the biotech sector, it was important that we devote a chapter to the history of medicine and followed its timeline from ancient Egypt to the present day so that you can develop an understanding of how we arrived at this juncture in the biotech/biopharma industry. It was also important to give an introductory lesson in biochemistry so that you gain an understanding how atoms, molecules, cells, nuclei, DNA, chromosomes and genes all sit in the scheme of things. There is a lot to absorb in Chapters 2 and 3 and it may require re-reading certain sections. The history of medicine was largely quackery for many centuries until the early 1800s after which life expectancy began to increase dramatically. Mass production of the first drug, quinine sulphate, was also around this time and marked the birth of the pharmaceutical industry, which developed different waves of drug types, the most important probably being antibiotics.

The biopharma industry was born in the mid-70s and since then some 400 products have been developed, accounting for about 40 per cent of all drugs sold around the world.

Having completed the timeline of medicine and the drug industry, Chapter 4 focused on the treatment and cure of disease. This is a long chapter because there is so much happening in therapeutics and so many companies developing treatments and cures to dozens of diseases that are today's biggest killers, especially ones that the elderly are more susceptible to contracting, such as dementia, Alzheimer's, heart disease and cancer.

There are literally thousands of companies out there all chasing their bioscience breakthrough but many of them will unfortunately amount to nothing, just like in the gold rush and dot com eras. We likened investing in biotech firms to investing in mining companies: there are many companies that show promise of striking gold; a great deal of up-front capital is required with no assurances of any returns to investors; only about 1 in 10 companies will get their lucky break. For these reasons, we caution investors to think twice before jumping into a biotech investment based on hype and rumour. We suggested quite a few that we believe are worthy of further consideration, especially companies that do not have all their eggs in one basket. In other words, investing in a company that is betting its entire future on one breakthrough arriving is incredibly risky, and so it is wiser to find one that has two or more promising products in the pipeline.

We also explained how pharmaceutical companies operate, starting with their R&D costs, their three phase trials and approvals by governmental bodies, namely the FDA in the US. We explained why the "hit and miss" approach to drug development has resulted in a successful drug costing around US$1 billion to get to market. We explained how patents work in the drug industry – where the filer of a proposed new product or process can be granted a 20-year exclusivity in the market – but because the patent has to be filed at the earliest stages of development, by the time the product has been through its three phases of clinical trials, it may only get about 8 or 9 cash cow years before the patent expires and it becomes a generic drug, open to all firms to copy and sell at knock-down prices. New blockbuster drugs are becoming increasingly rare and a new symbiotic business model has developed between the big pharmaceutical companies and the newer biotech firms, the latter being in need of cash to develop their big idea products, the former having cash but in need of the big idea products.

Following this, we dedicated an entire chapter to demographics. The rapid ageing of the human population is a phenomenon that is affecting the entire world and one that is going to be accelerating over the coming decades. The consequences of the changing global demographics will be felt in rich and poor countries alike. Although most of the rich world is already "older" than most developing countries, population ageing will be even more rapid in the developing nations, especially in the vast nation of China with its 1.34 billion people and a one-child policy whose effects will be felt this decade.

The oldest major economy, Japan, is a stark warning to other nations of what lies ahead if no action is taken to address the chronic ageing population problem.

The total human population is going to peak in the next two to three decades, after which there will be a small but steady decline. The proportion of elderly people in the world is also set to rise for the foreseeable future, creating unprecedented challenges to society as a whole. At the same time, there will be a handful of large nations and regions that have high-fertility rates and which pose a geopolitical challenge, because these nations tend to have high unemployment and a volatile history with the West. We discussed the implications of an old, rich world living alongside a young, poor one in Chapter 7 on disruptive changes. The coming decades will be the most disruptive ones yet in humankind's history, but fortunately more in a positive way than negative.

The advances in biotech and technology are excellent news against the backdrop of an ageing human population, and they will result in the birth of entirely new industries, some easier to anticipate than others. But it will also mean that some long-established businesses will become obsolete, downsized or side-lined. We try and provoke some thought into trying to anticipate what it will mean for the industry you currently work in and the potential opportunities that lie ahead.

A shrinking population of working age alongside a rapidly growing population of elderly people, both as a proportion of the population and in aggregate terms, will mean that there will not be enough people around to care for the elderly, especially the over-85s, who tend to need more care and assistance. That is where Chapter 8 on robotics can provide a solution. Given that Japan is already a world leader in robotics and is also the country with the most chronic ageing population problem, it has been investing heavily in the field of robotics in the hopes that in the next 10 years or so, there will be an affordable domestic helper robot to save the day. Honda is behind the most advanced robot today. Asimo has been a work in progress since the mid-1980s but major achievements have been made, such as its ability to walk, run and go up and down stairs. It is still some years away from being a household item, but over time it will be.

We decided to include a short chapter on health and lifestyle maintenance. Despite all the amazing drugs and technologies that we can expect to become available in the coming years, we still need to take reasonable care of ourselves. There are a lot books, journals and websites out there on this subject and we have pulled together some of our favourite tips on leading a healthy lifestyle. It is going to be a couple of decades before humans can expect to have nano-bots inside their bodies that will keep them in the best possible shape, and so in the meantime we have to do it ourselves manually.

We are entering a new chapter in human civilization and one that will dwarf all others combined. Although it may feel like the pace of technology is already advancing rapidly, it is about to feel even faster. Human forecasting abilities are only able to extrapolate into the future based on the past in a linear way, but the future pace of progress is accelerating. With computer processing power

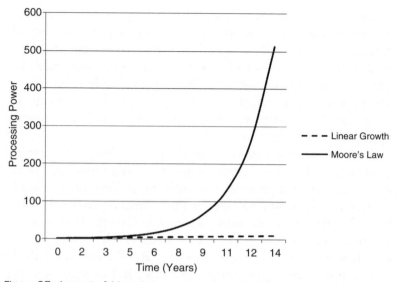

Figure 37: Impact of *Moore's Law* versus linear growth on processing power over time.

doubling every 18 months to 2 years, processing power today can perform tasks in minutes what used to take years just a decade ago. Like compound interest, its effects are not felt immediately, so for example a doubling of processing power every 18 months means a quadrupling in three years, a 16-fold increase in six years and a 64-fold increase in just nine years. Imagine what a processor 64 times faster can do compared to today's technology. Figure 37 is a simple chart to illustrate how in the first few years, exponential growth and linear growth follow similar paths but after around eight years, there is an inflection point after which the gap becomes vast and very apparent.

The invention of the transistor at Bells Labs in 1947 gave birth to the silicon age from which humankind has benefited enormously. After decades of ever faster chips, processing power is finally reaching a level that can be applied in a meaningful way in the field of biology. This will create an entirely new and exciting industry that will offer unparalleled benefits that will touch every aspect to our way of life.

The time taken to sequence a human genome is an excellent illustration of the impact of increased processing power. The original Human Genome Project took almost 15 years to sequence (most of) one human genome, and it cost some US$3 billion. Today, it can be done in just over a week at a cost of around US$4,000. In five years it will probably cost less than a thousand dollars and within 10 years it will be in the hundreds of dollars range and take a matter of minutes to sequence.

But sequencing a genome is just the beginning; the real work starts in analysing the genome and learning about what each part of the genome does, and again the faster the computer, the quicker this can be done.

The biotech field is not the only area that will benefit from faster processors, the technological advances made over the past half century are all around us and by far the most prevalent, visible and indispensable example is the mobile phone. Rich, poor, young and old, mobile phones (and their "smart" successors) are literally in the pockets of just about every person on the planet.

Yet only 20 years ago, just a handful of people had mobile phones and even then they were large, bulky contraptions that today would not qualify as being called mobile at all. Today they are one of, if not the, most useful tool we possess. They go far beyond being just a phone; they have seemingly never-ending additional functionality and applications that make our lives so much more convenient while on the move, such as cameras, maps, GPS, email, weather and of course access to the Internet, which offers virtually limitless information at our fingertips. This device will of course continue to evolve as it becomes faster, cheaper and smaller. Eventually, some-time in the next 20 years, they will end up as devices that are directly networked to our brain.

The future holds many more exciting gadgets and tools that will become indispensable to us, but the most important and exciting breakthroughs will be those that directly enhance, upgrade and extend the quality and quantity of our lives, so that living a long, healthy and pain-free life becomes the norm rather than the exception. We are already well on the way to realizing this seemingly ambitious goal.

In the same way that the lion's share of humankind's achievements so far can be attributed to the last 100 years, so will the next 50 years account for 95 per cent of all humankind's achievements.

If there is one take-away message from this book, it is that for the first time in human history we are within sight of being able to manipulate and synthesize the human body at a genomic level. The opportunities and implications to humankind are virtually limitless. As with any new, disruptive technology, it takes a long time for society to accept it into the mainstream. Remember that for thousands of years until around the time of the Renaissance in the 16th century, human life expectancy at birth was only around 30 years, yet today anybody who does not live until at least the age of 70 is considered to have had too short a life. Similarly in the next 20 years, anyone who does not make it to 110 years will be considered to have been unlucky.

Society will slowly become accustomed to people living to well beyond 100 years, and we will look back and be amazed at how short the average lifespan was in the early decades of the 21st century.

In the past, there was equal disbelief and even resistance to new technologies when they were first introduced; when electricity first became widely available in the home, it was viewed with suspicion, then resistance, then adoption. The same with the likes of the telephone, the television, even the Internet. It is human nature to resist change; some hold out longer than others but eventually everyone jumps in. What percentage of the population today still does not have an email address? Fifteen years ago, only tech savvy individuals and university students had them.

As with our other books, the subject matter is written to be thought-provoking, interesting and educational. This one has the added benefit of helping readers possibly add years to their life.

So far our track record in anticipating major trends has been quite accurate. In our *Wake Up!* and *Top 10* books:

- We foretold of the rise in *oil prices* when at the time oil was trading at around US$15 a barrel.
- We advised people to buy *gold* when it was selling for a few hundred dollars an ounce.
- We predicted the *debt crisis* in the rich world that would lead to a *weak US dollar* and long-term slump in the housing market.
- We also explained why *China* was set to boom and of the consequent *rise in commodity prices*.

Just as with our other books when they were first published, some of the predictions we made seemed to be a little remote and unlikely to happen; so it may appear to be the case with the exciting predictions we are making now for the bioscience and technology sectors.

However, we are totally convinced that the new technologies predicted in this book will become reality in the coming decades and that they will fundamentally transform the quality and length of our lives.

Glossary

Albinism: The congenital absence of pigmentation in the eyes and skin and hair.

Alkaloid: Any of a class of nitrogenous organic compounds of plant origin that have pronounced physiological actions on humans.

Allotrope: Each of two or more different physical forms in which an element can exist.

Amine: An organic compound derived from ammonia by replacement of one or more hydrogen atoms by organic radicals.

Anabolism: The synthesis of complex molecules in living organisms from simpler ones together with the storage of energy.

Atherosclerosis: A disease of the arteries characterized by the deposition of plaques of fatty material on their inner walls.

Atom: The basic unit of a chemical element.

ATP (Adenosine Triphosphate): A compound consisting of an adenosine molecule bonded to three phosphate groups, present in all living tissue. The breakage of one phosphate linkage (to form adenosine diphosphate, ADP) provides energy for physiological processes such as muscular contraction.

Autosome: Any chromosome that is not a sex chromosome.

Base pair: A pair of complementary bases in a double-stranded nucleic acid molecule, consisting of a purine in one strand linked by hydrogen bonds to a pyrimidine in the other.

Bioinformatics: The science of collecting and analysing complex biological data such as genetic codes.

Biologic: A medicinal product such as a vaccine, blood or blood component, allergenic, somatic cell, gene therapy, tissue, recombinant therapeutic protein or living cells that are used as therapeutics to treat diseases.

Bionic: Having particular physiological functions augmented or replaced by electronic or electromechanical components.

Bioscience: Any of the life sciences.

Blastocyst: A mammalian blastula in which some differentiation of cells has occurred.

Cancer: The disease caused by an uncontrolled division of abnormal cells in a part of the body.

Carbohydrate: Any of a large group of organic compounds occurring in foods and living tissues and including sugars, starch and cellulose. They contain hydrogen and oxygen in the same ratio as water (2:1) and typically can be broken down to release energy in the animal body.

Cardiomyocytes: Specialized muscle cells in the heart that play key roles in maintaining the heart's continuous beat in a rhythmical manner.

Catabolism: The breakdown of complex molecules in living organisms to form simpler ones, together with the release of energy.

Cell: The smallest structural and functional unit of an organism, typically microscopic and consisting of cytoplasm and a nucleus enclosed in a membrane. Microscopic organisms typically consist of a single cell, which is either eukaryotic or prokaryotic.

Cholesterol: A compound of the sterol type found in most body tissues, including the blood and the nerves. Cholesterol and its derivatives are important constituents of cell membranes and precursors of other steroid compounds, but high concentrations in the blood (mainly derived from animal fats in the diet) are thought to promote atherosclerosis.

Chromosome: A threadlike structure of nucleic acids and protein found in the nucleus of most living cells, carrying genetic information in the form of genes.

Cybernetics: The science of communications and automatic control systems in both machines and living things.

Cyborg: A person whose physical abilities are extended beyond normal human limitations by mechanical elements built into the body.

Cytoplasm: The material or protoplasm within a living cell, excluding the nucleus.

Deoxyribose: A sugar derived from ribose by replacing a hydroxyl group with hydrogen.

Diploid: Containing two complete sets of chromosomes, one from each parent.

DNA (Deoxyribonucleic Acid):   A self-replicating material present in nearly all living organisms as the main constituent of chromosomes. It is the carrier of genetic information.

Element: Each of more than one hundred substances that cannot be chemically interconverted or broken down into simpler substances and are primary constituents of matter. Each element is distinguished by its atomic number, that is, the number of protons in the nuclei of its atoms.

Emetine: An alkaloid present in ipecac and formerly used in the treatment of amoebic infections and as an emetic in aversion therapy.

Enzyme: A substance produced by a living organism that acts as a catalyst to bring about a specific biochemical reaction.

Ephedrine: A crystalline alkaloid drug obtained from some ephedras. It causes constriction of the blood vessels and widening of the bronchial passages and is used to relieve asthma and hay fever.

Epinephrine: A hormone secreted by the adrenal glands, especially in conditions of stress, increasing rates of blood circulation, breathing and carbohydrate metabolism and preparing muscles for exertion.

Eukaryotic: Cells with a high degree of internal organization, including a nucleus (genetic material surrounded by a membrane) and several other internal parts surrounded by membranes.

Fat: A soft greasy substance occurring in organic tissue and consisting of a mixture of lipids (mostly triglycerides).

GDP (Gross Domestic Product): A measure of economic output of a country or region.

Gene: A unit of heredity that is transferred from a parent to offspring and is held to determine some characteristic of the offspring.

Gene therapy: The transplantation of normal genes into cells in place of missing or defective ones in order to correct genetic disorders.

Genome: The complete set of genes or genetic material present in a cell or organism.

Glucose: A simple sugar that is an important energy source in living organisms and is a component of many carbohydrates.

Glycolysis: The breakdown of glucose by enzymes, releasing energy and pyruvic acid.

Gout: A disease in which defective metabolism of uric acid causes arthritis, especially in the smaller bones of the feet, deposition of chalkstones and episodes of acute pain.

Hayflick limit: The number of times a normal cell population will divide before it stops, presumably because the telomeres reach a critical length.

Hepatocytes: A liver cell.

Hyperlipidaemia: Presence of excess lipids in the blood.

Hyperplasia: The enlargement of an organ or tissue caused by an increase in the reproduction rate of its cells, often as an initial stage in the development of cancer.

Hypertension: High blood pressure.

Hypertrophy: The enlargement of an organ or tissue from the increase in size of its cells.

Laudanum: An alcoholic solution containing morphine, prepared from opium and formerly used as a narcotic painkiller.

LDL: Low density lipoprotein (the "bad" cholesterol), high levels of which in the body often cause cardiovascular disease.

Life Sciences: Any of the branches of natural science dealing with the structure and behaviour of living organisms.

Lipid: Any of a class of organic compounds that are fatty acids or their derivatives and are insoluble in water but soluble in organic solvents. They include many natural oils, waxes and steroids.

Liposome: A minute spherical sac of phospholipid molecules enclosing a water droplet, especially as formed artificially to carry drugs or other substances into the tissues.

Macromolecule: A molecule containing a very large number of atoms, such as a protein, nucleic acid or synthetic polymer.

Matter: A substance or material.

Median: Denoting the middle term of a series arranged in order of magnitude. For example, the median number of the series 55, 62, 76, 85, 93 is 76.

Meiosis: A type of cell division that results in four daughter cells each with half the number of chromosomes of the parent cell, as in the production of gametes.

Mitochondria: Structures found in cells that produce and regulate energy. They are the main energy source of cells. Mitochondria convert nutrients into energy and also perform many other specialized tasks.

Mitosis: A type of cell division that results in two daughter cells each having the same number and kind of chromosomes as the parent nucleus, typical of ordinary tissue growth.

Molecular Biology: The branch of biology that deals with the structure and function of the macromolecules (e.g., proteins and nucleic acids) essential to life.

Molecule: A group of atoms bonded together, representing the smallest fundamental unit of a chemical compound that can take part in a chemical reaction.

Moore's Law: The observation that the power of computers, since the early 1960s, has been doubling about every 2 years.

Mutagen: An agent, such as radiation or a chemical substance, that causes genetic mutation.

Mutations: The changing of the structure of a gene, resulting in a variant form that may be transmitted to subsequent generations, caused by the alteration of single base units in DNA, or the deletion, insertion or rearrangement of larger sections of genes or chromosomes.

Nanobot: A machine or robot whose components are at or close to the microscopic scale of a nanometre (1×10^{-9} metres).

Nucleotide: A compound consisting of a nucleoside linked to a phosphate group. Nucleotides form the basic structural unit of nucleic acids such as DNA.

Nucleus: A dense organelle present in most eukaryotic cells, typically a single rounded structure bounded by a double membrane, containing the genetic material.

OECD: Organization for Economic Cooperation and Development.

Oncogenes: A gene that in certain circumstances can transform a cell into a tumour cell.

Organelle: Any of a number of organized or specialized structures within a living cell.

Paracrine: Of, relating to, or denoting a hormone that has an effect only in the vicinity of the gland secreting it.

Phenylalanine: An amino acid widely distributed in plant proteins. It is an essential nutrient in the diet of vertebrates.

Phenylketonuria: An inherited inability to metabolize phenylalanine that causes brain and nerve damage if untreated.

Plasmid: A genetic structure in a cell that can replicate independently of the chromosomes, typically a small circular DNA strand in the cytoplasm of a bacterium or protozoan. Plasmids are much used in the laboratory manipulation of genes.

Pluripotent: Capable of giving rise to several different cell types.

Polymer: A substance that has a molecular structure consisting chiefly or entirely of a large number of similar units bonded together.

Polypeptides: A linear organic polymer consisting of a large number of amino-acid residues bonded together in a chain, forming part of (or the whole of) a protein molecule.

Prokaryote: A microscopic single-celled organism, including the bacteria and cyanobacteria, which has neither a distinct nucleus with a membrane nor other specialized organelles.

Protein: Any of a class of nitrogenous organic compounds that consist of large molecules composed of one or more long chains of amino acids and are an essential part of all living organisms.

Proteome: The entire complement of proteins that is or can be expressed by a cell, tissue or organism.

Proteomics: The branch of molecular biology concerned with determining the proteome.

R&D: Research and development.

Resveratrol: A natural compound found in grapes, mulberries, peanuts and other plants or food products, especially red wine, which may protect against cancer and cardiovascular disease by acting as an antioxidant, anti-mutagen and anti-inflammatory agent.

Ribosome: A minute particle consisting of RNA and associated proteins, found in large numbers in the cytoplasm of living cells. They bind messenger RNA and transfer RNA to synthesize polypeptides and proteins.

RNA (Ribonucleic Acid): A nucleic acid present in all living cells. Its principal role is to act as a messenger carrying instructions from DNA for controlling the synthesis of proteins, although in some viruses RNA rather than DNA carries the genetic information.

Soma: The parts of an organism other than the reproductive cells.

Stem cells: Cells that can both self-renew (make more stem cells by cell division) and differentiate into mature, specialized cells such as blood cells, nerve cells, muscle cells and so on.

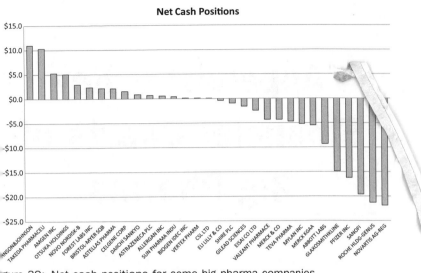

Figure 39: Net cash positions for some big pharma companies.
Source: Bloomberg

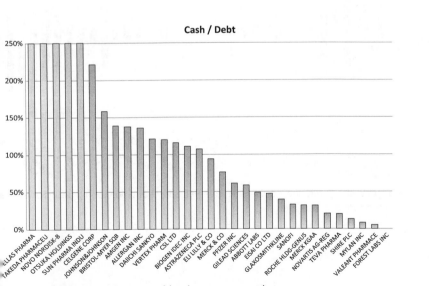

Figure 40: Cash/debt for some big pharma companies.
Source: Bloomberg

Telomerase: An enzyme that adds nucleotides to telomeres.

Telomere: A compound structure at the end of a chromosome.

Thrombosis: The formation of a blood clot inside a blood vessel.

Turing test: A test for intelligence in a computer, requiring that a human being should be unable to distinguish the machine from another human being by using the replies to questions put to both.

Tyrosine: A hydrophilic amino acid that is a constituent of most proteins and is important in the synthesis of some hormones.

Virosomes: A drug or vaccine delivery mechanism consisting of a unilamellar phospholipid bilayer vesicle incorporating virus-derived proteins to allow the virosomes to fuse with target cells. Virosomes are not able to replicate but are pure fusion-active vesicles.

ZFNs (Zinc Finger Nucleases): ZFNs are artificial restriction enzymes generated by fusing a zinc finger DNA-binding domain to a DNA-cleavage domain.

Zygote: A diploid cell resulting from the fusion of two haploid gametes; a fertilized ovum.

Appendix – Key Financial Charts Big Pharma

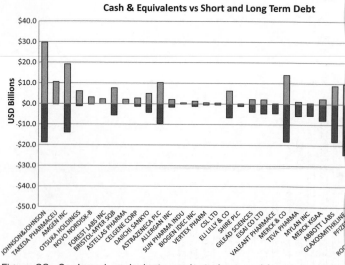

Figure 38: Cash and equivalents against short- and long-term debt big pharma companies.

Source: Bloomberg

References

Berrington de Gonzalez, Amy and Hartge, Patricia (2010) "Body-mass index and mortality among 1.46 million white adults", *New England Journal of Medicine*, 363: 2211–2219.

Jackson, Richard and Howe, Neil (2008) *The Graying of the Great Powers: Demography and Geopolitics in the 21st Century*, Center for Strategic & International Studies.

Kessler, Andy (2007) *The End of Medicine: How Silicon Valley (and Naked Mice) Will Reboot Your Doctor*, Collins.

Kurzweil, Ray (2006) *The Singularity is Near*, Gerald Duckworth & Co.

OECD (2011) *Pensions at a Glance 2011: Retirement-income systems in OECD and G20 Countries*, OECD Publishing; www.oecd.org/document/49/0,3746,en_2649_34757_42992113_1_1_1_1,00.html

United Nations (2010) *World Population Ageing 2009*, Department of Economic and Social Affairs, Population Division, United Nations.

United Nations Development Programme (2009) Human Development Report, United Nations.

Bibliography

Austad, Stephen N. (1999) *Why We Age: What Science is Discovering About the Body's Journey Through Life*, John Wiley & Sons, Inc.

"Australia to 2050: Future challenges". Circulated by The Hon. Wayne Swan MP, Treasurer of the Commonwealth of Australia.

Hamerman, David (2007) *Geriatric Bioscience: The Link between Aging and Disease*, Johns Hopkins University Press.

Jacoby, Susan (2011) *Never Say Die: The Myth and Marketing of the New Old Age*, Pantheon Books.

Kaku, Michio (2011) *Physics of the Future: How Science Will Shape Human Destiny and Our Daily Lives by the Year 2100*, Allen Lane.

Kubinyi, Hugo and Ravina, Enrique (2011) *The Evolution of Drug Discovery: From Traditional Medicines to Modern Drugs*, Wiley VCH.

Lane, Nick (2010) *Life Ascending: The Ten Great Inventions of Evolution*, Profile Books.

Mehta, Shreefal S. (2011) *Commercializing Successful Biomedical Technologies: Basic Principles for the Development of Drugs, Diagnostics and Devices*, Cambridge University Press.

Mukerjee, Siddhartha (2011) *The Emperor of all Maladies*, Fourth Estate.

Pisano, Gary P. (2006) *Science Business*, Harvard Business School Press.

Robbins-Roth, Cynthia (2001) *From Alchemy to IPO: The Business of Biotechnology*, Basic Books.

Shanks, Pete (2005) *Human Genetic Engineering: A Guide for Activists, Skeptics, and the Very Perplexed*, Nation Books.

Werth, Barry (1995) *The Billion-Dollar Molecule: One Company's Quest for the Perfect Drug*, Simon & Schuster.

Wikimedia Commons (www.commons.wikimedia.org)

Here is a list of websites that we found useful:

BBC News: www.bbcnews.com
Bio-IT World: www.bio-itworld.com
BioTime, Inc.: www.biotimeinc.com
BioWorld: www.bioworld.com
Business Insights: www.business-insights.com
Cowen and Company: www.cowen.com
The Economist: www.economist.com
The *FASEB* Journal: www.fasebj.org
FierceBiotech Research: www.fiercebiotechresearch.com
Institute for Global Futures: www.globalfuturist.com
Jefferies: www.jefferies.com
JP Morgan: www.jpmorgan.com
The Lancet: www.thelancet.com
National Center for Biotechnology Information:
    www.ncbi.nlm.nih.gov
Nature: www.nature.com
The *New England Journal of Medicine*: www.nejm.org
New Scientist: www.newscientist.com
OECD: www.oecd.org
Rodman & Renshaw: www.rodmanandrenshaw.com
Scientific American: www.scientificamerican.com
Singularity University: www.singularityu.org
Telome Health: www.telomehealth.com
United Nations World Population Ageing 1950–2050:
    www.un.org/esa/population/publications/
    worldageing19502050/
United Nations Development Programme:
    www.undp.org/hdr2009.shtml

Index

4 Gs of drug innovation 41, 70
23andMe 17–18, 163

A *see* adenine
accelerated development review, FDA
   82
accommodation design 210
Acorda Therapeutics 256, 287
ACE inhibitors 46–7
acne 153–5
ADD *see* Attention Deficit Disorder
addiction therapies 151
adenine (A) 27–8, 35
adenosine triphosphate (ATP) 29, 33–4
adult stem cells 166, 168
Afreeza (diabetes drug) 126–7
ageing 158–62, 240–4
"ageing" genes 89
ageing populations 181–8
   China 199–200
   investment 214–15
   Japan 185–6
   life expectancy 181–8
   monitor robots 223–8
   over 60s 184–8, 199–200
   over 80s 185–6
   psychological outlook 195–6
   retail goods/services 212–13
   social impact 195–6
   youth shortages 218
AI *see* artificial intelligence
airbags 233
airline industry 69
alcohol abuse 151
Aldebaran Robotics 226–7
Alexion 149
Allergan 249, 265, 283
allotropes 233
ALN-VSP (cancer drug) 261

Alnylam Pharmaceuticals 176, 256, 261,
   288
Alzheimer's disease 132–6
   APOE gene 160
   Aricept 88, 135
   FDA approval 82–3
   new drugs 135
   robotic pets 229, 231
America Invents Act 2011 78
Amgen 60–61, 69, 256–7, 288
   Denosumab 143, 257
   FTO principle 78
   oncolytic poxviruses 100
   Xgeva 156, 257
AmpliPhi Biosciences 113, 256, 279,
   294
Amylin Pharmaceuticals 122, 256, 288
anabolism 34
angina 45–6, 47, 131
angiogenesis inhibitors 94–5
animals 72
Antabloc (RA drug) 276
Anthera Pharmaceuticals 256, 294
anti-ageing medicine 243
antibiotics 43–4, 107–18
anti-cancer agents 48–50, 98–100
anticholinergic drugs 145
anti-depressants 42
antifungal drugs 109
anti-histamines 42–3, 47
anti-psychotic drugs 41–2, 150
antiretroviral drugs 115
antisense therapies 177–8, 256
antiviral drugs 109
apolipoprotein E (APOE) gene
   159–60
APP *see* beta-selective APP Cleaving
   Enzyme
Aricept (Alzheimer drug) 88, 135

Arrowhead Research
   company overview 295
   as investment choice 256, 279
   Nanotype 179–80
   obesity 123–4, 127
   siRNA 176–7
arsenical compounds 41
arthritis 48, 50, 139–43
artificial intelligence (AI) 5, 9–12
Asimo robot 224–5, 309
Asimov, Isaac 232
assisted living communities 210
Astellas Pharma 249, 267–8, 283
asthma 143–5
AstraZeneca 250, 261
atherosclerosis 159–60
atoms 24–35
ATP *see* adenine triphosphate
Attention Deficit Disorder (ADD) 263
attitude management 244
Avastin (cancer drug) 253
AVI BioPharma 295
Azilect (Parkinson's drug) 139

BACE *see* beta-selective APP Cleaving
   Enzyme
bacterial infections 109–10
Bafetinib (leukaemia drug) 277
balanced biopharma portfolio 280–1
Basilea Pharmaceutica 295
Bayh–Dole Act 1980, US 77
BCG vaccine 117
Benlysta (lupus drug) 141
beta blockers 46–7
beta-interferon (MS treatment) 137
beta-selective APP Cleaving Enzyme
   (BACE) 136
big pharma
   acquiring biotech firms 62–4
   and biopharma 58–73, 85
   developing world 251
   growth 253
   investment 248–56
   key financial charts 325–6
   notable companies 59
   reorganization 55–6
   see also individual companies;
   pharmaceutical industry
Biogen Idec 137–8, 256, 257–8, 289
bioinformatics 71, 165
biological networks 33–4

biologicals *see* biopharma
biologics 59, 62, 73, 85
biology and technology 1, 8, 13–21
   convergence of 1, 13–21
   genetic self-knowledge 16–18
   personalized medicine 16, 20
   synthetic biology 14–16
   tailor-made body parts 18–21
biomedical devices 223
Biondvax Pharmaceuticals 295
biopharma 23, 51–4, 247–304, 307
   balanced portfolio 280–1
   and big pharma 59–72
   business models 65
   company overviews 282–304
   conservative portfolio 279–80
   failures/successes 65
   favoured stocks 249
   investment 70, 247–304
   speculative portfolio 281–2
   startups 70–1
   top drugs 62
   see also individual companies;
   pharmaceutical industry
bio-printers 21
bio-rubber 21
bioscience 205–18
   disruptions 205–18
   food industry 213–14
   geopolitics 211–12
   healthcare 206–10
   influence of 205–18
   insurance 206–10
   investment 214–15
   the law 215–17
   politics 211
   real estate 210
   retail goods/services 212–13
   youth shortages 217–18
BioTime 179, 256, 278–9, 296
Black, James 47
bladders 179
Blagosklonny, Mikhail V. 238
blood tests 243
BMI *see* Body Mass Index
Boceprevir (hepatitis drug) 113
Body Mass Index (BMI) 236–7
body parts 18–21
bone disease 153–6
Botox 265
Boyer, Herbert 60

Brazil 251
Buettner, Dan 239
Business Insights research firm 96–7
Byetta (diabetes drug) 122

C *see* cytosine
Calment, Jeanne 182
calorie-restricted diets 161, 237–8
cancer 89–107
  angiogenesis inhibitors 94–5
  anti-cancer agents 48–50, 98–100
  causal links 91
  China 66–7
  common types 90
  companies to watch 104–6
  early detection 91
  epigenetic drugs 95–7
  Epizyme's approach 65
  FDA drug approval 80, 81, 83,
    92–3
  gene knockout 98–9
  gene patents 74
  Harvard Mouse 74
  immortality 158–9
  key drug sectors 93
  kinase inhibitors 102–4
  microchips 13
  pain relief 152–3
  PARP inhibitors 102–4
  pathway blockers 101–2
  promising prospects 106–7
  relapses 92
  targeted therapies 93–104
carbohydrates 25
carbon nanotubes 233–4
CardioFocus 303
cardiovascular disease 45–7, 88, 128–32,
    170
catabolism 34
CDAD *see Clostridium difficile* associated
    diarrhoea
Celgene 63–4, 256, 258, 289
cell culture 167
cell fusion 53
Cellceutix 256, 272, 296
cells 24–35, 53, 167
cellular biology 169
Cellular Dynamics 168–9, 303
Central Dogma of Molecular Biology 31
central nervous system (CNS) 150–3
Charles River Laboratories 72

China
  biopharma 251
  cancer 67
  demographic changes 188, 190–3, 196,
    198–200
  fertility rates 190–3
  geopolitical concerns 211–12
  labour pool 192
  one-child policy 199
  over 60s 199–200
  world labour pool 192–3
chlorpromazine 42
cholesterol 46, 128–31, 249
chromosomes 28–31
  see also telomeres
chronic kidney disease (CKD) 88, 123,
    127
Cisco Systems 5–6
CKD *see* chronic kidney disease
Claritin (anti-histamine) 42–3
cloning 18–19, 53
Clostridium (C.) difficile 110–12
Clostridium difficile associated diarrhoea
    (CDAD) 274
CNS *see* central nervous system
combinatorial chemistry 71
combinatorial probe-anchor ligation
    (cPAL) 164–5
companion diagnostics 255
company-based schools 218
Complete Genomics 163–5
computers
  Deep Blue 9
  processing power 221–2, 310
  quantum 4–5
  Watson 9–12
congenital diseases 207–8
consciousness 12
conservative biopharma portfolio 279–80
contraceptive pill 47–8
Contract Research Organizations (CROs)
    81
COPD respiratory disease 144–5
Cortisone 48
COX inhibitors 50
cPAL *see* combinatorial probe-anchor
    ligation
Crestor (statin) 130
Crick, Francis 27
CROs *see* Contract Research
    Organizations

Cubist Pharmaceuticals 256, 274, 289
Curagen 96
curing diseases 87–156, 307
Curis 97, 296
cybernetics 7
cyborgs 7–8
cytosine (C) 27–8, 35
cytotoxic drugs 93
CytRx 256, 277–8

da Vinci Surgical System 220–1
death 158–9
Deep Blue IBM computer 9
dementia *see* Alzheimer's disease
demographic changes 181–203, 308–9
    ageing populations 181–8, 195–6,
    199–200
    declining populations 186
    developed world 193–7
    government action 193, 200–3
    immigration 193–5
    impact of ageing 195–6
    Japan 185–6, 190–2, 194–5, 197–8
    life expectancy 181–8
    maximising workers 201
    support ratios 197–8
    sustainable policies 201–202
    United States 190–1, 193, 196–7
    world labour pool 191–3
Dendreon 100
Denosumab (osteoarthritis drug) 143, 257
deoxyribonucleic acid *see* DNA
depressive illnesses 150–1
dermatology 153–6
developing world 251
    see also China; India
diabetes 124–8
    China 66–7
    disease pathways 32
    gout 141–2
    hormones 48
    obesity 118–19, 122, 126–7
    stem cells 170
diarrhoea 274
diet 161, 237–8, 241–2
Dificid (CDAD drug) 274
digitalis (cardiovascular drug) 45
Dioscorides (Roman medic) 36, 49
diseases
    bone disease 153–6
    breakthroughs 88

cardiovascular disease 45–7, 88,
128–32, 170
curing disease 87–156, 307
dermatology 153–6
gastrointestinal disease 153–6
infectious diseases 37–41, 107–18,
275
kidney disease 88, 118, 123, 127
major categories 57–8
neurodegeneration 132–43
ophthalmology 153–6
pain relief 150–3
rare diseases 146–9
respiratory disease 143–6
rheumatology 132–3, 139–43
therapeutic prospects 87–156
    see also individual diseases; obesity
DMD *see* Duchenne Muscular
Dystrophy
DNA 23–32, 35
    discovery of 26–32
    gene patents 74–5
    genetic self-knowledge 17
    medical history 23–32
    nucleic acids 25, 27
    recombinant 52–3, 60–1
    synthetic biology 14–15
    ZFPTs 175
    see also genomes
DNA nanoballs (DNBs) 164–5
domestic robots 228–9
dopamine 132, 138
    see also Parkinson's disease
double helix structure 23–4, 27–8
DPP-IV inhibitors 125
drug industry 55–86
    drug development 71–86, 308
    drug targets 72
    FDA approval 58, 79–84, 92–3
    financial outlay 56–7
    model reinvention 55–86
    patents 56, 73–9, 308
    see also pharmaceutical industry
drugs
    FDA definition 56
    first true drugs 39
    see also individual drugs; medicine
Duchenne Muscular Dystrophy (DMD)
148
dyeing industry 39–40
Dynavax Technologies 256, 272–3, 297

Egyptian medicine 36
Ehrlich, Paul 40–1
electrophysiology (EP) 222
Eli Lilly 250
EMA *see* European Medical Agency
Embden–Mayerhof pathway 34
embryonic stem cells 166–7, 216
employer insurance 209
energy conservation 238
EP *see* electrophysiology
epidemics 37, 39, 109
epigenetic drugs 95–7
Epizyme 65
Escherichia Coli (*E. Coli*) 111
ETFs *see* exchange-traded funds
ethics and robots 232
eukaryotic cells 28–9
European Medical Agency (EMA) 58, 78
Evans, Dave 5–6
exchange-traded funds (ETFs) 248
exercise 242

Facebook 214
FDA *see* Food and Drug Administration
female life expectancy 182–3
fertility rates 187–91, 201–202, 217–18,
   308
Fleming, Alexander 43
Food and Drug Administration (FDA),
   US 307
   approval 58, 79–84, 92–3
   budget 72
   definition of "drug" 56
   fast tracking drugs 82
   obesity 120
food industry 213–14
Forest Laboratories 256, 266, 290
Fostamatinib (RA drug) 261
four Gs of drug innovation 41, 70
France 193–4
free radicals 161
Freedom to 0perate (FTO) principle 78
Friedman, Eby 4
FTO *see* Freedom to Operate principle
futurists 1–12, 305

G *see* guanine
Galen (Roman medic) 36
gastrointestinal disease 153–6
Gaucher's disease 147–8
gene therapy 89, 157, 170–8

antisense therapies 177–8
germ line therapy 171–2
investment 255
nanoparticles 173–4
retroviral vectors 172–3
somatic therapy 171–2
ZFPTs 174–5
Genentech 256
   angiogenesis inhibitors 94–5
   first biopharma company 59–60
   gene patents 75
   success 69
   VCs 67–8
genes
   "ageing" genes 89
   Alzheimer's disease 133–5
   APOE 159–60
   disease pathways 32–3
   DNA 29–33
   gene knockout 98–9
   life expectancy 239
   patents 74–6
   TP53 104
   see also gene...; Human Genome
   Project
genetic engineering 52
genetic self-knowledge 16–18
genetically-modified (GM) foods 214
genomes 14–17, 163–6
   see also human genome...
Genomic Health 297
genomics 157–80, 256
genotyping 17
Genzyme 260
geopolitics 211–12
germ line gene therapy 171–2
Germany 193
Gilead Sciences
   business models 63–4, 66,69
   company overview 290
   HIV/AIDS drugs 115
   as investment choice 256, 259
   Ranexa (drug) 131
GlaxoSmithKline (GSK) 108, 144–6, 249,
   252, 284
Gleevec kinase inhibitor 102–3
GLP-1 (hormone) 125–6
glycolysis 34
GM *see* genetically-modified foods
gout 34, 141–2
government action 193, 200–3

government bonds 215
Gram-negative infections 111–12
Greek medicine 36
GSK *see* GlaxoSmithKline
Guangdong Province, China 200
guanine (G) 27–8, 35

Hansen Medical 222, 297
Harvard Mouse 73
Hayflick Limit 160
health 305, 309
    see also lifestyle
healthcare 206–10
    demographic changes 193, 195, 198, 200
    insurance 206–10
    lifestyle choices 208–9
    medical insurance 209
    youth shortage 218
heart disease *see* cardiovascular disease
HeLa cells 158
Heparin, (cardiovascular drug) 45
hepatitis 107, 113–14, 272
Hepislav (hepatitis vaccine) 272
herbal remedies 37
Herceptin (cancer drug) 53–4, 253, 255
HGP *see* Human Genome Project
high blood pressure 128–30
    see also hypertension
high throughput screening (HTS) 35, 71
hIPS *see* induced pluripotent human stem
    cells
histamines 47
HIV/AIDS 107, 114–16, 275
HIVCide (HIV/AIDS drug) 275
Honda 224–6, 290, 309
hormones 33, 48, 161–2
housemaid robots 228–9
HPV *see* Human Papilloma Virus
HTS *see* high throughput screening
human cells 29–30
Human Genome Project (HGP) 30–1, 35, 71, 311
human genome sequencing 15–17, 310–11
    drug industry 70–1
    insurance 206–8
    the law 216–17
Human Papilloma Virus (HPV) 117–18
Hung, David 105
Hunter Syndrome 149
hydrogels 179

hypercholesterolemia 131
hyperplasia 24–5
hypertension 47, 129–31, 145
hypertrophy 25

IBM 4, 9–10
IBS (irritable bowel syndrome) 154
immigration 193–5
immortality 158–9
ImmunoGen 104
immunosuppressants 48
immunotherapeutics 99
implants 7–8
India
    biopharma 251
    demographic changes 189–93, 196
    fertility rates 189–91
    geopolitical concerns 211–12
    labour pool 192
induced pluripotent human stem cells
    (hIPS) 168–9
infectious diseases 37–41, 107–18
    epidemics 109
    hepatitis 107, 113–14
    HIV/AIDS 107, 114–16, 275
    malaria 116–7
    new antibiotics 107–18
    tuberculosis 117
    vaccines 116, 117–18
    worldwide mortality 108
Infinity Pharmaceuticals 273, 297
influenza 118
innovation, four Gs 41, 70
insulin 48, 53, 124–7
    see also diabetes
insurance 206–10
    employer insurance 209
    genome sequencing 206–8
    healthcare 206–10
    lifestyle choices 208–9
    pooled insurance 208
Intel 2, 4
Intuitive Surgical 221, 298
investment 214–15, 247–302
iRobot 228–9, 298
irritable bowel syndrome (IBS) 154
Isis Pharmaceuticals 178, 256, 260, 191

Japan 308–9
    ageing populations 185–6
    fertility rates 188, 190–1

immigration 194–5
labour pool 192
monitor robots 224–8
support ratios 197–8
"Jasmine Revolution" 216
Jenner, Edward 37
Johnson & Johnson 250, 284

Kekich, Dave 240
Keryx Biopharmaceuticals 298
Kessler, Andy 13
Kevetrin (cancer drug) 272
kidney disease 88, 118, 122–3, 127
kinase inhibitors 95, 102–4
Krystexxa (gout drug) 142
Kurzweil, Ray 2 5, 6

labour pool, world 191–5
Lasik eye surgery system 221
the law 215–17
Leonardo 174, 176
Levodopa (Parkinson's drug) 138–9
life expectancy 158–62, 181–8
    lifestyle 237–40
    longevity traits 238–40
    nine secrets 239–40
lifestyle 235–45, 309
    choices and insurance 208–9
    cure to ageing 240–4
    extending life 237–8
    longevity traits 238–40
    maintenance 235–45, 309
    obesity 235–7
    telomeres 244–5
Lilly 250
Linaclotide (gastrointestinal drug) 154
lipids 25–6, 46
Lipitor (cardiovascular drug) 129–30, 249
liposomes 174
Lister, Joseph 39, 51
longevity 238–40, 311–12
LSDs see lysosomal storage disorders
lupus 140–1
lysosomal storage disorders (LSDs) 147

MAbs see monoclonal antibodies
Macchiarini, Paolo 20
magic bullets 41
MAKO Surgical 222, 299
malaria 116–7
male life expectancy 182–3

managed funds 248
Manhattan Beach Project 240
Mannkind 126–7, 299
MAP 256
MDV3100 drug 105–6
medical devices 84
medical insurance 254
medical knowledge 182
medicine 23–54, 306–7
    atoms and cells 24–35
    DNA 23–32
    evolution of 23–54, 306–7
    personalized 16, 20
    pharmaceutical industry 36–54
    precision 16, 93–4
    targeted 93–104
Medicis Pharmaceutical 256, 264–5, 291
Medivation 104–6, 256, 267, 291
meiosis 30
Mendelian diseases 32
Merck & Co. 249, 251, 285
Merrimack Pharmaceuticals 106, 291
messenger RNA (mRNA) 30–1, 53,
    177–8
metabolism 33–4
Methylgene 299
micro RNA (miRNA) 173, 176
microchips 13
migraine 152
migration to warm climate 210
military robots
Mipomersen (cholesterol drug) 260
miRNA see micro RNA
mitochondria 29
mobile phones 311
molecules 24–5
monitor robots 223–8
    Asimo 224–5, 309
    Japan 224–8
    Nao 226–7
    nurse robots 223–8
    Stride Management Assist Device
    225–6
monoclonal antibodies (MAbs) 53–4,
    60–1, 70
Moore, Gordon 2–3
Moore's Law 2–4, 9, 10, 219, 305, 310
Morphine 39
mRNA see messenger RNA
MRSA 110, 112, 118
multiple sclerosis (MS) 132–3, 136–8

muscular dystrophy 148
mutations 32

nanotechnology 14, 219, 232–4
    allotropes 233
    nano medicine 170, 173–4
    nano-robots 223
    nanotubes 233–4
Nanotype 179–80
NanoViricides 115–16, 256, 275, 299
Nao robot 226–7
National Cancer Institute (NCI), US 92
Navidea Biopharmaceuticals 299
NDM-1 pathogen 111
Nektar Therapeutics 256, 271, 292
Neuralstem 300
neurodegeneration 83, 132–43
NicOx 300
non-steroidal anti-inflammatory drugs
    (NSAIDs) 50
notch pathway 101
Nova Nordisk 285
Novartis 249, 252, 285
Novelos Therapeutics 300
NSAIDs see non-steroidal anti-
    inflammatory drugs
nuclei 24
nucleic acids 25, 27
    see also DNA
nurse robots 223–8

obesity 118–27
    BMI 236–7
    diabetes 118–19, 122, 126–7
    FDA approval 120
    kidney disease 123
    lifestyle 235–7
    weight-loss drugs 119–23
OECD countries 197–8
oncolytic poxviruses 98–100
one-child policy, China 199
Onyx 256
ophthalmology 153–6
Opium 39
Optimer Pharmaceuticals 256, 274, 292
Orexigen Therapeutics 301
organ growth 178–80
organic nitrates 45
Orlistat (obesity drug) 120
orphan diseases 82, 146–9, 256
osteoarthritis 142–3
osteoporosis 155

Ott, Harold 19–20
overseas citizens 201–202
Oxycontin (pain drug) 152

P13K/AKT/mTOR pathway 101–2
p53 pathway 104
Pacific Biosciences 165–6, 256
Pacific Yew tree 49
pain relief 150–3
parasitic infections 40–1
paroxysmal nocturnal hemoglobinuria
    (PNH) 149
Parkinson's disease 132–3, 138–9, 172
Paro robotic pet 230–1
PARP inhibitors 102–4
partnerships 64, 81
patents 73–9, 308
    animals 74
    expiry 56
    genes 74–6
    length of life 77
pathways for disease 32–4, 101–4
Pearl, Raymond 160
PEG see polyethylene glycol
penicillin 43–4
pensions 187, 193, 200, 215
Perkin, William 39–40
personalized medicine 16, 20
pets (robotic) 229–32
Pfizer 135, 249, 251–3, 286
phage therapy 112–13
pharmaceutical industry 36–54
    birth of modern medicine 37–51
    early history 36–7
    FDA approval failures 82–3
    see also big pharma; biopharma; drug
    industry
Pharmacyclics 96, 301
phones (mobile) 311
Pleo robotic pet 231–1
Plethora Solutions Holdings 279, 301
pluripotent stem cells 167–9
PNH see paroxysmal nocturnal
    hemoglobinuria
politics 211
Poly ADP Ribose Polymerase see PARP
polyethylene glycol (PEG) 54
PolyMedix 112
precision medicine 16, 93–4
prediction of trends 312–13
price of drugs 254
price of food 213

price-earnings ratios 250–1
processing power of computers 221–2, 310
profitless prosperity 69
Prontosil (antibacterial drug) 41
prostate cancer 105–6
protein kinases 102
proteins 25–6, 26, 40
Prozac (SSRI) 42
psoriasis 155
pulmonary hypertension 145

quantum computers 4–5
quantum theory 162–3
Quinine sulphate (malaria drug) 39, 307

R&D *see* research and development
RA *see* rheumatoid arthritis
Ranexa (angina drug) 131
rare diseases 146–9
Rate of Living hypothesis 160
rational drug design (RDD) 71
rDNA *see* recombinant DNA
real estate 210
Reata Pharmaceuticals 123, 127, 304
receptors 26, 40, 72
recombinant DNA (rDNA) 52–3, 60–1
regeneration 157, 178–80
reproduction 161
research and development (R&D) 252, 255
respiratory disease 143–6
retail goods/services 212–13
retroviral vectors 172–4
rheumatoid arthritis (RA) 49, 50, 139
rheumatology 132–3, 139–43
ribonucleic acid *see* RNA
Rigel Pharmaceuticals 256, 261–2
Rituxan (lymphoma drug) 253, 257
RNA
    DNA 26–7, 30–2, 52
    gene therapy 175–7
    miRNA 173, 176
    mRNA 30–1, 53, 177–8
    Pacific Biosciences 166
    RNAi 121, 175–7
    siRNAs 98, 173, 175–7, 256
    see also DNA
RNA interference (RNAi) 121, 175–7
robotics 219–34, 309
    domestic assistance 228–9
    ethics 232
    monitors/nurses 223–8

pets 229–32
    surgery 220–3
Roche Holdings 249, 252, 253, 255–6, 286
Roman medicine 36–7
Russia 251

salmonella 111
Sangamo BioSciences 173, 301
sanitation 39
Sanofi 250–1, 287
Savient Pharmaceuticals 256, 292
scaffolds of organs 19–21
schizophrenia 149–50
serotonin reuptake inhibitors (SSRIs) 42
sex cells 29–30
Shire 256, 263–4, 293
short interfering RNA strands (siRNAs) 98, 173, 175–7, 256
signal transduction pathways 33
singularity hypothesis 5–7, 306
The Singularity is Near (Kurzweil) 2
Sinopharm Group 293
siRNAs *see* short interfering RNA strands
smallpox 37–8
social impact of ageing population 195–6
Soligenix 256, 302
somatic cells 29
somatic gene therapy 171–2
sonic hedgehog pathway 100–1
speculative biopharma portfolio 281–2
SSRIs *see* serotonin reuptake inhibitors
Star Scientific 256, 276–7, 302
startup firms 70–1
statins (cholesterol drugs) 46, 129–30
stem cells 157, 166–70
    embryonic 166–7, 216
    investment 256
    start of life 24
    WARF 76–7
stomach ulcers 47
stress management 244
Stride Management Assist Device 225–6
Stryker 222, 293
Summit 302
superbugs 44
superfoods 241
supplements 242–3
support ratios 197–8
surgery 220–3
    biomedical devices 223
    da Vinci Surgical System 220–1
    Hanson Medical 222

Lasik eye procedure 220
Lister 39
MAKO 222
nano-robots 223
procedures 220–3
TOGA 122
tracheal 20
Swaziland 182
Synergy Pharmaceuticals 303
synthetic biology 14–16, 306
synthetic life forms 12
systemic lupus erythematous 140–1

T *see* thymine
Tarceva (cancer drug) 95
targeted cancer therapies 93–104
tax 202–3, 254
Taxol (cancer drug) 49–50
technology *see* nanotechnology;
    transformational technologies
Telaprevir (hepatitis drug) 113, 262
telomerase 30, 160, 245
telomeres 30–1, 160, 244–5
Teva Pharmaceutical Industries 137,
    287
Thalidomide 50–1
Thomson, Jamie 77, 168
thought-controlled devices 8
three-dimensional bio-printers 21
thrombosis 131
thymine (T) 27–8, 35
TOGA *see* transoral gastroplasty
TP53 gene 104
tracheal surgery 20
transfection agents 173–4
transformational technologies 1–21,
    305–6
    AI 5, 9–12
    biology and technology 13–21
    consciousness 12
    future aspects 1–12
    synthetic biology 14–16, 306
transoral gastroplasty (TOGA) 122
trend predictions 312–13
Tri-Gate transistor chips 4
Triptans (migraine drugs) 152
Trojantec 98, 101, 304
Trypan Red dye 41
tuberculosis 117
Turing test 9
Tysabri (MS drug) 257

unemployment 212
United States (US)
    big pharma 254
    demographic changes 190–1, 193,
        196–7
    drug industry 57, 66–8, 73, 77–8
    geopolitical concerns 211–12
    obesity 118–19

vaccines 116, 117–18
    anti-cancer viruses 98–100
    BCG 117
    history of 37
    HIV/AIDS 116
    infectious diseases 116, 117–18
    malaria 116–7
Valium 43
variolation 37
VCs *see* venture capitalists
VEGF-Trap Eye (eye drug) 153
Ventnor, Craig 15
venture capitalists (VCs) 65, 67–8, 215
Vertex Pharmaceuticals 256, 262–3, 294
Viagra 55, 62
da Vinci Surgical System 220–1
Viread (HIV/AIDS drug) 259
viruses 98–100, 117–18
Vivus 303

WARF *see* Wisconsin Alumni Research
    Foundation
Warfarin (blood thinner) 16, 45, 76
Warwick, Kevin 7–8
Watson IBM computer 9–12
Watson, James 27, 35
wealth 305
weight-loss drugs 119–23
WikiLeaks 216–17
Wisconsin Alumni Research Foundation
    (WARF) 76–7

Xgeva (bone drug) 156

Yew trees 49
youth shortages 217–18

Zinc Finger Protein Transcription Factors
    (ZFPTs) 174–5

*Index compiled by Indexing Specialists (UK)
    Ltd*

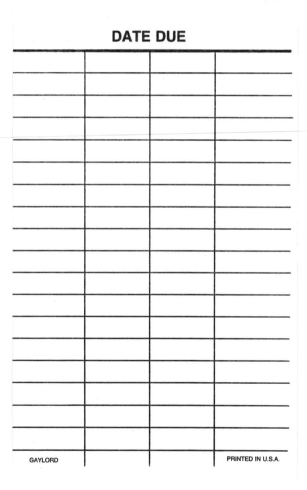

DATE DUE

GAYLORD			PRINTED IN U.S.A.